# ZION

## The Second Pillar of Zion
### The Oath & Covenant of the Priesthood

## LARRY BARKDULL

### Pillars of Zion Series Titles

**Introduction:** *Portrait of a Zion Person*

**Book 1:** *Zion—Our Origin and Our Destiny*

**Book 2:** *The First Pillar of Zion—The New and Everlasting Covenant*

**Book 3:** *The Second Pillar of Zion—The Oath and Covenant of the Priesthood*

**Book 4:** *The Third Pillar of Zion—The Law of Consecration*

**Book 5:** *The Pure in Heart*

**Book 6:** *No Poor among Them*

**Pillars of Zion Publishing**
Orem, Utah

## Copyright and Permission

## Contact

Contact us at info@pillarsofzion.com
Visit our Website at www.PillarsOfZion.com

## Disclaimer

This series is heavily documented with some 5,000 references and 400 works cited. Every effort has been made to achieve accuracy. This work is not an official publication of the Church of Jesus Christ of Latter-day Saints, and the views expressed within this work are the sole responsibility of the author and do not necessarily reflect the position of The Church of Jesus Christ of Latter-day Saints or any other entity.

## LICENSE USE

Library of Congress Cataloging Publication Data is on file at the Library of Congress.
ISBN: 978-1-937399-07-8

## Dedication
To Elizabeth Barkdull
Ron and Bonnie McMillan
David and Lorelea Anderson
Paul and Sharon Meyers

## Acknowledgments

My wife, Elizabeth, and I would like to acknowledge a number of people, who, in one way or another, lent their support for the creation of this project.

Lawrence and Georgia Shaw
Lance and Jozet Richardson
Blaine and Kathy Yorgason
Scot and Maurine Proctor
Clay Gorton
Ted Gibbons
Grover Cardon
Gary and Bonnie Leavitt
Bud and Barbara Poduska
Dee Jay Bawden
Steve Glenn
Gavon and Tanya Barkdull

## Production Staff

Thanks to Eschler Editing for editorial and design work.

Editors—Jay A. Parry and Michele Preisendorf
Graphic Artist—Douglass Cole
Typesetter—Sean Graham

## Note about The Three Pillars of Zion

The complete Zion series contains seven books. The full bibliography, and index are included in each of the books for ease of referencing and navigation. Each volume includes its own table of contents except for the Introduction book, *Portrait of a Zion Person*, includes the table of contents for each volume in order to introduce the entire series.

# Table of Contents

## Book 3
## The Second Pillar of Zion—The Oath and Covenant of the Priesthood

Introduction ..........................................................................................................1

**Section 1**
**The Holy Priesthood after the Order of the Son of God** ........................................3

The Doctrines of the Priesthood As They Apply to Men and Women          4
Melchizedek, the Title and the Man                                       4
King Benjamin, a Type of Melchizedek                                     7
The Restoration of the Priesthood                                        12
Elijah Restores the Sealing Keys of the Patriarchal Order of the Priesthood   12
Elijah Restores the Fulness of the Priesthood                            13
Moses Restores Priesthood Keys of Family Gathering                       14
Elias Restores Priesthood Keys                                           14
The Joint Missions of Elias and Elijah                                   15
Building One Priesthood Power upon Another                               16
Rescuing This Generation                                                 17
Eternal Principle of Power                                               17
Premortal Qualification for the Priesthood                               18
The Obligation of Zion Priesthood Holders                                19
Our Priesthood Work Then and Now                                         20
The Covenant of the Priesthood                                           21
The Lesser and Greater Portions                                          22
The Patriarchal Order                                                    22
Differing Purposes and Powers                                           23
Grand Purposes of the Priesthood                                         24
Priesthood Blessings                                                     24
The Blessings of Adam                                                    25
The Blessings of Abraham                                                 26
Abraham's Qualifications and Desire                                      28
Blessings of the Priesthood                                              29
The Prize Is Worth the Price                                             30
The Authority and Keys of the Priesthood                                 31
Doctrine of the Priesthood                                               33
"As My Father Hath Sent Me, Even So Send I You"                          35
Summary and Conclusion                                                   35

## Section 2

**The Oath and Covenant of the Priesthood—Our Agreements** ...................................39

| | |
|---|---|
| If We Are Faithful | 41 |
| If We Magnify Our Calling | 43 |
| Magnifying the Calling and Callings | 44 |
| Three Ways to Magnify Our Calling | 46 |
| Obtaining Gospel Knowledge | 46 |
| Personal Righteousness | 47 |
| Dedicated Service | 51 |
| Grace to Grace by Grace for Grace | 52 |
| If Any of You Lack | 54 |
| Magnifying Our Priesthood Calling by Bearing Testimony | 55 |
| The Ultimate Magnification of Our Calling | 57 |
| The Three Stages of the Priesthood Covenant | 58 |
| Summary and Conclusion | 59 |

## Section 3

**The Oath and Covenant of the Priesthood**

**The Father's Oath, Instructions, and Promises** ...........................................63

| | |
|---|---|
| The Father's Two Oaths Guaranteeing Us the Blessings of Abraham | 64 |
| Sanctification by the Spirit unto the Renewing of Our Bodies | 66 |
| The Progression of the Renewing of Our Bodies | 67 |
| Power Given to the Renewed and Sanctified | 69 |
| Blessings Given to the Renewed and Sanctified | 70 |
| "I Sanctify Myself, That They Also Might Be Sanctified" | 74 |
| The Sons of Moses and of Aaron | 76 |
| The Seed of Abraham | 78 |
| The Church and Kingdom of God | 79 |
| The Elect of God | 79 |
| Calling and Election Made Sure | 81 |
| Receiving Christ and the Father | 85 |
| "All That My Father Hath" | 88 |
| Ministering and Protection of Angels | 90 |
| The Father's Instructions: Be Careful and Be Diligent | 94 |
| "And the Father Teacheth Him of the Covenant" | 95 |
| The Promise of Eternal Life | 98 |
| Penalties for Neglecting or Rejecting the Covenant of the Priesthood | 102 |
| Summary and Conclusion | 103 |

**Section 4**

**The Constitution of the Priesthood—Why Many Are Called but Not Chosen** ........107

Two Groups                                                                108
A Satanic Strategy                                                        109
A Test of Loyalties                                                       109
Restoration of the Constitution of the Priesthood                         110
The Marriage of the King's Son                                            111
"Many Will Say to Me in That Day"                                         113
Called and Chosen for Eternal Life                                        114
Abiding Zion's Celestial Law in Babylon's Telestial Setting               116
The End Purpose of Our Calling                                            117
Distinctions between Those Who Are Called and Those Who Are Chosen         118
Building a Sure House                                                      119
Mortal Tests That Challenge Our Calling                                   120
The Daunting Test of Riches                                               122
Safety and Perfection in Consecration                                     123
The Sacrifice of All Things—A "Hard Thing"                                123
Safety in the "Royal Law"                                                 124
The Dangers of Rationalization and Postponement                          125
The Law of Restitution—An Hundredfold Reward                             126
Babylon among Us                                                          127
Walking in Darkness at Noon-day                                           130
The Test of Praise                                                        131
"Rights of the Priesthood"                                                134
"Inseparably Connected"—Righteousness and Priesthood Power               135
Connecting to the True Vine                                               135
Amen to the Priesthood                                                    137
Summary and Conclusion                                                    139

## Section 5

**The Constitution of the Priesthood—Instructing the Chosen Few**...........143

Stages of Progression within the Covenant                                                  144

No Power or Influence Can or Ought to Be Maintained by Virtue of the Priesthood    145

Zion's Approach to Agency                                                                   146

Persuasion versus Babylon's Counterparts                                                    147

Zion's Patient Persuasion                                                                   147

Patience and Long-suffering                                                                 147

Patience                                                                                    148

Long-suffering                                                                              150

Gentleness and Meekness                                                                     151

Feigned and Unfeigned Love                                                                  153

What Is "True Love"?                                                                        155

To Love First                                                                               156

Love Perfected                                                                              157

No Fear in Love                                                                             158

Love—The Greatest Power                                                                     158

Kindness                                                                                    159

Pure Knowledge versus False Knowledge                                                       159

Zion's Approach to "Pure Knowledge"                                                         164

Wisdom and Pure Knowledge                                                                   167

Reproving the Lord's Way                                                                    168

Reproving with Love                                                                         169

Cords of Death and Bonds of Love                                                            170

Charity toward All Men and the Household of God                                             171

Let Virtue Garnish Thy Thoughts Unceasingly                                                 172

Garnishing Our Thoughts with Virtue                                                         173

Summary and Conclusion                                                                      173

## Section 6

**The Constitution of the Priesthood—The Rewards for the Chosen Few** .................175

The Rewards 175

"Then Shall Thy Confidence Wax Strong in the Presence of God" 176

Now Is the Time 177

A Change of Paradigm 178

Turning the Key 179

Obtaining, at Last, a Perfect Knowledge of the Savior 180

Receiving the Greatest Comfort 181

Regaining the Presence of God—The End Purpose of the Priesthood 182

The Revealed Process for Standing in the Presence of God 182

The Priesthood Is the Power to Stand in God's Presence 183

"The Doctrine of the Priesthood Shall Distil upon Thy Soul" 184

The Rights and the Doctrine of the Priesthood 186

The Doctrine of the Priesthood and the Law of Asking 187

Lesser and Greater Portions of the Doctrine of the Priesthood 189

The Necessity and Power of Priesthood Ordinances 189

The Doctrine of the Priesthood and Revelatory "Keys" 191

"The Holy Ghost Shall Be Thy Constant Companion" 193

The Holy Spirit of Promise 194

Scepters and Dominions—The Holy Interview 194

Priests and Kings, Priestesses and Queens 197

Becoming Members of the Church of the Firstborn 200

Angelic Ministers from the Church of the Firstborn 202

The Order of the Son of God 204

The Order of the Son of God and Marriage 206

The Fulness of the Priesthood 208

Power in the Priesthood 208

"Without Compulsory Means It Shall Flow unto Thee Forever" 210

Summary and Conclusion 211

Postlude 214

**Bibliography** ..................................................................215

**Index and Concordance** ..................................................225

**About the Author** ..........................................................249

# Book 3
## The Second Pillar of Zion— The Oath and Covenant of the Priesthood

# Introduction

*"We ought to have the building up of Zion as our greatest object."*[1]—*Joseph Smith*

In this third book of The Three Pillars of Zion series, we will examine in depth the second pillar of Zion: The Oath and Covenant of the Priesthood. We recall that the "Law of the Church"(D&C 42) states that three covenants are sufficient to establish us as Zion people: "And ye shall hereafter receive church covenants, such as shall be sufficient to establish you, both here and in the New Jerusalem."[2] These covenants are:

1. The New and Everlasting Covenant. (D&C 132:4–7)
2. The Oath and Covenant of the Priesthood. (D&C 84:33–44)
3. The Law of Consecration. (D&C 82:11–15)

In book 1, we learned that Zion was our origin and will be our destiny. She is our ideal and the antithesis of Babylon. Moreover, Zion is the standard among celestial and celestial-seeking people.[3] Brigham Young said, "[Zion] commences in the heart of each person."[4] Clearly, the responsibility to become Zion people rests upon each of us individually.

That responsibility begins with formally accepting the Atonement by receiving the new and everlasting covenant by way of baptism. The new and everlasting covenant is the *umbrella covenant*, consisting of two primary covenants: the covenant of baptism, and the oath and covenant of the priesthood. The priesthood covenant is magnified by (1) ordination for worthy men; (2) temple covenants and ordinances for worthy men and women; and (3) the temple sealing covenant, which is called the Covenant of Exaltation,[5] for worthy men and women.

---

1    Smith, *Teachings of the Prophet Joseph Smith*, 60.
2    D&C 42:67.
3    D&C 105:5.
4    Young, *Discourses of Brigham Young*, 118.
5    Nelson, *The Power within Us*, 136; Smith, *Doctrines of Salvation*, 2:58. Note: Elder McConkie stated that men make a covenant of exaltation twice: once upon ordination to the Melchizedek Priesthood and again at the time of the marriage sealing: "Ordination to office in the Melchizedek priesthood and entering into that 'order of the priesthood' named 'the new and everlasting covenant of marriage' are both occasions when men make the covenant of exaltation, being promised through their faithfulness all that the Father hath (D&C 131:1–4; 84:39–41; 132; Num. 25:13)" (*Mormon Doctrine*, 167).

The new and everlasting covenant not only provides a way to be cleansed from sin and separated from the world, it provides us a way to receive God's authority, power, and knowledge—everything we need to become like him and inherit all that he has. This is the essence of the second pillar of Zion—the oath and covenant of the priesthood.

As we will learn, the principles in this book apply to both worthy men and women. The priesthood covenant is received by men at the time of ordination, but its principles are expansive and eventually lead to the temple. There, faithful men and women are washed clean and anointed, purified and sanctified, then endowed with priesthood covenants and ordinances that culminate at a marriage altar. An editorial in the *Improvement Era* noted: "Now, as far as the Church of Christ is concerned, this oath and covenant is made first in baptism, when the Holy Ghost is given, and more especially when the Priesthood is conferred. It is, secondly, repeated by partaking of the Sacrament, and by entering into special covenants in holy places [the temple]."[6] Elder Bruce R. McConkie said, "This covenant, made when the priesthood is received, is renewed when the recipient enters the order of eternal marriage."[7] Clearly, both men and women are involved in the doctrines of the priesthood.

In this section, we will examine the history of the priesthood and men who were great examples of righteousness in the priesthood. We will discuss priesthood keys and their importance in the restored Church of Jesus Christ. Then we will survey our covenantal agreements and the Father's oath, instructions, and promises. Following these sections, we will examine what President Stephen L Richards called "The Constitution of the Priesthood,"[8] found in Doctrine and Covenants 121. We will discuss why many are called to eternal life, but few are chosen. We will also study the Lord's instructions and rewards for the chosen few who keep their covenants. In the end, we come to understand that receiving the priesthood is more than an ordination; it is a way of life and the power to pursue that life. Without the priesthood and its guiding principles, neither a man nor a woman could achieve Zion in his or her life and thus attain the ultimate form of salvation, *exaltation* in the celestial kingdom.

---

6    Editor's Note, "The Bondage of Sin," *Improvement Era,* Feb. 1923.
7    McConkie, *A New Witness for the Articles of Faith,* 313.
8    Richards, Conference Report, Apr. 1955, 12.

# Section 1
# The Holy Priesthood after the Order of the Son of God

*Note: The first time we refer to a covenant or unique doctrine, we may capitalize it to call special attention to it. Thereafter, we will lowercase the name of the covenant or doctrine with two exceptions: (1) If the name is capitalized in a quotation from another source, we will leave it as found in that source; and (2) if we are referring to the new and everlasting covenant by the shorthand of "the Covenant," we will capitalize it in that setting.*

Priesthood is power, said President Marion G. Romney.[9] To receive that power—the power of God—is to be set apart and authorized as the most honored of God's sons. But we also have the greatest responsibility. We should be diligent in learning all we can about this great power. Nevertheless, despite our best efforts through prayer, study, and faithful performance of our duties, we will not fully comprehend the priesthood in this life. But what we do learn and experience will leave us in awe. Brigham Young said, "The Priesthood of the Son of God . . . is the law by which the worlds are, were, and will continue forever and ever. It is that system which brings worlds into existence and peoples them, gives them their revolutions—their days, weeks, months, years, their seasons and times and by which they are rolled up as a scroll, as it were, and go into a higher state of existence."[10]

From the days of Adam until Melchizedek, the priesthood was called The Holy Priesthood after the Order of the Son of God. "But out of respect or reverence to the name of the Supreme Being, to avoid the too frequent repetition of his name, they, the church, in ancient days, called that priesthood after Melchizedek, or the Melchizedek Priesthood."[11] As we learned in book 2, this high priesthood is received with the Father's oath and our covenant.[12] The oath and covenant of the priesthood is the second pillar

---

9   Romney, "Priesthood," 43.
10   Young, *Discourses of Brigham Young*, 130.
11   D&C 107:3–4.
12   D&C 84:33–44.

of Zion. The oath and covenant of the priesthood is also the second of two covenants (baptism being the first) that comprise the Covenant of Mercy.

## The Doctrines of the Priesthood As They Apply to Men and Women

This section will explore the priesthood covenant in depth as it applies to both men and women. Elder James E. Talmage wrote, "It is a precept of the Church that women of the Church share the authority of the Priesthood with their husbands, actual or prospective; and therefore women, whether taking the endowment for themselves or for the dead, are not ordained to specific rank in the Priesthood. Nevertheless there is no grade, rank, or phase of the temple endowment to which women are not eligible on an equality with men. . . . Within the House of the Lord the woman is the equal and the help-meet of the man."[13]

Previously (in book 2) we discussed the fact that the priesthood covenant cannot deliver power without our magnifying our calling in the priesthood. As we will explain, that calling is the call to eternal life. We magnify that calling progressively by (1) ordination to the priesthood, (2) receiving temple ordinances, (3) being married in the temple. Because women are included the last two criteria, they are clearly involved in the doctrines of the priesthood.

With that in mind, let us make the following examination.

## Melchizedek, the Title and the Man

Melchizedek, as we discussed in book 1, is a title as well as a name, which, in Hebrew means "King of Righteousness." The identity of the man who originally bore this title is the subject of much conjecture. What we do know about the man Melchizedek is of importance to every man who desires to become a Zion person and thus take upon himself the high priesthood. Melchizedek "represents the scriptural ideal of one who obtains the power of God through faith, repentance, and sacred ordinances, for the purpose of inspiring and blessing his fellow beings."[14] Because the man Melchizedek was so righteous and faithful "in the execution of his high priestly duties . . . he became a prototype of Jesus Christ (Heb. 7:15)."[15]

Men who receive the high priesthood by ordination assume the title of "Melchizedek." Becoming a part of that order, they are expected to do the works of Melchizedek and of Jesus Christ, the two great exemplars of what a priesthood holder should be. They are to become *kings of righteousness* to their posterity.

In Melchizedek's life we see an example of what we should become. His ministry is a model that we should apply to our own priesthood service. In the first place, because the new and everlasting covenant has been available to all of God's sons and daughters, Melchizedek would have received that Covenant by baptism and thereafter would have made each additional covenant, received every ordinance, and endured in faith until he

---

13    Talmage, *The House of the Lord,* 79.
14    *Encyclopedia of Mormonism,* 879–80.
15    *Encyclopedia of Mormonism,* 879–80.

finally received the ultimate promise of salvation. From the beginning, he would have desired to progress in the Covenant and become a savior to his people in the similitude of the Savior. Therefore, at some point, he would have sought for his ordination to the Holy Priesthood after the Order of the Son of God so that he might administer the blessings of the Covenant to help save his people.

The scripture reads: "Now this Melchizedek was a king over the land of Salem and his people had waxed strong in iniquity and abomination; yea, they had all gone astray; they were full of all manner of wickedness; but Melchizedek having exercised mighty faith, and received the office of the high priesthood according to the holy order of God, did preach repentance unto his people." Like Enoch, Melchizedek was enormously successful and taught his people the principles of Zion until they, too, became Zion people: "And behold, they did repent; and Melchizedek did establish peace in the land in his days; therefore he was called the prince of peace, for he was the king of Salem; and he did reign under his father."[16] From this account, we learn that "Melchizedek was a man of faith, who wrought righteousness. . . . And his people wrought righteousness, and obtained heaven, and sought for the city of Enoch [they became Zion people and were likewise translated]."[17] This is our priesthood model as holders of the Melchizedek Priesthood.

Again, we emphasize the fact that Melchizedek would have progressed as we all must: by baptism, by receiving the high priesthood with an oath and covenant, and by receiving all temple blessings, culminating with eternal marriage, which is the patriarchal order or the highest order of the priesthood.[18] We know that Melchizedek progressed in this manner because he is described as being both a king and a priest unto God,[19] meaning that he received a fulness of the priesthood. The titles *king* and *priest* and their associated blessings are possible only by receiving the fulness of temple ordinances.[20] This is the *fulness* that defines Zion people.

"What was the power of Melchizedek?" asked the Prophet Joseph Smith. "Those holding the fulness of the Melchizedek Priesthood are kings and priests of the Most High God, holding the keys of power and blessings. In fact, that Priesthood is a perfect law of theocracy, and stands as God to give laws to the people, administering endless lives to the sons and daughters of Adam."[21] Zion marriages, families, and priesthood societies function under the Melchizedek Priesthood, which is the "perfect law of theocracy." Through Melchizedek's righteousness and faith, he received the keys of power and blessings, ruled as a king of righteousness, administered *endless lives* (the covenants and ordinances of eternal life) to his people, and brought them back into the presence of God. This is the power of the Melchizedek Priesthood and the purpose and expectation of our ordination. Everything about the priesthood points to establishing Zion in life, marriage, family, and in a priesthood society.

---

16    Alma 13:17–18.
17    JST, Genesis 14:26, 34.
18    D&C 131:1–4.
19    Alma 13:17–18; JST, Hebrews 7:3.
20    McConkie, Conference Report, Oct. 1950, 15–16; Smith, *The Words of Joseph Smith,* 304.
21    Smith, *Teachings of the Prophet Joseph Smith,* 322.

Because Melchizedek was an authorized servant of the Lord, he had the keys to ordain Abraham to the priesthood. Moreover, Melchizedek administered to Abraham the new and everlasting covenant, tutored him in the doctrine of the priesthood,[22] and, of great importance, gave him authority to effect the ordinance of eternal marriage and perpetuate the patriarchal order, "a system that would make [Abraham] the Father of the Faithful from that day onward as long as the earth should stand."[23]

Additionally, Melchizedek kept "the storehouse of God," where the "tithes for the poor" were held,[24] as is typical of a Zion priesthood society. We read that Melchizedek gave priesthood blessings to individuals such as Abraham[25]; he preached repentance[26]; and he administered the ordinances of the new and everlasting covenant to his people "after this manner, that thereby the people might look forward on the Son of God . . . for a remission of their sins, that they might enter into the rest of the Lord."[27]

Melchizedek ministered with "extraordinary goodness and power, . . . diligently administered in the office of high priest and 'did preach repentance unto his people. And behold, they did repent; and Melchizedek did establish peace in the land in his days' (Alma 13:18). Consequently, Melchizedek became known as 'the prince of peace' (JST, Gen. 14:33; Heb. 7:1–2; Alma 13:18). 'His people wrought righteousness, and obtained heaven' (JST, Gen. 14:34)."[28] Clearly, all of this is indicative of Zion, and, therefore, establishing Zion is the goal and the outcome of the oath and covenant of the priesthood.

Alma noted that it was this "order" of the high priesthood, coupled with faith, "that gave Melchizedek the power and knowledge that influenced his people to repent and become worthy to be with God. . . . Those ordained to this order were to 'have power, by faith,' and, according to 'the will of the Son of God,' to work miracles. Ultimately, those in this order were 'to stand in the presence of God' (JST, Gen. 14:30–31). This was accomplished by participating in the ordinances of this order (Alma 13:16; D&C 84:20–22). The result was that 'men having this faith, coming up unto this order of God, were translated and taken up into heaven' (JST, Gen. 14:32). Accordingly, the Prophet Joseph Smith taught that the priesthood held by Melchizedek had 'the power of endless lives.'"[29]

If we ever hope to become Zion-like people, we must follow the example of Melchizedek in our individual lives, marriages, and families, as well as in our callings. Like Melchizedek, we must enter into the new and everlasting covenant, follow it to its conclusion, and live worthily so that we might receive a fulness of the priesthood. We must seek the blessings of the priesthood for the purposes of individual salvation and for the salvation of those in our stewardships. We must become kings and priests unto God by means of temple ordinances and "kings of righteousness" to our families and to those in our stewardships. We must use the priesthood, which is the perfect law of theocracy,

---

22    D&C 84:14; JST, Genesis 14:40.
23    McConkie, *A New Witness for the Articles of Faith,* 36.
24    JST, Genesis 14:37–38.
25    JST, Genesis 14:18, 25, 37.
26    Alma 13:18.
27    Alma 13:16; JST, Genesis 14:17.
28    *Encyclopedia of Mormonism,* 879.
29    *Encyclopedia of Mormonism,* 879.

to preach repentance, administer endless lives, and bring our charges back into the presence of God. We must set an example of righteousness by exemplifying Jesus Christ, "that thereby the people might look forward on the Son of God . . . for a remission of their sins, that they might enter into the rest of the Lord."[30] We must become princes of peace by entering the order of the Son of God and in every way typifying Jesus Christ, whose authority we hold. As Melchizedek Priesthood holders, we take upon ourselves the title of Melchizedek and must become even as Jesus Christ is.[31] Because Melchizedek was able to achieve Zion by virtue of the priesthood, we who take upon ourselves the title of Melchizedek and who hold that same authority, must strive to achieve Zion in our lives, marriages, families, and stewardships.

## King Benjamin, a Type of Melchizedek

If Melchizedek is an ideal of a priesthood holder in the Bible, King Benjamin is an ideal in the Book of Mormon. Both kings used their priesthood to facilitate a spiritual rebirth of their people and managed to bring them into the presence of the Lord.

BYU professor M. Catherine Thomas wrote, "The power to play a saving role is the most sought-after power among righteous priesthood holders in time and eternity. The greater the soul, it seems, the deeper the desire to labor to bring souls to Christ through causing them to take his name upon them."[32] King Benjamin was such a priesthood holder, a king and a priest after the order of Melchizedek. Because we are likewise kings and priests to our people—our families, our home teaching families, our quorums, wards, stakes, or otherwise—we can glean priesthood saving principles from the example of King Benjamin and thus learn how to establish the principles of Zion in the lives of those over whom we have stewardship.

One of the first things we learn about King Benjamin is that he followed in the tradition of great priesthood holders before him. What he desired and accomplished for his people was not new. As we learned in book 1, Adam set the example. The Prophet Joseph Smith taught, "[Adam] wanted to bring [his people] into the presence of God. They looked for a city . . . 'whose builder and maker is God' (Hebrews 11:10)."[33] Later, Enoch, Noah, and Melchizedek followed this pattern. Now Benjamin, who "held the keys of power and blessing for his community," prayed earnestly for priesthood power to endow his people with spiritual blessings and make them Zion-like people. Of priesthood holders' preparation to enact such a change in their people, Catherine Thomas wrote:

> A priesthood holder's office is to sanctify himself and
> stand as an advocate before God seeking blessings for
> his community in the manner of the Lord Jesus Christ

---

30   Alma 13:16; JST, Genesis 14:17.
31   3 Nephi 27:27; 28:10.
32   Thomas, "Benjamin and the Mysteries of God," 279.
33   Smith, *Teachings of the Prophet Joseph Smith*, 159.

himself (see John 17:19), whether the community be
as small as a family or as large as Benjamin's kingdom.
A righteous priesthood holder can work by faith to
provide great benefits to his fellow beings (see Mosiah
8:18). He can, in fact, exercise great faith in behalf of
others of lesser faith, "filling in" with faith for them;
thus a prophet [or any priesthood holder] and a people
together can bring down blessings for even a whole
community (for example, see Ether 12:14). The Lord
seems to be interested not only in individuals but also
in groups of people who wish to establish holy cities and
unite with heavenly communities. Like the ancients,
one who holds the holy priesthood is always trying to
establish a holy community, is always "look[ing] for a
city" (Hebrews 11:10, 16). So it was with Benjamin.[34]

Imagine if every priesthood holder approached his stewardship, metaphorically, always "looking for a city." If such were the case, Zion could begin to more fully be established in families, quorums, wards, and stakes. The Lord said, "The power and authority of the higher, or Melchizedek Priesthood, is to hold the keys of all the spiritual blessings of the church—to have the privilege of receiving the mysteries of the kingdom of heaven, to have the heavens opened unto them, to commune with the general assembly and church of the Firstborn, and to enjoy the communion and presence of God the Father, and Jesus the mediator of the new covenant."[35] If Melchizedek Priesthood holders do not instigate and disseminate spiritual blessings, those blessings will remain forever unknown and unclaimed.

What did King Benjamin do that is worthy of our emulation? First, he lived a Christlike life, the covenantal obligation of all priesthood holders, having labored ceaselessly in the service of his people and his God.[36] Next, he prepared his people for the blessings of salvation by fighting for them and doing all that he could to "triumph over the powers of evil—over 'enemies.'" Catherine Thomas wrote, "This is the pattern: the priesthood holder labors with all his faculties to rout Satan from his loved ones as that enemy is manifested in contention, mental warfare, and physical violence among the people. For any priesthood holder to become a prince of peace, he must in some degree wrest his kingdom, great or small, from the adversary and halt the plans of the destroyer on behalf of his loved ones." Establishing peace is absolutely essential for spiritual progress and "to receive greater spiritual blessings."[37] Thus, Melchizedek and Abraham were called princes of peace[38] after the order to Jesus Christ, *the* Prince of Peace.

---

34    Thomas, "Benjamin and the Mysteries of God," 281–82.
35    D&C 107:18–19.
36    Mosiah 2:10–16.
37    Thomas, "Benjamin and the Mysteries of God," 282–83; Mosiah 4:14.
38    Alma 13:17–18; Abraham 1:2.

Another priesthood action of King Benjamin worthy of our emulation is that he sanctified himself and prayed earnestly for priesthood power to bring his people into the presence of the Lord. We cannot overemphasize this step. As we have discussed in book 2, the process of sanctification is to purify (eliminate contaminants) and then change the purpose of something. For example, we take common bread and water, sanctify them by the purifying power of the priesthood, and thus change their purpose to become the sacred emblems of the sacrament. King Benjamin sanctified himself to move from king and protector to prophet and priest, or, more specifically, to savior in the similitude of the Savior.

In response to his prayer, an angel appeared, giving the king permission to gather the people for the purpose of bestowing upon them a great spiritual endowment, along with instructions for how to do it. "The Lord hath heard thy prayers," the angel said, "and hath judged of thy righteousness, and hath sent me to declare unto thee that thou mayest rejoice; *and that thou mayest declare unto thy people, that they may also be filled with joy.*"[39] These were "glad tidings of great joy," the very thing Benjamin had wanted for his people. The message of the angel would distinguish this group of people "above all the people which the Lord hath brought out of the land of Jerusalem."[40] Catherine Thomas explained, "Perhaps this was the first time among all the people brought out from the land of Jerusalem that a king and priest—in the tradition of Adam, Enoch, and Melchizedek—had succeeded in bringing his people to this point of transformation actually to receive the name of Christ."[41]

What exactly happened for them to "actually receive the name of Christ"? The process of taking upon ourselves the name of Christ begins at baptism,[42] and our subsequent partaking of the sacrament indicates our *willingness* to take upon ourselves the name of Jesus Christ,[43] but to actually do so usually lies in the future. Elder Bruce R. McConkie explained,

> Mere compliance with the formality of the ordinance of baptism does not mean that a person has been born again. No one can be born again without baptism, but the immersion in water and the laying on of hands to confer the Holy Ghost do not of themselves guarantee that a person has been or will be born again. The new birth takes place only for those who actually enjoy the gift or companionship of the Holy Ghost, only for those who are fully converted, who have given themselves without restraint to the Lord. Thus Alma addressed himself to his "brethren of the church," and pointedly asked them if they had "spiritually been born of God,"

---

39   Mosiah 3:3–4; emphasis added.
40   Mosiah 1:11.
41   Thomas, "Benjamin and the Mysteries of God," 290–91.
42   2 Nephi 31:13.
43   Moroni 4:3; D&C 20:37.

> received the Lord's image in their countenances, and
> had the "mighty change" in their hearts which always
> attends the birth of the Spirit. (Alma 5:14, 31.)[44]

Beyond the ordinance of baptism and ordination to the priesthood for men, fully taking upon ourselves the name of Christ requires at least three things: (1) intervention by the priesthood (as explained below), (2) receiving all of the temple covenants and ordinances, and (3) living worthy of all that we have received.

King Benjamin understood his priesthood role to act as an advocate for the people and to facilitate a spiritual experience whereby they could receive a greater endowment of the Spirit in a temple setting. We must realize that the responsibility of the priesthood is to bring people to the Holy Ghost, whose responsibility is to bring people to Jesus Christ—whose responsibility is to bring people to the Father. King Benjamin sanctified himself, thus changing his purpose from being king and protector to becoming a savior to his people. The priesthood is the power to facilitate a conversion opportunity for those of one's stewardship, to bring people to Christ so that they might more fully take upon themselves his name, and to unlock the mysteries of the kingdom of heaven that can be learned only by revelation. This astounding idea links priesthood authority, the name of Christ, and unlocking blessings for those whom we serve.

King Benjamin adhered to this priesthood principle, prayed, and received the angel's permission to proceed with the promise that his people might "rejoice with exceedingly great joy,"[45] and be "filled with joy,"[46] which terms, according to Catherine Thomas, are synonymous with being born again.[47] Then he gathered his people to the temple, where he administered to them something akin to the temple endowment. He covered such temple themes as "the creation, fall, Atonement, consecration, and covenant making. Benjamin's last words pertain to being 'sealed' to Christ and receiving eternal life (see Mosiah 5:15)." The result was as astonishing as anything else we read in scripture. These people became Zion people; they "received an endowment of spiritual knowledge and power which took them from being good people to Christlike people—all in a temple setting. What they experienced through the power of the priesthood was a revelation of Christ's nature and the power to be assimilated to his image."[48] That is, by King Benjamin's priesthood intervention, they fully took upon themselves the name of Jesus Christ and consummated their journey to full rebirth. Now they were Zion people.

The connection of the priesthood, temple, and receiving the name of Christ should not escape us. The scriptures teach us that the temple is a house for "the name" of the Lord.[49] The Kirtland Temple was a place where "thy name shall be put upon this house."[50] Clearly, the temple is where we fully receive the name of Jesus Christ through the saving

44   McConkie, *Mormon Doctrine*, 101.
45   Mosiah 3:13.
46   Mosiah 4:3.
47   Thomas, "Benjamin and the Mysteries of God," 285–86.
48   Thomas, "Benjamin and the Mysteries of God," 292.
49   1 Kings 3:2; 5:5; 8:16–20, 29, 44, 48; 1 Chronicles 22:8–10, 19; 29:16; 2:4; 6:5–10, 20, 34, 38.
50   D&C 109:26.

covenants and ordinances we make there. Our leaders have taught that when we partake of the sacrament, we indicate our willingness to make our way to the temple to take upon ourselves fully the name of Christ and receive the blessings of exaltation. These include the highest blessings associated with the name of Christ given to those who live righteously against all hazards.[51]

Priesthood holders are specifically commissioned to help people take upon themselves the name of Christ. Beyond administering the ordinances of baptism and the Holy Ghost, priesthood holders are responsible to get us to the temple, where we take upon us the name of Christ more fully. Then priesthood holders are to teach those exalting covenants and to set an example of righteous covenantal living. The result helps make their charges Zion people and eventually gods. Elder Bruce R. McConkie wrote, "God's name is God. To have his name written on a person is to identify that person as a god. How can it be said more plainly? Those who gain eternal life become gods!"[52] To fully take upon us the name of Jesus Christ—which we do through the endowment, an event that can happen only in a temple—opens the door for our nomination as a candidate for exaltation. For King Benjamin's people, this pivotal experience resulted in a "profound transformation from basic goodness to something that exceeded their ability to even describe. This much did they say, 'The Spirit of the Lord Omnipotent . . . has wrought a mighty change in us, or in our hearts, that we have no more disposition to do evil, but to do good continually' (Mosiah 5:2)."[53]

Who can underestimate a priesthood holder's power and responsibility to help to establish Zion principles in his people? Catherine Thomas concluded, "It is the privilege and responsibility of a community's priesthood leader, through exercising mighty faith and laboring with his people, to bring them to a higher spiritual plane in their quest to return to God. Benjamin had been praying that the Lord would send power to bring to pass a spiritually transforming experience for his people. The Lord sent his angel to declare to the king that power would be given to cause the people to be spiritually reborn, to become sons and daughters of Christ, and to receive the sacred name forever. . . . The people tasted of the glory of God and came to a personal knowledge of him; through the power of the Holy Spirit they experienced the mighty change of heart and the mystery of spiritual rebirth."[54]

No other priesthood responsibility should take precedence over this. It has everything to do with establishing Zion in one life or many lives. President Benson said, "When we awake and are born of God, a new day will break and Zion will be redeemed."[55] That is what Benjamin did with his priesthood—that is what priesthood holders must do: awaken the people so that they are born of God; seek for a new day, so that Zion will be redeemed. This is the "city" we look for, the city "whose builder and maker is God."[56]

This, then, is the priesthood model that draws people toward perfection and the ideal of Zion. This model calls for priesthood holders to sanctify themselves, as did King Benja-

---

51   Oaks, "Taking Upon Us the Name of Jesus Christ," 80–83.
52   McConkie, *Doctrinal New Testament Commentary*, 3:459.
53   Thomas, "Benjamin and the Mysteries of God," 290.
54   Thomas, "Benjamin and the Mysteries of God," 293.
55   Benson, *A Witness and a Warning*, 66.
56   Hebrews 11:10.

min, so that they might have a redeeming effect on those they serve. This model also calls for the followers of such righteous priesthood holders to take advantage of the conversion opportunity proffered them. Joseph Smith said, "The nearer man approaches perfection, the clearer are his views, and the greater his enjoyments, till he has overcome the evils of his life and lost every desire for sin; and like the ancients, arrives at that point of faith where he is wrapped in the power and glory of his Maker and is caught up to dwell with Him."[57]

## The Restoration of the Priesthood

Joseph Smith said, "All Priesthood is Melchizedek, but there are different portions or degrees of it."[58] That is, there is but one priesthood, which is Melchizedek, and it is "the highest and holiest priesthood, and is after the order of the Son of God, and all other priesthoods are only parts, ramifications, powers and blessings belonging to the same, and are held, controlled, and directed by it."[59] The Melchizedek Priesthood has a variety of *orders,* among which are Aaronic, Melchizedek, and Patriarchal.[60] After the great Apostasy, each of these priesthood orders needed to be restored. Because establishing Zion in the life of an individual, a marriage, a family, or a priesthood society is impossible without the Melchizedek Priesthood, and because Zion must be established for the Lord to come,[61] the priesthood must exist upon the earth.

The earliest recorded reference to priesthood restoration was in 1823, when Moroni appeared to Joseph Smith and prophesied, "I will reveal [restore] unto you the priesthood by the hand of the Elijah."[62] But to which order of the priesthood was Moroni referring?

The restoration of the priesthood began on May 15, 1829, with the appearance of John the Baptist, who restored the Aaronic Priesthood.[63] Shortly thereafter, in June 1829, it is assumed, Peter, James, and John restored the Melchizedek Priesthood, including the keys to the kingdom of God.[64] These priesthood and keys authorize men to perform the ordinances of salvation, and give those priesthood holders the right and the commission to preach the gospel of salvation throughout the world.[65] Now the Aaronic and Melchizedek priesthoods had been restored, but in 1823 Moroni had prophesied that Elijah would come and reveal priesthood. The fact that Elijah had not yet appeared indicates that there was still more of the priesthood to be revealed.

## Elijah Restores the Sealing Keys of the Patriarchal Order of the Priesthood

A few years later, as recorded in Doctrine and Covenants 110, Elijah would return and reveal, or restore, the sealing keys associated with what is called the patriarchal order

---

57    Smith, *Teachings of the Prophet Joseph Smith,* 51.
58    Smith, *Teachings of the Prophet Joseph Smith,* 180.
59    Smith, *Teachings of the Prophet Joseph Smith,* 166–67.
60    *Encyclopedia of Mormonism,* 1067–68.
61    Whitney, Conference Report, Oct. 1928, 60.
62    D&C 2:1.
63    D&C 13.
64    Benson, "What I Hope You Will Teach Your Children about the Temple," 6–10.
65    Mark 16:15; McConkie, *Mormon Doctrine,* 220.

of the priesthood, which was restored in a preceding vision by Elias. But prior to those events, a temple had to be built. Joseph Smith learned that the patriarchal order could not be restored unless it took place in a temple. Once, while expounding on the various priesthood orders, the Prophet made the following statement: "[This] . . . Priesthood is Patriarchal authority. Go to and finish the temple, and God will fill it with power, and you will then receive more knowledge concerning this priesthood."[66]

Shortly after the dedication of the Kirtland Temple, on April 3, 1836, Elijah appeared to Joseph Smith and Oliver Cowdery and committed to them the sealing keys associated with the patriarchal order of the priesthood.[67] This priesthood had power "to turn the hearts of the fathers to the children, and the children to the fathers."[68] This patriarchal order of the priesthood is entered into by husbands and wives when they are sealed in the temple. "The patriarchal order is, in the words of Elder James E. Talmage, "a condition where 'woman shares with man the blessings of the Priesthood,' where husband and wife minister, 'seeing and understanding alike, and cooperating to the full in the government of their family kingdom.' A man cannot hold this priesthood without a wife, and a woman cannot share the blessings of this priesthood without a husband, sealed in the temple."[69]

To turn the hearts of parents and children to each other means, according to Joseph Smith, *sealing* their hearts together: "Elijah shall reveal the covenants to *seal* the hearts of the fathers to the children, and the children to the fathers."[70] To make possible this linkage, Elijah restored the keys that bind "the covenants of the fathers in relation to the children, and the covenants of the children in relation to the fathers."[71] That is, Elijah restored the sealing keys of the priesthood whereby covenants and ordinances made and performed are bound on earth and in heaven,[72] and therefore they carry "efficacy, virtue, or force in and after the resurrection of the dead."[73]

With regard to Zion, the message is clear: Zion is defined by the priesthood, by couples and families gathering to temples to obtain the covenants and ordinances of salvation, by entering into the patriarchal order of the priesthood through marriage, and by having those marriages and families sealed together forever.

## Elijah Restores the Fulness of the Priesthood

Elijah's mission was greater still; Elijah's charge was also to restore the "fulness of the priesthood," which includes the fulness of the temple covenants and the ordinances of the house of the Lord.[74] Therefore, the Lord commanded the Saints to build a temple for the purpose of endowing them with power from on high: "Yea, verily I say unto you,

---

66    Smith, *History of the Church,* 5:554–55.
67    Tvedtnes, *The Church of the Old Testament,* 34.
68    D&C 110:15.
69    Talmage, *Young Woman's Journal* 25:602–3; *Encyclopedia of Mormonism,* 1067.
70    Smith, *Teachings of the Prophet Joseph Smith,* 323.
71    Brown, *The Gate of Heaven,* 215; Roberts, *Comprehensive History of the Church,* 5:530.
72    D&C 127:7; 128:8.
73    D&C 132:7.
74    Benson, "What I Hope You Will Teach Your Children About the Temple," 6–10; Smith, *Teachings of the Prophet Joseph Smith,* 308.

I gave unto you a commandment that you should build a house, in the which house I design to *endow* those whom I have chosen with *power from on high*."[75] To endow means to present as a gift of honor; to award, bestow, confer, give, grant.[76] When a college receives an endowment, the principal is typically placed in a fund where it spins off income perpetually; that is, the endowment is structured to continually give. Just so, God endows us in the temple with knowledge and power that bless us eternally. By drawing upon the Lord's endowment and by growing in our understanding of it, we receive progressively greater power to bless our families and others of God's children.

Of the connection between the ordinances associated with the temple endowment and the fulness of the priesthood, Elder Bruce R. McConkie wrote, "It is *only through the ordinances* of his holy house that the Lord deigns to 'restore again that which was lost unto you, or which he hath taken away, even *the fulness of the priesthood*.'"[77] And Joseph Smith said: "If a man gets a fulness of the priesthood of God he has to get it in the same way that Jesus Christ obtained it, and that was by keeping all the commandments and obeying all the ordinances of the house of the Lord."[78]

Again, we see Zion in these descriptions. Zion people are endowed with power from on high; they receive all the ordinances of salvation, which culminates with temple marriage and the fulness of the priesthood. Their eternal standing and blessings are confirmed by revelation and by ordinance.

## Moses Restores Priesthood Keys of Family Gathering

Elijah's appearance in the Kirtland Temple was preceded by the appearances of the Savior, Moses, and Elias. That Moses and Elias came to restore priesthood keys should hold enormous significance for parents in Zion. Moses committed the keys of the gathering of both the dead and the living of the family of Israel. This suggests that individually we now are in possession of priesthood powers to gather our families "from the four parts of the earth."[79]

For what purpose is the gathering of families? Elder McConkie wrote, "Israel gathers for the purpose of building temples in which the ordinances of salvation and exaltation are performed for the living and the dead."[80] On an individual level, this statement suggests that Zion people now have power to gather, or call, their families to the temple to receive the crowning ordinances of salvation.

## Elias Restores Priesthood Keys

Elias, whose office is that of forerunner,[81] appeared after Moses and "committed the dispensation of the gospel of Abraham, saying that in us and our seed all generations after

75    D&C 95:8; emphasis added.
76    *American Heritage Dictionary*, s.v. "endow."
77    D&C 124:28; 127:8; 128:17; McConkie, *Mormon Doctrine*, 637; emphasis added.
78    Smith, *Teachings of the Prophet Joseph Smith*, 308.
79    D&C 110:11.
80    McConkie, *A New Witness for the Articles of Faith*, 539.
81    *Encyclopedia of Mormonism*, 449.

us should be blessed."[82] President Joseph Fielding Smith said, "Elias came, after Moses had conferred his keys, and brought the gospel of the dispensation in which Abraham lived. Everything that pertains to that dispensation, the blessings that were conferred upon Abraham, the promises that were given to his posterity, all had to be restored, and Elias, who held the keys of that dispensation, came."[83] This is the power to organize families into eternal units.[84] That is, because of Elias, our children and grandchildren can now be blessed with the gospel of Abraham (the new and everlasting covenant), blessings of which include the rights to receive the priesthood, all gospel blessings, ordinances, and sealings, including the sealing of eternal marriage and the sealing to eternal life. These rights flow to children who are born in the covenant to parents in Zion because those parents, like Abraham, Isaac, Jacob, and their wives, have entered into the new and everlasting covenant and progressed until they entered into the new and everlasting covenant of marriage.[85] Elder McConkie wrote, "That same day 'Elias appeared, and committed the dispensation of the gospel of Abraham,' meaning the great commission given to Abraham that he and his seed had a right to the priesthood, the gospel, and eternal life. Accordingly, Elias promised those upon whom these ancient promises were then renewed that in them and in their seed all generations should be blessed. (D&C 110:12–16.) Thus, through the joint ministry of Elijah, who brought the sealing power, and Elias, who restored the marriage discipline of Abraham, the way was prepared for the planting in the hearts of the children of the promises made to the fathers. (D&C 2:2.) These are the promises of eternal life through the priesthood and the gospel and celestial marriage.[86]

## The Joint Missions of Elias and Elijah

Joseph Fielding McConkie wrote, "Simply stated, Elijah was sent to restore the keys of the patriarchal order of priesthood, rights which had not yet been fully operational in this dispensation. Elijah restored the keys whereby families (organized in the patriarchal order through the keys delivered by Elias) could be bound and sealed for eternity."[87] Why is the patriarchal priesthood important to Zion people? Because patriarchal priesthood is *family* priesthood; entering into this order of the priesthood directly affects and eternally empowers fathers and mothers to do the work of redemption among their posterity. President Joseph Fielding Smith said, "Through the power [keys] of this priesthood which Elijah bestowed, husband and wife may be sealed, or married for eternity; children may be sealed to their parents for eternity; thus the family is made eternal, and death does not separate the members. *This is the great principle that will save the world from utter destruction.*"[88]

---

82    D&C 110:12.
83    Smith, *Doctrines of Salvation*, 3:127; emphasis added.
84    Millet and McConkie, *The Life Beyond*, 96.
85    D&C 131:2.
86    McConkie, *A New Witness for the Articles of Faith*, 322.
87    Robert L. Millet and Joseph Fielding McConkie, *The Life Beyond*, 96. For other references stating that Elijah restored the sealing keys of the patriarchal priesthood, see Tvedtnes, *The Church of the Old Testament*, 33–35; Smith, *Teachings of the Prophet Joseph Smith*, 172: "Elijah's mission was to 'restore the authority and deliver the keys of the priesthood. . . . Why send Elijah? Because he holds the keys of the authority to administer in all the ordinances of the priesthood.'"
88    Smith, *Doctrines of Salvation*, 2:118; emphasis added.

Imagine Moses, Elias, and Elijah laying their hands upon your head to give you a blessing. First, Moses blesses you with the ability to gather with your family to the kingdom of God and the holy temple. Then Elias blesses you and your spouse and children to organize into an eternal family. He offers you the same covenant of the gospel that Abraham received—the new and everlasting covenant. When you agree to its terms, Elias blesses you with everything that was promised to Abraham: you and your posterity will have the eternal "right to the priesthood, the gospel, and eternal life."[89] Central to those blessings is "the marriage discipline of Abraham,"[90] meaning the promise that your marriage will be eternal, through your faithfulness, and that you and your spouse will enjoy the blessing of eternal posterity. Additionally, you are promised, as was Abraham, that you and your posterity will receive a promised land in this world and a promised inheritance in the celestial world to come.

Now that you have entered into the new and everlasting covenant, which includes eternal marriage, Elijah confirms these blessings with a *seal*, a "welding link,"[91] that cannot be broken. Then, as a final blessing, because you have proven faithful at all hazards, Elijah seals upon you the *fulness of the priesthood,* which, in the ultimate sense, means that he seals you up unto eternal life; that is, Elijah makes everything with which you have been blessed *more sure.*[92] Now, because of your righteousness, Elijah extends to you a promise for your children. The promise is this: As you turn your heart to your children, their hearts will turn to you and the Covenant you have made. Elijah's blessing guarantees that no matter what happens in time or eternity, these children are yours. Then, when Elias and Elijah finish their blessings upon your head, the Savior steps forward and receives you into his embrace. You are home at last, and your spouse and children are there with you.

## Building One Priesthood Power upon Another

Of the interwoven tapestry of the restoration of the priesthood, Joseph Fielding McConkie wrote,

> Joseph Smith taught that ultimate salvation is found
> only in the eternal union of man and woman. Every
> priesthood, grace, power, and authority restored to
> the Prophet Joseph Smith centers in the salvation of
> the family. Peter, James, and John restored the Holy
> Priesthood, thereby authorizing men to perform the
> ordinances of salvation; Elias restored the ordinance of
> eternal marriage and the promise of an endless seed;
> and Elijah restored the sealing power and the fulness

---

89    McConkie, *A New Witness for the Articles of Faith,* 322.
90    McConkie, *A New Witness for the Articles of Faith,* 322.
91    D&C 128:18.
92    Smith, *Teachings of the Prophet Joseph Smith,* 337–38.

of the priesthood by which husband, wife, and children are bound eternally. These doctrines build on the assurance of the Book of Mormon that the resurrection is corporeal and thus that women will be resurrected as women and men as men, the bond of their love ever intact. Thus, as baptism is the gate to the strait and narrow path leading to eternal life, eternal marriage becomes the door through which all who inherit that glory must enter. None enter alone. The man and the woman must stand side by side. Couples in turn must be bound in eternal covenant with their righteous progenitors and with their posterity. In that eternal and restored system we know as The Church of Jesus Christ of Latter-day Saints, salvation is a family affair.[93]

## Rescuing This Generation

Joseph Smith said, "How shall God come to rescue this generation? He will send Elijah the Prophet. . . . *Elijah shall reveal the covenants to seal* the hearts of the fathers to the children, and the children to the fathers."[94] Achieving Zion is impossible without eternal marriages and families. On a family level, the Lord will rescue *this* generation by sending Elijah the prophet to seal the hearts of the fathers to the children, and the children to the fathers. Elijah's sealing power is the crowning blessing of the priesthood.

We see the blessings of the priesthood unfold in the pattern set forth in Doctrine and Covenants 110. First, the Savior comes. He directs the work of salvation and exaltation. His Atonement makes eternal marriage and family possible. Then comes Moses, whose keys gather a couple and a family to the temple. Then comes Elias, whose keys bless a couple and their children with saving and exalting ordinances. Finally, Elijah comes and seals or confirms "more sure" all that has happened. The generation of that couple is rescued, and Zion is established.

## Eternal Principle of Power

"Like God himself," taught Elder McConkie, "the Melchizedek Priesthood is eternal and everlasting in nature."[95] Joseph Smith said, "The priesthood is an everlasting principle, and existed with God from eternity, and will to eternity, without beginning of days or end of years."[96] That is, the priesthood had no beginning and will have no end. When the authority of God is conferred on a worthy man, he will always possess it as long as he remains true to the covenant associated with the priesthood.

---

93    McConkie, *Joseph Smith: The Choice Seer*, chapter 20.
94    Smith, *Teachings of the Prophet Joseph Smith*, 323.
95    McConkie, *Mormon Doctrine*, 475–83.
96    Smith, *Teachings of the Prophet Joseph Smith*, 157–58, 323; D&C 84:17; JST, Hebrews 7:1–3.

Beyond authority, the priesthood becomes power when a man exercises righteousness. Moses revealed, "[Every man] being ordained after this order and calling should have power, by faith, to break mountains, to divide the seas, to dry up waters, to turn them out of their course; to put at defiance the armies of nations, to divide the earth, to break every band, to stand in the presence of God; to do all things according to his will, according to his command subdue principalities and powers; and this by the will of the Son of God which was from before the foundation of the world."[97] Clearly, priesthood is power.

What is this ideal Zion like? In the last days, we are told, it will be a place of refuge in a doomed world. "It shall be called the New Jerusalem, a land of peace, a city of refuge, a place of safety for the saints of the Most High God; . . . and the terror of the Lord also shall be there, . . . and it shall be called Zion" (D&C 45:66–67). At that time, "every man that will not take his sword against his neighbor must needs flee unto Zion for safety" (D&C 45:68). And the wicked shall say that Zion is terrible. Terrible because it is indestructible. Her invulnerability makes her an object of awe and terror. As Enoch said, "Surely Zion shall dwell in safety forever. But the Lord said unto Enoch: Zion have I blessed, but the residue of the people have I cursed" (Moses 7:20). So Zion, in Enoch's day, was taken away and the rest of the world was destroyed. Zion itself is never in danger; on the contrary, it alone offers safety to the world, "that the gathering together upon the land of Zion, and upon her stakes, may be for a defense, and for a refuge from the storm, and from wrath when it shall be poured out without mixture upon the whole earth" (D&C 115:6). It would seem that Zion enjoys the complete security of a bit of the celestial world and that nothing can touch it as long as it retains its character. But a *celestial* order it must be.[98]

## Premortal Qualification for the Priesthood

As a rule, we who strive to live celestial laws and are thus judged worthy to be ordained to the Melchizedek Priesthood were qualified to hold that authority in the premortal life, which Alma calls the "first place."[99] Quoting Alma and Joseph Smith, Elder McConkie taught that worthy priesthood holders were "'on the same standing with their brethren,' meaning that initially all had equal opportunity to progress through righteousness. But while yet in the eternal worlds, certain of the offspring of God, 'having chosen good, and exercising exceeding great faith,' were as a consequence 'called and prepared from the foundation of the world according to the foreknowledge of God' to enjoy the blessings and powers of the priesthood. These priesthood calls were made 'from the foundation of the world,' or in other words faithful men held priesthood power and authority first in pre-existence and then again on earth. 'Every man who has a calling to minister to the inhabitants of the world was ordained to that very purpose in the Grand Council of heaven before this world was.'"[100]

---

97    JST, Genesis 14:30–31.
98    Nibley, *Approaching Zion*, 6–7.
99    Alma 13:3.
100   McConkie, *Mormon Doctrine*, 475–83; Alma 13:3, 5; Smith, *Teachings of the Prophet Joseph Smith*, 365.

Our premortal calling to and preparation in the priesthood, Alma says, was "on account of [our] exceeding faith and good works." Having chosen independently to embrace the good and eschew evil, and to exercise "exceedingly great faith," we received the authority of God, which qualified us for a "preparatory redemption."[101] That is, in the "first place," we earned the blessings of redemption, which guaranteed that we would be offered those blessings again in the flesh. Unless we chose otherwise in this life, the blessings of redemption would be ours forever.

## The Obligation of Zion Priesthood Holders

"Priesthood is the great governing authority in the universe," writes M. Catherine Thomas, assistant professor emeritus of ancient scripture at Brigham Young University. "It unlocks spiritual blessings of the eternal world for the heirs of salvation."[102] The priesthood is always conferred upon us with the understanding that we will minister among God's children, offer them the blessings of the plan of redemption, and bring them to Christ for the purpose of establishing Zion in their lives.[103] This is modeled in the scriptures by Enoch leaving the land of Cainan to preach the gospel to the people, offer the ordinances of salvation, and bring them to Zion.[104] Likewise, Melchizedek preached the gospel, administered the ordinances, and achieved Zion: "And his people wrought righteousness, and obtained heaven, and sought for the city of Enoch which God had before taken, separating it from the earth, having reserved it unto the latter days, or the end of the world."[105]

The Book of Mormon offers another example: "And it came to pass that the thirty and fourth year passed away, and also the thirty and fifth, and behold the disciples of Jesus had formed a church of Christ in all the lands round about. And as many as did come unto them, and did truly repent of their sins, were baptized in the name of Jesus; and they did also receive the Holy Ghost. *And it came to pass in the thirty and sixth year, the people were all converted unto the Lord, upon all the face of the land, both Nephites and Lamanites,* and there were no contentions and disputations among them, and every man did deal justly one with another."[106]

Catherine Thomas writes, "The power to play a saving role is the most sought-after power among righteous priesthood holders in time or in eternity. The greater the soul, it seems, the deeper the desire to labor to brings souls to Christ. . . . A brief look at the history of the priesthood on the earth reveals that men like [King] Benjamin have stood in this priesthood channel unlocking the blessings of salvation for their people since the days of Adam. Adam, in fact, was the great prototype of priesthood holders who strove to bring their communities and their posterity into at-one-ment with the Lord Jesus Christ. Adam blessed his posterity because, the Prophet Joseph taught, 'he wanted to bring them into the presence of God. They looked for a city . . . 'whose builder and maker is God' (Hebrews 11:10)."

---

101   Alma 13:3.
102   Thomas, "Benjamin and the Mysteries of God," 279.
103   Eyring, "Faith and the Oath and Covenant of the Priesthood," 61–64.
104   Moses 6:41; see Moses 6–7.
105   JST, Genesis 14:34.
106   4 Nephi 1:1–2; emphasis added.

As we have said, a priesthood holder is under obligation to sanctify himself so that he can advocate for his people, as did Adam, Enoch, Melchizedek, Moses, King Benjamin, and Joseph Smith. Dr. Thomas explains the duties of a priesthood holder: "A priesthood holder's office is to sanctify himself and stand as an advocate before God seeking blessings for his community in the manner of Jesus Christ (see John 17:19), whether the community be as small as a family or as large as Benjamin's kingdom. A righteous priesthood holder can work by faith to provide great benefits to his fellow beings (see Mosiah 8:18). He can, in fact, exercise great faith in behalf of others of lesser faith, 'filling in' with faith for them. . . . The Lord seems interested not only in individual but in groups of people who wish to establish holy cities and unite with heavenly communities. Like the ancients, one who holds the holy priesthood is always trying to establish a holy community, is always 'look[ing] for a city' (Hebrews 11:10, 16)."[107]

## Our Priesthood Work Then and Now

Our works on earth are an extension of the works we did in the premortal world. Alma explained that our premortal calling to the priesthood set us apart from others in that realm, those who hardened their hearts against the gospel and thus forfeited their privileges: "And thus they [priesthood holders] have been called to this holy calling on account of their faith, while others would reject the Spirit of God on account of the hardness of their hearts and blindness of their minds, while, if it had not been for this they might have had as great privilege as their brethren." Clearly, we distinguished ourselves in the premortal life by embracing the gospel and the principles of Zion, and therefore we were rewarded in that "first place" with the priesthood: "Thus this holy calling [was] prepared from the foundation of the world for such as would not harden their hearts, being in and through the Atonement of the Only Begotten Son."

Having received the priesthood, we became part of the same order as the Son of God and went about doing his work, the work of Zion:

> And thus being called by this holy calling, and ordained
> unto the high priesthood of the holy order of God, to
> teach his commandments unto the children of men, that
> they also might enter into his rest—this high priest-
> hood being after the order of his Son, which order was
> from the foundation of the world; or in other words,
> being without beginning of days or end of years, being
> prepared from eternity to all eternity, according to his
> foreknowledge of all things—Now they were ordained
> after this manner—being called with a holy calling, and
> ordained with a holy ordinance, and taking upon them
> the high priesthood of the holy order, which calling, and

107   Thomas, "Benjamin and the Mysteries of God," 280–82.

> ordinance, and high priesthood, is without beginning
> or end—thus they become high priests forever, after the
> order of the Son, the Only Begotten of the Father, who is
> without beginning of days or end of years, who is full of
> grace, equity, and truth. And thus it is. Amen.[108]

Clearly, our past experience with the priesthood will be exceeded only by a glorious future experience. Moreover, our priesthood work now is an extension of our work then, and our work in the priesthood will continue into the eternities: "The faithful elders of this dispensation, when they depart from mortal life, continue their labors in the preaching of the gospel of repentance and redemption, through the sacrifice of the Only Begotten Son of God."[109]

The work we assumed so long ago—the work of redemption—is the work that helps to establish Zion in the lives of people. This work is as eternal as is the priesthood. The priesthood vitalizes the plan of redemption and makes possible the establishment of Zion. The priesthood of God is the power by which the foundation of Zion (the Atonement) and the three pillars of Zion function together. Upon this sure foundation and its pillars, Zion rises to form "the highest order of priesthood society."[110]

## The Covenant of the Priesthood

"When we receive the Melchizedek Priesthood," Elder Bruce R. McConkie testified, "we enter into a covenant with the Lord. It is the covenant of exaltation. . . . There neither is nor can be a covenant more wondrous and great."[111]

After we receive the new and everlasting covenant by baptism, the Spirit begins to purify us and change our nature. The Spirit also urges us to progress in the Covenant, and our desire migrates from selfish to selfless. The more we become Zion-like, the more we yearn to share the Covenant with others and to invite them to become Zion-like. The only authoritative way to bless other people with the Covenant is to seek the priesthood, as did Abraham, and receive it by covenant. This is the second pillar of Zion—the oath and covenant of the priesthood. It emerges from the Covenant of Mercy, which likewise emerges from the new and everlasting covenant.

We seek to enter the priesthood covenant for both personal and universal reasons. The priesthood offers us supernal individual gifts, such as individual salvation, keys to the knowledge and power of God, and eternal marriage, none of which can be obtained in any other manner. But the priesthood is also the "power and authority of God" that

---

108    Alma 13:4–9.
109    D&C 138:57.
110    Kimball, *Teachings of Spencer W. Kimball,* 125.
111    McConkie, *A New Witness for the Articles of Faith,* 312–13. Note: In *Doctrines of Salvation,* 2:58, Joseph Fielding Smith reminded us that the marriage covenant is also called the covenant of exaltation. "The marriage covenant flows from the covenant of the priesthood; the marriage covenant is the order of the priesthood (Patriarchal) that allows us to become like God. Therefore, in the marriage covenant, all the blessings of exaltation contained in the priesthood covenant are renewed and pronounced upon both the man and the woman."

allows us "to minister to other beings to bring about their happiness."[112] Let us examine the priesthood and its covenant that allow us these privileges.

## The Lesser and Greater Portions

"All priesthood is Melchizedek," said the Prophet Joseph Smith, "but there are different portions or degrees of it."[113] The lesser "portion," or the preparatory priesthood, is called the Aaronic, or Levitical Priesthood, one of the blessings of which is the key to the ministering of angels. The higher "portion" of the priesthood is the Melchizedek Priesthood, one of the blessings of which is that righteous men and women have the ability "to speak with God face to face."[114] This privilege is descriptive of Zion people, with whom the Lord makes his abode.[115] Elder McConkie taught that these two orders of the priesthood are received by covenant, but only the Melchizedek Priesthood is received with the Father's oath.

The covenant regarding the Aaronic Priesthood, said Elder McConkie, states that a worthy man must promise to forsake the world, magnify his calling, minister and give service to others, and obey the commandments. In return, the Lord promises to magnify the priesthood holder in his position and prepare him in every way to receive the Melchizedek Priesthood.

Elder McConkie continued by saying that the covenant regarding the Melchizedek Priesthood is that a worthy man promises to magnify his calling, obey the commandments, be an example of Jesus Christ, serve as the Lord would serve, "live by every word that proceedeth forth from the mouth of God" (D&C 84:44), and marry in the temple for time and eternity. In return, the Father promises *with an oath* that he will give that man all that the Father has, which is the definition of eternal life. These covenantal blessings comprise the promises of exaltation, godhood, eternal marriage, and endless posterity.[116]

## The Patriarchal Order

In addition to the Aaronic and Melchizedek orders of the priesthood is the patriarchal order. Neither Zion nor Zion people can be established without the patriarchal order of the priesthood. This order is not a separate priesthood but rather the highest order of the Melchizedek Priesthood.[117] According to Elder McConkie, this is the Lord's eternal patriarchal order, or the priesthood order of the gods. This order exists only in the highest degree of the celestial kingdom, and it is the priesthood order by which husbands and wives, who have been sealed for time and eternity, may enjoy eternal increase of spirit

---

112   Riddle, "The New and Everlasting Covenant," 231.
113   Smith, *Teachings of the Prophet Joseph Smith,* 180.
114   Smith, *Teachings of the Prophet Joseph Smith,* 180.
115   Moses 7:21; Psalm 132:13.
116   McConkie, "The Doctrine of the Priesthood," 32; D&C 131:1–4.
117   *Encyclopedia of Mormonism,* 1067.

children in the Resurrection.[118] This is the order of priesthood government that exists in heaven among all glorified fathers and mothers who preside over their vast families.

Elder McConkie wrote: "'This order was instituted in the days of Adam, and came down by lineage.' It was designed 'to be handed down from father to son.' It came down in succession; it is priesthood government; it is the government of God both on earth and in heaven. And even today, it 'rightly belongs to the literal descendants of the chosen seed, to whom the promises were made.' (D&C 107:40–41.) *That it is not now in full operation simply means that fallen men have departed from the ancient ways and are now governing each other as they choose.*"[119] That is, the patriarchal order of the priesthood presently functions within righteous marriages and families by virtue of the husband and wife's marriage covenant and sealing, but it does not yet function as it did in the beginning as the government of the Church. This form of priesthood government exists in the celestial kingdom.[120]

## Differing Purposes and Powers

The Aaronic and Melchizedek priesthoods administer different elements of the gospel. The Aaronic Priesthood holds "the keys of the ministering of angels, and to administer in outward ordinances, the letter of the gospel, the baptism of repentance for the remission of sins, agreeable to the covenants and commandments."[121] In other words, this is a temporal priesthood, a priesthood that *cannot* establish Zion because "Zion is heaven. It is where God lives."[122] The ideal of Zion people is to enjoy the presence of God: "For without [the ordinances of the Melchizedek Priesthood] no man can see the face of God, even the Father, and live."[123]

When the Melchizedek Priesthood, its ordinances, and principles of Zion are neglected or rejected by a covenant person, the Lord swears in his wrath that that person risks losing the blessings of eternal life. The Melchizedek Priesthood and its blessings cease to function in such a person. He is left with a preparatory gospel, and he is in danger of losing his blessings altogether, as did the Nephites and Jaredites. The ancient Israelites are an example of a people who lost their blessings due to neglect or rejection of the priesthood. "Now this Moses plainly taught to the children of Israel in the wilderness, and sought diligently to sanctify his people that they might behold the face of God; but they hardened their hearts and could not endure his presence; therefore, the Lord in his wrath, for his anger was kindled against them, swore that they should not enter into his rest while in the wilderness, which rest is the fulness of his glory. Therefore, he took Moses out of their midst, and the Holy Priesthood also; and the lesser priesthood continued, which priesthood holdeth the key of the ministering of angels and the preparatory gospel; which gospel is the gospel of repentance and of baptism, and the remission of sins, and the law of carnal commandments, which the Lord in his wrath caused to continue with the house of Aaron among the children of Israel."[124]

---

118    McConkie, "The Doctrine of the Priesthood," 32; D&C 131:1–4.
119    McConkie, *A New Witness for the Articles of Faith*, 35; emphasis added.
120    McConkie, *Mormon Doctrine*, 559.
121    D&C 107:20.
122    Nibley, *Approaching Zion*, 6–7.
123    D&C 84:22.
124    D&C 84:23–27.

Zion people embrace the Melchizedek Priesthood, which "administereth the gospel and holdeth the key of the mysteries of the kingdom, even the key of the knowledge of God."[125]

## Grand Purposes of the Priesthood

As we can see, the Melchizedek Priesthood has two grand purposes: to administer the gospel (meaning to preside) and the covenants and ordinances of salvation; and to enable its holders to stand in the presence of God and receive personal revelation directly from him. This eminent level of revelation enjoyed by Zion people, is made possible only by the ordinances of the Melchizedek Priesthood: "Therefore, in the ordinances thereof, the power of godliness [i.e., the power to become Godlike] is manifest. And without the ordinances thereof, and the authority of the priesthood, the power of godliness is not manifest unto men in the flesh; for without this [the power to become Godlike] no man can see the face of God, even the Father, and live."[126]

This information about the priesthood is of profound significance. To hold the authority of God, to wield his power, and to stand in his presence, are definitive characteristics of Zion and of eternal life. Of Zion, Enoch declared, "Surely Zion shall dwell in safety forever," whereupon the Lord answered, "Zion have I blessed." Moses wrote, "The Lord came and dwelt with his people, and they dwelt in righteousness." He continued with "Zion, in the process of time, was taken into heaven. And the Lord said unto Enoch: Behold mine abode forever."[127]

## Priesthood Blessings

If men desire to become Zion-like, they must be ordained to the Melchizedek Priesthood and abide in the covenant of the priesthood. If women desire to become Zion-like, they must also embrace the principles of the covenant of the priesthood by receiving the ordinances of the priesthood, including eternal marriage, thereby entering into the patriarchal order of the priesthood with their husbands. Here, we must keep in mind that Zion is a journey. That single men and women might presently lack temple marriage does not discount their ability to qualify now as Zion people. As with all gospel ideals, it is the direction in which we are headed that qualifies us for blessings. The Lord's grace allows him to reward us *as if* we had met all of the requirements. We simply must do the best we can with present realities.

For men, this process begins with the Father's invitation. He offers them the priesthood by swearing a sacred oath; then they enter into a covenant with him. If they remain faithful to that covenant, it will lead them to eternal life. They progress in the priesthood covenant by ordination, receiving temple covenants and ordinances, and temple marriage, at which time the Father's oath given in the priesthood covenant is renewed.[128] Only by progressing in this way can men ever hope to obtain the blessings of Zion, stand

---

125    D&C 84:19.
126    D&C 84:20–22.
127    Moses 7:16, 20–21.
128    McConkie, *A New Witness for the Articles of Faith*, 313.

in the presence of God, receive intelligence and instructions from him, become in every way as God is, and inherit what he has.

And the blessings of the priesthood multiply.

When men have received the priesthood ordination and the temple covenants and ordinances, they then possess the authority to administer the same to others of God's children. They become saviors on Mount Zion[129] for both the living and the dead. They are authorized to assist in the eternal redemptive work of God, which is to bring people to Christ so that those people might also receive the blessings of immortal glory and "eternal lives."[130] Therefore, as we have said, men receive the priesthood for two reasons: "for your sake, and not for your sake only, but for the sake of the whole world."[131]

## The Blessings of Adam

Joseph Smith taught: "The Priesthood was first given to Adam; he obtained the First Presidency, and held the keys of it from generation to generation. The Priesthood is an everlasting principle. The keys have to be brought from heaven whenever the Gospel is sent. When they are revealed from heaven, it is by Adam's authority."[132] The "Holy Priesthood after the order of the Son of God"[133] provided for the promises that God made to Adam[134]—to provide a Savior to redeem him and his children from their fallen condition,[135] and restore them to a Zion-like condition through the new and everlasting covenant, which includes the oath and covenant of the priesthood. This covenantal relationship forms the foundation of the plan of salvation God gave to Adam, and this plan was determined from the beginning to be administered by "the order of the Son of God." Adam was first taught by God and angels, and then he taught his children by the authority of the priesthood how to become Zion-like in character and how to regain God's presence.

The holy priesthood offered Adam the greatest promises of personal blessings, but perhaps more importantly, it also gave Adam the necessary authority to minister those blessings to his family.[136] Among those blessings is the establishment of Zion. Adam's righteousness summoned the Lord to establish the foundations of Adam-ondi-Ahman, the first Zion priesthood society.[137] It was there that Adam eventually succeeded in bringing his faithful posterity back into the presence of the Lord.[138]

We see in Adam's example the redemptive power of the priesthood and the exalting power of Zion-like principles that are incorporated in the priesthood. It was by means of

---

129    Obadiah 1:21.
130    Smith, *Teachings of the Prophet Joseph Smith*, 322; Moses 1:39.
131    D&C 84:48.
132    Smith, *History of the Church*, 3:385–86.
133    D&C 107:3.
134    Moses 5:6–10.
135    Alma 13:2.
136    Smith, *Teachings of the Prophet Joseph Smith*, 159.
137    Bruce R. McConkie wrote, "In our popular Latter-day Saint hymn which begins, 'Glorious things are sung of Zion, Enoch's city seen of old,' we find William W. Phelps preserving the doctrine that 'In Adam-ondi-Ahman, Zion rose where Eden was.' And in another hymn, written by the same author in the days of the Prophet Joseph Smith, we find these expressions; 'We read that Enoch walk'd with God, Above the power of mammon, While Zion spread herself abroad, And Saints and angels sang aloud, In Adam-ondi-Ahman'" (*Mormon Doctrine*, 20).
138    D&C 107:53–54.

the power of the priesthood, specifically the power of the ordinances of the Melchizedek Priesthood,[139] that Adam was able to accomplish these supernal feats. President Benson asked, "How did Adam bring his descendants into the presence of the Lord? The answer: Adam and his descendants entered into the priesthood order of God. Today we would say they went to the House of the Lord and received their blessings."[140] We may follow the example of Adam by going to the house of the Lord and entering into "the order of the Son of God" that we, too, might obtain power to bring ourselves, our children, and those for whom we are responsible into the presence of God.

There is great power in the Melchizedek Priesthood and its ordinances—power to ask for and receive blessings, which is personal revelation at the highest level. Adam and Eve exemplified the pattern of asking and receiving. Finding themselves estranged from God, they offered mighty prayer at an altar. In that sacred setting, they sought for reconciliation, for knowledge, and for the power to return to the Lord's presence. When God determined that they qualified for the blessings they were seeking, the veil was rent and "an angel of the Lord appeared" with the promise of a Savior and deliverance.[141] Eventually, Adam would receive additional priesthood ordinances so that he might receive the knowledge of God, power to counsel with and ask him questions directly, and power to return to his presence.

This is a priesthood journey that every son or daughter of Adam and Eve must make—the journey out of Babylon to Zion. No power except "the order of the Son of God"—the Melchizedek Priesthood and its ordinances—has the ability to bring us to God and teach us how to ask for and receive revelation so that we might successfully make the journey. President Ezra Taft Benson taught, "To enter into the order of the Son of God is the equivalent today of entering into the fullness of the Melchizedek Priesthood, which is only received in the house of the Lord."[142] If men and women endure in faith, they can qualify to receive the fulness of the priesthood in the temple, where they receive the covenants and ordinances of the priesthood and enter into the highest order of the priesthood—eternal marriage. Zion, in the ultimate sense, can be established in no other way, and Adam and Eve are our models.

## The Blessings of Abraham

Whereas Adam and Eve were the parents of the human race, Abraham and Sarah were the parents of the faithful. Like Adam and Eve, whose faith was so great that they were able to approach God in mighty prayer and receive his assurance of a Savior and plan of salvation for their family,[143] Abraham and Sarah also had great faith as they approached God in mighty prayer and received the promises of the new and everlasting covenant and the perpetual rights to priesthood for their family. They received the promise that the

---

139   D&C 84:19–22.
140   Benson, *Teachings of Ezra Taft Benson,* 257.
141   Moses 5:6–9.
142   Benson, *Teachings of Ezra Taft Benson,* 257.
143   Moses 5:6–12.

Savior would come through their lineage and, that through the combined ministries of the Savior and their family, all of the children of Adam and Eve could be blessed with the Covenant.

Abraham and Sarah's heritage was Zion, and Zion was what they desired to reestablish as a legacy.[144] Reading the records of his fathers, Abraham knew that he had a right to the priesthood and therefore was of the heritage of Zion.[145] For the purpose of placing the priesthood power to become Zion into Abraham's hands, the Lord guided him to Melchizedek, whose people were Zion-like.[146] Later, Melchizedek and his people in Salem were translated and taken from the earth, as had been Enoch and his people. Then, we assume, Abraham and Sarah were left behind as the surviving Zion people on the earth.

As we have learned, the new and everlasting covenant comprises all gospel blessings, including eternal marriage and eternal posterity. The familial right to this Covenant was given to this wonderful couple. Because we are literally their children, or adopted into their family by baptism, we are heirs to their blessings. Abraham received the blessings of the new and everlasting covenant, the priesthood, temple blessings, and eternal marriage in an unbroken chain from Melchizedek back to Noah, to Enoch, to Adam. Of Abraham, Elder McConkie wrote,

> He was called by the Lord to "be a father of many nations." To him the Lord said: "I will establish my covenant [the gospel covenant] between me and thee and thy seed after thee in their generations for an everlasting covenant, to be a God unto thee and to thy seed after thee." (Genesis 17:4, 7.) "And in thy seed shall all the nations of the earth be blessed" (Genesis 22:18), meaning that all who thereafter believed what Abraham believed and lived as Abraham lived would bless themselves through the everlasting gospel covenant. The Lord promised Abraham, "Thou shalt be a blessing unto thy seed after thee," the Lord promised Abraham, "that in their hands they shall bear this ministry and Priesthood unto all nations." This is the very thing the seed of Abraham is commencing to do in these last days. "I will bless them [all nations] through thy name," the Lord continues, "for as many as receive this Gospel shall be called after thy name, and shall be accounted thy seed, and shall rise up and bless thee, as their father." Even the believing Gentiles shall cleave unto Abraham, account him as their father, and be adopted

---

144    Hebrews 11:9, 16.
145    Abraham 1:2–3, 31.
146    Clark, *The Blessings of Abraham,* 136–41.

into his family. "And I will bless them that bless thee," saith the Lord, "and curse them that curse thee; and in thee (that is, in thy Priesthood) and in thy seed (that is, thy Priesthood), for I give unto thee a promise that this right shall continue in thee, and in thy seed after thee (that is to say, the literal seed, or the seed of the body) shall all the families of the earth be blessed, even with the blessings of the Gospel, which are the blessings of salvation, even of life eternal." (Abraham 2:9–11.)[147]

Has there ever been such a promise? If we are faithful, we, the children of Abraham, receive the blessings of Abraham. "The seed of Abraham shall take the gospel and the priesthood to all nations, and those who accept the divine word shall become as though they too were the chosen seed." Abraham's children "have a right to hear the gospel, and if they accept it, to receive the priesthood, to have their own family units continue everlastingly so that they with Abraham shall have eternal life."[148] When Zion is established by the Lord in the case of a person, a family, or a priesthood society, it is through the ministry of Abraham's authorized children.

Adam and Eve and Abraham and Sarah are our models. At various points of the temple experience, we see them exemplified. We see them as they seek for and secure blessings for themselves and for us, their children. When we set out on our journey to find redemption, we are like Adam and Eve, who set the example for that experience. When we kneel with our sweethearts at a temple altar to be married for eternity, we assume, then follow, the example of Abraham and Sarah, receiving all the blessings that were given to them in the same culminating temple ordinance. These blessings define and exalt Zion people.

## Abraham's Qualifications and Desire

Abraham knew something about the priesthood that we need to know. He knew that achieving the celestial kingdom was not possible unless he took someone with him, and he knew that taking someone with him was not possible without the priesthood. Therefore, he diligently sought the priesthood so that he could bless others: "I sought after the right," he said, "whereunto I should be ordained *to administer the same.*"[149]

Blessing other people, we are taught, results in one of the highest attainments of joy: If we cry repentance, the Lord says, "How great shall be your joy with him in the kingdom of my Father!"[150] Abraham knew that the priesthood offered him "greater happiness and peace and rest,"[151] and *rest*, of course, is the fulness of the glory of the Lord.[152]

---

147  McConkie, *A New Witness for the Articles of Faith*, 36.
148  McConkie, *A New Witness for the Articles of Faith*, 37.
149  Abraham 1:2.
150  D&C 18:15.
151  Abraham 1:2.
152  D&C 84:24.

Abraham spared no effort or expense in seeking the blessings of the priesthood. His quest required that he move away from a wicked environment,[153] a quest every Zion person must make. In seeking the priesthood, Abraham exemplified these qualifications and desires:

- He had been a follower of righteousness.
- He had a desire to become a *greater* follower of righteousness.
- He had a desire for great knowledge.
- He had a desire to possess a *greater* knowledge.
- He had a desire to become a father of many nations (an eternal father).
- He had a desire to become a prince of peace, like Melchizedek and the Savior.
- He had a desire to receive instructions from God.
- He had a desire to keep the highest revealed commandments of God.

Abraham was, by birth, a rightful heir to the priesthood, as we, his children, are. That he had to qualify for his appointment to the priesthood by desire and righteousness should be a lesson for all of us. Abraham's journey to receive the priesthood took him from Ur to Hebron to Salem, where he finally met Melchizedek, the only man on earth who had the keys to confer upon him the holy priesthood and its blessings. Now Abraham's faith, faithfulness, patience, and endurance were rewarded. He was ordained a high priest, and his authoritative ministry began. We, who are Abraham's children, have been commanded to do likewise: "Go ye, therefore, and do the works of Abraham; enter ye into my law and ye shall be saved."[154]

## Blessings of the Priesthood

Now ordained and empowered, having covenanted to be obedient to "every word that proceedeth forth from the mouth of God,"[155] to sacrifice all things,[156] and to remain faithful in the Covenant, Abraham received blessings that every worthy priesthood holder might expect to receive: a revelation of the Creation and all the works of God; an endowment of divine knowledge and power; a specially proffered gift; and God's setting him apart for a special commission. Abraham's journey in the priesthood would lead him to coronation; he would become a king and a priest unto God forever, and he would be set in his kingdom by the ordinance of eternal marriage. Because the priesthood temple ordinances are also available to the daughters and adopted daughters of Abraham, worthy women also may qualify to receive these blessings.

This is the priesthood journey of our parents, Adam and Eve and Abraham and Sarah, which journey is symbolized in the sacred setting of the temple. Our journey to celestial glory is like theirs. Every power in the priesthood, every covenant, ordinance, instruction, and honor, even the privilege of eternal marriage and entering into the patriarchal order of the Gods—everything that was given to these, our parents, is offered to us if we, too, desire, qualify, sacrifice, and endure.

---

153   Abraham 1:1.
154   D&C 132:32.
155   D&C 84:44.
156   Smith, *Lectures on Faith,* 6:7.

In both Adam's and Abraham's examples, we see the ultimate blessing of the priesthood: to stand in the presence of God. Of Adam, it is recorded: "Three years previous to the death of Adam, he called Seth, Enos, Cainan, Mahalaleel, Jared, Enoch, and Methuselah, who were all high priests, with the residue of his posterity who were righteous, into the valley of Adam-ondi-Ahman, and there bestowed upon them his last blessing. *And the Lord appeared unto them,* and they rose up and blessed Adam, and called him Michael, the prince, the archangel."[157] Centuries later, Abraham wrote: "I, Abraham . . . prayed unto the Lord, and the Lord appeared unto me." In that vision, the Lord declared, "I am the Lord thy God; I dwell in heaven; the earth is my footstool; I stretch my hand over the sea, and it obeys my voice; I cause the wind and the fire to be my chariot; I say to the mountains—Depart hence—and behold, they are taken away by a whirlwind, in an instant, suddenly. My name is Jehovah, and I know the end from the beginning; therefore my hand shall be over thee." When the vision had ended, Abraham exclaimed, "Thy servant has sought thee earnestly; now I have found thee."[158]

## The Prize Is Worth the Price

In our day, the Prophet Joseph Smith recorded a similar experience after he and Sidney Rigdon had seen in vision the Father and the Son. "Great and marvelous are the works of the Lord, and the mysteries of his kingdom which he showed unto us, which surpass all understanding in glory, and in might, and in dominion; which he commanded us we should not write while we were yet in the Spirit, and are not lawful for man to utter; neither is man capable to make them known, for they are only to be seen and understood by the power of the Holy Spirit, which God bestows on those who love him, and purify themselves before him; *to whom he grants this privilege of seeing and knowing for themselves;* that through the power and manifestation of the Spirit, *while in the flesh,* they may be able to bear his presence in the world of glory."[159]

This is the sum of gospel teaching: God's sons and daughters can return to him *while in the flesh!* And the priesthood is the power that makes it all possible. Zion, indeed!

Here, then, we see the purposes of the new and everlasting covenant and the oath and covenant of the priesthood—the first and second pillars of Zion. The Lord calls us out of the world and places us under covenant to become new people. To that end he begins to purify us of sin and sanctify us for a new and holy purpose. He places upon us his name and authority, then prepares us to receive our kingdom by cleansing (purifying) and anointing (sanctifying) us for coronation. He clothes us in a way that our body becomes a temple, then endows us with the keys of divine knowledge and power, and teaches us how to ask for and receive blessings so that we know how to enter his presence. In the process, we receive from him a special gift or intelligence, and he gives us a commission. Ultimately, he draws us into his kingdom, where we receive from him our eternal kingdom in the patriarchal order of the gods.

---

157    D&C 107:43–53; emphasis added.
158    Abraham 2:6–8, 12.
159    D&C 76:114–18; emphasis added.

Do we appreciate our priesthood blessings? Are we applying the principles of the priesthood to seek the Lord diligently, as did Abraham, so that we, too, might find him? Or are we neglectful, sitting on a plateau, and taking our privileges for granted? President Kimball succinctly stated the purposes of the priesthood: "Priesthood is the means to exaltation. The priesthood is the power and authority of God delegated to man on earth to act in all things pertaining to the salvation of men. It is the means whereby the Lord acts through men to save souls. Without this priesthood power, men are lost. Only through this power does man 'hold the keys of all the spiritual blessings of the church,' enabling him to receive 'the mysteries of the kingdom of heaven, to have the heavens opened' unto him (see D&C 107:18–19), enabling him to enter the new and everlasting covenant of marriage and to have his wife and children bound to him in an everlasting tie, enabling him to become a patriarch to his posterity forever, and enabling him to receive a fullness of the blessings of the Lord."[160]

The quality of Zion cannot be achieved in a person, marriage, family, or society without the priesthood. Elias Higbee asked Joseph Smith, "What is meant by the command in Isaiah, 52nd chapter, 1st verse, which saith: Put on thy strength, O Zion—and what people had Isaiah reference to?" The Prophet answered, "He had reference to those whom God should call in the last days, who should hold the power of priesthood to bring again Zion, and the redemption of Israel; and to put on her strength is to put on the authority of the priesthood, which she, Zion, has a right to by lineage; also to return to that power which she had lost."[161]

## The Authority and Keys of the Priesthood

The authority of God is God's to give, and it is conferred by covenant to his worthy sons. The Apostle Paul taught, "No man taketh this honour unto himself but he that is called of God, as was Aaron."[162] Elder McConkie listed four criteria concerning the doctrine of priesthood authority:

1. There is a God in heaven whose powers and authority are infinite. He is the author and creator of salvation, and he has offered salvation to men on his own terms and on no others.
2. The Lord's house is a house of order. He has given a law unto all things, and all blessings come by obedience to those laws upon which their receipt is predicated.
3. Salvation is available to men through the gospel. The gospel is, in fact, the plan of salvation, and in it are set forth the terms and conditions upon which God offers salvation to men.
4. Deity calls his own prophets, his own ministers, and his own legal administrators to preach his gospel and to administer the affairs of his earthly kingdom, all so that salvation may be made available to his earthly children.[163]

---

160   Kimball, *Teachings of Spencer W. Kimball*, 494.
161   D&C 113:7–8.
162   Hebrews 5:4.
163   McConkie, *A New Witness for the Articles of Faith*, 306.

According to Elder McConkie, the best statement on the doctrine of priesthood authority is found in Doctrine and Covenants 132:7—"All covenants, contracts, bonds, obligations, oaths, vows, performances, connections, associations, or expectations, that are not made and entered into and sealed by the Holy Spirit of promise, of him who is anointed, both as well for time and for all eternity, and that too most holy, by revelation and commandment through the medium of mine anointed, whom I have appointed on the earth to hold this power, . . . are of no efficacy, virtue, or force in and after the resurrection from the dead; for all contracts that are not made unto this end have an end when men are dead."

Elder McConkie adds this statement: "Men can do what they please and make any assumptions they like as to the validity of any of their acts in this life. But as the Lord lives, nothing they do will endure in heaven unless it meets the divine standard here set forth. It must be done in righteousness; it must be approved by the Spirit; and it must be performed and sealed by a legal administrator."[164]

Becoming a Zion person is impossible without the priesthood and its covenants and ordinances. The Lord's house is a house of order and not a house of confusion.[165] "We believe that a man must be called of God, by prophecy, and by the laying on of hands by those who are in authority, to preach the gospel and administer in the ordinances thereof."[166] A man's personal salvation is tied to his discharge of his priesthood responsibilities: to preach the gospel and to administer the ordinances of salvation to God's children.

All priesthood authority flows to us by means of the delegated *keys of authority* that come directly from the President of the Church, who holds all of the administrative keys. When we are called by prophecy to a responsibility by an authorized priesthood leader who holds the keys of authority, we in turn receive the necessary authority to fulfill our duty. We receive "the right and power to speak for the Lord, to state what he wants stated, to say what he would say if he personally were here!" We receive "divine power, the power to perform the ordinances of salvation. . . ! Without [priesthood keys and authority], there is no true gospel, no divine church, no salvation for fallen man."[167]

"The keys of the priesthood," continues Elder McConkie, "are the right and power of presidency. They are the directing, controlling, and governing power. Those who hold them are empowered to direct the manner in which others use their priesthood. Every ministerial act performed by a priesthood holder must be done at the proper time and place and in the proper way. The power of directing these labors constitutes the keys of the priesthood."[168] When the priesthood society of Zion is established on the earth, it will be under the direction of the President of the Church, who holds the authoritative keys to do so. When Zion is established in the life of an individual, in a marriage, or in a family, it is done by the power of the priesthood, which comes from priesthood ordinances and righteousness.

---

164   McConkie, *A New Witness for the Articles of Faith*, 307.
165   D&C 132:7–8.
166   Articles of Faith 1:5.
167   McConkie, *A New Witness for the Articles of Faith*, 308.
168   McConkie, *A New Witness for the Articles of Faith*, 309.

## Doctrine of the Priesthood

Elder Bruce R. McConkie taught that personal revelation is the only way to know the doctrine of the priesthood.[169] By charity and virtue, we gain "confidence to stand in the presence of God,"[170] and "the Father teacheth [us] of the covenant."[171] The Lord's language in the oath and covenant of the priesthood bears a strict injunction: "For you shall live by every word that proceedeth forth from the mouth of God."[172] Because this is a covenant, the assumed promise is that God will reveal his word to us. By this covenant priesthood relationship we receive and live by *every* word that proceeds from God, an amazing principle that unlocks the "mystery of godliness"[173] and those things that "eye has not seen, nor ear heard, nor yet entered into the heart of man."[174]

The doctrine of the priesthood will "distil" upon our souls "as the dews from heaven," the scripture says.[175] If we were to walk through dewy grass in the early morning, we would soon be drenched in moisture. Tens of thousands of tiny, almost imperceptible droplets combining together would eventually create a veritable flood. The distillation process of the priesthood settles upon those who love and serve God with all their "heart, might, mind, and strength."[176] According to Elder McConkie, this process occurs line upon line and precept upon precept by the power of the Holy Ghost. If we are "full of charity towards all men, and to the household of faith" and if virtue garnishes our thoughts unceasingly, the doctrine of the priesthood will distil upon us until we are saturated in it.[177]

What, then, is this doctrine of the priesthood that pivots on charity and virtue? Elder McConkie lists the following:

- The priesthood is the actual power of God, and the actual name of the power of God. It is the power by which he created and creates the heavens, and it is the power by which he governs, sustains, and preserves all things. To become as he is, we must exercise his priesthood, or power, as he does.

- The priesthood is the power of faith—faith is power and power is priesthood. Faith is a true belief or knowledge that is acted upon.[178] The priesthood is useless unless put into action; thus the combination of faith, truth, virtue, and priesthood results in actual power. By faith, then, priesthood becomes power "to put at defiance the armies of nations, to divide the earth, to break every band, to stand in the presence of God; to do all things according to his will,

---

169   McConkie, "The Doctrine of the Priesthood," 32.
170   D&C 121:45.
171   D&C 84:48.
172   D&C 84:44.
173   D&C 19:10.
174   D&C 76:10.
175   D&C 121:45.
176   D&C 98:12.
177   McConkie, "The Doctrine of the Priesthood," 32; D&C 121:45.
178   Alma 32:21.

according to his command, subdue principalities and powers; and this by the will of the Son of God" (JST, Genesis 14:31).[179] To the extent that we act with our priesthood in faith, according to charity and virtue, we become like God, who is the perfection of faith, priesthood, and power. By this means, we can lay hold on eternal life.

- The priesthood is the doctrine that "God lives and is and ever shall be. He is the Everlasting Elohim who dwells in heaven above. He is our Father, the father of our spirits; we are his children, the offspring of his begetting. He has a glorified body of flesh and bones; he lives in the family unit; and he possesses all power, all might, all dominion, and all truth. The name of the kind of life he lives is eternal life [that is, he lives in the family unit]."[180]

- The priesthood provides us the knowledge that our Heavenly Father enjoys an exalted status of glory, perfection, and power because his faith and his priesthood are perfect and infinite.

- The priesthood of God is *after the order of his Son,* which power, like God himself, is infinite and eternal. We who receive this endowment of power become of that same order.

- The priesthood is a system of orders, the highest of which is named *The New and Everlasting Covenant of Marriage* (see D&C 131:2)[181] or the patriarchal order. Only in this order can we become like God, creating for ourselves eternal family units patterned after the family of God.

- The doctrine of the priesthood is that we can progress until we obtain the priesthood's *fulness,* which increasingly gives us power by faith to govern and control all temporal and spiritual things, to effect miracles, to help to perfect God's children, to stand in Father's presence, and to become like him, having developed his faith, perfections, and power.

- The priesthood is the power to do all things that are expedient: move mountains, control the elements, cast away evil spirits, defeat every enemy, conquer any adversity, provide protection, cure disease, raise the dead, bind together marriages and families, and ultimately to achieve glorious immortality in the celestial kingdom of God.[182]

---

179    JST, Genesis 14:31.
180    McConkie, *A New Witness for the Articles of Faith,* 704.
181    D&C 131:2.
182    McConkie, "The Doctrine of the Priesthood," 32.

## "As My Father Hath Sent Me, Even So Send I You"[183]

The priesthood separates us for a holy purpose: "for your sake, and not for your sake only, but for the sake of the whole world."[184] By covenant, when we receive the priesthood, we agree to seek our own salvation and to seek the salvation of others by bringing people to Christ and becoming to them saviors on Mount Zion.[185] We have a model. As the Father sent his Son into the world (Babylon) to raise the standard or banner of Zion, set an example, and call people out of the world, so the Son sends us, his sons, back into Babylon to do likewise. For the sons of God, Babylon is what we are to battle, not what we are to embrace; we are to overcome Babylon, not to be overcome by it. Zion is who we are; Zion is what we are to proclaim. We, like Jesus Christ, our spiritual father, are to raise the standard of Zion, set the example of Zion, and call the sons and daughters of God to Zion. We are sent by Jesus Christ into the world to minister to God's children and to declare to them in word, deed, and example that God's kingdom is at hand. We, who hold the priesthood of God and are authorized to act in his name are commissioned to be living proof that the kingdom of God has indeed come!

During his mortal ministry, Jesus ordained the Seventy, gave them power to use his name, and then sent them into the world on missions. Their charge was to provide service with the priesthood in the name of the Lord as a sign that the kingdom of heaven was finally among the people. The Seventy were commissioned to be the kingdom's representatives. Jesus instructed them, "Heal the sick therein, and say unto them, The kingdom of heaven is come nigh unto you [i.e., We have come with power as authorized servants of the kingdom of heaven, and we have authority to use the name of Jesus Christ to bless you]." When the Seventy returned from their missions, they were astonished at the power of the priesthood and the name of Jesus Christ: "And the seventy returned again with joy, saying, Lord, even the devils are subject unto us *through thy name.*"[186]

Neither the priesthood nor its commission has changed since that time. We, the Lord's servants, represent him and the kingdom; we minister, bless, cast out vexing spirits, and call people to Zion in his name. We are Zion!

## Summary and Conclusion

Zion is built on the foundation of the Atonement, upon which three pillars stand: The new and everlasting covenant, the oath and covenant of the priesthood, and the law of consecration. Upon this sure foundation and its pillars rises Zion, "the highest order of priesthood society."[187] Like the other pillars, the oath and covenant of the priesthood has a singular purpose in making Zion possible for each of us, both men and women.

---

183    John 20:21.
184    D&C 84:48.
185    Obadiah 1:21.
186    Luke 10:9, 17; emphasis added.
187    Kimball, *Teachings of Spencer W. Kimball,* 125.

The priesthood is our heritage; it is this authority and power that we qualified for in the "first place," or the premortal world. In this life, we must qualify again to receive the priesthood and its blessings, as did Adam, Melchizedek, Abraham, and others. Like these righteous individuals, we too receive the priesthood by covenant with the Father.

This covenant is the oath and covenant of the priesthood, and is often referred to as the covenant of exaltation. The Father's guarantees are so sacred that he swears to deliver them with an oath, putting his godhood on the line. Likewise, with similar determination, we must swear to him our promise to keep the priesthood covenant. If we meet the conditions of the covenant of the priesthood, exaltation will be ours by virtue of the Father's personal guarantee.

Our primary covenantal promise is to magnify our eternal calling, which includes receiving the Melchizedek Priesthood; receiving Christ, the Father, and the Father's kingdom; living by every word that proceeds forth from the mouth of God; and marrying for eternity, which is the patriarchal order of the priesthood and which places us in the patriarchal order of the Gods. This patriarchal priesthood order provides that we, like Melchizedek, can become kings and priests and queens and priestesses, thereby becoming gods. Only this priesthood order provides us the blessing of eternal lives, or endless posterity. Because the blessings of the priesthood ultimately involve the temple blessings and the marriage covenant, and because both the priesthood and marriage covenants are called the covenant of exaltation, the call to eternal life that we must magnify carries significance for both men and women.

Upon receiving the priesthood, the Lord calls us out of the world and places us under covenant to become new people. The covenant associated with the Melchizedek Priesthood surpasses the privileges of the Aaronic Priesthood. This supernal authority and power is that which allows righteous men and women "to speak with God face to face,"[188] a privilege that is descriptive of Zion people, with whom the Lord makes his abode.[189] Adam was the first to receive the oath and covenant of the priesthood, and by applying its principles, he was able to secure for his posterity the blessings of a Savior and the plan of salvation. Likewise, Abraham sought the blessings of the priesthood, and by applying priesthood principles, he was able to secure the Lord's promise that his children would have a right to the blessings of the gospel and priesthood forever. He also received the promise that through us, his children, all of the nations of the earth would be blessed with the gospel and priesthood blessings. As we follow Adam and Eve's and Abraham and Sarah's examples, we too can qualify for their blessings. As we grow in charity and virtue, the doctrine of the priesthood will distil upon our souls, line upon line, until we have power to stand in the presence of God and receive instructions, intelligence, blessings, and, ultimately, coronation.

Beyond the priesthood's personal privileges, the priesthood is the authority and power to bless other souls with the new and everlasting covenant and the blessings of the priesthood. In a great way, our blessing other people is representative of the environment

---

188   Smith, *Teachings of the Prophet Joseph Smith*, 180.
189   Moses 7:21; Psalm 132:13.

of Zion. Our covenant commission in the priesthood is to become saviors on Mount Zion. If a person neglects his or her responsibility to bring the living and the dead to Christ, that person's priesthood and priesthood blessings cease to function. Therefore, we take upon ourselves the priesthood with a covenant to assume the Lord's work as our own. This work is the eternal work of redemption. This work is not new to us; it is an extension of our premortal work, and it will be our work hereafter and forever. We came from Zion, our earthly heritage is Zion, our immediate aim is Zion, and our eternal future is Zion. And Zion is, and always has been, a product of the priesthood

# Section 2
# The Oath and Covenant
# of the Priesthood
## Our Agreements

The second pillar of Zion is the oath and covenant of the priesthood, and our agreements in that covenant are faithfulness, obtaining the Aaronic Priesthood and Melchizedek priesthoods, and magnifying our calling in the priesthood.[190] Additionally, we agree to receive Christ and his Father and to live by every word that proceeds from the mouth of God, both of which we will discuss. Although these initial chapters on the priesthood apply to worthy men, faithful women, as we will see, take part in this covenant with their husbands. Again, faithful single men and women are not exempted from the blessings of Zion. Blessings are predicated on what we do with what we have. Blessings are not withheld by what we lack. Therefore, single men *and* women should become conversant with priesthood principles.

Our leaders have said that the purpose of the Melchizedek Priesthood centers on obtaining eternal life. We receive the priesthood by covenant and with the Father's immutable oath. Inasmuch as the covenant of baptism is renewed in the covenant of the sacrament, the covenant of the priesthood is renewed in the temple ceremonies. Failure to make the covenant of the priesthood or neglecting to keep the covenant after we have received it brings severe penalties and tragic consequences. But if we are trying to do our best we need not fear; embedded in the covenant is God's promise that he will sustain us, help us live the covenant, and bless us with success.[191]

The priesthood comes to us by the Father's invitation. We are "called by this holy calling," Alma taught, "and ordained unto the high priesthood of the holy order of God."[192] The Father offers us the priesthood through his authorized servants. That fact alone is evidence that we have been chosen and called by God. Our responsibility is to

---

190  D&C 84:33.
191  Eyring, "Faith and the Oath and Covenant of the Priesthood," 61–64.
192  Alma 13:6.

qualify by becoming worthy of the honor. Remember, the Apostle Paul taught, "No man taketh this honour unto himself but he that is called of God, as was Aaron."[193] And, as the fifth Article of Faith declares, "We believe that a man must be called of God, by prophecy, and by the laying on of hands by those who are in authority, to preach the gospel and administer in the ordinances thereof."[194]

To be chosen and called of God, to receive his authority, power, and name to speak authoritatively as would God, to have the power to do what God would do, and to act in the capacity of the Savior are honors without equal. That the Father seeks us out, chooses and calls us, offers us the covenant of the priesthood, and then swears his covenantal promise with an oath are indications of his anxiousness to bestow upon us exalted blessings. Moreover, by offering us the priesthood, he is furthering his work: "to bring to pass the immortality and eternal life of man."[195] He knows that the quality of immortality called eternal life can be achieved only by our receiving and living worthy of the oath and covenant of the priesthood. No wonder, then, that Elder McConkie called the priesthood covenant "the covenant of exaltation."[196]

The oath and the covenant of the priesthood is set forth in Doctrine and Covenants 84:33–44:

> For whoso is faithful unto the obtaining these two priesthoods of which I have spoken, and the magnifying their calling, are sanctified by the Spirit unto the renewing of their bodies. They become the sons of Moses and of Aaron and the seed of Abraham, and the church and kingdom, and the elect of God.
>
> And also all they who receive this priesthood receive me, saith the Lord; for he that receiveth my servants receiveth me; and he that receiveth me receiveth my Father; and he that receiveth my Father receiveth my Father's kingdom; therefore all that my Father hath shall be given unto him.
>
> And this is according to the oath and covenant which belongeth to the priesthood. Therefore, all those who receive the priesthood, receive this oath and covenant of my Father, which he cannot break, neither can it be moved. But whoso breaketh this covenant after he hath received it, and altogether turneth therefrom, shall not have forgiveness of sins in this world nor in the world to come. And wo unto all those who come not unto this priesthood which ye have received, which I now confirm

---

193    Hebrews 5:4.
194    *Articles of Faith* 1:5.
195    Moses 1:39.
196    McConkie, *A New Witness for the Articles of Faith*, 312–13.

upon you who are present this day, by mine own voice
out of the heavens; and even I have given the heavenly
hosts and mine angels charge concerning you.

And I now give unto you a commandment to beware concerning yourselves, to give diligent heed to the
words of eternal life. For you shall live by every word
that proceedeth forth from the mouth of God.

This covenant, like all other covenants, contains *if-then* clauses: *If* we fulfill our obligations, *then* the Father will fulfill his oath—guaranteed! Here are our covenantal promises:

## If We Are Faithful . . .

Faithfulness or righteousness is the first promise that we make in the oath and covenant
of the priesthood. Abraham is a model of faithfulness; he made himself good so that he
could do good. Therefore, he worked to make his righteousness equal to his desire to
receive the priesthood.[197] Righteousness not only qualifies a man to receive this honor, but
it also is the principle upon which the priesthood functions: "The rights of the priesthood
. . . cannot be controlled nor handled only upon the principles of righteousness." Without
righteousness, "the heavens withdraw themselves; the Spirit of the Lord is grieved; and
when it is withdrawn, Amen to the priesthood or the authority of that man."[198]

The requirement of righteousness is self-evident. By receiving the priesthood, we
receive the Lord's name,[199] and therefore we are called to become models of him whose
name we bear. As ambassadors of Jesus Christ, said President Joseph Fielding Smith, we
are commissioned to represent him. We who hold the holy priesthood must live lives and
do all things as the Lord would do them if he were personally present.[200] Elder McConkie
wrote, "[Melchizedek Priesthood holders] pray and minister in the place and stead of their
Master."[201] That is, we become the hands, arms, and voice of Jesus Christ. For example,
Edward Partridge was told by the Lord, "I will lay my hand upon you by the hand of my
servant Sidney Rigdon."[202] In a similar manner, priesthood holders are the arms of Jesus
Christ: "And their arm shall be my arm."[203] Likewise, the Lord emphasizes his willingness
to support us when we, through the priesthood, minister in his name and thus become his
voice: "What I the Lord have spoken, I have spoken, and I excuse not myself; and though
the heavens and the earth pass away, my word shall not pass away, but shall all be fulfilled,
whether by mine own voice or by the voice of my servants, it is the same."[204] That is, we
(as an interpretation) who are the Lord's authorized servants on a local basis may speak in

197    Abraham 1:2.
198    D&C 121:36–37.
199    Abraham 1:18.
200    Smith, "Our Responsibility As Priesthood Holders," 49.
201    McConkie, *A New Witness for the Articles of Faith,* 379.
202    D&C 36:2; emphasis added.
203    D&C 35:14.
204    D&C 1:38; emphasis added.

the name of Jesus Christ as moved upon by the Holy Ghost, and minister in our stewardships as do the Apostles and Prophets, who are authorized to use His name on a global
basis, and the Lord will likewise validate what we say in His name.

Clearly, faithfulness empowers us to fulfill our priesthood commission. That is essential. While priesthood authority is conferred upon us at the time of ordination, priesthood *power* comes only when priesthood *authority* is exercised in righteousness.[205] Being
good precedes doing good.

If We Obtain the Aaronic and the Melchizedek Priesthoods . . .

Following the requirement of righteousness is the requirement of receiving the Aaronic and Melchizedek orders of the priesthood.[206] As we have noted, both of these two
orders of the priesthood are received by covenant, but only the Melchizedek Priesthood
is received with the Father's oath.[207] Also, as we have discussed, the covenant regarding the Aaronic Priesthood is that we promise to forsake the world, magnify our calling,
minister to God's children by preaching, teaching, and giving service, and by obeying
God's commandments. In return, the Lord promises to magnify us in the Aaronic Priesthood and to prepare us in every way to receive the Melchizedek Priesthood. This is the
covenant of the Aaronic, or preparatory priesthood.

The covenant regarding the Melchizedek Priesthood is that we promise to live
faithfully to the Aaronic and Melchizedek priesthoods' covenants, magnify our calling,
obey the commandments, be an example of Jesus Christ, serve as the Lord would serve,
"live by every word that proceedeth forth from the mouth of God" (D&C 84:44), and
marry in the temple for time and eternity. In return, the Father promises us *with an oath*
that he will give us all that he has, which by definition is eternal life. This is the Lord's
promise of exaltation, godhood, eternal marriage, and endless posterity.[208]

We receive these two priesthoods for various common and some diverse reasons.
For example, both priesthoods carry the responsibilities of preaching, teaching, expounding, exhorting, and, in the case of Aaronic Priesthood priests, the responsibilities of
baptizing and administering the sacrament—these by delegation of the Apostles.[209] Both
priesthoods carry the responsibilities of inviting all people to come unto Christ and to
watch over the Church by visiting, exhorting, and strengthening the members. But only
the Melchizedek Priesthood "confirm[s] the church by the laying on of the hands, and
the giving of the Holy Ghost; and to take the lead of all meetings."[210]

As mentioned previously, the Aaronic Priesthood holds "the keys of the ministering
of angels, and to administer in outward ordinances, the letter of the gospel, the baptism
of repentance for the remission of sins, agreeable to the covenants and commandments."[211]
This priesthood has the power to prepare us, or a person to whom we are ministering, for

---

205    Nelson, "Personal Priesthood Responsibility," 44; emphasis added.
206    We note here that the Melchizedek Priesthood encompasses the Aaronic Priesthood. If a man is ordained only to the
        Melchizedek Priesthood, he can also function in the Aaronic Priesthood and enjoy those blessings.
207    McConkie, "The Doctrine of the Priesthood," 32; D&C 131:1–4.
208    McConkie, "The Doctrine of the Priesthood," 32; D&C 131:1–4.
209    D&C 20:38–39, 40.
210    D&C 20:44. Note: A priest may take the lead in meetings in the absence of an elder (see D&C 20:49).
211    D&C 107:20.

the higher, exalting ordinances of the gospel. Again, both priesthoods are received for the purposes of personal salvation and the salvation of others: "for your sake, and not for your sake only, but for the sake of the whole world."[212]

The scripture reads, the Melchizedek Priesthood "administereth the gospel and holdeth the key of the mysteries of the kingdom, even the key of the knowledge of God."[213] That is, the high priesthood has two grand purposes: (1) to administer the gospel, meaning to preside, and to administer the covenants and ordinances of salvation; and (2) to stand in the presence of God, and receive personal revelation directly from him. "Therefore, in the ordinances thereof, the power of godliness [i.e., the power to become Godlike] is manifest. And without the ordinances thereof, and the authority of the priesthood, the power of godliness is not manifest unto men in the flesh; for without this [the power to become Godlike] no man can see the face of God, even the Father, and live."[214]

Moreover, the high priesthood is the "power and authority of God" that allows us "to minister to other beings to bring about their happiness."[215] The high priesthood is the power to become saviors on Mount Zion[216] for both the living and the dead, and to receive and administer the blessings of "endless lives."[217]

## If We Magnify Our *Calling* . . .

Possibly, the central agreement of the covenant of the priesthood is to magnify our calling. Of interest, the covenant states that we agree to magnify our *calling* rather than our *callings*. There is a difference between the calling *of* the priesthood and callings *in* the priesthood. What, then, is the singular *calling* to which the covenant refers?

A review might be in order. As we have learned, Alma said that our experience with the priesthood began premortally, in the "first place,"[218] where we were "*called* and prepared from the foundation of the world according to the foreknowledge of God, on account of [our] exceeding faith and good works."[219] In that premortal setting, we qualified to be *called* and elected (selected) for eternal life. In this life, when we are baptized and enter into the new and everlasting covenant—we are "*called* into the fellowship of Jesus Christ."[220] Then, as we progress in the Covenant and receive the oath and covenant of the priesthood, we are *called* again to eternal life. Therefore, our *calling* in the priesthood is the call to eternal life, or, in other words, to become like God. And therefore, the Lord said, "All they who receive this priesthood receive me, saith the Lord; . . . and he that receiveth me receiveth my Father."[221]

---

212    D&C 84:48.
213    D&C 84:19.
214    D&C 84:20–22.
215    Riddle, "The New and Everlasting Covenant," 231.
216    Obadiah 1:21.
217    Smith, *Teachings of the Prophet Joseph Smith*, 322.
218    Alma 13:3.
219    Alma 13:3–5.
220    1 Corinthians 1:9, 26–27; Hebrews 3:1.
221    D&C 84:35, 37.

## Magnifying the *Calling* and *Callings*

Of course, magnifying our *calling* assumes that we will magnify all of our priesthood *callings*. According to the *Encyclopedia of Mormonism*, we magnify each of our callings by taking our responsibilities seriously, making them honorable in the eyes of God's children, and making them glorious to the Lord.[222] Additionally, we magnify our callings by functioning faithfully under the guidance of priesthood leadership and the instruction of the Holy Ghost.[223] Our various priesthood callings—like our singular *calling*—hearkens back to the premortal world: "Every man who has a calling to minister to the inhabitants of the world," said Joseph Smith, "was ordained to that very purpose in the grand council of heaven before this world was."[224] It is the magnification of our singular *calling* and our various callings that provides the key to our eventual glory; that is, the end result of our present labors is to become like God.

The seriousness of magnifying our *calling* is set out in Doctrine and Covenants 121:34, 40: "Many are called, but few are chosen." That is, "many are called to the priesthood, but few are chosen for eternal life."[225] Institute instructor S. Brent Farley taught,

> One who magnifies his calling to the priesthood will understand that "the rights of the priesthood are inseparably connected with the powers of heaven, and that the powers of heaven cannot be controlled nor handled only upon the principles of righteousness." He will know that "no power or influence can or ought to be maintained by virtue of the priesthood, only by persuasion, by long-suffering, by gentleness and meekness, and by love unfeigned; by kindness, and pure knowledge, which shall greatly enlarge the soul without hypocrisy, and without guile." (D&C 121:36, 41–42.) One whose service is characterized by those qualities is magnifying his priesthood *calling*, and he has the foundation for success for the various priesthood tasks and offices he may hold throughout his life. He will also use these principles in his home.[226]

Interestingly, the word *virtue* means both "moral excellence" and "power." The phrase "by virtue of the priesthood" means "by the power of the priesthood," and that power is developed only by virtue of character, or moral excellence. A terrifying chain of events occurs when moral virtue slips. According to Doctrine and Covenants 121, when our

---

222   *Encyclopedia of Mormonism,* 850.
223   Riddle, "The New and Everlasting Covenant," 232.
224   Smith, *Teachings of the Prophet Joseph Smith,* 365.
225   McConkie, *Mormon Doctrine,* 482.
226   Farley, "The Oath and Covenant of the Priesthood," 42–43; emphasis added.

hearts are set upon the things of this world and we aspire to the honors of men, we will then attempt to cover our sins, gratify our pride and our vain ambitions, and then we will begin to exercise unrighteous dominion. These conditions result in the heavens withdrawing, the Spirit of the Lord being grieved, and the cessation of priesthood authority and power. The cycle leads to breaking our covenant to magnify our priesthood calling. On the other hand, when our hearts are set on the things of God and we aspire for God's approval, we will repent, seek first for the things of the kingdom of God, and demonstrate charity. These conditions result in the heavens drawing near, the Spirit of the Lord becoming our constant companion, and receiving an increase of priesthood power. Now we are fulfilling our covenant to magnify our priesthood calling.

What does it mean to magnify a calling in the priesthood? Elder McConkie explained: "Now, to magnify as here used means to enlarge or increase, to improve upon, to hold up to honor and dignity, to make the calling noble and respectable in the eyes of all men by performing the mission which appertains to the calling in an admirable and successful manner. So to magnify a calling in the ministry requires brethren first to learn what duties go with their respective offices and callings and then to go to with their might and do the work assigned them. By doing this, which includes within it the requirement to 'give diligent heed to the words of eternal life,' and to 'live by every word that proceedeth forth from the mouth of God' (D. & C. 84:43–44), they are assured of an eventual inheritance of eternal life in the kingdom of God.[227]

Again we see the connection of our various priesthood *callings* to our singular overriding priesthood *calling*. Our leaders teach us that there are four ways that we magnify our various callings in the priesthood:

- By learning our responsibility and fully accomplishing it.[228]
- By doing our very best in our assignments.
- By consecrating our time, talents, and resources to the Lord and his work as our leaders request and as the Spirit whispers.[229]
- By teaching and being an example of the truth.[230]

The Book of Mormon prophet Jacob described the result of faithfully magnifying a calling in the priesthood: "We did magnify our office unto the Lord, taking upon us the responsibility, . . . [teaching] them the word of God with all diligence; . . . [and] laboring with our might."[231]

Melchizedek also set an example of magnifying a priesthood calling: "Now this Melchizedek was a king over the land of Salem; and his people had waxed strong in iniquity and abomination; yea, they had all gone astray; they were full of all manner of wickedness; but Melchizedek having exercised mighty faith, and received the office of the high priesthood according to the holy order of God, did preach repentance unto his people. And

227    McConkie, *Mormon Doctrine*, 481.
228    D&C 107:99–100.
229    Kimball, "Becoming the Pure in Heart," 5.
230    Asay, "The Oath and Covenant of the Priesthood," 43.
231    Jacob 1:19.

behold, they did repent; and Melchizedek did establish peace in the land in his days; therefore he was called the prince of peace."[232] "And his people wrought righteousness, and obtained heaven."[233]

Because we are of the same order of the priesthood as Melchizedek, and because we take upon ourselves the title *Melchizedek* when we receive the priesthood, we, by covenant, are expected to magnify our *calling* and *callings* as did this "great high priest."[234]

As the high priesthood pertains to Zion, we note the following item of interest: The priesthood order of Melchizedek is "after the order of Enoch, which was after the order of the Only Begotten Son."[235] Enoch's order is the order of Zion, which order is also the order of Melchizedek and the order of the Only Begotten Son. We become Zion people by entering into priesthood covenants and by magnifying our priesthood *calling*, as did Melchizedek, Enoch, and Jesus Christ.

## Three Ways to Magnify Our Calling

President Marion G. Romney explained that magnifying our singular priesthood *calling* consists of at least three steps:
1. Obtaining gospel knowledge.
2. Personal righteousness by compliance with gospel standards.
3. Giving dedicated service.[236]

## Obtaining Gospel Knowledge

We cannot magnify our *calling* without searching the scriptures and the words of the prophets. Especially important is the Book of Mormon, which contains "the fulness of the gospel of Jesus Christ."[237] The Book of Mormon, said the Prophet Joseph, is "the most correct of any book on earth, and the keystone of our religion, and a man would get nearer to God by abiding by its precepts, than by any other book."[238] How could we expect to be on the Lord's errand, minister to his people, represent him to the covenant people and the inhabitants of the world, stand in his stead, speak his words, and teach his children the words of eternal life, if we are not conversant in his words?

The Nephite prophet Jacob drew a connection between priesthood power and gospel knowledge: "Wherefore, we search the prophets, and we have many revelations and the spirit of prophecy; and having all these witnesses we obtain a hope, and our faith becometh unshaken, insomuch that *we truly can command in the name of Jesus* and the very trees obey us, or the mountains, or the waves of the sea."[239] Power in the priesthood,

---

232    Alma 13:17–18.
233    JST, Genesis 14:34.
234    D&C 107:2.
235    D&C 76:57.
236    Romney, "'The Oath and Covenant Which Belongeth to the Priesthood,'" 43.
237    D&C 20:9.
238    Smith, *History of the Church,* 4:461.
239    Jacob 4:6–7; emphasis added.

Jacob said, comes by searching "the prophets," that is, by searching the scriptures. By so doing, we become familiar with the voice of the Spirit, we enjoy "many revelations," and we develop the "spirit of prophecy." Jacob stated that "all these witnesses" from the Spirit increase our hope, faith, and spiritual experience until our confidence in Jesus Christ and his name become "unshaken," and we truly can perform many mighty miracles. Clearly, obtaining and applying gospel knowledge serves to magnify our priesthood *calling.*

## Personal Righteousness

We cannot magnify our priesthood *calling* if we "undertake to cover our sins, or to gratify our pride, our vain ambition, or to exercise control or dominion or compulsion upon the souls of the children of men, in any degree of unrighteousness" or to "exercise unrighteous dominion."[240] How can we expect to represent and exemplify the Lord, as the covenant of the priesthood requires, if our personal lives are contrary to his? We might gain a trivial knowledge of gospel facts, but if we do not live the gospel, "Amen to the priesthood or the authority of that man."[241]

Personal righteousness describes a Zion person, and personal righteousness consists of pure knowledge, pure actions, and pure motives. Zion is the pure in heart.[242] "Zion is pure," writes Hugh Nibley, "which means 'not mixed with any impurities, unalloyed'; it is all Zion and nothing else."[243] The covenantal deportment of a Zion-like priesthood holder is set forth in the scriptures: "No power or influence can or ought to be maintained by virtue of the priesthood, only by persuasion, by long-suffering, by gentleness and meekness, and by love unfeigned; by kindness, and pure knowledge, which shall greatly enlarge the soul without hypocrisy, and without guile—reproving betimes with sharpness, when moved upon by the Holy Ghost; and then showing forth afterwards an increase of love toward him whom thou hast reproved, lest he esteem thee to be his enemy."[244]

In the oath and covenant of the priesthood, we covenant to "keep the commandments of God, to live by every word that proceedeth forth from the mouth of Deity, and to walk in paths of righteousness and virtue."[245] These criteria are absolutely essential if we wish to magnify our priesthood *calling.*

To attain to personal righteousness is to exemplify the Master, whom we must come to know and love. We do this by serving him and keeping his commandments[246]: "If thou lovest me thou shalt serve me and keep all my commandments."[247] It is a principle with promises: "And unto him that keepeth my commandments I will give the mysteries of my kingdom, and the same shall be in him a well of living water, springing up unto everlasting life."[248] Attaining personal righteousness leads to receiving the fulness of the priest-

---

240   D&C 121:37, 39.
241   D&C 121:37.
242   D&C 97:21.
243   Nibley, *Approaching Zion,* 26–27.
244   D&C 121:41–43.
245   McConkie, *Mormon Doctrine,* 480.
246   D&C 42:29.
247   D&C 42:29.
248   D&C 63:23.

hood: "And no man receiveth a fulness unless he keepeth his commandments. He that keepeth his commandments receiveth truth and light, until he is glorified in truth and knoweth all things."[249] Can we not see the essence of Zion in these promises?

As a model for magnifying our *calling* through our personal conduct, President Romney directs us to Doctrine and Covenants 42, the "Law of the Church,"[250] which comprises the law of Zion. There are at least twenty points made in this revelation that paint a portrait of a Zion person.

1. The Lord's "first commandment" in Doctrine and Covenants 42 is to "go forth in my name." The covenant of the priesthood commissions us and makes it possible for us to lift up our voices, "preaching the gospel . . . with the sound of a trump," declaring the word of God like unto the angels.[251]

2. Our sights should be set upon becoming Zion people, so that we might become the Lord's people.[252]

3. We are to accept priesthood assignments and stand in the offices to which we are called.[253]

4. We are to "observe the covenants and church articles to do them," and use them as our text when teaching, as directed by the Spirit.[254]

5. We are to strive to receive the Spirit before attempting to teach.[255]

6. We are to boldly speak and prophesy according to the promptings of the Spirit.[256]

7. We will not kill, steal, lie, commit adultery, or speak evil—nor will we avoid repentance.[257]

8. We will love our wives with all our heart, cleave unto none else, and lust after no other women.[258]

9. With special regard to Zion, we will "remember the poor, and consecrate [our] properties for their support that which [we] have to impart unto them," agreeing that we are stewards over the Lord's property and accountable for our discharge of our stewardship.[259]

10. We will consecrate our surplus to the bishop "to administer to the poor and the needy" and for the building up of the Church and the establishment of Zion.[260]

11. We are to forsake pride and costly apparel, and create beautiful things with our own hands.[261]

12. We are to do all things in cleanliness before the Lord.[262]

249   D&C 93:27–28.
250   D&C 42, section heading.
251   D&C 42:4, 6.
252   D&C 42:9.
253   D&C 42:10.
254   D&C 42:13.
255   D&C 42:14.
256   D&C 42:16–17.
257   D&C 42:19–21, 24–25.
258   D&C 42:22–23.
259   D&C 42:30–32.
260   D&C 42:34.
261   D&C 42:40.
262   D&C 42:41.

13. We are to be industrious.[263]

14. We are to minister in the Lord's name by healing the sick, blessing the afflicted, and nourishing and bearing the infirmities of those who are of weaker faith until they are made whole.[264]

15. We are to stand in our stewardship and not take anything from a brother without paying him fairly.[265]

16. We are to ask the Lord for intelligence with the expectation of receiving revelation, knowledge, and the mysteries of the kingdom.[266]

17. We are to be faithful to everything that the Lord reveals.[267]

18. We agree to become Zion people by taking upon us the new and everlasting covenant, the oath and covenant of the priesthood, and the law of consecration.[268]

19. If we lack anything, we are to ask of God, who will give to us liberally.[269]

20. If someone offends us, we are to "take him or her between him or her and thee alone; and if he or she confess thou shalt be reconciled. . . . And thus ye shall conduct in all things."[270]

Personal righteousness allows one to be a representative of Zion and therefore a vessel of blessedness. The Beatitudes given by the Lord to his disciples in Jerusalem and later to the Nephites describe this state of blessedness.[271] President Harold B. Lee called these sermons that contain the Beatitudes "the constitution for a perfect life."[272] Additionally, President Romney directed us to the instructions for personal conduct given in Doctrine and Covenants sections 59 and 88. These instructions include at least twenty-two points of personal conduct that describe Zion-like righteousness:

1. "Thou shalt love the Lord thy God with all thy heart, with all thy might, mind, and strength."[273]

2. "In the name of Jesus Christ thou shalt serve him."[274]

3. "Thou shalt love thy neighbor as thyself."[275]

4. "Thou shalt not steal . . . "[276]

5. "Neither commit adultery, nor kill, nor do anything like unto it" [i.e., we should avoid any type of sexual sin or anything that approaches the taking of life].[277]

6. "Thou shalt thank the Lord thy God in all things. . . . And in nothing doth man

---

263   D&C 42:42.
264   D&C 42:43–52.
265   D&C 42:53–54.
266   D&C 42:56, 61–62, 65.
267   D&C 42:66.
268   D&C 42:67.
269   D&C 42:68.
270   D&C 42:88–93.
271   Matthew 5:1–11; 3 Nephi 12:1–12.
272   Lee, *Decisions for Successful Living,* 56–57.
273   D&C 59:5.
274   D&C 59:5.
275   D&C 59:6.
276   D&C 59:6.
277   D&C 59:6.

offend God, or against none is his wrath kindled, save those who confess not his hand in all things, and obey not his commandments."[278]

7.  "Thou shalt offer a sacrifice unto the Lord thy God in righteousness, even that of a broken heart and a contrite spirit."[279]

8.  "And that thou mayest more fully keep thyself unspotted from the world, thou shalt go to the house of prayer and offer up thy sacraments upon my holy day."[280]

9.  "And as all have not faith, seek ye diligently and teach one another words of wisdom; yea, seek ye out of the best books words of wisdom; seek learning, even by study and also by faith."[281]

10.  "Organize yourselves."[282]

11.  "Prepare every needful thing."[283]

12.  "Cease from all your light speeches, from all laughter, from all your lustful desires, from all your pride and light-mindedness, and from all your wicked doings."[284]

13.  "Appoint among yourselves a teacher, and let not all be spokesmen at once; but let one speak at a time and let all listen unto his sayings, that when all have spoken that all may be edified of all, and that every man may have an equal privilege."[285]

14.  "See that ye love one another."[286]

15.  "Cease to be covetous."[287]

16.  "Learn to impart one to another as the gospel requires."[288]

17.  "Cease to be idle."[289]

18.  "Cease to be unclean."[290]

19.  "Cease to find fault one with another."[291]

20.  "Cease to sleep longer than is needful; retire to thy bed early, that ye may not be weary; arise early, that your bodies and your minds may be invigorated."[292]

21.  "And above all things, clothe yourselves with the bond of charity, as with a mantle, which is the bond of perfectness and peace."[293]

22.  "Pray always, that ye may not faint, until I come."[294]

The Lord promises that "he who doeth the works of righteousness shall receive his reward, even peace in this world, and eternal life in the world to come."[295]

---

278   D&C 59:7, 21.
279   D&C 59:8.
280   D&C 59:9.
281   D&C 88:118.
282   D&C 88:119.
283   D&C 88:119.
284   D&C 88:121.
285   D&C 88:122.
286   D&C 88:123.
287   D&C 88:123.
288   D&C 88:123.
289   D&C 88:124.
290   D&C 88:124.
291   D&C 88:124.
292   D&C 88:124.
293   D&C 88:125.
294   D&C 88:126.
295   D&C 59:23.

## Dedicated Service

We cannot magnify our priesthood *calling* without freely offering charitable, selfless service—a central hallmark of a Zion person. The Lord said, "Men should be anxiously engaged in a good cause, and do many things of their own free will, and bring to pass much righteousness; for the power is in them."[296] While anyone can give charitable service, only men and women of the Covenant can give charitable service *that has the power to save another person.* Such saving service is a priesthood privilege and a priesthood responsibility, according to President Marion G. Romney, which "can be done properly only by men who are magnifying their priesthood—who know the gospel, conform their lives to its standards, and enthusiastically give dedicated service."[297] Of course, the same could be said of women who are living their covenants.

Service is the lifeblood of Zion. The selfishness of Babylon must give way to the *selflessness* of Zion in order that Zion-like attributes might be established in a covenant person. The spirit of charitable service cannot be mandated; that spirit is a condition of the heart that motivates a person to lift another. It is no wonder, then, that Zion is described as having no poverty of any kind. Zion people can neither tolerate lack nor endure poverty abiding among them. They attack misery wherever they find it. They abolish every form of scarcity, hurt, impairment, injustice, illness, and sorrow. They think of their brethren like unto themselves, and they are familiar with all and free with their substance, that others might be rich like unto themselves.[298] Therefore, they insist on having "all things common among them; therefore there [are] not rich and poor, bond and free, but they [are] all made free and partakers of the heavenly gift." Consequently, there never could be a happier people.[299]

Zion people "love one another and serve one another." They "succor those that stand in need of [their] succor," and they "administer of [their] substance unto him that standeth in need." They "will not suffer that the beggar [put] up his petition to [them] in vain, and turn him out to perish."[300] Zion people "bear one another's burdens, that they may be light," and they "are willing to mourn with those that mourn; yea, and comfort those that stand in need of comfort."[301]

King Benjamin pointed out that there are blessings that flow only from dedicated service. These things we must learn if we hope to become Zion-like. For example, service allows us to retain "a remission of [our] sins from day to day, that [we] may walk guiltless before God." Therefore, King Benjamin exhorted us, "I would that ye should impart of your substance to the poor, every man according to that which he hath, such as feeding the hungry, clothing the naked, visiting the sick and administering to their relief, both spiritually and temporally, according to their wants."[302] And, of course, the profound

---

296   D&C 58:27–28.
297   Romney, "'The Oath and Covenant Which Belongeth to the Priesthood,'" 43.
298   Jacob 2:17.
299   4 Nephi 1:3, 16.
300   Mosiah 4:15–16.
301   Mosiah 18:8–9.
302   Mosiah 4:26.

statement regarding service: "When ye are in the service of your fellow beings ye are only in the service of your God."[303]

In Doctrine and Covenants 42, "the law of the Church," we read the following verse: "For inasmuch as ye do it unto the least of these, ye do it unto me."[304] The implication is intriguing. Because God lacks for nothing and is in no need of our service to him, he passes our desire to serve *him* to serving his children, who *do* need our help. As we transfer our service from him to his children, he does not forget our wanting to express our love to him. He counts our service to his children as service to him, and he rewards us accordingly.

As we have discussed, God is in debt to no one. When we serve him by serving one of his children, he "doth immediately bless [us]; and therefore he hath paid [us]. And [we] are still indebted unto him, and are, and will be, forever and ever."[305] To arrest any hint of debt or imbalance in the checks and balances of heaven, God quickly erases any claim by immediately blessing us in excess of our service. Therefore, we live forever in his debt. We are always awarded more blessings than we expend in service, and for that reason we are gratefully "unprofitable servants."[306]

It is upon the principle of service that we progress toward perfection. By receiving grace (the Lord's help) *for* grace (our service and blessings to others), we grow *from* grace (light, truth, power, and perfection) *to* grace (more light, truth, power, and perfection). According to John the Baptist's testimony, Jesus grew in grace (light, truth, power, and perfection) by giving grace (service and blessings to others): "And I, John, saw that he received not of the fulness at first, but received grace *for* grace. And he received not of the fulness at first, but continued from grace *to* grace, until he received a fulness."[307] Likewise, we progress toward a fulness incrementally—grace *to* grace—by keeping the commandments and giving service, for which the Lord blesses us—grace *for* grace: "For if you keep my commandments you shall receive of his fulness, and be glorified in me as I am in the Father; therefore, I say unto you, you shall receive grace *for* grace."[308] Clearly, giving and receiving grace is central to the priesthood covenant.

## Grace *to* Grace by Grace *for* Grace

The above definitions of grace are in addition to the common definition: the Lord's help, strength, or enabling power.[309] Jesus' grace is ever evident in the unequalled service he proffers. Here is a formula for receiving his help or grace: *We come unto Christ in humility and faith, having done all we can do,*[310] *and then he makes up the difference.* Consequently, we will never lack. In this, we again hear overtones of Zion: *no lack* and *divine help* to accomplish our work.

---

303    Mosiah 2:17.
304    D&C 42:38.
305    Mosiah 2:24.
306    Mosiah 2:21.
307    D&C 93:12–13; emphasis added.
308    D&C 93:20; emphasis added.
309    Bible Dictionary, "Grace," 697.
310    2 Nephi 25:23: "for we know that it is by grace that we are saved [helped], after all we can do."

Pertaining to the concept of *no lack*, we recall again the Lord's abundant grace to the wandering Israelites, as recorded by the prophet Nehemiah: "This is thy God that brought thee up out of Egypt, and had wrought great provocations; yet thou in thy manifold mercies *forsookest them not* in the wilderness: the pillar of the *cloud departed not* from them by day, to lead them in the way; *neither the pillar of fire* by night, to shew them light, and the way wherein they should go. Thou gavest also thy good spirit to *instruct them,* and withheldest not thy *manna* from their mouth, and gavest them *water* for their thirst. *Yea, forty years didst thou sustain them* in the wilderness, [so that] they *lacked nothing;* their *clothes waxed not old, and their feet swelled not.*"[311]

The Lord never forsook them. He was with them both day and night. He constantly instructed them. He provided manna and water to sustain them. For four decades of wandering, they lacked nothing! Amazingly, neither their clothing nor their shoes wore out. The Israelites experienced the Lord's grace.

We see these two elements of grace—no lack and divine help—in an incident in the Savior's life. Just before Jesus entered Gethsemane, he reminded his Apostles of their early missions when he had purposely placed them in a condition of lack by sending them out with neither purse nor scrip. He had expected them to give grace (service) by means of his grace, that is, by relying completely on him and on nothing else. Now he asked them, "When I sent you without purse, and scrip, and shoes, lacked ye any thing? And they said, Nothing."[312]

They needed to internalize this lesson in order to fulfill their priesthood assignments. They had learned from that experience that what had initially appeared to be a condition of lack was not one after all; the Lord had provided his grace (divine help) to sustain them in proportion to the grace (service) they proffered to the people. The situation had been carefully orchestrated by the Lord to teach them to trust him while they served. Their service would produce blessings of sustenance for the people, and by serving they (the servants) would never lack. The Apostles needed to understand the inherent safety and security that derives from the new and everlasting covenant and the oath and covenant of the priesthood. These covenants contain the Lord's promise of sustaining grace. Therefore, the Apostles needed firsthand experience to see that the Lord would be true to his promise. Without his grace, they could neither survive nor gain the necessary power to fulfill their priesthood calling.

Similarly, we need experience with the Lord and the covenants. We need to know that our lack is resolved by service; as we give grace, we receive grace. That is the formula. When we experience a lack of something, we can go to the Lord and he will proffer us grace in proportion to how we  because we have extended grace to his children. Moreover, because we are under covenant to represent and emulate the Lord, we must demonstrate by word and deed that we, like Jesus, will abide in the new and everlasting covenant and the oath and covenant of the priesthood by giving his children help, strength, and enablement. The Lord is clearly our example of priesthood service, and by covenant we have agreed to do as he would do.

---

311    Nehemiah 9:18–21; emphasis added.
312    Luke 22:35.

## If Any of You Lack

James, the Lord's brother, offered a solution for those of us who lack in a specific way: "If any of you lack wisdom, let him ask of God, that giveth to all men liberally, and upbraideth not, and it shall be given him."[313] Personalized, this scripture could read: "If I lack *anything*, I can ask of God, who will give to me *abundantly*, and he will never chastise me for having asked for his help. Instead, he will help me." This is the promise of grace!

Grace allows our lack to be swallowed up in Christ's abundance. We come unto him in humility and faith, we do all we can do—which *must* include offering service—and then we have the assurance that he will make up the difference. By living this principle, we never need lack for anything. Our lack might include any physical, emotional, or spiritual deficit. Also, we might experience lack when we minister to the Lord's children. In any of these situations, when we experience lack and attempt to remedy the situation, we almost certainly will come up short; that is the condition of mortality. In some way, we will lack sufficient ability or resources to counter the lack. Both the new and everlasting covenant and the oath and covenant of the priesthood provide that we can draw upon the Savior's resources and power as we minister to his children.

On two remarkable occasions, the Apostles experienced the Lord's grace when they came up short in attempting to minister to people who lacked something—when Jesus fed the five thousand and later the four thousand.[314] In each case, hungry people were in immediate need of help, and the Apostles could manage only scant resources. Jesus' response was identical in both cases: "Bring all that you have or your best effort to me; I will bless it; you will have enough to feed the people until they are filled. Then, when it is your turn to eat, you will have enough. In fact, you will have more than you started with. Your responsibility is to feed my sheep, not to worry about having enough. Just go forth and minister, and I will multiply your efforts so that you never lack."

When we go to the Savior for his grace, we will not encounter someone who is lacking in grace. The Savior is *full* of grace.[315] We can obtain a fulness of grace as the Savior did—by extending grace to others. We grow in our capacity to give grace by covenanting to consecrate our best efforts and resources to the Lord, taking those efforts and resources to the Lord and asking for his blessing and help, and then going forth in faith to feed the Lord's sheep. In return, he multiplies our efforts and resources, thus providing us with more grace to give away. It is a formula that applies to other gospel principles: "Blessed are the merciful: for they shall obtain mercy."[316] We could say, "Blessed are those who extend grace, for they shall obtain more grace." Elder Mark E. Petersen said, "Love and understanding—cooperation and brotherhood—will reproduce themselves in the hearts of others when given willingly and sincerely."[317]

---

313    James 1:5; emphasis added.
314    Mark 6:35–44; 1–9.
315    D&C 93:11.
316    Matthew 5:7.
317    Petersen, Conference Report, Oct. 1967, 67.

For instance, if we were given a kernel of corn and ate it, the kernel would be gone forever. But if we were to plant the kernel and nourish it, the kernel would soon grow into a stalk with several ears and many kernels. Then, if we were to eat just a few of the kernels and plant the rest, the kernels would become a field of corn and a huge harvest. And it all began with a single kernel!

As we humbly seek and receive the Lord's grace, then extend that grace to others, the Lord will give us more grace, and the cycle of receiving and giving will continue until we are filled with grace. If we do not stop the cycle by hoarding the Lord's blessings, we will grow from grace to grace by giving grace for the grace until we are perfected by grace. Elder Boyd K. Packer said, 'As you give what you have, there is a replacement, with increase!"[318] Of charitable service, President Gordon B. Hinckley promised that we cannot extend merciful blessings to God's children and not experience a harvest of merciful blessings in return.[319]

## Magnifying Our Priesthood Calling by Bearing Testimony

We cannot overemphasize the fact that God calls us to the priesthood for the express purpose of assisting him in doing his work: "to bring to pass the immortality and eternal life of man."[320] Because this work is the work of God, it requires the authority and power of God, and we must exercise our priesthood to accomplish it. President Wilford Woodruff said, "We [priesthood holders] have a labor laid upon our shoulders . . . and we will be condemned if we do not fulfill it."[321] He also said, "If we . . . , bearing the priesthood, use that priesthood for any purpose under heaven but to build up the Kingdom of God, . . . our power will fail."[322]

Part of our priesthood responsibility is bearing testimony of the truth. The following verse lies adjacent to the oath and covenant of the priesthood: "Therefore, go ye into all the world; and unto whatsoever place ye cannot go ye shall send, that the testimony may go from you into all the world unto every creature."[323] It is our priesthood obligation to raise our voices in testimony.[324] A testimony is a "declaration made under oath or affirmation by a witness in court to establish a fact—a public avowal . . . to give witness—a firsthand account."[325] Effectively, we are saying, "I put my character on the line to avow that what I say is true." Therefore, the opposite of testimony would be perjury.

Bearing testimony fulfills the law of witnesses.[326] Effectively, we are saying, "We add our witness to others that have been given." For example, Alma "began to speak unto [Zeezrom], and to establish the words of Amulek."[327] And we read, "Moses did not only

318   Packer, "The Candle of the Lord," 54–55.
319   Hinckley, "Blessed Are the Merciful," 68.
320   Moses 1:39.
321   Woodruff, *Discourses of Wilford Woodruff*, 102
322   Woodruff, Conference Report, Apr. 1880, 83.
323   D&C 84:62.
324   Eyring, "Faith and the Oath and Covenant of the Priesthood," 61–64.
325   *American Heritage Dictionary*, s.v. "Testimony."
326   Deuteronomy 19:15.
327   Alma 12:1.

testify of these things, but also all the holy prophets, from his days even to the days of Abraham."[328] And to this group we add our testimonies. Clearly, the weight of multiple testimonies serves to establish the truth.

We do God's work by bearing testimony. By covenant, we are to stand as witnesses of God at all times.[329] To that end, the Lord has placed upon us the "testimony of the covenant."[330] President Joseph Fielding Smith wrote, "People are converted by their hearts being penetrated by the Spirit of the Lord when they humbly hearken to the testimonies of the Lord's servants."[331] Zion is established, and we establish ourselves as Zion people, by bearing testimony.[332] On the other hand, those who are "not valiant in the testimony of Jesus" forfeit their celestial inheritance and their "crown over the kingdom of our God."[333] The terrestrial kingdom is their likely destiny.

The result of our bearing testimony is sanctification and renewal: "Nevertheless, ye are blessed, for the testimony which ye have borne is recorded in heaven for the angels to look upon; and they rejoice over you, and your sins are forgiven you."[334] That is, our sincere testimony becomes part of the record of heaven and simultaneously purifies the heart! In another place we read, "Whosoever shall confess me before men, him shall the Son of man also confess before the angels of God."[335] Our testimony of Christ summons his testimony of us! And in still another place, "Whosoever shall confess that Jesus is the Son of God, God dwelleth in him, and he in God."[336] Our testimony makes us one with God. Clearly, God blesses those who bear testimony in word and example.

Why does God give such honor to sincere testimony? Because bearing testimony is an act of charity; that is, because we love him, we are willing to advocate and endorse him—and if we love our fellowmen, we will want to help them find the truth. Mormon wrote, "If a man be meek and lowly in heart, and confesses by the power of the Holy Ghost that Jesus is the Christ, he must needs have charity; for if he have not charity he is nothing; wherefore he must needs have charity."[337] Significantly, the ultimate testimony that we can bear is the testimony we bear with our lives.[338]

The law of increase has impact on the bearing of testimony. By bearing testimony, a testimony grows. Brigham Young said, "A man who wishes to receive light and knowledge, to increase in the faith of the Holy Gospel, and to grow in the knowledge of the truth as it is in Jesus Christ, will find that when he imparts knowledge to others he will also grow and increase. Be not miserly in your feelings, but get knowledge and understanding by freely imparting it to others. . . . Wherever you see an opportunity to do good, do it, for that is the way to increase and grow in the knowledge of the truth."[339]

---

328   Helaman 8:16.
329   Mosiah 18:9.
330   D&C 109:38.
331   Smith, *Church History and Modern Revelation*, 1:36–37.
332   D&C 58:13.
333   D&C 76:79.
334   D&C 62:3.
335   Luke 12:8.
336   1 John 4:15.
337   Moroni 7:44.
338   D&C 135:1.
339   Young, *Discourses of Brigham Young*, 335.

Clearly, the bearing of testimony magnifies our priesthood calling and thus sanctifies and renews us. Our sins are forgiven, our witness is recorded as part of the eternal record of the truth, we are made one with God, and the Lord in turn commends us to the hosts of heaven. Ultimately, the bearing of testimony is an act of love, one in which we unashamedly stand forth, place our character and reputation on the line, and give solemn testimony of God. Bearing testimony is a confession of truth that summons great blessings from God.

## The Ultimate Magnification of Our *Calling*

Beyond every calling in the priesthood, the one calling that stands supreme is to become like God. That calling can be accomplished only through the ordinances of the temple. It is by means of these priesthood ordinances that "the power of godliness is manifest." Only these sacred ordinances hold "the key of the mysteries of the kingdom, even the key of the knowledge of God." Without these ordinances, "no man can see the face of God, even the Father, and live [eternal life]."[340] If we expect to become like God, "overcome" all things, become part of "the church of the Firstborn . . . into whose hands the Father has given all things"; become "priests and kings, who have received of his fulness, and of his glory; . . . priests of the Most High, after the order of Melchizedek, which was after the order of Enoch, which was after the order of the Only Begotten Son"; and become "gods, even the sons of God," among those of whom it is said, "all things are theirs, whether life or death, or things present, or things to come, all are theirs and they are Christ's, and Christ is God's"[341]—we must magnify our priesthood *calling*. We do that by going to the temple to receive the holy ordinances, including the endowment of priesthood knowledge and power.[342] These ordinances culminate with eternal marriage and the fulness of the priesthood.

Elder McConkie said, "In setting forth as much as can, with propriety, be spoken outside of the temple, the Lord says that 'the fulness of the priesthood' is received only in the temple itself. This fulness is received through washings, anointings, solemn assemblies, oracles in holy places, conversations, ordinances, endowments, and sealings. (D&C 124:40.) It is in the temple that we enter into the patriarchal order, the order of priesthood that bears the name 'the new and everlasting covenant of marriage' [D&C 131:2]."[343] So, temple ordinances and eternal marriage lead to the "fulness of the priesthood," and only by receiving that fulness can we ultimately magnify, or enlarge, our *calling* and progress to become like God. This is exactly how Jesus magnified his *calling*. Joseph Smith said, "If a man gets a fullness of the priesthood of God he has to get it in the same way that Jesus Christ obtained it, and that was by keeping all the commandments and obeying all the ordinances of the house of the Lord."[344]

---

340   D&C 84:19–22.
341   D&C 76:53–60.
342   D&C 95:8.
343   McConkie, *A New Witness for the Articles of Faith*, 315.
344   Smith, *Teachings of the Prophet Joseph Smith*, 308.

A man might serve faithfully in the Church and have numerous callings, but if he is capable and has the opportunity, and then chooses to neglect (1) to make temple covenants and receive temple ordinances, and (2) to marry for eternity in the temple and thus enter into the patriarchal order of the priesthood, he has *not* magnified his priesthood, and he is violating the terms of the oath and covenant of the priesthood.[345] Zion is established in the life of an individual by fulfilling these essential priesthood qualifications; because they lead to divine knowledge, power, and an eternal kingdom, they also lead to Zion and eventual exaltation.

## The Three Stages of the Priesthood Covenant

We take upon ourselves the oath and covenant of the priesthood and magnify our calling in three stages:
1. Ordination to the priesthood.
2. Temple endowment.
3. Temple marriage.

Note that two of the three stages involve both worthy men and women. The following information comes from an address given by BYU professor Chauncey Riddle at the Sperry Symposium in 1989:

> There are three stages by which one takes upon himself the oath and covenant of the holy priesthood and receives the power and authority of the Son of God [see D&C 68:2–4]. The first stage is to receive the priesthood, which one does by receiving ordination, being set apart to a calling, and by functioning faithfully in that calling under the guidance and instruction of the Holy Spirit. Those who thus function carry out the mind and the will of God. If they do this faithfully, they will be given progressively greater power and responsibility in their stewardships, but this does not necessarily mean church position [see Matthew 25:14–30]. To receive the priesthood does mean that one fully accepts the priesthood authority of The Church of Jesus Christ of Latter-day Saints and that one will be subject to those who preside over him in that priesthood.
>
> The second stage of receiving the oath and covenant of the holy priesthood is to receive one's personal endowment in the holy temple of God. First, the endow-

---

345    D&C 84:41–42.

ment consists of special blessings that are given to the person so that he can bear the power of God in this world without being destroyed by the abundant evil that will confront and oppose his labors to do the work of God in the power of God. Second, the endowment is a set of instructions and understandings that assist the person to understand mortality and his role therein. Third, the endowment involves covenants that the person makes, special promises to bear the burden of the work of the Lord in righteousness and purity. These promises are covenants of the oath and covenant of the priesthood [see D&C 84:39]. The oath is action taken by God, who cannot lie nor sin in any way. Men, who can and do sin and lie, make covenants with God that they might escape sinning altogether and wield the power of God in righteousness, and they do this altogether for the glory of God, as part of their worship of him for his goodness, for his righteousness [see D&C 82:19].

The third part of the oath and covenant of the holy priesthood is to receive the covenant of marriage in the temple. This is God's marriage, eternal marriage, the establishment of a new eternal kingdom in the pattern of godliness, to do the supreme work of godliness eternally. Blessings are bestowed, covenants are made, and power and authority to act in the priesthood roles of husband and wife, father and mother, are given [see D&C 131:1–4].[346]

As we achieve each stage of the oath and covenant of the priesthood, we progressively receive more responsibility and more power. That power speaks to the reasons we entered into the covenant of the priesthood in the first place: (1) to become like Christ, and (2) to have the power to bring people to Christ. These reasons are central to becoming a Zion person.

## Summary and Conclusion

The second pillar of Zion, the oath and covenant of the priesthood, is the covenant of exaltation. Our agreements in the covenant are faithfulness, obtaining the Aaronic and Melchizedek priesthoods magnifying our *calling*, receiving Christ and his Father, and living by every word that proceeds from the mouth of God. The Father's oath states that he will exalt us and give us all that he has.

---

346   Riddle, "The New and Everlasting Covenant," 232–33.

The priesthood covenant comes to us by the Father's invitation through his authorized servants. We are "called by this holy calling, and ordained unto the high priesthood of the holy order of God."[347] To be chosen and called of God, to receive his authority, power, and name to speak authoritatively as would God, to have the power to do what God would do, and to act in the capacity of the Savior, are honors without equal. By offering us the priesthood, he is offering us the opportunity to assume his name and further his work: "to bring to pass the immortality and eternal life of man."[348]

The oath and covenant of the priesthood contains *if-then* clauses: If we fulfill our obligations *then* the Father will fulfill his oath. The covenantal promises are:

- *If we are faithful*—Faithfulness or righteousness is the first promise that we make in the priesthood covenant. By receiving the priesthood, we receive the Lord's name, and therefore we are called to become models of him. Faithfulness empowers us to fulfill our priesthood commission.
- *If we obtain the Aaronic and the Melchizedek priesthoods*—We are required to progress in the priesthood until we receive a fulness of the priesthood. Both the Aaronic and Melchizedek orders of the priesthood are received by covenant, but only the Melchizedek Priesthood is received with the Father's oath.
- *If we magnify our calling*—A central agreement in the oath and covenant of the priesthood is magnifying our singular calling to eternal life, which impacts our various callings in mortality. We received that calling in the premortal world. There, we qualified to be *called* and elected (selected) for eternal life. It is the magnification of our singular calling and our various callings that provide the key to our eventual exaltation. Magnifying our singular priesthood *calling* consists of at least three steps:
    1. Obtaining gospel knowledge.
    2. Personal righteousness by compliance with gospel standards.
    3. Giving dedicated service.[349]

Magnifying our calling is ultimately dependent upon the principle of giving dedicated service. By giving service we progress toward perfection. However, giving adequate service, which is called *grace* (in one meaning of the word), lies beyond our ability; we need the Lord's help, which is also called *grace*. By receiving the Lord's grace (his help, light, truth, power, and perfecting principles), we grow in grace (ability to help, give light, truth, power, and perfecting principles to others), which enables us to give more grace to other people. In other words, we come unto Christ in humility and faith, having done all we can do,[350] and then he makes up the difference. Consequently, we will never lack grace. This is a condition of Zion people—*no lack*. The Lord takes care of us in proportion to how we take care of his children.

347   Alma 13:6.
348   Moses 1:39.
349   Romney, "The Oath and Covenant Which Belongeth to the Priesthood,'" 43.
350   2 Nephi 25:23: "for we know that it is by grace that we are saved [helped], after all we can do."

One way that we magnify our priesthood calling is by bearing testimony of the Lord. This act serves to sanctify and renew us. By bearing testimony our sins are forgiven, our witness is recorded as part of the eternal record of the truth, we are made one with God, and the Lord in turn bears testimony of us. Ultimately, bearing testimony is an act of love. It is a confession of truth that summons some of God's greatest blessings.

The calling in the priesthood that stands supreme is to become like God. That calling can be accomplished only through the ordinances of the temple, which culminate with eternal marriage and the fulness of the priesthood. We take upon ourselves the priesthood covenant and magnify our calling in three stages:

1. Ordination to the priesthood.
2. Temple endowment.
3. Temple marriage.

Of significance, two of the three stages include worthy women. We enter into the priesthood covenant and receive its blessings to become like Christ and to bring people to Christ. Only by receiving the new and everlasting covenant and thereafter receiving the oath and covenant of the priesthood, the first and second pillars of Zion, can we become Zion people and one day attain to the covenantal priesthood society of Zion.

# Section 3
# The Oath and Covenant
# of the Priesthood
## The Father's Oath, Instructions, and Promises

The oath and covenant of the priesthood, the second pillar of Zion, contains a remarkable feature—the Father swears this oath upon a man's ordination to the Melchizedek Priesthood. In the most sacred language, the Father promises us that we will be sanctified by the Spirit unto the renewing of our bodies and that we will become "the sons of Moses and of Aaron and the seed of Abraham, and the church and kingdom, and the elect of God." Our making the covenant of the priesthood signals that we are willing to receive Jesus Christ and the Father; the Father promises in his oath that upon our faithfulness he will give us his kingdom—meaning all that he has—which allows us to become all that he is, which is eternal. Furthermore, upon our making the priesthood covenant, Jesus assigns the heavenly hosts and his angels charge concerning us.[351] To assure that we learn the doctrine and workings of the priesthood covenant, the Father personally takes charge of our education concerning it. These promises combined constitute the Father's oath.

In discussing these sublime truths, we run the risk of feeling overwhelmed and unworthy. Such is not the intention of this book. Like ensigns, ideals are set on high mountains, waving loftily in the winds of hope, beckoning us to make the climb. Because no one can ascend without divine help, the Savior wrought the Atonement to clear the obstacles and make the journey possible. Elder McConkie taught that persisting in the strait and narrow path guarantees our arriving at our goal of eternal life.[352] Therefore, our success is a given, assuming that we persist in faith and faithfulness. Nevertheless, as we mount toward that ideal, we often will feel stretched and weighed down by the reality of our present weaknesses. During such times, we might remember that all gospel blessings derive from a principle

---

351   D&C 84:33–38, 42.
352   McConkie, "The Probationary Test of Mortality," 11.

of progress referred to as "line upon line," or "from grace to grace." We have been taught repeatedly that the direction we are heading is as important as arriving.

As we have mentioned, faithful women have every reason to become familiar with these principles. Although the priesthood is conferred upon worthy men, both men and women receive all of the blessings of the Father's oath when it is repeated at the time they are married.[353] Just so, single women have been promised repeatedly by the prophets that they simply need remain worthy to receive every blessing they have been denied in this season of their existence. When the opportunity for eternal marriage comes, a couple enters into the patriarchal order of the priesthood with all the blessings of Abraham, Isaac, and Jacob. Included in those blessings are the rights to the gospel and priesthood for the couple's posterity. A woman claims these priesthood blessings alongside her husband. Therefore, it is fitting that both the oath and covenant of the priesthood and the covenant of eternal marriage are simultaneously called the covenant of exaltation.[354]

Therefore, let us examine the Father's oath and the ideal of the oath's associated blessings with the confidence that as we progress in the oath and covenant of the priesthood, we, both men and their wives, will eventually qualify for every reward.

## The Father's Two Oaths Guaranteeing Us the Blessings of Abraham

Because of his righteousness, Abraham received the honor of becoming the "father of the faithful."[355] The Lord promised Abraham *with an oath* that he would bless and multiply him.[356] The Lord promised further:

> And I will make of thee a great nation, and I will bless thee above measure, and make thy name great among all nations, and thou shalt be a blessing unto thy seed after thee, that in their hands they shall bear this ministry and Priesthood unto all nations; and I will bless them through thy name; for as many as receive this Gospel shall be called after thy name, and shall be accounted thy seed, and shall rise up and bless thee, as their father; and I will bless them that bless thee, and curse them that curse thee; and in thee (that is, in thy Priesthood) and in thy seed (that is, thy Priesthood), for I give unto thee a promise that this right shall continue in thee, and in thy seed after thee (that is to say, the literal seed, or the seed of the body) shall all the families of the earth be blessed, even with the blessings of the Gospel, which are the blessings of salvation, even of life eternal.[357]

353    McConkie, *A New Witness for the Articles of Faith,* 313.
354    McConkie, *Mormon Doctrine,* 167.
355    D&C 138:41.
356    Hebrews 6:13–15.
357    Abraham 2:9–11.

Thus we see that Abraham and his children, including those who are adopted into Abraham's family, have a "*right* to the priesthood, to the gospel, and to eternal life."[358] This is the right and condition of every Zion person.

Abraham's blessings, which were renewed with Isaac and Jacob, are the "promises made to the fathers" that Moroni prophesied would be restored in this dispensation.[359] The fulfillment of that prophecy occurred in the Kirtland Temple on April 3, 1836,[360] when Moses, Elias, and Elijah appeared and delivered their sacred priesthood keys. The crowning promise given to the fathers was the blessing that the Savior, Jesus Christ, would come through their lineage,[361] in part to ensure that the terms of the new and everlasting covenant would be set in motion to save the fathers' children—*us!*

To do the work of salvation, the Savior needed the priesthood. Jesus is our great Exemplar; what he did to obtain the priesthood we must also do. To understand, we must look back to an ancient time.

In the premortal world, Jesus lived in a way to qualify to receive the priesthood. So did we. Of course, the priesthood is inherent in Jesus; nevertheless, in this life, he again was "called of God an high priest after the order of Melchisedec."[362] Evidently Jesus received the priesthood by covenant and by the Father's oath. Elder McConkie explained that this was the first of two oaths concerning the priesthood that the Father swore. The Father swore an oath that his Son would be a "high priest forever."[363] When we receive the priesthood, the Father swears the same oath to us. The second oath states that we will become priests and kings unto God forever, we will inherit all that the Father has, and we will become all that the Father is, just like his Beloved Son.

The author of Hebrews wrote, "All those who are ordained unto this priesthood are made like unto the Son of God, abiding a priest continually."[364] And at another time he wrote: "God, willing more abundantly to shew unto the heirs of promise the immutability of his counsel, confirmed it by an oath: That by *two immutable things [two oaths]*, in which it was impossible for God to lie, we might have a strong consolation, who have fled for refuge to lay hold upon the hope set before us."[365] In other words, the Father swore the oath first to his Son and then to us, thereby confirming to us, the children of Abraham and heirs of the promise, the immutability of his oath! Elder McConkie taught: "Because the blessings of Abraham exceed anything else on earth or in heaven, Deity uses the most solemn language known to man to confirm their verity. That is, he swears with an oath in his own name that these blessings shall rest upon the faithful forever. . . . When men anciently swore with an oath in the Lord's name to perform an act, they thereby made God their partner; and because God does not fail, they were then bound to perform the act or lay down their lives in the attempt. When God himself swears with an oath,

358   McConkie, *A New Witness for the Articles of Faith*, 317.
359   D&C 2:2.
360   D&C 110.
361   Galatians 3:16.
362   Hebrews 5:4–10.
363   Hebrews 6:16–20.
364   JST, Hebrews 7:1–3.
365   Hebrews 6:17–18; emphasis added.

he puts his own Godhood on the line: either what he promises shall come to pass or he ceases to be God. . . . God swore not one oath but two that the promises made to Abraham—that he and his seed had a right to the priesthood, to the gospel, and to eternal life—would surely come to pass."[366]

Two oaths guaranteeing the promise of eternal life!

## Sanctification by the Spirit unto the Renewing of Our Bodies

Zion is the pure in heart,[367] they who are purified and sanctified. We recall our definition that purification is the process of ridding something of impurities and that sanctification is the process of changing the purpose of something. A Zion person is someone whom the Spirit has purified and whom the Spirit has changed into a new creature[368] in the similitude of God's Only Begotten Son.[369] We agree to this process, which is called the baptism of fire, when we enter into the new and everlasting covenant. The purifying and sanctifying process accelerates when we enter into the oath and covenant of the priesthood. It is in the priesthood covenant that the Father promises renewal of our bodies.[370] This renewal will reach its highest manifestation in the celestial resurrection[371] when we become gods[372] and can fully assume the work of the Father.[373]

The Spirit sanctifies and renews the body in a variety of ways, such as when we undergo adversity or give service, and when our minds and hearts are infused with intelligence and peace. The process of sanctification also renews our bodies at covenant-making and covenant-renewing occasions. Baptism, confirmation, partaking of the sacrament, receiving the priesthood, receiving temple ordinances, and eternal marriage are examples. The Father's oath at the time of priesthood conferral heightens the process of sanctification that was set in motion at the time of baptism and confirmation. Now the Holy Ghost begins to purify "not only the minds of worthy priesthood holders, but also their bodies, until they are enlivened and strengthened to minister among the nations of the earth."[374] We see in these descriptions the condition and the work of Zion people. Receiving the priesthood carries with it a call for us to minister among God's children and become saviors on Mount Zion. This is the work of God and therefore is beyond our normal capability. In order to accomplish such a work, we must experience sanctification; our bodies must be renewed, reformed, rejuvenated, and empowered. Otherwise, left to our natural fallen condition, we could never achieve success.

In advance of his mission, Moses learned that he would need the sanctifying support of the Spirit to retool his body for the work he had been called to do. Without the Spirit's sanctifying renewal, he would have been left significantly impotent and weak.[375]

---

366   McConkie, *A New Witness for the Articles of Faith*, 317.
367   D&C 97:21.
368   2 Corinthians 5:17.
369   Moses 1:6, 13.
370   D&C 84:33.
371   D&C 88:28–29.
372   D&C 132:19–31.
373   Moses 1:39.
374   *Encyclopedia of Mormonism*, 1019.
375   Moses 1:9–11.

We deceive ourselves if we suppose that we, without the Spirit, are independently powerful.[376] It is the doctrine of the anti-Christ that man, of himself, "fare[s] in this life according to the management of the creature . . . prosper[s] according to his genius, and that every man conquer[s] according to his strength."[377] Jesus clearly tells us that he is the source of life[378] and the True Vine[379] from whom we draw sanctifying strength and power. It is through him that our bodies are renewed and fashioned so that we might become instruments in his hands.

Therefore, the hearts of Zion people are purified and sanctified by covenant and the reception of the Holy Ghost. Their bodies are renewed by the Spirit to enable them to engage and persist in the work of God, which otherwise would be beyond their ability. Neither Zion people nor Zion communities can be created in any other way; they must be renewed.

## The Progression of the Renewing of Our Bodies

President Faust taught that renewal, or sanctification, is linked to our desires and efforts to become holy.[380] Such desires and efforts invite the Holy Ghost to do his sanctifying work. Sanctification, as we have learned, leads to a change of heart.[381] According to the Apostle Paul, we prepare our hearts to be changed with "the words of faith and of good doctrine."[382] These "words" lead us to the covenants and ordinances of the priesthood, which further change our hearts. Thus, King Benjamin taught, "Because of the covenant which ye have made . . . *your hearts are changed through faith on his name.*"[383] President Faust said that it is the combination of faith, obedience, and adherence to the covenants and ordinances of the gospel that paves the way for the Spirit to purify our hearts and purge us of all that is unholy. The result of this purifying effort is sanctification, or holiness, which, he said, is the soul's true source of strength.[384]

Sanctification unto the renewing of the body is another manifestation of being born again. The Father's promise—"sanctification by the Spirit unto the renewing of [our] bodies"[385]—enumerates both the process and the eventual outcome of the Holy Ghost's sanctifying motions. Of course, we are sanctified by degrees. We begin by having faith in Christ, which always leads to repentance. We are motivated because we hope for the blessings of eternal life that we see distantly. By faith and repentance, our hearts are changed; we are *renewed and reborn*, and we seek to enter the kingdom by covenant. Baptism and confirmation are the entrance ordinances. Upon receiving the Holy Ghost, our hearts are further changed; we are *renewed and reborn* to a greater degree, and we begin to feel willing and anxious to sacrifice and consecrate all that we have and are to sustain and defend

376   D&C 88:5–13.
377   Alma 30:17.
378   John 11:25.
379   John 15:1; 1 Nephi 15:15; Alma 16:17.
380   Faust "Standing in Holy Places," 62.
381   Eyring, "Faith and the Oath and Covenant of the Priesthood," 61–64.
382   1 Timothy 4:6.
383   Mosiah 5:7; emphasis added.
384   Faust, "Standing in Holy Places," 62.
385   D&C 84:33.

the kingdom of God. We feel the fallen, natural part of us give way to the saintly man or woman. Now our nature becomes "as a child, submissive, meek, humble, patient, full of love, willing to submit to all things which the Lord seeth fit to inflict upon him."[386]

Further sanctification and renewal occur when we receive the oath and covenant of the priesthood. This covenant leads us to and includes the sacred ordinances of the temple. Successively, these ordinances cleanse and purify us again; they renew and empower our bodies, member by member, for more exalted purposes. Now, to a greater degree, we are separate from the telestial order of things.[387] More than ever before, we are Zion-like. We are anointed and consecrated for a holy purpose, which is to become like God. Therefore, our bodies are renewed and thus prepared to receive a kingdom in this life that will span eternity. In every way, our bodies become a temple.

The sanctification and renewal process continues as we receive the more impressive ordinances of the temple, which Moroni indicated was the revelation of the priesthood.[388] These sacred covenants and ordinances orient us toward eternal life and change our hearts. They serve to instruct us more perfectly "in theory, in principle, and in doctrine"[389] concerning our relationship to the Father, his plan of salvation, and the celestial system of laws that govern Zion people.

Our temple experience renews our bodies by heightening former covenants. *The Encyclopedia of Mormonism* states, "The words set forth eternal principles to be used in solving life's dilemmas, and they mark the way to become more Christlike and progressively qualify to live with God. There, the laws of the new and everlasting covenant are taught—laws of obedience, sacrifice, order, love, chastity, and consecration."[390] In the temple, we once again, *and more specifically*, promise to exercise strict obedience to all of the commandments,[391] including obedience to every word that proceeds forth from God's mouth.[392] We agree to sacrifice anything and everything to sustain and defend the kingdom of God,[393] which is the vehicle to prepare for the establishment of Zion.[394] We agree to live a unique celestial lifestyle called *chastity*,[395] which is to hold sacred, within the bond of legal and lawful matrimony, the power of procreation, which is God's power of "eternal lives."[396] We agree to consecrate all that we are and have for the building up of God's kingdom on the earth,[397] which kingdom is the custodian of the priesthood and the new and everlasting covenant,[398] and we do all of this to promote the cause of Zion in our personal lives, marriages, families, and the Church.

---

386    Mosiah 3:19.
387    2 Corinthians 6:17; Alma 5:57.
388    D&C 2:1.
389    D&C 97:14.
390    *Encyclopedia of Mormonism*, 1449.
391    Moroni 4:3; D&C 20:77.
392    D&C 84:44.
393    Smith, *Lectures on Faith*, 6:7.
394    Roberts, *Seventy's Course of Theology*, 1:10.
395    Exodus 20:14; 22:16; Leviticus 18:6–23; Matthew 5:27–28; 3 Nephi 12:27–28; Jacob 2:28, 31–35; Alma 39:5; Moroni 9:9; D&C 42:23–26; 63:16; 76:103.
396    Clark, *Messages of the First Presidency*, 6:176.
397    D&C 42.
398    Smith, *Teachings of the Prophet Joseph Smith*, 271–74.

We experience even greater sanctification, renewal, and change by marrying for time and eternity and entering into the patriarchal order of the priesthood. Now the power of procreation is legitimatized, and our bodies are sanctified and renewed to become authorized and empowered life-giving agents in the similitude of God the Father.

Finally, when we have proven that we will abide in our covenants "at all hazards," we experience an extraordinary renewal referred to as making one's "calling and election sure."[399] Having faithfully kept our covenantal promises, and having overcome all things by faith, we are privileged to receive the Father's personal assurance that we will receive an inheritance in the celestial kingdom. This blessing is described in Doctrine and Covenants 76:58: "Wherefore, as it is written, they are gods, even the sons of God." The various levels of renewal ultimately culminate in the celestial Resurrection, when our bodies are like God's and capable of doing all that He can do.

## Power Given to the Renewed and Sanctified

The result of sanctification is power—the renewing strength and capacity to magnify our *calling* and callings in the priesthood, the vitality and vigor associated with Zion. We learn a lesson of renewal and sanctification from Enos, the Book of Mormon prophet. Enos began the process of sanctification by repenting. Then, yearning for the promise of eternal life and knowing that no unclean thing could dwell in God's presence,[400] he wrestled before God to receive a remission of his sins: "And my soul hungered; and I kneeled down before my Maker, and I cried unto him in mighty prayer and supplication for mine own soul. . . . And there came a voice unto me, saying: Enos, thy sins are forgiven thee, and thou shalt be blessed."[401]

Notice that coupled with the Lord's assurance of forgiveness was his promise to Enos of future blessings. Now, having achieved a higher level of renewal, Enos immediately began to seek for those promised blessings, which included the ability to obtain priesthood power so that he could engage in the work of redemption and influence an increasing number of people. Enos had experienced *renewal;* he was stronger in the Spirit than he had ever been. Now he had more confidence to approach the Lord, who had told him: "Whatsoever thing ye shall ask in faith, believing that ye shall receive in the name of Christ, ye shall receive it."[402]

Enos's renewal and sanctification led him to the point that he now had power to ask the Lord to bless his people: "I began to feel a desire for the welfare of my brethren, the Nephites; wherefore, I did pour out my whole soul unto God for them."[403] The Lord's subsequent promise to bless Enos's family resulted in Enos experiencing greater sanctification and renewal. Consequently, his power to do the work of God increased. This is an important principle of Zion: *The sanctified gain increasing power to become saviors on Mount Zion for an increasing number of people.*

---

399   Smith, *Teachings of the Prophet Joseph Smith,* 150.
400   3 Nephi 27:19; Moses 6:57.
401   Enos 1:5.
402   Enos 1:15.
403   Enos 1:9.

Now that Enos's faith "began to be unshaken in the Lord,"[404] he prayed for his enemies—those estranged family members who opposed him: "I prayed unto [God] with many long strugglings for my brethren, the Lamanites. And it came to pass that after I had prayed and labored with all diligence, the Lord said unto me: I will grant unto thee according to thy desires, because of thy faith."[405] The Lord's response to that prayer had eternal implications that would transcend Enos's mortal life and extend to the coming forth of the Book of Mormon. Such were the renewing blessings the Spirit laid upon a Zion-like man who persisted in the sanctification process and gained power through prayer to call down the blessings of the gospel and priesthood upon his troubled family.

This is the same sanctifying and renewing process Melchizedek employed to draw upon the Spirit to do the work of Zion among his people. These were individuals who "had waxed strong in iniquity and abomination; yea, they had all gone astray; they were full of all manner of wickedness; but Melchizedek having exercised mighty faith, and received the office of the high priesthood according to the holy order of God, did preach repentance unto his people. And behold, they did repent; and Melchizedek did establish peace in the land in his days."[406]

Similarly, Joseph, who was sold into Egypt, remained true to the priesthood covenant as he was sanctified and renewed by the Spirit during his fourteen-year ordeal in Pharaoh's prison. The result was Joseph's power in the priesthood to bless numerous people. Catherine Thomas wrote, "Our ancestor and patriarch Joseph who was sold into Egypt was the model for us as he sanctified himself to have a sanctifying influence on his very troubled family and, like his Savior, exercised a saving power on his brethren."[407] We who are Joseph's children (whether born or adopted into Israel) enjoy the blessings of Joseph's renewing sanctification. Just so, we who are willing to accept the Spirit's sanctifying motions experience renewal and empowerment so that we might do the redemptive work of Zion, which includes the power to pray for sanctifying blessings for many souls for many generations.

## Blessings Given to the Renewed and Sanctified

In teaching Adam the essentials of the new and everlasting covenant, the Lord revealed that the process of renewal and sanctification follows the pattern of physical birth—water, spirit, and blood. This pattern is repeated at the time of our spiritual birth, when we are *born again* into the kingdom of heaven. The Lord explained that by means of this second birth, which consists of baptism (water), reception of the Holy Ghost (spirit), and the Atonement of Jesus Christ (blood), we emerge cleansed and sanctified of all sin. Now our new life provides that we might "enjoy the words of eternal life in this world, and eternal life in the world to come, even immortal glory."[408] The ultimate manifestation

---

404    Enos 1:11.
405    Enos 1:11–12.
406    Alma 13:17–18.
407    Thomas, "Alma the Younger, Part 1," n.p.
408    Moses 6:59.

of the "words of eternal life" is the "more sure word of prophecy."[409] This is the Father's pronouncement that our place in his kingdom is *made sure*; that is, our exaltation is sealed upon us[410] "by revelation and the spirit of prophecy through the power of the Holy Priesthood."[411]

Because the oath and covenant of the priesthood mandates that we "give diligent heed to the words of eternal life,"[412] we must understand and submit to the process of sanctification, which renews our bodies. Let us remember here that the sanctified are the pure in heart, the people of Zion, those who have been born again into the kingdom of God through the new and everlasting covenant, and those who strive for a greater level of renewal by entering into the oath and covenant of the priesthood.

The Lord explained to Adam that obedience to the pattern of sanctification—rebirth by water, Spirit, and blood—justifies us for the blessings of eternal life. These blessings are available only to those who are renewed by the Spirit and thus sanctified: "For by the water ye keep the commandment; by the Spirit ye are justified, and by the blood ye are sanctified."[413] In other words, by baptism in water we keep the commandment to pursue a new life in Christ. The Spirit justifies both that action and our continuing obedience to God's laws so that we might receive promised blessings. Although the Holy Ghost is the purifying and sanctifying agent, ultimately the blood of Christ makes the sanctification process possible.

But there is more. The Lord taught Adam that his being justified by the Spirit and sanctified by the blood of Christ lead to unequalled blessings: "Therefore it is given to abide in you; the record of heaven; the Comforter; the peaceable things of immortal glory; the truth of all things; that which quickeneth all things, which maketh alive all things; that which knoweth all things, and hath all power according to wisdom, mercy, truth, justice, and judgment."[414]

This list of blessings describes the effects of spiritual birth through obedience to the pattern of sanctification. Our names are written in the "record of heaven." This entails the promise of eternal life delivered by "another comforter . . . even the Holy Spirit of promise."[415] There could be no greater comfort than to receive this promise. The scripture reads: "Behold, this is pleasing unto your Lord, and the angels rejoice over you; the alms of your prayers have come up into the ears of the Lord of Sabaoth, and are recorded in the book of the names of the sanctified, even them of the celestial world. Wherefore, I now send upon you another Comforter, even upon you my friends, that it may abide in your hearts, even the Holy Spirit of promise; which other Comforter is the same that I promised unto my disciples, as is recorded in the testimony of John. *This Comforter is the promise which I give unto you of eternal life, even the glory of the celestial kingdom.*"[416]

---

409    D&C 131:5.
410    McConkie, *Mormon Doctrine*, 217; emphasis added.
411    D&C 131:5.
412    D&C 84:43.
413    Moses 6:60.
414    Moses 6:61.
415    D&C 88:2–4.
416    D&C 88:2–4; emphasis added.

And the blessings to those whose bodies are renewed multiply: "If thou shalt ask, thou shalt receive revelation upon revelation, knowledge upon knowledge, that thou mayest know the mysteries and peaceable things—that which bringeth joy, that which bringeth life eternal."[417] Combined, these scriptures give us a glimpse of the Lord's blessings to those who obey the commandment, who are justified by the Spirit, and who are sanctified by the blood of Christ.

These blessings correspond with other blessings given to the renewed and sanctified. For example, in Doctrine and Covenants 50, the Lord promises priesthood holders an exalted status among men, provided that men humble themselves, as did the Savior, and use that exalted status to minister among God's children: "He that is ordained of God and sent forth, the same is appointed to be the greatest, notwithstanding he is the least and the servant of all."[418] Moreover, the Lord confirms the promises of the oath and covenant of the priesthood on the condition of our striving to be cleansed and purified: "Wherefore, [the priesthood holder] is possessor of all things; for all things are subject unto him, both in heaven and on the earth, the life and the light, the Spirit and the power, sent forth by the will of the Father through Jesus Christ, his Son. But no man is possessor of all things except he be purified and cleansed from all sin."[419] The result is power given to men to ask for and receive blessings and, additionally, power over all spirits: "And if ye are purified and cleansed from all sin, ye shall ask whatsoever you will in the name of Jesus and it shall be done. But know this, it shall be given you what you shall ask; and as ye are appointed to the head, the spirits shall be subject unto you."[420]

As great as are these blessings, could any blessings be greater than those listed in Doctrine and Covenants 76? Therein are the promises to those who are "washed and cleansed from all their sins, and receive the Holy Spirit by the laying on of the hands of him who is ordained and sealed unto this power; and who overcome by faith, and are sealed by the Holy Spirit of promise, which the Father sheds forth upon all those who are just and true":[421]

> They are they who are the church of the Firstborn.
> They are they into whose hands the Father has given
> all things—They are they who are priests and kings,
> who have received of his fulness, and of his glory;
> and are priests of the Most High, after the order of
> Melchizedek, which was after the order of Enoch, which
> was after the order of the Only Begotten Son.
> Wherefore, as it is written, they are gods, even the
> sons of God—wherefore, all things are theirs, whether
> life or death, or things present, or things to come, all

---

417    D&C 42:61.
418    D&C 50:26.
419    D&C 50:27–28.
420    D&C 50:29–30.
421    D&C 76:52–53.

are theirs and they are Christ's, and Christ is God's. And they shall overcome all things.

Wherefore, let no man glory in man, but rather let him glory in God, who shall subdue all enemies under his feet.

These shall dwell in the presence of God and his Christ forever and ever. These are they whom he shall bring with him, when he shall come in the clouds of heaven to reign on the earth over his people. These are they who shall have part in the first resurrection. These are they who shall come forth in the resurrection of the just. These are they who are come unto Mount Zion, and unto the city of the living God, the heavenly place, the holiest of all. These are they who have come to an innumerable company of angels, to the general assembly and church of Enoch, and of the Firstborn. These are they whose names are written in heaven, where God and Christ are the judge of all. These are they who are just men made perfect through Jesus the mediator of the new covenant, who wrought out this perfect Atonement through the shedding of his own blood. These are they whose bodies are celestial, whose glory is that of the sun, even the glory of God, the highest of all, whose glory the sun of the firmament is written of as being typical.[422]

These are the blessings given to those who receive the priesthood unto the renewing of their bodies. This is the pattern the Lord revealed to Adam—the pattern from which supernal blessings flow. This pattern makes our hearts pure so that we can become Zion people. This pattern contains the essence of the plan of salvation. By this pattern we may become sons of God. The Lord told Adam:

And now, behold, I say unto you: This is the plan of salvation unto all men, through the blood of mine Only Begotten, who shall come in the meridian of time. . . .

And thus he [Adam] was baptized, and the Spirit of God descended upon him, and thus he was born of the Spirit, and became quickened in the inner man.

And he heard a voice out of heaven, saying: Thou art baptized with fire, and with the Holy Ghost. This is the record of the Father, and the Son, from henceforth

---

422   D&C 76:54–70.

and forever; and thou art after the [priesthood] order of
him who was without beginning of days or end of years,
from all eternity to all eternity. Behold, thou art one in
me, a son of God; and thus may all become my sons.
Amen.[423]

## "I Sanctify Myself, That They Also Might Be Sanctified"

A primary purpose of the priesthood is to obtain power to save God's children. As we
shall see, Jesus exemplified the fact that our effort to sanctify ourselves has a direct sanctifying effect upon others for whom we are praying or are trying to help. Such a sanctifying effort is Zion-like in nature, and such Zion-like people will be motivated to sanctify
themselves to help others through charity, the pure love of Christ.

Sanctification, we have learned, results in a changed and renewed heart. That renewal, in great part, is defined by charity.[424] Charity is "the end of the commandment,"[425]
and "the crowning virtue"[426] without which we could not do the Lord's work.[427] Charity,
of course, is one of the hallmarks of Zion. Equality, unity, the abolition of poverty, and
Christlike love define Zion people. We understand that charity is not merely love; it is
*saving* love—the pure love of Christ; it is the love that characterizes Zion, which never
fails and endures forever.[428]

Without charity, we are useless to God, because the covenant of the priesthood
calls for us to care for others.[429] Moreover, without charity we are useless to ourselves
as well—if we are proud, selfish, and without empathy, the scripture tells us, "Except ye
have charity ye can in nowise be saved in the kingdom of God."[430]

Charity, or saving love, is not something we come by naturally. Charity is a spiritual
gift we must first seek and then develop.[431] Therefore, it is incumbent upon those who
make the covenant of the priesthood to pursue the covenant's promised renewal of the
body to become vessels of charity.

We look to Jesus' example to understand the process and purposes of sanctification
and how sanctification renews the body and creates a new heart that is filled with saving
love. In his great intercessory prayer, the Savior taught us that personal sanctification
is *the most important* principle by which one person might save another. Just moments
before entering Gethsemane, Jesus made the following statement: "For their sakes I sanctify myself that they also might be sanctified."[432] In other words, the first action, *personal*

423   Moses 6:62, 65–68.
424   Eyring, "Faith and the Oath and Covenant of the Priesthood," 61–64.
425   1 Timothy 1:5.
426   McConkie, *Mormon Doctrine,* 121.
427   D&C 12:8; 18:19; see also D&C 4:5.
428   2 Nephi 26:30; Moroni 7:47; 8:25–26.
429   Eyring, "Faith and the Oath and Covenant of the Priesthood," 61–64.
430   Moroni 10:20–21.
431   Moroni 7:48; 1 Corinthians 16:14; 1 Timothy 4:12; 2 Timothy 2:22; Titus 2:2; 2 Peter 1:7; 2 Nephi 33:7–9; Alma 7:24;
      D&C 121:45; 124:116.
432   John 17:19.

*sanctification*, makes possible the second, *the saving of another*. We often think of sanctification in the context of being cleansed from sin—and it is certainly that—but here we see Jesus, who had no sin, sanctifying himself for the express purpose of saving others.

So how did Jesus sanctify himself? We learn the answer in the context of the seventeenth chapter of John. Jesus sanctified himself through strict obedience, partaking of the sacrament, entering into a fast, making a sacrifice, and offering mighty prayer, which might be defined as prayer preceded by sacrifice. The result of Jesus' sanctification was that he obtained power to overcome everything that stood between his people and eternal life, including the promise of a glorious resurrection—the ultimate expression of corporeal renewal.

Likewise, we offer *Saviorlike* sacrifice when we enter the temple and perform proxy ordinances for people who cannot achieve salvation otherwise. Certainly, by offering these sacred sacrifices, we are indeed acting in a Zion-like way. In the process, we experience a greater degree of sanctification in that we are *offering up* ourselves as a proxy sacrifice in the similitude of Christ. By means of that sacrifice, we, like Jesus, effectively break down the obstacles that stand between the deceased and eternal life. When we understand that by pursuing this sanctifying process Jesus gained immeasurable power to ask for and receive blessings, is it any wonder that we, after making a vicarious sacrifice, might also approach the Father with power and, in the precincts of the most sacred location of his house, offer mighty prayer and receive blessings?

Clearly, to symbolically lend our sanctified body, which has been prepared and renewed by the Spirit for this purpose, to someone who is disembodied, to act and speak in the stead of the deceased, to offer our time and effort to someone who has no power to receive saving ordinances in a physical world where these things must be done—to do all of these unselfish acts counts as Christlike sacrifice and love. Sacrificing for someone who is powerless to help himself—that is, standing in the stead of another—is the highest form of love because it is the most Christlike. This is the love that is found in Zion: pure, unselfish, saving love. Zion-like love *lifts us toward the likeness of God and Jesus Christ*.[433] This is the Savior's pattern of sanctification; it is the renewal of the body for a holy purpose. His motivation was love. The result was the renewing of his body. In performing his mission on earth, he conformed himself into the image of the Father in order to do the Father's will, and he conformed himself into our image, so to speak, so that he could anticipate the entirety of our experience and make a corresponding sacrifice in our behalf. Then he received the ultimate renewal of the body: celestial resurrection.

Jesus is our exemplar, and we must follow his pattern. Unless we seek sanctification and the renewal of the body, we may fall short in our priesthood duties and many of our assignments may go unfinished.[434] Therefore, the Father makes an oath that faithful priesthood holders will be "sanctified by the Spirit unto the renewing of their bodies." They will be made clean through the power of the Holy Ghost, and then they will be given the Spirit's "operative power giving guidance for life's activities."[435]

---

433   Widtsoe, Conference Report, Apr. 1943, 38; emphasis added.
434   Asay, "The Oath and Covenant of the Priesthood," 43.
435   Farley, "The Oath and Covenant of the Priesthood," 44.

## The Sons of Moses and of Aaron

In the gospel, we enter into a variety of relationships that have reference to family. For example, by birth or adoption we are the children of Abraham, Isaac, and Jacob, and thus are entitled to the blessings of the gospel and the priesthood.[436] Additionally, we become sons and daughters of Jesus Christ when we are baptized.[437] Accepting the Atonement of Jesus Christ makes us, in the fullest sense, the "sons of God."[438] With the conferral of the Aaronic and Melchizedek priesthoods we become the sons of Aaron and of Moses, which relationship, writes LDS scholar S. Brent Farley, "denotes belonging to a family and having certain rights as a member and as an heir." He continues, "Becoming a son implies the acceptance of the person and principles of the one designated as the father. To become a son of Moses and Aaron, then, would imply accepting them and their principles so that we would have a relationship and as heirs, receive certain rights, including the rights of the priesthood."[439]

According to the oath and covenant of the priesthood, we become sons of these two great priesthood brethren by "obtaining these two priesthoods,"[440] and by doing the works of Moses and Aaron. What were their works? Farley answers, "Aaron was a spokesman for Moses and an assistant to him, Moses having the greater calling and Aaron the lesser. The lesser, or preparatory, priesthood was named after Aaron. (D&C 84:18, 26–27.) The sons of Aaron today are those who accept the preparatory, or Aaronic, Priesthood and live its principles, thus proving worthy of greater blessings as they enter the Order of the Melchizedek Priesthood. They learn to accept all who are called as spokesmen (those other local and general authorities who help accomplish the Lord's work) under the direction of the prophet. They are also willing themselves to serve as spokesmen in priesthood capacities when called to do so."[441]

The Aaronic Priesthood also holds the key of "the gospel of repentance, and of baptism by immersion for the remission of sins."[442] This key punctuates our priesthood covenant to teach and preach the gospel, bring people to Jesus Christ through repentance, initiate them into the kingdom of God by means of baptism and the new and everlasting covenant—all of which set God's children on the path to eternal life. Clearly, receiving the Aaronic Priesthood is a call to serve with the authority to do so.

Moses was called of God as the prophet to gather Israel, lead them from Egyptian bondage, and establish them as an independent and strong people. (Exodus 3:10–17.) He was the prophet, the mouthpiece of the Lord to Israel; by following his inspired direction the people could obtain exaltation. Those who become sons of Moses today are those who accept the mouthpiece of the Lord who has been called to deliver modern Israel from the bondage of worldliness in order to become established as a strong and indepen-

---

436    Abraham 2:8–11.
437    Mosiah 5:7.
438    D&C 35:2; 45:8; 76:58.
439    Farley, "The Oath and Covenant of the Priesthood," 44.
440    D&C 84:14–33.
441    Farley, "The Oath and Covenant of the Priesthood," 45.
442    D&C 13:1.

dent people and be led toward exaltation. They too participate in the gathering of Israel, the keys of which Moses committed to Joseph Smith and Oliver Cowdery in the latter-day restoration (D&C 110:11). The sons of Moses have a right "to the Holy Priesthood," "which priesthood continueth in the church of God in all generations, and is without beginning of days or end of years." (D&C 84:6, 17.) Moses sought diligently to prepare his people for this right to be worthy of the presence of God through the authority, ordinances, and power of the priesthood. (D&C 84:19–23.) The sons of Moses today hearken to the one called of God to guide them in their preparation to behold His presence.

Thus, the sons of Moses and of Aaron today are faithful priesthood holders. In the course of their progress, they will become worthy temple recommend holders. They will "offer an acceptable offering and sacrifice in the house of the Lord" (D&C 84:31) by receiving their own temple endowment and performing work for the dead. "And the sons of Moses and of Aaron shall be filled with the glory of the Lord, upon Mount Zion in the Lord's house, whose sons are ye; and also many whom I have called and sent forth to build up my church." (D&C 84:32).[443]

A most significant prelude to the oath and covenant of the priesthood references the temple as the focal point of the priesthood. Only through the ordinances of the temple can we "prepare to achieve the goal sought by Moses for his people: to enter the Lord's presence."[444] The revelation reads: "Now this [the Melchizedek Priesthood doctrine, covenants, and ordinances] Moses plainly taught to the children of Israel in the wilderness, and sought diligently to sanctify his people that they might behold the face of God."[445] The Israelites rejected this higher law despite the fact that Moses taught them that it was the only way to bring about their personal sanctification. Elder McConkie noted that "the greatest blessings [of the priesthood covenant] are reserved for those who obtain 'the fulness of the priesthood,' meaning the fullness of the blessings of the priesthood. These blessings are found only in the temples of God."[446] Every covenant and ordinance received in the temple—the purpose and power of which is to bring us into God's presence—is included in the oath and covenant of the priesthood—the second pillar of Zion.

It is the mission of the latter-day sons of Aaron and Moses to follow in the footsteps of their *fathers*. They support their leaders, serve as spokesmen in priesthood capacities, and watch over the Church. They teach the gospel of repentance, then go forth to gather Israel, preaching and teaching the doctrine of the priesthood. They bring people to Christ to receive their temple blessings so that the people might be sanctified and enter into the presence of the Lord.[447] Farley concludes, "The corollary between the mission of Moses in ancient Israel and the mission of the sons of Moses in modern Israel is not coincidental."[448]

---

443   Farley, "The Oath and Covenant of the Priesthood," 44.
444   Farley, "The Oath and Covenant of the Priesthood," 45.
445   D&C 84:23.
446   McConkie, *Mormon Doctrine,* 482.
447   D&C 84:2.
448   Farley, "The Oath and Covenant of the Priesthood," 45–46.

## The Seed of Abraham

The oath of the priesthood stipulates that our receiving the priesthood fulfills the Father's oath to Abraham, who was promised that the rights to the gospel and priesthood would perpetually belong to him and his seed. Whether we are a blood descendant of Abraham or adopted into his family, when we receive the covenant of the priesthood, the Father deems us "the seed of Abraham,"[449] and thus we, by birthright, are entitled to all of the associated blessings.

As we have learned, we who are of the bloodline of Abraham qualified premortally to be elected (selected) in this life (1) to receive the blessings of the gospel and priesthood for our own salvation, and (2) to go forth and bless others with these same blessings.[450] These blessings are the blessings Abraham sought and received; they include our children's right as "lawful heirs" to be offered the fulness of the gospel and the priesthood "according to the flesh."[451]

Abraham is our priesthood model. He made himself worthy so that he could qualify to receive the priesthood by covenant; he magnified his calling; he received both Jesus Christ and the Father in the fullest sense; and he gave strict diligence to every word that proceeded forth from the mouth of God. Ultimately, by means of the Melchizedek Priesthood and the temple covenants and ordinances, he entered into the presence of God and eventually achieved godhood.[452] We are heirs to Abraham's blessings; if we follow his example, we will receive the same blessings. Elder McConkie wrote, "Abraham and his seed (including those adopted into his family) shall have all of the blessings of the gospel, of the priesthood, and of eternal life,"[453] including eternal increase. The Lord revealed, "This promise is yours also, because ye are of Abraham. . . . Therefore . . . do the works of Abraham."[454]

"Elder McConkie noted that 'what we say for Abraham, Isaac, and Jacob we say also for Sarah, Rebekah, and Rachel, the wives . . . who with them were true and faithful in all things,' for, as President Joseph Fielding Smith taught, 'the Lord offers to his daughters every spiritual gift and blessing that can be obtained by his sons.'"[455] The connection of women to the oath and covenant of the priesthood is, of course, vital to the progression of both men and women, and we will more fully address this subject later on.

Concerning our being the seed of Abraham and thus entitled to his blessings, Brent Farley taught, "In order to enjoy the full blessings of the oath and covenant of the priesthood, a man must marry for time and eternity in the house of the Lord. Elder McConkie explained that 'this covenant, made when the priesthood is received, is renewed when the recipient enters the order of eternal marriage.' Further, 'when he is married in the temple for time and for all eternity, each worthy member of the Church enters personally into the

---

449    D&C 84:34.
450    Romans 9:11; 11:5, 7, 28.
451    D&C 86:8–11; 113:6.
452    D&C 132:37.
453    McConkie, *A New Witness for the Articles of Faith,* 505.
454    D&C 132:31–32.
455    Farley, "The Oath and Covenant of the Priesthood," 46.

same covenant the Lord made with Abraham. This is the occasion when the promises of eternal increase are made, and it is then specified that those who keep the covenants made there shall be inheritors of all the blessings of Abraham, Isaac, and Jacob.'"[456]

## The Church and Kingdom of God

The priesthood inseparably links us to The Church of Jesus Christ of Latter-day Saints, which is God's kingdom on earth. Elder McConkie wrote, "The church is a kingdom; it is God's kingdom, the Kingdom of God on earth, and as such is designed to prepare men for an inheritance in the kingdom of God in heaven, which is the celestial kingdom."[457] As priesthood holders, we represent the Church and kingdom wherever we are. The priesthood makes us bright beacons who draw people to Christ. Jesus taught: "Let your light so shine before men, that they may see your good works, and glorify your Father which is in heaven."[458] The priesthood is associated with light, the power of light, and the light of Christ, which is "the law by which all things are governed."[459] By virtue of our priesthood calling, the Lord shines his light on us that we might stand as sources of guidance, inspiration, and power. We are the standard bearers of that light to the nations.[460]

As ministers of Jesus Christ, we are authorized to bless the Father's children in the name of Jesus Christ. The Lord instructed the Seventy, "Heal the sick therein, and say unto them, *The kingdom of heaven is come nigh unto you.*"[461] That is, "We, who represent the kingdom, are come to bless you." We bearers of the priesthood are *of* the kingdom and, more importantly, we *are* the kingdom. We are the Church and kingdom of God. We magnify our calling in the priesthood, according to President J. Reuben Clark, by building up the kingdom of God, which is done by blessing God's children, and that can only be done by faith in Jesus Christ and the authority of the priesthood.[462]

## The Elect of God

Zion people are the elect of God. Elder Bruce R. McConkie explains, "The *elect of God* comprise a very select group, an inner circle of faithful members of The Church of Jesus Christ of Latter-day Saints. These are the portion of Church members who are striving with all their hearts to keep the fulness of the gospel law in this life so that they can become inheritors of the fulness of gospel rewards in the life to come." Faithful Melchizedek Priesthood holders are among the elect of God. Of this group, Elder McConkie said, they are those who "keep 'the oath and covenant which belongeth to the priesthood,' and are rewarded with the fulness of the Father's kingdom."[463] The elect of God qualify

---

456  Farley, "The Oath and Covenant of the Priesthood," 46; McConkie, A New Witness for the Articles of Faith, 313, 508; D&C 131:1–3.
457  McConkie, A New Witness for the Articles of Faith, 335.
458  Matthew 5:16.
459  D&C 88:13.
460  D&C 115:5.
461  Luke 10:9; emphasis added.
462  Clark, Conference Report, Oct. 1950, 169–71.
463  McConkie, Mormon Doctrine, 217; emphasis added.

to enter into the Lord's rest, meaning the fulness of his glory.[464] In the perfection of the term, the elect *receive* the Father and his kingdom, and therefore they receive all that the Father has.[465] President Marion G. Romney described the elect of God as those who live worthy of every trust; who live by every word of God; who hunger and thirst after righteousness; who make their calling and election sure.[466]

These descriptions of the elect are of those who make covenants, who exhibit profound faithfulness, who overcome the world, and who surmount their fallen condition so that they might be exalted on high; they are wholly Zion-like. These live celestial laws in a telestial setting. They hold up the celestial standard, beckoning all to abandon telestial complacencies and filth and come up to Zion to be saved by the King of Zion. They are Zion people, the pure-hearted, the elect of God.

The word *elect* suggests "election," or "selection." As we have learned, our selection for exaltation began in the premortal world. There we embraced the ideal of Zion. Because of our righteousness, we were both *called* and *elected* for eternal life. The scripture states that we were "*called* and prepared from the foundation of the world according to the foreknowledge of God, on account of [our] exceeding faith and good works."[467] That is, we were *called* and elected (selected) to receive the priesthood in the premortal world, an ordination that qualified us to receive the priesthood in this life. In the premortal world, we who entered into the holy order of the priesthood "elected to become gods" and to "come to earth and learn the work of redemption in apprenticeship to the Lord Jesus Christ." Therefore, we elected, and were *selected*, to come to mortality as heirs of special blessings, to embrace the ideal of Zion *again*, and to continue to do the work of redemption here so that we would someday "qualify to live with the Gods in the eternal worlds."[468] This was our premortal calling and election.

Elder McConkie wrote, "If the full blessings of salvation are to follow, the doctrine of election must operate twice. First, righteous spirits are elected or chosen to come to mortality as heirs of special blessings. Then, they must be called and elected again in this life, an occurrence which takes place when they join the true Church. (D&C 53:1.) Finally, in order to reap eternal salvation, they must press forward in obedient devotion to the truth until they make their 'calling and election sure' (2 Pet. 1:10), that is, are 'sealed up unto eternal life.' (D&C 131:5.)"[469]

In this life, we are called and elected once more. Through baptism, we are *called* into the fellowship of Jesus Christ,[470] that is, we receive our "calling and election in the church."[471] That calling leads to our being *called* to receive our calling to and in the priesthood. The oath and covenant of the priesthood requires that we magnify that calling, which is to become like God. That goal is accomplished only by obedience, sacrifice,

---

464    D&C 84:24.
465    D&C 84:35–38.
466    Romney, Conference Report, Apr. 1974, 116.
467    Alma 13:3–5; emphasis added.
468    Thomas, "Alma the Younger, Part 1," n.p.
469    McConkie, *Mormon Doctrine*, 217.
470    1 Corinthians 1:9, 26–27; Hebrews 3:1.
471    D&C 53:1.

and living by "every word that proceedeth forth from the mouth of God."[472] If, after we have lived our covenants against all odds by persisting in the new and everlasting covenant and the oath and covenant of the priesthood—the first and second pillars of Zion—we will eventually receive the Lord's guarantee of eternal life, and our provisional calling and election will now be made *sure*.[473] Then we are "sealed up unto eternal life"[474] and become, in the fullest sense, the elect of God, who have been called and *selected* by God's own oath and the promise of the certainty of eternal life.

## Calling and Election Made Sure

Describing the elect of God, Elder McConkie said they are members of the Church who "devote themselves wholly to righteousness."[475] Joseph Smith explained the journey to becoming the elect, and the ideal description of that term: "After a person has faith in Christ, repents of his sins, and is baptized for the remission of his sins and receives the Holy Ghost, (by the laying on of hands), which is the first Comforter, then let him continue to humble himself before God, hungering and thirsting after righteousness, and living by every word of God, and the Lord will soon say unto him, Son, thou shall be exalted. When the Lord has thoroughly proved him, and finds that the man is determined to serve him at all hazards, then the man will find his calling and election made sure, then it will be his privilege to receive the other Comforter."[476]

Here the Prophet links the calling and election made sure with becoming worthy to come into the presence of the Lord and receive his comfort. Joseph Smith said, "Then it will be [our] privilege to receive the other Comforter. Now what is this other Comforter? It is no more nor less than the Lord Jesus Christ himself; . . . when any man obtains this last Comforter, he will have the personage of Jesus Christ to attend him, or appear unto him from time to time, and even he will manifest the Father unto him, and they will take up their abode with him, and the visions of the heavens will be opened unto him, and the Lord will teach him face to face, and he may have a perfect knowledge of the mysteries of the Kingdom of God."[477]

Elder McConkie gives the following definition of the calling and election made sure: "To have one's calling and election made sure is to be sealed up unto eternal life; it is to have the unconditional guarantee of exaltation in the highest heaven of the celestial world; it is to receive the assurance of godhood; it is, in effect, to have the day of judgment advanced, so that an inheritance of all the glory and honor of the Father's kingdom is assured prior to the day when the faithful actually enter into the divine presence to sit with Christ in his throne, even as he is 'set down' with his 'Father in his throne.' (Rev. 3:21.) But when the ratifying seal of approval is placed upon someone whose calling and

---

472    D&C 84:44.
473    Lee, Conference Report, Oct. 1970, 116; 2 Peter 1:10.
474    D&C 131:5.
475    McConkie, *Mormon Doctrine*, 217.
476    Smith, *Teachings of the Prophet Joseph Smith*, 149–51.
477    Smith, *Teachings of the Prophet Joseph Smith*, 150–51; John 14:16:23; D&C 88:3–4; 130:3.

election is thereby made sure—because there are no more conditions to be met by the obedient person—this act of being sealed up unto eternal life is of such transcendent import that of itself it is called being sealed by the Holy Spirit of Promise, which means that in this crowning sense, being so sealed is the same as having one's calling and election made sure."[478] Obviously, no greater promise can be made by God through the Holy Ghost than the promise of eternal life.

Another term emerges from the scriptures in connection with the calling and election made sure: *the more sure word of prophecy*.[479] Elder McConkie explains that the elect of God, in the ultimate sense, are those who "receive *the more sure word of prophecy*, which means that the Lord seals their exaltation upon them while they are yet in this life."[480] The fact that our exaltation is "sealed" upon us suggests a priesthood ordinance by means of the sealing keys. The Doctrine and Covenants describes this term: "The more sure word of prophecy means a man's knowing that he is sealed up unto eternal life, by revelation and the spirit of prophecy through the power of the Holy Priesthood."[481] We immediately see the link between the more sure word of prophecy and the oath and covenant of the priesthood, which stipulates that we must "give diligent heed to the words of eternal life."[482] Clearly, the ultimate manifestation of those *words* of eternal life is the more sure *word* of prophecy that the Father seals upon us through his anointed servant, promising us that we will be called up to his kingdom and that our place in it is made sure.

Elder McConkie expounds: "Those so favored of the Lord are sealed up against all manner of sin and blasphemy except the blasphemy against the Holy Ghost and the shedding of innocent blood. That is, their exaltation is assured; their calling and election is made sure, because they have obeyed the fulness of God's laws and have overcome the world."[483]

Although having our calling and election made sure stands at the summit of gospel blessings, it is nevertheless remarkably within reach, more so than we might imagine. For example, "on May 16, 1843, Joseph Smith, William Clayton, and company were traveling through Carthage and stopped for the night at the farm of Benjamin F. Johnson in Ramus, Illinois. That evening Joseph instructed the group in detail on the principle of eternal marriage. As Benjamin and his wife listened, the air lavish with the sweet words of life, Joseph put his hand on the knee of William Clayton and promised him: 'Your life is hid with Christ in God, and so are many others. Nothing but the unpardonable sin can prevent you from inheriting eternal life for you are sealed up by the power of the priesthood unto eternal life, having taken the step necessary for that purpose. William Clayton was twenty-eight years old when Joseph avowed to him the irrevocable promise of eternal life. He had been a member of the Church for a little more than five years."[484]

478    McConkie, *Doctrinal New Testament Commentary*, 3:336.
479    D&C 131:5; 2 Peter 1:19.
480    McConkie, *Mormon Doctrine*, 217; emphasis added.
481    D&C 131:5.
482    D&C 84:43.
483    McConkie, *Mormon Doctrine*, 109–10.
484    Summerhays, "The Stripling Elect," Feb. 20, 2009, referencing Allen, *No Toil Nor Labor Fear: The Story of William Clayton*, 129–30.

In an article entitled, "The Stripling Exalted," James T. Summerhays, an editor at *BYU Studies*, writes, "A recurring motif in Joseph Smith's discourse is the principle of calling and election. 'There is some grand secret here,' Joseph said, and he wanted to reveal 'the secret and grand key' that would unlock 'the most glorious principle of the Gospel of Jesus Christ.'"[485]

Continuing, Summerhays says,

> In my mind, four words divulge the secret: *Spiritual blessings are timely*. That's it. That's the key. Imagine the absurdity of being given the sword of valor only after you slay the dragon, or being received into a house of refuge only after the storm is passed. Instead, the promise has a more timely purpose: "Having this promise [of eternal life] sealed unto them," spoke Joseph, "it was an anchor to the soul, sure and steadfast. Though the thunders might roll and lightnings flash, and earthquakes bellow, and war gather thick around, yet this hope and knowledge would support the soul in every hour of trial, trouble and tribulation" (*History of the Church*, 5:401).
>
> I see a clear chronology to Joseph's statement: first, the promise is given to make the receiver strong, and then the thunders roll. My instinct tells me that this is why Heber C. Kimball and many others were given the promise so early in life: it was to shore up their courage for the coming storm and fury.
>
> The "calling and election made sure" fulfills a more expedient and satisfying purpose—it was not intended to be only a capstone to a life of faithfulness; nor is it a final prize to be given out after the race of life is already won.
>
> Imagine the peace of mind that would come if we already knew that God had signed our names in the Book of Life. No surprises at Judgment Day, no sudden and everlasting thrusting down to the dark abyss. Being able to almost taste salvation, we might become much more light-hearted, jovial, and resilient in the face of trials and sorrows that must come but now seem so trifling in the eternal scheme of things. We could be ablaze with confidence, having internalized the words of Peter which say, "Make your calling and election

---
485   Smith, *Teachings of the Prophet Joseph Smith*, 298.

> sure: for if ye do these things, ye shall never fall" (2
> Peter 1:10).
>
> Above all, being unshackled with worries over
> personal salvation, we would feel free and wholly avail-
> able to give ourselves to the salvation of others. In other
> words, we will have made a cosmic leap forward in
> being more like God, who is not too worried about him-
> self but whose whole glory rests upon bringing "to pass
> the immortality and eternal life of man" (Moses 1:39).[486]

Clearly, we need not have arrived at perfection to experience our calling and election made sure. Rather, it is a step in our progression that makes perfection possible. It comes after the Lord tries our faith and determines that we will remain in the Covenant at all hazards. It becomes the ultimate comfort that provides us strength to face and endure the trials of mortality, providing us knowledge that our future is secure with God.

Blaine Yorgason explained that having our calling and election made sure is both a revelation and an ordinance called the "more sure word of prophecy." "Scriptural evidence seems to indicate that one's calling and election can be made sure in either of two ways, though it seems likely that both are interrelated. They are (1) receiving the voice of God in a personal revelation wherein the promise of exaltation is given; and (2) receiving by ordinance the fullness of the priesthood through the more sure word of prophecy by 'him who is anointed' (D&C 132:7)."[487] Evidently, we can receive either the revelation or the ordinance first, but eventually we will receive both. In either case, the revelation and the ordinance deliver the assurance of attaining eternal life.

That said, too many of us flounder because we do not seek this revelation when in fact the Holy Spirit of Promise may have already set his seal upon us. We may be like the converted Lamanites who had been "baptized with fire and with the Holy Ghost, and they but knew it not."[488] We suppose that this blessing comes only to the venerable aged, and then only by ordinance; therefore, we fail to seek the personal revelation from the Holy Ghost that would provide us with comfort and with the strength to pursue our lifes' missions.

Many blessings flow from having our calling and election made sure. To the elect of God, the Lord has promised the ultimate sanctification and renewal of the body: "Ye shall come forth in the first resurrection. . . . They shall pass by the angels, and the gods, which are set there, to their exaltation and glory in all things, as hath been sealed upon their heads, which glory shall be a fulness and a continuation of the seeds forever and ever. Then shall they be gods, because they have no end; therefore shall they be from everlasting to everlasting, because they continue; then shall they be above all, because all things are subject unto them. Then shall they be gods, because they have all power, and the angels are subject unto them."[489]

---

486    Summerhays, "The Stripling Exalted," Feb. 20, 2009.
487    Yorgason, *I Need Thee Every Hour*, 387–88.
488    3 Nephi 9:20.
489    D&C 132:19–20.

The elect of God are Zion people forever in an eternal Zion priesthood society. No wonder, then, that Joseph Smith exhorted the Saints "to go on and continue to call upon God until you make your calling and election sure for yourselves, by obtaining this more sure word of prophecy, and wait patiently for the promise until you obtain it."[490]

## Receiving Christ and the Father

Monte S. Nyman writes: "Through receiving the priesthood, a person is receiving Jesus Christ because the recipient is taking the name of Christ and acting with his authority. And those who receive Jesus are actually receiving the Father because all that Jesus does is by divine investiture of the Father. Those who receive the Father receive his kingdom; they receive the fullness of the glory of the Father. 'Therefore all that [the] Father hath shall be given unto [them]' (D&C 84:34–38). In short, they shall receive eternal life. All that the Father has was given to Jesus, and he is willing to give the same to the faithful priesthood holder (John 15:16)."[491]

The language of the oath and covenant of the priesthood has overtones of courtship—a plea from God, who wants us to join with him. In the priesthood covenant we hear him yearning for us to choose to love him as he loves us, to give to him our hearts, to take upon us his name (priesthood), and to enter into a marriage-like covenant whereby we fully *receive* him: "And also all they who receive this priesthood receive me, saith the Lord; for he that receiveth my servants receiveth me; and he that receiveth me receiveth my Father."[492] Notice that the Father endows us with all that he has, just as a husband endows his bride with all that he possesses or will possess. Both the husband and the Father make that consecration with a solemn oath.

The marriage motif continues. Whereas a husband and wife are sealed together as one, so we are invited in the priesthood covenant to become one with the Father as the Father and the Son are one. The vehicle by which we become one with them is entering into their same order of the priesthood. Of such, Farley writes, "Such unity was the Savior's desire when he prayed: 'Holy Father, keep through thine own name those whom thou hast given me, that they may be one, as we are. . . . Father, I will that they also, whom thou hast given me, be with me where I am; that they may behold my glory, which thou hast given me.' (John 17:11, 24.) The oath and covenant of the priesthood is the means for the fulfilment of that prayer. . . . Herein is the fulfillment of heirship."[493]

Because the oath and covenant of the priesthood approximates the marriage covenant, and because the oath and covenant of the priesthood is the second pillar of Zion, the condition of Zion is very much like a marriage. As husbands and wives *receive* each other in the covenant of marriage, we similarly *receive* the Father and Jesus Christ. In each relationship, we grow together until we become one. In both relationships, we

---

490   Smith, *History of the Church,* 6:365; 5:388–89.
491   Nyman, "Priesthood, Keys, Councils, and Covenants," 125.
492   D&C 84:35–37.
493   Farley, "The Oath and Covenant of the Priesthood," 46.

mature in appreciation and love for our *beloved*. And, over time, we, become more and more like each other.

Joseph Smith explained this process of growing together in love: "And all those who keep his commandments shall grow up from grace to grace, and become heirs of the heavenly kingdom, and joint-heirs with Jesus Christ; possessing the same mind, being transformed into the same image or likeness, even the express image of him who fills all in all; being filled with the fulness of his glory, and become one in him, even as the Father, Son and Holy Spirit are one. . . . A sure reward [is] laid up for them in heaven, even that of partaking of the fullness of the Father and the Son through the spirit. As the Son partakes of the fullness of the Father through the Spirit, so the saints are, by the same Spirit, to be partakers of the same fullness, to enjoy the same glory; for as the Father and the Son are one, so, in like manner, the saints are to be one in them. Through the love of the Father, the mediation of Jesus Christ, and the gift of the Holy Spirit, they are to be heirs of God, and joint heirs with Jesus Christ."[494]

Our receiving God leads to our knowing and seeing God. These privileges are some of the "rights of the priesthood."[495] As we have learned, only the priesthood ordinances revealed in the temple have the power to provide a man or a woman with these consummate blessings: "For without this [the power of godliness that is facilitated through temple ordinances] no man can see the face of God, even the Father, and live."[496] Elder McConkie wrote:

> What greater personal revelation could anyone receive than to see the face of his Maker? Is not this the crowning blessing of life? . . . There is a true doctrine on these points, a doctrine unknown to many and unbelieved by more, a doctrine that is spelled out as specifically and extensively in the revealed word as are any of the other great revealed truths. There is no need for uncertainty or misunderstanding; and surely, if the Lord reveals a doctrine, we should seek to learn its principles and strive to apply them in our lives. This doctrine is that mortal man, while in the flesh, has it in his power to see the Lord, to stand in his presence, to feel the nail marks in his hands and feet, and to receive from him such blessings as are reserved for those only who keep all his commandments and who are qualified for that eternal life which includes being in his presence forever.[497]

---

494   Smith, *Lectures on Faith*, 5:2–3.
495   D&C 121:36.
496   D&C 84:22.
497   McConkie, *A New Witness for the Articles of Faith*, 492.

If we are true and faithful to the oath and covenant of the priesthood, where will it lead us? The focal point of the priesthood, the reason that we enter into this covenant, the motivation that drives us to bring others to Christ, is to regain the presence of God—to *receive* him. Having personally experienced that blessing, Joseph Smith exclaimed, "Great and marvelous are the works of the Lord, and the mysteries of his kingdom which he showed unto us, which surpass all understanding in glory, and in might, and in dominion; which he commanded us we should not write while we were yet in the Spirit, and are not lawful for man to utter; neither is man capable to make them known, for they are only to be seen and understood by the power of the Holy Spirit, which God bestows on those who love him, and purify themselves before him; *to whom he grants this privilege of seeing and knowing for themselves*; that through the power and manifestation of the Spirit, while in the flesh, they may be able to bear his presence in the world of glory."[498]

"While in the flesh!" proclaims Elder McConkie. "For those who 'purify themselves before him,' this is the time and the day and the hour when they have power to see their God!"[499] This "right" of the priesthood is, of course, dependent on our allowing the Holy Ghost to purify our hearts, for only Zion people, the pure in heart, may see and receive God.[500] This "right" of the priesthood also reminds us of two words in the priesthood covenant we have discussed: *calling* and *elect*.[501] Elder McConkie said, "Brethren whose calling and election is made sure always hold the holy Melchizedek Priesthood. Without this delegation of power and authority they cannot be sealed up unto eternal life."[502]

Ultimately, *receiving* Christ and the Father means receiving the "fulness of the priesthood,"[503] the ordinance involving the more sure word of prophecy, which we have discussed. Blaine M. Yorgason writes:

> Peter calls this ordinance, which was to be restored to the earth through priesthood authority in the Nauvoo Temple, "the more sure word of prophecy"; Elder McConkie calls it "the fulness of the sealing power"; and the Prophet Joseph Smith referred to it as both "the patriarchal power," and "the keys of knowledge and power." It is all the same—the sealing up of individuals to eternal life through the authorized priesthood ministrations of the Lord's mouthpiece or those he may have appointed. . . . When the president of the Church is instructed "by revelation and commandment" to exercise these keys of sealing power in their fulness in behalf of worthy Church members, his blessings or pronouncement of fullness of the priesthood is called

---

498   D&C 76:114–18; emphasis added.
499   McConkie, *A New Witness for the Articles of Faith*, 495.
500   3 Nephi 12:8; Matthew 5:8.
501   D&C 84:33–34.
502   McConkie, *The Promised Messiah*, 587.
503   D&C 124:28.

in the scripture "the more sure word of prophecy"; that is, it is a prophetic declaration as if from the mouth of God that will not fail, for, as the Lord says, "Whether by mine own voice or by the voice of my servants, it is the same." The Lord declares, "The more sure word of prophecy means a man's *knowing* that he is sealed up unto eternal life, by revelation and the spirit of prophecy through the power of the Holy Priesthood." Thus Joseph said, "I anointed [Judge James Adams] to the patriarchal power—to receive the keys of knowledge and power, by revelation to himself."[504]

All of these blessings are associated with receiving Jesus Christ and the Father. This is both a stipulation and a blessing stated in the oath and covenant of the priesthood. Zion people must understand and embrace this commandment if they are to become one with the Father and Jesus Christ. In a most beautiful way, our receiving them is symbolic of the marriage covenant. "And this is according to the oath and covenant which belongeth to the priesthood."[505]

## "All That My Father Hath"

Our Heavenly Father sets the example of consecration. With no selfish motive, he offers each of us, *indivisibly*, all that he has. Just how much is all that he has? To Moses, who was given a panoramic view of the universe, the Lord said, "And worlds without number have I created . . . innumerable are they unto man; but all things are numbered unto me, for they are mine and I know them. . . . The heavens, they are many, and they cannot be numbered unto man; but they are numbered unto me, for they are mine. And as one earth shall pass away, and the heavens thereof even so shall another come; and there is no end to my works, neither to my words."[506]

A quantity so vast that it would appear numberless unto man is beyond our comprehension, even with the aid of modern technology. That the Father promises us with an oath that, upon the condition of our faithfulness, he will give us the totality of his kingdom is equally beyond our comprehension. The Father's promise of our eventual exaltation is so expansive and glorious that it defies explanation.[507]

To attempt to grasp the extent of the Father's creations, let us examine what we know about the heavens. In 1983, before the Hubble telescope and modern computer technology, the National Geographic Society published an article and a map of the

504    Yorgason, *I Need Thee Every Hour,* 395–98, quoting 2 Peter 1:19; McConkie, *Mormon Doctrine,* 217; Smith, *Teachings of the Prophet Joseph Smith,* 325; D&C 1:38; 131:5; emphasis added; Smith, *Teachings of the Prophet Joseph Smith,* 326.
505    D&C 84:39–40.
506    Moses 1:33–38.
507    Asay, "The Oath and Covenant of the Priesthood," 43.

known universe.[508] The editors explained that our solar system has a radius of 150 million kilometers, or .000016 light years. A light year is the distance that light travels (at 186,000 miles per second) for a year: 5,878,625,373,183.61 miles—almost 6 trillion miles per year! Our solar system resides on the outskirts of the Milky Way galaxy in a *neighborhood* of twenty nearby stars. The radius of this neighborhood is twenty light years, or 120 trillion miles. This tiny grouping of stars is only a pinpoint in the enormous Milky Way, which has a radius of 50,000 light years, and, by one estimate, is made up of some 100–200 billion stars like our sun. On a clear night, when we gaze up into the heavens, we see, but we cannot comprehend, the vastness of our galaxy. Traveling at 220 kilometers per second, our sun makes one revolution around the center of our galaxy every 230 million years!

As incomprehensible as are these numbers, the Milky Way galaxy is still only a pinpoint in the ocean of the known universe. Consider this—our galaxy is one of a *cluster* of twenty nearby galaxies of like size. This cluster is called a "Local Group" containing 2 to 4 trillion stars. The radius of our Local Group is two million light years. But it is only a dot in the universe. Local Groups tend to congregate in "Local Superclusters," which are the largest of celestial formations. Each "Local Supercluster" may be comprised of thousands of member galaxies. The Local Supercluster in which we reside has a radius of 75 million light years. As incredible as these numbers might seem, nothing is more unfathomable than the fact that our Local Supercluster is still a mere speck in the known universe. And there is no visible end to these creations! When this *National Geographic* article was written in 1983, astronomers could not have imagined that the dots in far reaches of space they were mapping would one day be identified as numerous Superclusters. With the help of advanced technology, astronomers now estimate that the *known* universe is comprised of some 125 billion galaxies, and, as Enoch exclaimed to the Lord, "Thy curtains are stretched out still!"[509]

If by means of modern telescopes we are able see to this extent, imagine what Moses was able to see by the power of God! And yet God had to limit that vision of his creations in order to keep Moses in the flesh.[510] Enoch saw this same vision. Within that context, he viewed the eternal resting place of his Zion people, and, in a universal sense, he saw his Zion in relation to all the creations of God. In awe, he exclaimed, "And thou hast taken Zion to thine own bosom, *from all thy creations,* from all eternity to all eternity."[511]

All of this the Father offers us. Clearly, we who strive to become Zion-like will be richly rewarded for our investment of faithfulness. The scriptures describe our reward as inheriting "thrones, kingdoms, principalities, and powers, dominions, all heights and depths." We will move on from this telestial realm to surmount the heavens and "pass by the angels, and the gods, which are set there, to [our] exaltation and glory in all things, as hath been sealed upon [our] heads, which glory shall be a fulness and a continuation

508   "Galaxy Map," *National Geographic Society,* June 1983.
509   Moses 7:30.
510   Moses 1:4.
511   Moses 7:31; emphasis added.

of the seeds forever and ever."[512] Numberless worlds, innumerable posterity, and eternal, exalted life—such are the blessings of the oath and covenant of the priesthood! Failing to find adequate language to describe these blessings, the Apostle Paul conceded, "Eye hath not seen, nor ear heard, neither have entered into the heart of man, the things which God hath prepared for them that love him."[513]

These are Father's gifts that he guarantees us in his oath. By revelation, the Prophet wrote, "Wherefore, all things are theirs. . . . These shall dwell in the presence of God and his Christ forever and ever. . . . They who dwell in his presence are the church of the Firstborn; . . . and he makes them equal in power, and in might, and in dominion."[514] This is the condition and destiny of Zion people.

## Ministering and Protection of Angels

The oath and covenant of the priesthood contains the Lord's special promise of angelic help, counsel, and protection to accomplish our work upon the earth: "I have given the heavenly hosts and mine angels charge concerning you."[515] In that same revelation, the Lord adds, "And whoso receiveth you, there I will be also, for I will go before your face. I will be on your right hand and on your left, and my Spirit shall be in your hearts, and mine angels round about you, to bear you up."[516] Zion people are continually blessed by and become conversant with angels.

Angelic ministrations may come as visitations or promptings, but in any case, these ministrations occur under the direction of the Holy Ghost, for "angels speak by the power of the Holy Ghost."[517] According to the scriptures, angelic ministrations are for the purposes of:

- Delivering messages.[518]
- Ministering and prophesying.[519]
- Teaching doctrines of salvation.[520]
- Calling us to repentance.[521]
- Rescuing us from peril.[522]
- Helping us to fight our battles.[523]
- Guiding us in the performance of our work.[524]
- Helping us to find and bless others with the gospel.[525]

---

512    D&C 132:19.
513    1 Corinthians 2:9.
514    D&C 76:59, 62, 94–95.
515    D&C 84:42.
516    D&C 84:88.
517    2 Nephi 32:3; see also 1 Nephi 17:45.
518    Luke 1:11–38.
519    Acts 10:1–8, 30–32.
520    Mosiah 3.
521    Moroni 7:31.
522    1 Nephi 3:29–31; Daniel 6:22.
523    2 Kings 6:15–17.
524    Genesis 24:7.
525    Matthew 24:31.

- Helping us to perform all needful things relative to God's work.[526]
- Comforting us, as the angel comforted Jesus in his Gethsemane.[527]

The promise of angelic ministration includes several different types of beings broadly classed as "heavenly hosts."[528] These beings are members of the Church of the Firstborn, another name for Zion, the heavenly church whose faithful members are prepared by the earthly Church of Jesus Christ of Latter-day Saints,[529] also another name for Zion, or Zion in process. The Church of the Firstborn is made up of resurrected beings, translated beings, premortal spirits, spirits of the deceased (who are called "just men made perfect"[530]) and righteous mortal beings. Each being can function as an angel, and each type of being has specific powers. If we are worthy, we will "have the rights of fellowship and communion 'with the general assembly and church of the Firstborn' (D&C 107:19), meaning those faithful members whose names 'are written in heaven' (Hebrews 12:23), referring to Saints on both sides of the veil."[531] *Angels!*

Zion-like people, people of the Covenant, they who have received the holy priesthood by covenant, are *never* left alone. And neither are their children. Embedded in Jesus' instructions on ministering to his little ones is the comforting phrase: "In heaven their angels do always behold the face of my Father which is in heaven."[532] Angels are continually around us, serving, blessing, and protecting us. Joseph Smith taught, "The spirits of the just are exalted to a greater and more glorious work; hence they are blessed in their departure to the world of spirits. Enveloped in flaming fire, they are not far from us, and know and understand our thoughts, feelings, and motions, and are often pained therewith."[533]

Who are these ministering angels? Often they are our deceased relatives, friends, and people with whom we have labored in the work of the Lord. President Joseph F. Smith said, "When messengers are sent to minister to the inhabitants of this earth, they are not strangers, but from the ranks of our kindred, friends, and fellow-beings and fellow-servants. . . . Our fathers and mothers, brothers, sisters and friends who have passed away from this earth, having been faithful, and worthy to enjoy these rights and privileges, may have a mission given them to visit their relatives and friends upon the earth again, bringing from the divine Presence messages of love, of warning, or reproof and instruction, to those whom they had learned to love in the flesh."[534] In President Smith's vision of the spirit world, he declared, "I beheld that the faithful elders [and sisters] of this dispensation, when they depart from mortal life, continue their labors in the preaching of the gospel of repentance and redemption, through the sacrifice of the Only Begotten Son of God, among those who are in darkness and under the bondage of sin in the great world of the spirits of the dead."[535]

526   Moroni 7:29–33.
527   Luke 22:42-43.
528   D&C 84:42.
529   McConkie, *Mormon Doctrine*, 139–40.
530   D&C 76:69; 129:3; Hebrews 12:23.
531   Farley, "The Oath and Covenant of the Priesthood," 50.
532   Matthew 18:10.
533   Burton, *Discourses of the Prophet Joseph Smith,* 128.
534   Smith, *Gospel Doctrine,* 435.
535   D&C 138:57.

To discount the reality of the constant ministering by angels is to deny one of the supernal blessings of Zion and the restored gospel—a central blessing pertaining to both the Aaronic and Melchizedek priesthoods. As Moroni was closing the Book of Mormon, he quoted his father, Mormon, who exhorted us to believe in miracles and in the ministering of angels: "Wherefore, if these things [miracles and the ministering of angels] have ceased wo be unto the children of men, for it is because of unbelief, and all is vain."[536] In other words, without heavenly help we are left to ourselves to struggle through life without a shield to deflect the adversary's blows. Without this help we are alone and trying to find meaning in life is vain.

Because we are children of God, we have planted within our souls the innate desire to do the work of God. But in our fallen condition we can do very little. When it comes to redeeming others and bringing them to Zion, we are often limited to loving and exhorting them, praying for them, and bearing testimony—that is, we can only attempt to create an atmosphere in which the Spirit can function. We are not equipped to change a person's heart, provide him a spiritual experience, or rescue him from spiritual death. That is the special work of the Godhead. To achieve any spiritual goal, we must order our lives according to our covenants and petition the Father in the name of Christ for help. His response will come by the Holy Ghost, who may deliver God's messages and blessings to us through the ministering of angels, who are other Zion-like people sent to help us become Zion people.

Of our exhortation to believe in the ministration of angels and expect their help, LDS writer and family life specialist H. Wallace Goddard, wrote,

> When we impose mortal constraints on eternal doings, we are surely selling heaven short. As the Prophet Joseph observed, "It is the constitutional disposition of mankind to set up stakes and set bounds to the works and ways of the Almighty." If we limit heaven's doings by our rules and assumptions, we will shortchange Heaven and ourselves. Maybe a set of laws very different from those we know for mortality governs the doings of immortals. My propositions for the laws that govern immortals include the following:
> 1. Immortals love us and yearn to be a part of our lives. There is nothing they enjoy more than serving the family and friends who literally mean everything to them.
> 2. Those who live in eternity are not everlastingly at odds with time. While those in the spirit world may not be fully free of the constraints of time, surely they do not struggle with time the way we do.

---

536    Moroni 7:37.

3. Immortals can only participate fully in our lives when we allow them to. They are not allowed to intrude on our lives uninvited but may take part as we appropriately invite them to take part.
4. They will not violate our agency (nor do our chores), but they gladly teach us, love us, reassure us, and guide us according to heavenly wisdom.
5. Though it may take us years to learn to hear their language, they already know us and our language.[537]

President James E. Faust taught that angelic ministration is the common right and experience of all Zion people in every dispensation. Angels have always appeared or prompted the Saints by giving instruction, warning, and direction. We underestimate the extent to which they affect our lives. Their ministry has always been an important part of the gospel.[538]

Our entrance into the new and everlasting covenant through baptism and confirmation blesses us with the gift of the ministering of angels through the gift of the Holy Ghost. These two gifts are inseparable. As we partake of the sacrament and renew the Covenant, the blessing of the Lord's Spirit—the Holy Ghost—to always be with us is renewed and confirmed. This promise of the Holy Ghost's companionship carries with it the promise of angelic ministration. When worthy men receive the Aaronic Priesthood, the promise of ministering angels is renewed, confirmed, and magnified. This priesthood holds the "keys of the ministering of angels."[539] This additional promise of angelic ministration now provides us with heavenly help to do our priesthood duty.

We receive the promise of angelic help again when we are ordained to the Melchizedek Priesthood. Once more, that promise is renewed, confirmed, and magnified in the oath and covenant of the priesthood. This time we receive the promise of angelic help with the Father's oath.[540] With the Melchizedek Priesthood, the blessings of angelic ministration multiply. Through the ministering of angels, Melchizedek priesthood holders who are worthy have "the privilege of receiving the mysteries of the kingdom of heaven, to have the heavens opened unto them, to commune with the general assembly and church of the Firstborn, and to enjoy the communion and presence of God the Father, and Jesus the mediator of the new covenant."[541] These supernal blessings—the promise of angelic ministration and continuing help from the hosts of heaven—are associated with the oath and covenant of the priesthood.

Such are the promises given to Zion people—"they who are come unto Mount Zion, and unto the city of the living God, the heavenly place, the holiest of all . . . they who have come to an innumerable company of angels, to the general assembly and church of Enoch, and of the Firstborn."[542]

---

537   Goddard, "Blessed by Angels"; quoting Smith, *Teachings of the Prophet Joseph Smith*, 320.
538   Faust, "A Royal Priesthood," 50–53.
539   D&C 13:1.
540   D&C 84:39–42.
541   D&C 107:18–19.
542   D&C 76:66–67.

## The Father's Instructions: *Be Careful and Be Diligent*

With such great potential for blessings, it comes as no surprise that by way of commandment, as stated in the priesthood covenant, the Father charges us to beware—to be careful or to take care—concerning our diligence to the words of eternal life. Why? Because the oath and covenant of the priesthood carries the promise of exaltation: "And I now give unto you a commandment to beware [be careful] concerning yourselves, to give diligent heed to the words of eternal life."[543] Carelessness, negligence, or rejection of the priesthood covenant results in the Father's condemnation and the cessation of the priesthood rights and promises.[544] On the other hand, President Romney said, obedience, or giving careful diligence to the words of eternal life, entitles us to the priesthood covenant's blessings and rewards.

Expounding on the commandment to be careful and give diligent heed to the words of eternal life, Farley says, "This verse is a key verse within the oath and covenant of the priesthood. It leads one to an understanding of how to obtain the fulness of the oath and covenant of the priesthood."[545] This commandment precedes the Father's instruction: "For you shall live by every word that proceedeth forth from the mouth of God."[546] This instruction suggests that we are obligated to search and learn the revealed word of the Lord. And where are the words of eternal life found? In the standard works; in the teachings of the prophets and apostles; in the inspired words of parents, teachers, and local leaders; and in direct revelation from the Holy Ghost. In each case, as we search and learn the words of eternal life, the Holy Ghost will confirm them to us by personal revelation.[547]

Brother Farley says, "How one receives these words is next explained in a chain of logic: 'For the word of the Lord is truth, and whatsoever is truth is light, and whatsoever is light is Spirit, even the Spirit of Jesus Christ. And the Spirit giveth light to every man that cometh into the world; and the Spirit enlighteneth every man through the world, that hearkeneth to the voice of the Spirit.' Elder McConkie explained that the light of Christ 'is the instrumentality and agency by which Deity keeps in touch and communes with all his children, both the righteous and the wicked. It has an edifying, enlightening, and uplifting influence on men. . . . It is the means by which the Lord invites and entices all men to improve their lot and to come unto him and receive his gospel.'"[548]

Thus, we are commanded to be careful and diligent to the words of eternal life because they are essential to our becoming Zion people. The words of eternal life flow to us by our sincerely searching the scriptures and the prophets, and these words are confirmed to us by testimony of the Holy Ghost. The result of this process is coming unto God, which is the premier purpose of the Melchizedek Priesthood. Quoting Doctrine and Covenants 84:47, Farley says, "'And every one that hearkeneth to the voice of the Spirit cometh unto God, even the Father.' Elder McConkie explained: 'By following

---

543    D&C 84:43.
544    D&C 84:41.
545    Farley, "The Oath and Covenant of the Priesthood," 51.
546    D&C 84:44.
547    Asay, "The Oath and Covenant of the Priesthood," 43.
548    Farley, "The Oath and Covenant of the Priesthood," 51, quoting McConkie, *A New Witness for the Articles of Faith,* 258, 260.

the light of Christ, men are led to the gospel covenant, to the baptismal covenant, to the church and kingdom. There they receive the Holy Ghost.' Those who are sensitive to the Holy Ghost continue to learn the words of God and direct their lives according to his counsel. Faithful brethren are led by this process to the oath and covenant of the priesthood."[549] By following this process to its perfect conclusion, being careful and giving diligent heed, Zion people ultimately receive the fulness of the priesthood covenant's promise: eternal life.

## "And the Father Teacheth Him of the Covenant"

As we have learned, it is with the Father that we make the oath and covenant of the priesthood. He is the one who takes both the responsibility and the initiative to teach us concerning the priesthood covenant. Herein lies the predominant key to learning the covenant's doctrine and scope. The Father's promise reads: "And the Father teacheth him of the covenant which he has renewed and confirmed upon you."[550]

The covenantal promise contained in this clause speaks to the Father's taking direct charge of our priesthood education. Through our faithfulness and by personal revelation, line upon line, distilling intelligence upon us as the dews from heaven, the Father rains priesthood knowledge upon our souls until we are saturated in it. This doctrine is unknown in the world and not widely known in the Church, Elder McConkie taught. The priesthood information that the Father distils upon us cannot fully be learned in the scriptures or even in the teachings of the prophets. God reserves the right to teach the doctrine of the priesthood by the Holy Ghost to those who love and serve him completely.[551] Farley taught, "Sufficient scriptural information is given to place a brother upon the pathway of exaltation, but the printed word in the standard works is not the culmination point. It is an aid in helping one to progress to the point where *revelation is the key* in magnifying a calling and in learning more about the oath and covenant of the priesthood."[552] The doctrine of the priesthood, therefore, is one of the sublime mysteries of the kingdom that we are entitled to learn through personal revelation by means of Melchizedek Priesthood ordinances.[553]

We insert a stipulation and a caution here. It is the Father's prerogative—not ours—to reveal to us the covenant and doctrine of the priesthood. That he may choose to instruct us through his authorized servants in the order of the priesthood is a distinct possibility, but, as Elder McConkie stated, this sacred information is so individualized that it cannot be fully learned even in the scriptures or through the prophets. It is learned by revelation. Therefore, because the Father's revelations are tailor-made to our needs, and because they are his to give, we must be careful how and from whom we choose to receive them. The Father has specifically commanded, "Thou shalt have no

---

549   Farley, "The Oath and Covenant of the Priesthood," 51, quoting McConkie, *A New Witness for the Articles of Faith,* 258, 260.
550   D&C 84:48.
551   McConkie, "The Doctrine of the Priesthood,' 32.
552   Farley, "The Oath and Covenant of the Priesthood," 52; emphasis added.
553   D&C 84:19–22.

other gods before me."[554] To set another person before God, from whom we would receive this specialized education, is to step into idolatry. Our effort should be to live righteously and to hone the essential spiritual skills so as to invite personal revelation. On this subject Brigham Young said,

> There is one principle that I wish the people would understand and lay to heart. Just as fast as you will prove before your God that you are worthy to receive the mysteries, if you please to call them so, of the Kingdom of heaven—that you are full of confidence in God—that you will never betray a thing that God tells you—that you will never reveal to your neighbor that which ought not to be revealed, as quick as you prepare to be entrusted with the things of God, there is an eternity of them to bestow upon you. Instead of pleading with the Lord to bestow more upon you, plead with yourselves to have confidence in yourselves, to have integrity in yourselves, and know when to speak and what to speak, what to reveal, and how to carry yourselves and walk before the Lord. And just as fast as you prove to him that you will preserve everything secret that ought to be—that you will deal out to your neighbors all which you ought, and no more, and learn how to dispense your knowledge to your families, friends, neighbors, and brethren, the Lord will bestow upon you, and give to you, and bestow upon you, until finally he will say to you, "You shall never fall; your salvation is sealed unto you; you are sealed up unto eternal life and salvation, through your integrity."[555]

Of retaining integrity to the revelations of God, Alma explained, "It is given unto many to know the mysteries of God; nevertheless they are laid under a strict command that they shall not impart only according to the portion of his word which he doth grant unto the children of men, according to the heed and diligence which they give unto him." Mysteries are things that can be received only by revelation. Because they might exceed the general doctrines set forth by prophets and in the scriptures, we are under "strict command" to not impart them, so as not to step in front of our file leaders—and so that we don't share them with those who are not ready. We are only allowed to impart "according to the portion of his word which he doth grant unto the children of men," and then only "according to the heed and diligence which they give unto him." But seek

554    Exodus 20:3.
555    Young, *Discourses of Brigham Young*, 93.

the mysteries we must, for in them lies the Father's instruction on the doctrine of the priesthood. Alma said, "And therefore, he that will harden his heart, the same receiveth the lesser portion of the word; and he that will not harden his heart, to him is given the greater portion of the word, until it is given unto him to know the mysteries of God until he know them in full. And they that will harden their hearts, to them is given the lesser portion of the word until they know nothing concerning his mysteries; and then they are taken captive by the devil, and led by his will down to destruction. Now this is what is meant by the chains of hell."[556] Clearly, our protection and salvation depend upon our seeking and receiving the Father's instruction.

This level of divine education the Father provides is not possible, of course, unless we exercise the priesthood properly. Therefore, the Lord directs: "Let thy bowels also be full of charity towards all men, and to the household of faith, and let virtue garnish thy thoughts unceasingly; then shall thy confidence wax strong in the presence of God; *and the doctrine of the priesthood shall distil upon thy soul as the dews from heaven.*"[557] This instruction is the key that opens the door to the Father's priesthood education and the means by which we progress within the oath and covenant of the priesthood.

Concerning personal revelation, Joseph Smith taught John Taylor, "If you be true to [the Spirit's] whisperings it will in time become in you a principle of revelation, so that you will know all things."[558] The Prophet also taught, "A person may profit by noticing the first intimation of the spirit of revelation; for instance, when you feel pure intelligence flowing into you, it may give you sudden strokes of ideas, so that by noticing it, you may find it fulfilled the same day or soon; (i.e.) those things that were presented unto your minds by the Spirit of God, will come to pass; and thus by learning the Spirit of God and understanding it, you may grow unto the principle of revelation, until you become perfect in Christ Jesus."[559] The Father teaches us the doctrine of the priesthood in this way.

In time, the day will come when we will be able to stand in his presence and receive intelligence from him face-to-face. This ultimate blessing is a right and part of the doctrine of the priesthood and of Zion people. To this end, the Lord commands: "Sanctify yourselves that your minds become single to God, and the days will come that you will see him; *for he will unveil his face unto you,* and it shall be in his own time, and in his own way, and according to his own will."[560] And again, "And *seek the face of the Lord always,* that in patience ye may possess your souls, and ye shall have eternal life."[561] Such is the condition of Zion people, for we read: "The Lord came and dwelt with his people, and they dwelt in righteousness."[562]

---

556   Alma 12:9–11.
557   D&C 121:45.
558   Taylor, *Journal of Discourses,* 19:154.
559   Smith, *Teachings of the Prophet Joseph Smith,* 151.
560   D&C 88:68; emphasis added.
561   D&C 101:38; emphasis added.
562   Moses 7:16.

## The Promise of Eternal Life

Over and over, the oath and covenant of the priesthood points us to the promise of eternal life, the outcome of making our calling and election sure. This promise is such a prevalent theme in the priesthood covenant that we are obliged to consider it as the focal point. To accomplish this lofty goal, the Lord reveals to us a sacred pattern to follow and endows us with power from on high to pursue that pattern. As we have discussed, sacred revelatory privileges and powers—"keys," as Joseph Smith called them[563]—are granted to faithful Melchizedek Priesthood holders. The most powerful manifestation of these "keys" is found in the temple ordinances. The scripture reads: "[The Melchizedek Priesthood] holdeth the key of the mysteries of the kingdom, even the key of the knowledge of God. Therefore, in the ordinances thereof, the power of godliness is manifest."[564] As the Father teaches us the intricacies of the priesthood covenant, he also reveals to us the uses, powers, and blessings of these "keys."

Blaine Yorgason notes that the definition of the word *keys* has somewhat migrated since the early days of the Restoration. "The Lord, His modern prophets, and others who have been closely associated with them frequently refer to the ordinances of the priesthood, as administered in the temple, as 'keys' or 'keys of the priesthood.' In our day, however, such usage has become more narrowly or carefully defined. Now the word 'keys' or the phrase 'keys of the priesthood,' . . . refer specifically to the powers and authority held in fullness by the president of the Church and passed down from him by ordination or setting apart through specific lines of priesthood authority."[565]

These ordinances, or keys (speaking in the earlier sense), are the ordered manner by which we may obtain the power to speak with God in his presence—the ultimate form of revelation. In fact, these keys are the only way to return to God's presence and "enter into his rest, which rest is the fulness of his glory"[566]—eternal life. This quality of *rest* is the condition in which Zion and its people reside. Once again, we encounter the subject of making our calling and election sure in the oath and covenant of the priesthood. This is the revealed promise of our eventual exaltation or the guarantee of eternal life that Elder Romney confirmed comes only by a divine witness.[567] Our faithful persistence in the priesthood covenant leads to this revelation. To teach this truth, Elder McConkie wrote a fourth verse to the hymn, "Come Listen to a Prophet's Voice." It reads:

> Then heed the words of truth and light
> That flow from fountains pure.
> Yea, keep His law with all thy might
> Till thine election's sure,
> Till thou shalt hear the holy voice

---

563    Smith, *History of the Church,* 4:608; 5:1–2; Smith, *Teachings of the Prophet Joseph Smith,* 226; *Juvenile Instructor,* June 1, 1892, 345; Smith, *The Words of Joseph Smith,* 54, footnote 19.
564    D&C 84:19–20.
565    Yorgason, *I Need Thee Every Hour,* 367.
566    D&C 84:22–24.
567    Romney, Conference Report, Oct. 1965, 20.

> Assure eternal reign,
> While joy and cheer attend thy choice,
> As one who shall obtain.[568]

Alma said it this way: "And whosoever doeth this [repentance and baptism], and keepeth the commandments of God from thenceforth, the same will remember that I say unto him, yea, he will remember that I have said unto him, *he shall have eternal life.*"[569]

Joseph Smith received the promise of eternal life by revelation: "For I am the Lord thy God, and will be with thee even unto the end of the world, and through all eternity; for verily I seal upon you your exaltation, and prepare a throne for you in the kingdom of my Father, with Abraham your father."[570] We recall that the calling and election made sure is both a revelation and an ordinance associated with the more sure word of prophecy. Of the revelation, Blaine Yorgason writes, "Throughout history, even when the blessings of receiving the fullness of the priesthood have not been readily available, righteous men and women who have progressed spiritually to the fullest extent possible have obtained the voice of God declaring their callings and elections to be sure. Thus Moses taught, '[The approval of God] was delivered unto men by *the calling of his own voice,* according to his own will, unto as many as believed on his name' (JST, Genesis 14:29)."[571]

A survey of the scriptures and historical journals reveals multiple ways whereby this promise of eternal life is delivered. Each communication may be as unique as its recipient. For example, James T. Summerhays writes:

> On June 9, 1830, the newly restored Church held its first conference. About thirty members attended. After singing and prayer, many began to prophesy, when several had the visions of heaven unveiled to them. So overcome were these visionaries that it was necessary to find beds or some location to safely lay them down. One of these, Newel Knight, could not understand why his fellow Saints were making such a fuss to lay him on a bed; his spirit was soaring so high that he did not notice that his body was helpless. As they lay him down, a vision burst upon his view. "He saw heaven opened, and beheld the Lord Jesus Christ, seated at the right hand of the majesty on high," recounts Joseph Smith, "and had it made plain to his understanding that the time would come when he would be admitted into His presence to enjoy His society for ever and ever."

---

568   McConkie, "Come Listen to a Prophet's Voice," fourth verse, *Hymns,* no. 21.
569   Alma 7:16; emphasis added.
570   D&C 132:49.
571   Yorgason, *I Need Thee Every Hour,* 387–88 emphasis added.

The Colesville Branch of the Church, having lived in the relative civility of New York and Ohio, followed the call to resettle on the frontier in Jackson County, Missouri. At first, the branch had neither tents nor implements to farm with. They had little to eat but some beef and cornmeal made by rubbing ears of corn against an old tin grater. Yet when the Prophet visited them, he found them in a lively mood. Amid what for lesser people would have been a plight of abject misery, the Colesville Branch welcomed their Prophet as had those that once shouted Hosanna at Christ's triumphal entry into Jerusalem; they rejoiced as the ancient Saints had when Paul returned from his long dispersion. Joseph, overcome with their greatness of soul and generosity of heart, gathered them together and did something that caused a considerable stir among those that witnessed it—he sealed up the branch, all present, to Eternal Life.[572]

Of his own experience, Heber C. Kimball wrote:

I returned to Far West, April 5th. My family having been gone about two months, during which time I heard nothing from them; our brethren being in prison; death and destruction following us everywhere we went; I felt very sorrowful and lonely. The following words came to my mind, and the Spirit said unto me, 'write,' which I did by taking a piece of paper and writing on my knee as follows: FAR WEST, April 6th, 1839. A word from the Spirit of the Lord to my servant, Heber C. Kimball: Verily I say unto my servant Heber, thou art my son, in whom I am well pleased; for thou art careful to hearken to my words, and not transgress my law, nor rebel against my servant Joseph Smith, for thou hast a respect to the words of mine anointed, even from the least to the greatest of them; *therefore thy name is written in heaven, no more to be blotted out for ever,* because of these things; and this Spirit and blessing shall rest down upon thy posterity for ever and ever; for they shall be called after thy name, for thou shalt have many

---

572    Summerhays, "The Stripling Exalted," Feb. 20, 2009, quoting Smith, *History of the Church,* 1:85; Jessee, "Joseph Knight's Recollection of Early Mormon History," 39.

more sons and daughters, for thy seed shall be as numerous as the sands upon the sea shore; therefore, my
servant Heber, be faithful, go forth in my name and I
will go with you, and be on your right hand and on your
left and my angels shall go before you and raise you up
when you are cast down and afflicted; remember that
I am always with you, even to the end, therefore be of
good cheer, my son, and my spirit shall be in your heart
to teach you the peaceable things of the kingdom.[573]

Notice that the Lord repeated to Elder Kimball the oath given in the covenant of the
priesthood. The Lord also confirmed that Elder Kimball would obtain eternal life, as
the covenant promises. In this man's case, the Lord revealed the assurance of exaltation
directly to Elder Kimball's mind. In the case of Mary Elizabeth Rollins Lightner, Joseph
Smith, as an authorized servant of God, delivered the revelation to her and others. In an
address at Brigham Young University in 1905, she said,

Joseph looked around very solemnly. It was the first
time some of them had ever seen him. Said he, "There
are enough here to hold a little meeting." They got a
board and put it across two chairs to make seats. Martin Harris sat on a little box at Joseph's feet. They sang
and prayed. Joseph got up and began to speak to us.
As he began to speak very solemnly and very earnestly,
all at once his countenance changed and he stood
mute. Those who looked at him that day said there
was a search light within him, over every part of his
body. I never saw anything like it on the earth. I could
not take my eyes off him; he got so white that anyone
who saw him would have thought he was transparent.
I remember I thought I could almost see the cheek
bones through the flesh. I have been through many
changes since but that is photographed on my brain. I
shall remember it and see in my mind's eye as long as
I remain upon the earth. He stood some moments. He
looked over the congregation as if to pierce every heart.
He said, "Do you know who has been in your midst?"
One of the Smiths said an angel of the Lord. Martin
Harris said, "It was our Lord and Savior, Jesus Christ."
Joseph put his hand down on Martin and said: "God
revealed that to you Brethren and sisters, the Spirit of

573   Whitney, *Life of Heber C. Kimball*, 241–242; emphasis added.

God has been here. The Savior has been in your midst
this night and I want you to remember it. There is a
veil over your eyes for you could not endure to look
upon Him. You must be fed with milk, not with strong
meat. I want you to remember this as if it were the last
thing that escaped my lips. *He has given all of you to me
and has sealed you up to everlasting life that where he is,
you may be also.* And if you are tempted of Satan say,
'Get behind me, Satan.'" These words are figured upon
my brain and I never took my eye off his countenance.
Then he knelt down and prayed. I have never heard
anything like it before or since. I felt that he was talking
to the Lord and that power rested down upon the congregation. Every soul felt it. The spirit rested upon us
in every fiber of our bodies, and we received a sermon
from the lips of the representative of God.[574]

Expounding on the Father's oath and promise of eternal life, Farley says, "As the Lord
confirmed the priesthood by his own voice out of the heavens to his servants (D&C
84:42), so may he confirm the promise of eternal life [to us], whether in this life or the
next. The fulfillment of that promise of eternal life is the grand purpose of the oath and
covenant of the priesthood. Every worthy priesthood holder may qualify if he will keep
the covenants of the priesthood."[575]

President Joseph Fielding Smith taught that no promises are more glorious than
those given to us in the oath and covenant of the priesthood.[576] The Father's oath brings
to pass the noblest goal of existence: "For behold, this is my work and my glory—to bring
to pass the immortality and eternal life of man."[577]

## Penalties for Neglecting or Rejecting the Covenant of the Priesthood

Sobering consequences follow those who take their priesthood covenant lightly or who
break it after they have made it. Equally grave penalties await those who refuse to accept
the covenant once they have been offered it. The Lord warns: "But whoso breaketh this
covenant after he hath received it, and altogether turneth therefrom, shall not have
forgiveness of sins in this world nor in the world to come."[578] And to those who refuse to
enter into the priesthood covenant, the Lord cautions: "And wo unto all those who come
not unto this priesthood."[579] The word *wo* suggests condemnation, distress, misery, and

---

574    Lightner, Address at Brigham Young University, 1905, 1; emphasis added.
575    Farley, "The Oath and Covenant of the Priesthood," 53.
576    Smith, Conference Report, Oct. 1970, 92.
577    Moses 1:39.
578    D&C 84:41.
579    D&C 84:42.

calamity.[580] Whatever leads to a person's choice for neglecting this covenant, the dire consequence is the same.[581]

Although this is a solemn declaration, it is not necessarily equated to becoming a son of perdition. Elder McConkie wrote: "This has never been interpreted by the Brethren to mean that those who forsake their priesthood duties, altogether turning therefrom, shall be sons of perdition; rather, the meaning seems to be that they shall be denied the exaltation that otherwise might have been theirs."[582] Farley writes: "President Joseph Fielding Smith explained that there is a chance to repent if a man has not altogether turned from the priesthood. If he does altogether turn from it, however, there is no forgiveness."[583] The meaning of these two condemnations, said President Smith, is that a man who neglects or rejects the covenant will be denied forever the privilege of exercising the priesthood and thus achieving eternal life. That man will no longer be associated with Zion. He will forfeit Zion's blessings, the holy priesthood, and the privileges associated with exaltation—and he will never again be offered those blessings![584] Brother Farley concludes, "As the priesthood is the only source and channel through which exaltation may be obtained from the Lord, it follows that those who avoid it also avoid their only chance for eternal happiness in the celestial kingdom."[585]

## Summary and Conclusion

We who strive to become worthy Zion-like men seek for the Melchizedek Priesthood and its blessings by entering into the oath and covenant of the priesthood. Our primary qualification is to have received, and been faithful to, the new and everlasting covenant—the first pillar of Zion, which contains the first promise of eternal life. Thereafter, we must have lived worthy to have received the Aaronic Priesthood by covenant. Then, having proven worthy of these two covenants and having prepared ourselves through righteous living, the Father, through his authorized servant, will offer us the Melchizedek Priesthood, the authority of God. We receive this priesthood by means of the oath and covenant of the priesthood—the second pillar of Zion, which contains the second promise of eternal life.

The oath and covenant of the priesthood repeats our previous *callings* and *elections* (selections) to and for eternal life. These we received premortally and when we were baptized. These callings and elections were provisional and needed to be made *sure*. A primary purpose of the oath and covenant of the priesthood is to obtain personal salvation—to make our calling and election *sure*. The second purpose of the priesthood covenant is to do the work of God by bringing people to Christ. We could not accomplish this work without the authority of God. The priesthood obligates and empowers us to raise our voices in testimony, which is a vehicle for conveying the Spirit to others and

---

580   *American Heritage Dictionary*, s.v. "woe."
581   Eyring, "Faith and the Oath and Covenant of the Priesthood," 61–64.
582   McConkie, *A New Witness for the Articles of Faith*, 232.
583   Farley, "The Oath and Covenant of the Priesthood," 50.
584   Smith, Conference Report, Oct. 1970, 92.
585   Farley, "The Oath and Covenant of the Priesthood," 50.

to bless the Father's children with the covenants, ordinances, and blessings of the new and everlasting covenant.

We enter the oath and covenant of the priesthood by agreeing to be faithful, by obtaining the Aaronic and Melchizedek priesthoods, by receiving Christ and his Father, by living by every word that proceeds from the mouth of God, and by magnifying our singular priesthood *calling*.[586] Three ways to magnify our calling are:

1. Obtaining gospel knowledge.
2. Personal righteousness by compliance with gospel standards.
3. Giving dedicated service.[587]

Ultimately, to magnify our priesthood calling means to become like God. To do that we must make temple covenants, receive temple ordinances, and marry for eternity. Then we must endure worthily in these covenants to the end. Zion's purity, ideal, and eternal life can be achieved in no other way.

The Father enters the covenant of the priesthood with us by swearing an oath. In doing so, he places his godhood on the line in warranting that every promise he makes in the priesthood covenant will be fulfilled, contingent on our faithfulness to the covenant. The Father promises us all of the blessings of our fathers, Abraham, Isaac, and Jacob. He promises that the Holy Ghost will sanctify us and renew our bodies so that we might become capable of fulfilling our priesthood calling and callings, and that we might be made fit for eternal life.

We receive the Melchizedek Priesthood for two reasons: "for your sake, and not for your sake only, but for the sake of the whole world."[588] As we sanctify ourselves and as the Spirit sanctifies us, we gain power upon power in the priesthood. Then, as we bless others with the blessings God gives us, we grow from grace *to* grace by giving grace *for* grace. Increasingly, we become more and more like the Savior; we become saviors on Mount Zion[589] for both the living and the dead, authorized and empowered to assist in the eternal redemptive work of God. We gain heightened ability to bring people to Christ so that they, too, might receive the blessings of immortal glory and "eternal lives."[590] The process of receiving blessings and giving them away sanctifies, renews, and magnifies us until we become like God, can stand in his presence, receive all that he has, and become all that he is. The Spirit's sanctification renews our heart so that it is filled with saving love, or charity—"the end of the commandment"[591] and "the crowning virtue."[592]

In the oath and covenant of the priesthood, the Father promises that we will become the sons of Moses and of Aaron, and thus we are eternally identified with these great brethren and authorized to do their works. Moreover, he promises that we will become the seed of Abraham with the reconfirmed assurance that we, and our children

---

586   D&C 84:33.
587   Romney, "'The Oath and Covenant Which Belongeth to the Priesthood,'" 43.
588   D&C 84:48.
589   Obadiah 1:21.
590   Smith, *Teachings of the Prophet Joseph Smith,* 322; Moses 1:39.
591   1 Timothy 1:5.
592   McConkie, *Mormon Doctrine,* 121.

through us, will retain and have rights to all of the gospel blessings, including the new and everlasting covenant and the oath and covenant of the priesthood. Additionally, the Father declares that we are his Church and kingdom. Wherever we go and whatever we do, we represent him and his Church. Because we hold the high priesthood, by which he places upon us his name, we literally are the kingdom of God. As we minister among his children, we, like the Seventy of old, can say to the people with authority, "The kingdom of heaven is come nigh unto you."[593]

In the priesthood covenant, the Father promises us angelic ministration and protection as we function in the priesthood. He promises that we will become his elect—called and selected on account of our good works. Our priesthood calling in the flesh is an extension of the work we engaged in the premortal world: the work of redemption. Now we are once again authorized and empowered to continue that work. As we continue our work, magnify our priesthood calling and callings, and give diligent heed to the words of eternal life, the day will come when the Father, by revelation, will declare our calling and election *sure*. The associated ordinance called "the more sure word of prophecy" will either precede or follow that revelation. That revelation fulfills his oath, guaranteeing to us all that he has. Moreover, he promises to make us equal to him in might, power, and dominion. In all these supernal blessings, Jesus Christ is our model. As he became the Son of God, so we, by following his example, become the sons of God and joint heirs to the Father's kingdom with him.

The Father makes these promises to us in the oath and covenant of the priesthood with a charge that we should beware, or be careful, and give diligent heed to the words of eternal life. These words are found in the scriptures, the counsel of the prophets and apostles, the holy temple, and in the language of the priesthood covenant. Moreover, these words are the intelligence we receive through personal revelation, for we have covenanted to "live by every word that proceedeth forth from the mouth of God."[594] The Father promises that he will teach us of the priesthood covenant by the gift of the Holy Ghost, pointing us to the day when we can stand in God's presence and receive his instructions and counsel face-to-face. The Father's warning to be cautious and diligent forebodes harsh penalties that will be suffered by those who neglect or reject the oath and covenant of the priesthood. God will not be mocked; he takes this covenant and our word seriously. The only safe path to eternal life is to make this priesthood covenant and then keep it with all our heart, might, mind, and strength.

No greater promise is contained in the oath and covenant of the priesthood than the Father's oath guaranteeing eternal life to those who keep the covenant. If we are faithful, he promises "thrones, kingdoms, principalities, and powers, dominions, all heights and depths." We will "pass by the angels, and the gods, which are set there, to [our] exaltation and glory in all things, as hath been sealed upon [our] heads, which glory shall be a fulness and a continuation of the seeds forever and ever."[595] "Wherefore, all things are theirs," the Father promises. "These shall dwell in the presence of God and

---

593    Luke 10:9.
594    D&C 84:44.
595    D&C 132:19.

his Christ forever and ever. . . . They who dwell in his presence are the church of the Firstborn; . . . and he makes them equal in power, and in might, and in dominion."[596]

Such are the blessings of the oath and covenant of the priesthood—the second pillar of Zion.

---

[596]   D&C 76:59, 62, 94–95.

# Section 4
# The Constitution of the Priesthood
## Why Many Are Called but Not Chosen

President Stephen L Richards called Doctrine and Covenants 121:34–46 "The Constitution of the Priesthood."[597] This is that constitution:

> Behold, there are many called, but few are chosen. And why are they not chosen?
>
> Because their hearts are set so much upon the things of this world, and aspire to the honors of men, that they do not learn this one lesson—that the rights of the priesthood are inseparably connected with the powers of heaven, and that the powers of heaven cannot be controlled nor handled only upon the principles of righteousness.
>
> That they may be conferred upon us, it is true; but when we undertake to cover our sins, or to gratify our pride, our vain ambition, or to exercise control or dominion or compulsion upon the souls of the children of men, in any degree of unrighteousness, behold, the heavens withdraw themselves; the Spirit of the Lord is grieved; and when it is withdrawn, Amen to the priesthood or the authority of that man.
>
> We have learned by sad experience that it is the nature and disposition of almost all men, as soon as they get a little authority, as they suppose, they will immediately begin to exercise unrighteous dominion.
>
> Hence many are called, but few are chosen.

---

597   Richards, Conference Report, Apr. 1955, 12.

No power or influence can or ought to be maintained by virtue of the priesthood, only by persuasion, by long-suffering, by gentleness and meekness, and by love unfeigned; by kindness, and pure knowledge, which shall greatly enlarge the soul without hypocrisy, and without guile—

Reproving betimes with sharpness, when moved upon by the Holy Ghost; and then showing forth afterwards an increase of love toward him whom thou hast reproved, lest he esteem thee to be his enemy; that he may know that thy faithfulness is stronger than the cords of death.

Let thy bowels also be full of charity towards all men, and to the household of faith, and let virtue garnish thy thoughts unceasingly; then shall thy confidence wax strong in the presence of God; and the doctrine of the priesthood shall distil upon thy soul as the dews from heaven.

The Holy Ghost shall be thy constant companion, and thy scepter an unchanging scepter of righteousness and truth; and thy dominion shall be an everlasting dominion, and without compulsory means it shall flow unto thee forever and ever.

This constitution contains some the greatest blessings and one of the harshest indictments pronounced by the Lord upon priesthood holders. Endowed women are not exempt. The denouncement, "Behold, there are many called, but few are chosen," applies equally to them. Anyone who has entered into the new and everlasting covenant and received the priesthood blessings of the temple should understand the principles contained in the Constitution of the Priesthood. Therefore, as with other sections of this book describing priesthood principles, women can benefit from the discussion.

## Two Groups

In the Constitution of the Priesthood, the Lord divides the totality of priesthood holders into two groups: (1) those who respond to the call to eternal life,[598] magnify their calling to eternal life, and thereafter obtain the promise of exaltation, and (2) those who neglect or reject the call to eternal life, take casually or ignore that calling, and forfeit exaltation. There are only two choices, and each of us, male or female, belongs to one of these two groups. Why would many be placed in the second group? The Lord gives us the answer: "Because their hearts are set so much upon the things of this world, and [they] aspire to the honors of men."[599]

---

598    McConkie, *Mormon Doctrine,* 482.
599    D&C 121:35.

*Love of money!*
*Love of power!*
*Love of popularity, which is attention, recognition, and influence!*

We could divide and define the groups as Zion people and Babylon people. Hugh Nibley taught that these two groups are mutually exclusive; they represent two opposite directions. We cannot belong to both.[600] To attempt to do so summons the Lord's ominous denouncement: "Amen to the priesthood or the authority of that man!"[601] This statement hangs over our heads like a sword. The implication is *amen to the exaltation of that man!*

## A Satanic Strategy

Looking forward to our day, Nephi saw a frightening satanic strategy to carefully deceive men and women. Nephi saw Satan lulling us into supposed carnal security and thereby convincing us to abandon our birthright blessings, take our eyes off Zion, and quietly persuade us to sacrifice the promise of eternal life. Satan's strategy was designed to trick us into minimizing our covenants, including the oath and covenant of the priesthood. His tactic is one he employed anciently, one he taught Cain. He has successfully used it ever since, convincing untold thousands that they can simultaneously focus on money and Zion. Because it is impossible to serve both God and mammon, Satan knows that he can dupe us into setting aside and abandoning our priesthood covenant, which will cause us to spiral downward into temporal and spiritual destruction.

Here is what Nephi foresaw, in his words: "And others will he pacify, and lull them away into carnal security, that they will say: All is well in Zion; yea, Zion prospereth, all is well— and thus the devil cheateth their souls, and leadeth them away carefully down to hell."[602]

Few prophecies are repeated more often by Latter-day Saints. We quote this verse regularly in classes; we trumpet it from the pulpit; and yet many of us will fall into the devil's snare, thinking that the scripture applies to others. If we are not careful, we may fail in our priesthood calling, forfeit Zion, and fall short of eternal life. The chosen few are not those who place the god of money, power, and recognition before the one true God. On the other hand, the prophesied result to the many who were called but not chosen will be "Amen to the priesthood or the authority of that man."

## A Test of Loyalties

President Ezra Taft Benson taught, 'When we put God first, all other things fall into their proper place or drop out of our lives. Our love of the Lord will govern the claims of our affection, the demands on our time, the interests we pursue, and the order of our priorities."[603]

---

600    Nibley, *Approaching Zion*, 18–19.
601    D&C 121:37; emphasis added.
602    2 Nephi 28:21.
603    Benson, *Teachings of Ezra Taft Benson*, 349–50.

To Moses, the Lord revealed our covenantal relationship to God: "Thou shalt have no other gods before me. Thou shalt not make unto thee any graven image, or any likeness of any thing that is in heaven above, or that is in the earth beneath, or that is in the water under the earth: Thou shalt not bow down thyself to them, nor serve them: for I the LORD thy God am a jealous God. . . . Thou shalt not take the name of the LORD thy God in vain; for the LORD will not hold him guiltless that taketh his name in vain."[604]

These first three commandments allow no wiggle room; they demand our total allegiance to God. We are allowed no other affections before God—no idolizing, adoring, or worshipping anything or anyone in front of God, and no taking upon us his name and then dishonoring him by placing our loyalties elsewhere. In no uncertain terms, the Lord said we would not be held guiltless for such actions. We cannot suppose that we can enter the priesthood covenant, replace it in our minds and hearts with other affections, and then receive a few stripes at the Day of Judgment and go on to inherit eternal life. God demands our total loyalty to at least the same degree that a wife demands total loyalty from her husband. "Thou shalt have no other gods before me."

A common hypocrisy is to expect total loyalty from God while not returning that same loyalty to him. Mortality is a perfect environment in which to test the depth of these loyalties. A pivotal test is the choice between God and mammon. Hugh Nibley explains that the Hebrew word *mammon* means "financial activity of any kind."[605] The Savior warned that we cannot choose both: "Ye cannot serve God and Mammon."[606] Some try to simultaneously choose both God and mammon, but that defines them as mammon choosers, which categorizes them among the many who are called but not chosen. Gospel writers Leaun G. Otten and C. Max Caldwell explained: "There are many brethren who are called and given the rights or authority of the priesthood, but few of them are also chosen for an inheritance of eternal life. Those who are to receive eternal lives must first learn and apply the fundamental principles upon which the priesthood must function."[607] One of the first principles on that list would be fierce loyalty to God.

Zion people are classified as the few who are both called *and* chosen, those who distinguish themselves from the many by choosing and serving God over mammon and remaining loyal to the end, enduring in the covenants "at all hazards."[608]

## Restoration of the Constitution of the Priesthood

As we have mentioned, the verses contained in Doctrine and Covenants 121:34–46 have been referred to as the Constitution of the Priesthood. These verses are among the "plain and precious"[609] parts of the gospel the Lord restored in the dispensation of the fulness of times. Elder Neal A. Maxwell explained that this section contains an "elaboration [that]

---

604   Exodus 20:3–7.
605   Nibley, *Approaching Zion*, 20–21.
606   Matthew 6:24; 3 Nephi 13:24.
607   Otten and Caldwell, *Sacred Truths of the Doctrine and Covenants*, 2:305.
608   Smith, *History of the Church*, 3:379, 380.
609   1 Nephi 13:34.

is given nowhere else in scripture! It is a significant part of the fulness of the Restoration and includes counsel on how human foibles can keep us from gaining access to the powers of heaven and how power and authority are to be exercised."[610]

Of the many who are called to eternal life, evidently only a few will distinguish themselves in the priesthood by abiding the principles of the Constitution of the Priesthood and thereby earn their reward.

## The Marriage of the King's Son

The "elaboration" mentioned above by Elder Maxwell reminds us of the Savior's parable of the royal feast found in Matthew 22:1–10. In this parable, "a certain king" sends his servants out to "call them that were bidden to a marriage for his son." Elder James E. Talmage writes, "The invitation of a king to his subjects is equivalent to a command. The marriage feast was no surprise event, for the selected guests had been bidden long aforetime; and, in accordance with oriental custom were notified again on the opening day of the festivities." As we shall see, this parable delineates those who are called from those who are chosen.

According to custom, the select guests who had been invited to the marriage would have included the king's family and close friends. In Jewish custom, such guests are first honored by the king's sending them an invitation and subsequently are more honored when they arrive at the wedding. They comprise the king's inner circle, those whom he knows and loves best. When they arrive at the wedding, the king has them clothed in beautiful wedding garments and treated with great respect. Sadly, in the case of this "certain king," "many of the bidden guests refused to come when formally summoned; and of the tolerant king's later and more pressing message they made light and went their ways, while the most wicked turned upon the servants who brought the royal summons, mistreated them cruelly, and some of them they killed."

The latter-day interpretation of this parable should be obvious. These select guests, who are members of the King's family and his closest friends, are they who have taken upon them his name, and who profess to love him and his Son, and who have a right to attend this most sacred event. They are the Church—*us!* Only those who have covenanted their allegiance to the King could be invited to the marriage of his Beloved Son. Elder Talmage concurs: "The guests who were bidden early, yet who refused to come when the feast was ready, are the covenant people."[611]

We should note that, according to Elder McConkie, the bride of the Bridegroom is also *us,* or "the Church composed of the faithful saints who have watched for his return," the Saints whom the Bridegroom will come to claim. We are the Lord's *bride,* that is, the few who are called *and* chosen.

The marriage supper of the Lamb described in this parable is an actual future event. Elder McConkie explained: "The elders of Israel by preaching the message of the restora-

---

610    Maxwell, *Men and Women of Christ,* 123.
611    Talmage, *Jesus the Christ,* 499.

tion are inviting men to come to that supper. 'For this cause I have sent you,' the Lord says to his missionaries, 'that a feast of fat things might be prepared for the poor; yea, a feast of fat things, of wine on the lees well refined, that the earth may know that the mouths of the prophets shall not fail; yea, a supper of the house of the Lord, well prepared, unto which all nations shall be invited. First, the rich and the learned, the wise and the noble; and after that cometh the day of my power; then shall the poor, the lame, and the blind, and the deaf, come in unto the marriage of the Lamb, and partake of the supper of the Lord, prepared for the great day to come.' (D. & C. 58:6–11; 65:3.)" Of that event, Elder McConkie also wrote: "Soon the scripture shall be fulfilled which saith: 'The marriage of the Lamb is come, and his wife hath made herself ready. And to her was granted that she should be arrayed in fine linen, clean and white: for the fine linen is the righteousness of saints. And he saith unto me, Write, Blessed are they which are called unto the marriage supper of the Lamb.' (Rev. 19:7–9.)"[612]

In the parable of the royal feast, we are awed by the honor extended to the many, who were called to the marriage, and we are simultaneously appalled that so few responded. Some of them had actually grown so hardened against the king that they reacted in open rebellion. Of course, only a small number of Latter-day Saints would be in that company. However, the group that should frighten us most is the one that "made light" of the invitation, those who "went their ways, one to his farm, another to his merchandise."[613] Of this group, Elder Talmage writes, "The turning away by one man to his farm and by another to his merchandise is in part an evidence of their engrossment in material pursuits to the utter disregard of their sovereign's will; but it signifies further an effort to deaden their troubled consciences by some absorbing occupation; and possibly also a premeditated demonstration of the fact that they placed their personal affairs above the call of their king."[614] Unfortunately, many will belong to this group and thus forfeit their call to the wedding.

Will the King allow his Son's marriage to go unattended? No.

Elder Talmage writes: "Finding the guests who had some claim on the royal invitation to be utterly unworthy, the king sent out his servants again, and these gathered in from the highways and cross-roads, from the byways and the lanes, all they could find, irrespective of rank or station, whether rich or poor, good or bad; 'and the wedding was furnished with guests.'" Elder Talmage concludes, "The children of the covenant will be rejected except they make good their title by godly works; while to the heathen and the sinners the portals of heaven shall open, if by repentance and compliance with the laws and ordinances of the gospel they shall merit salvation."[615]

Were it not for modern revelation, we might assign this parable solely to the Jews in the meridian of time. But a phrase in this parable links it to us, we who would be the Zion people of the latter-days; that phrase is "many are called, but few are chosen."[616] In

---

612    McConkie, *Mormon Doctrine*, 469.
613    Matthew 22:5.
614    Talmage, *Jesus the Christ*, 499.
615    Talmage, *Jesus the Christ*, 501.
616    Matthew 22:14; D&C 121:34.

1833, the Lord commanded the brethren to attend to their priesthood duties, saying, "There are many who have been ordained among you, whom I have called but few of them are chosen. They who are not chosen have sinned a very grievous sin, in that they are walking in darkness at noon-day. . . . If you keep not my commandments, the love of the Father shall not continue with you, therefore you shall walk in darkness."[617] That "grievous sin" is a result, in part, from our straying from the ordinances and thus breaking the everlasting covenant: "They seek not the Lord to establish his righteousness, but every man walketh in his own way, and after the image of his own god, whose image is in the likeness of the world, and whose substance is that of an idol, which waxeth old and shall perish in Babylon, even Babylon the great, which shall fall."[618]

The marriage of the king's son contains imagery that reminds us of the conflict between Zion and Babylon. The king had called many guests to the wedding. These people were friends and family, those who should have shown the most interest and who should have exhibited the greatest loyalty. Nevertheless, the many would not make the time or spurned the invitation outright. We see in their actions Babylon captivating the children of Zion and seducing them with idolatry, the love of mammon over the love of God. In the end, only a few of the called actually attended the wedding. How we choose to respond to the King's call will determine our loyalties and identify the group to which we will belong.

## "Many Will Say to Me in That Day"

When we examine the parable of the royal feast, we shudder when we read of the guest who tried to enter the marriage without a wedding garment.[619] Perhaps he was attempting to enter without submitting to the laws governing the wedding, or maybe he had received the garment and then removed or rejected it. In any case, a terrible wo is pronounced upon such who mock the King: "And [the king] saith unto him, Friend, how camest thou in hither not having a wedding garment? And he was speechless. Then said the king to the servants, Bind him hand and foot, and take him away, and cast him into outer darkness; there shall be weeping and gnashing of teeth. For many are called, but few are chosen."[620]

There is a lesson here concerning Zion. All are invited to become Zion people and to gain an inheritance in Zion; all are called to eternal life when they receive the new and everlasting covenant. But only they who keep the Covenant have actual claim to the blessings of Zion. No one can enter illegitimately. No citizen of Babylon is welcome. Because a person professes to be part of Zion does not mean that he actually is a Zion person. How he honors his *garment,* which symbolizes his devotion to his Covenant, determines his place at the royal wedding. They who treat the Covenant lightly, who go "their ways, one to his farm, another to his merchandise," will be excluded and replaced.

---

617   D&C 95:5–6, 12.
618   D&C 1:15–16.
619   Matthew 22:11.
620   Matthew 22:13–14.

They who refuse to submit to the laws of the wedding and pay homage to other gods rather than to the one true God will be cast out. Sadly, the people who make up these groups seem to be "many."

Of the many, they who are invited to the wedding, the Lord says, "Many will say to me in that day, Lord, Lord, have we not prophesied in thy name? and in thy name have cast out devils? and in thy name done many wonderful works? And then will I profess unto them, I never knew you: depart from me, ye that work iniquity."[621] We should note here that priesthood holders are included in this scripture. We have established the fact that the many are they who have been called to eternal life but have forfeited their calling through neglect or disobedience. In this scripture, they, the many, will perform all sorts of marvelous works and yet in the end come up short. The Lord says that they have spent their days working iniquity, which is that "grievous sin" which we discussed above—the love of money, power, and popularity. We know that sin so well, for it is common to Babylon. The many have attempted to embrace both God and mammon, they have sought power and recognition while professing Zion, and in the process they have abandoned their calling, forfeited the blessings of the priesthood, and will be excluded from the wedding feast.

In their works of iniquity, their grievous sin was idolatry, which places love of God second to love of money, power, and popularity. These things always result in oppressive class distinction and inequality, strife, and persecution; they stand in stark contrast to the unity, equality, peace, and charity required by the celestial law of Zion.[622] Therefore, the Lord said, "But it is not given that one man should possess that which is above another, *wherefore the world lieth in sin.*"[623] Clearly, many of us will forfeit our invitation to the wedding because we "go [our] way" and love our "merchandise" more than we love God and his needy children. Thus, even now, many of us are staggering under the weight of the Lord's condemnation. When we treat lightly our covenants and spend our time and effort pursuing vain ambitions, our minds become darkened with unbelief and neglect, and we run the risk of losing our calling. Then when the time of the wedding arrives, many of us may find ourselves under condemnation. This condition of darkness is apparently so widespread that the Lord's condemnation "resteth upon the children of Zion, even all."[624] *The many!* Pray, therefore, that we come to ourselves and strive to become the few who are both called *and* chosen.

## Called and Chosen for Eternal Life

Zion people are the few. Zion people are they who live celestial laws in the telestial environment of Babylon. Zion people are the elect who are invited to the marriage of the Lamb and who attend joyfully dressed in holy garments. Zion people are the "chosen,"

---

621    Matthew 7:22–23.
622    D&C 105:5.
623    D&C 49:20; emphasis added.
624    D&C 84:54–56.

meaning "chosen for eternal life."[625] Zion people fully embrace the oath and covenant of the priesthood, the objective of which is to bring us to the point that we can be, as discussed earlier, "chosen," and receive all the blessings the Father offers us in that covenant. To be chosen from among those who are called depends upon our magnifying our calling. Then, when we have proven faithful, the announcement will come that we have been *elected*, that is, *selected* for eternal life.

Joseph of Egypt is an example of someone who was called and then chosen (elected) by embracing the principles of Zion, that is, by worthily living the new and everlasting covenant and the oath and covenant of the priesthood. Commenting, Kent P. Jackson and Robert L. Millet, wrote, "Joseph chose righteousness and the Lord chose him; this redounded to the everlasting blessing of all his literal and spiritual posterity. The far-sighted Pharaoh recognized something in this stalwart slave not found in most ordinary men—i.e., the attributes of godliness. Said he, 'Can we find such a one as this is, a man in whom the spirit of God is?' Without waiting for the answer, he turned to Joseph, 'Thou shalt be over my house, and according unto thy word shall all my people be ruled: only in the throne will I be greater than you.'"[626] The question posed by Pharaoh concerning Joseph could be asked of us: "Can we find such a one as this is, a man in whom the spirit of God is?"

If we enter into the oath and covenant of the priesthood and keep it in every respect, the priesthood covenant will lead to our eventually being chosen for eternal life. This announcement, as we have discussed, is conveyed in a variety of ways, but it always involves the voice of God through the Holy Ghost. The Lord said: "I speak unto you with my voice, even the voice of my Spirit."[627] Elder McConkie wrote, "As is well known, many are called to the Lord's work but few are chosen for eternal life. So that those who are chosen may be sealed up unto eternal life, the scripture says: 'It shall be manifest unto my servant, by the voice of the Spirit, those that are chosen; and they shall be sanctified.' (D&C 105:36.) They are chosen by the Lord, but the announcement of their calling and election is delivered by the Spirit."[628] Therefore, the call goes out to all, a few respond, which distinguishes them from the many, and eventually, through faithfulness, the announcement of the surety of that calling and *chosenness* (election) will be delivered by the voice of the Spirit.

It may seem a stretch to imagine the President of the Church issuing a directive that all Saints give diligent heed to become designated as the few by striving to make their calling and election sure. And yet such a call was given by the leaders of both the meridian of time and the dispensation of the fulness of times. Peter admonished the ancient Saints to "give diligence to make your calling and election sure: for if ye do these things, ye shall never fall: For so an entrance [into the celestial kingdom] shall be ministered unto you abundantly into the everlasting kingdom of our Lord and Saviour Jesus

---

625    McConkie, *Mormon Doctrine*, 482.
626    Jackson and Millet, *Studies in Scripture*, 3:69, quoting Genesis 41:38, 40.
627    D&C 97:1.
628    McConkie, *A New Witness for the Articles of Faith*, 270.

Christ."[629] And Joseph Smith exhorted the Saints, "Oh! I beseech you to go forward, go forward and make your calling and your election sure; and if any man preach any other Gospel than that which I have preached, he shall be cursed."[630] Because these appeals were universally given by the Presidents of the Church, we should perhaps rethink our position and consider the calling and election made sure as an attainable event in our gospel progression, one that is as important as receiving the ordinances of the temple or eternal marriage.

In a landmark article entitled "What I Hope You Will Teach Your Children about the Temple," President Ezra Taft Benson invoked God's blessings upon us that we seek and receive every blessing associated with Elijah so that our calling and election could be made sure.[631] Perhaps we should cease considering this event beyond our mortal reach and begin to study and pursue it with careful diligence. In the final analysis, the few who are called and elected to eternal life may well be those who have received the revelation that their calling and election has been made sure, and, in a broader sense, these few might actually total an even greater number of people whose salvation has been guaranteed without their having thought to ask if it is so.

## Abiding Zion's Celestial Law in Babylon's Telestial Setting

The challenge of convincing those who professed to be Zion people to live the celestial laws of Zion weighed continually upon Joseph Smith's mind. His purpose seemed to be riveted upon creating a Zion people who would be defined by their overcoming Babylon and ultimately becoming a nation of priests and kings unto God.[632] In a speech given to the Relief Society in 1842, the Prophet admonished the sisters to live up to their covenants; to strive for the unity that is found in Zion; to become separate from Babylon; and to become virtuous, holy, and thus "select"—chosen. The purpose of God, he said, was to make a Zion, as in Enoch's day—a holy kingdom of priests.

All difficulties we encounter must be surmounted. Though the soul be tried, the heart faint, and the hands hang down, we must not retrace our steps; there must be decision of character. When instructed, we must obey that voice, observe the laws of the kingdom of God, that the blessings of heaven may rest down upon us. All must act in concert, or nothing can be done, and we should move according to the ancient Priesthood; hence the Saints should be a select people, separate from all the evils of the world—choice, virtuous, and holy. The Lord was going to make of the Church of Jesus Christ a kingdom of priests, a holy people, a chosen generation, as in Enoch's day, having all the gifts they had.[633]

At another time Joseph said, "I have tried for a number of years to get the minds of the Saints prepared to receive the things of God; but we frequently see some of them,

629    2 Peter 1:10–11.
630    Smith, *Teachings of the Prophet Joseph Smith*, 366.
631    Benson, "What I Hope You Will Teach Your Children about the Temple," 6.
632    Exodus 19:5–6. Note: Women become priestesses and queens unto their husbands.
633    Smith, *Teachings of the Prophet Joseph Smith*, 202.

after suffering all they have for the work of God, will fly to pieces like glass as soon as anything comes that is contrary to their traditions: they cannot stand the fire at all. *How many will be able to abide a celestial law, and go through and receive their exaltation, I am unable to say, as many are called, but few are chosen.*"[634]

Decidedly, it is difficult to step away from Babylon and its allurements. "Even if we try to leave Babylon," wrote Elder Maxwell, "some of us endeavor to keep a second residence there, or we commute on weekends."[635] But leave Babylon we must. Zion lies in the opposite direction, and soon, straddling the ever-widening gulf between Babylon and Zion will become impossible and we will have to jump to one side or the other. The unavoidable truth is that leaving Babylon is the sacrifice we make and the price we pay for eternal life. Upon the decision to leave Babylon, we create a broken heart and a contrite spirit.

Former BYU religion instructor, Rodney Turner, writes, "One reason many are called and few are chosen is that *they fail the test—which is to live celestial principles in a telestial setting. Insofar as circumstances permit, we are expected to do the eternally natural thing under unnatural conditions.* . . . However, we can take heart from the fact that those things which call for sacrifice and sheer grit in mortality will be accomplished with ease and unmitigated joy in eternity. But first we must demonstrate our love of righteousness by practicing it in adversity. Doing the easy and the convenient thing proves nothing, for it does not call for effort, self-denial or any strength beyond our own. Only after we have been tried successfully in the refining fires of human weakness and worldly opposition can we abide the eternal burnings of celestial glory—for 'our God is a consuming fire.'"[636]

## The End Purpose of Our Calling

As we have mentioned, our *calling,* which was first extended to us in the premortal world, has always been the call to eternal life. In this life, we are called to eternal life again when we enter the new and everlasting covenant through baptism.[637] Then we are called once more to eternal life when we enter into the oath and covenant of the priesthood. Brother Farley says, "Alma repeatedly associates the word *called* or *calling* with the priesthood itself (as contrasted with particular priesthood assignments), teaching that men are 'called by this holy calling, and ordained unto the high priesthood of the holy order of God.' (Alma 13:6.)"[638]

All priesthood *callings* point us toward our being *chosen* for eternal life, but they do not guarantee that reward. That supernal blessing depends upon our giving "diligent heed to the words of eternal life."[639] President James E. Faust wrote, "We are called when hands are laid upon our heads and we are given the priesthood, but we are not chosen until we demonstrate to God our righteousness, our faithfulness, and our commitment."[640]

---

634    Smith, *History of the Church,* 6:184–85; emphasis added.
635    Maxwell, *A Wonderful Flood of Light,* 47.
636    Turner, *Woman and the Priesthood,* 235; emphasis added.
637    D&C 55:1.
638    Farley, "The Oath and Covenant of the Priesthood," 42–43.
639    D&C 84:43.
640    Faust and Bell, *In the Strength of the Lord,* 394.

Elder Neal A. Maxwell gives an elegant explanation of why many are called but few are chosen: "It makes sense to me that the Lord would choose out of the world those who are (or who could become) different from the world and, therefore, could lead the world to a different outcome. We must be different in order to make a difference."[641] Zion people comprise the few who are different and who make a difference.

To that end, we are commanded to magnify our singular calling. Magnification of our calling exceeds obeying the commandments, which are the means and not the end to achieving the glory of Zion. President Kimball taught, "The faithful in the priesthood are those who fulfill the covenant by 'magnifying their calling' and living 'by every word that proceedeth forth from the mouth of God.' (D&C 84:33, 44.) Far more seems to be implied in these requirements than token obedience—far more is needed than mere attendance at a few meetings and token fulfillment of assignments. *The perfection of body and spirit are implied, and that includes the kind of service that goes far beyond the normal definition of duty. 'Behold, there are many called, but few are chosen.' (D&C 121:34.)"[642] Ultimately, to magnify our priesthood calling, which is the call to eternal life, is to marry in the temple and thereby enter into the order of the Gods; it is to achieve exaltation and inherit eternal lives.[643] Clearly, these statements point to the magnificent end purpose of the priesthood covenant. Those few who fully respond to their priesthood calling are those who will be chosen for eternal life.

## Distinctions between Those Who Are Called and Those Who Are Chosen

Elder Maxwell reminded us that premortal worthiness is simply the first of several tests of worthiness we must pass in order to obtain eternal life: "Just because we were chosen 'there and then,' surely does not mean we can be indifferent 'here and now.' Whether foreordination for men, or foredesignation for women, those called and prepared must also prove 'chosen and faithful.'"[644] The difference, he said, between the "many called" and the "few chosen" is the faithfulness and submission to the celestial laws that make the priesthood operative. He stated, "One reason for the distinction between being 'called' and being 'chosen' is that the latter can understand this next reality: the powers of heaven are accessed and controlled only upon the principles of righteousness (D&C 121:36)."[645] The principles of righteousness, which the Lord wishes to call to our attention, are these:

> No power or influence can or ought to be maintained
> by virtue of the priesthood, only by persuasion, by
> long-suffering, by gentleness and meekness, and by love
> unfeigned; by kindness, and pure knowledge, which

---

641    Maxwell, *Deposition of a Disciple*, 55.
642    Kimball, *Teachings of Spencer W. Kimball*, 496.
643    D&C 132:24.
644    Maxwell, *The Neal A. Maxwell Quote Book*, 127.
645    Maxwell, *But for a Small Moment*, 113.

shall greatly enlarge the soul without hypocrisy, and
without guile—

Reproving betimes with sharpness, when moved
upon by the Holy Ghost; and then showing forth
afterwards an increase of love toward him whom thou
hast reproved, lest he esteem thee to be his enemy; that
he may know that thy faithfulness is stronger than the
cords of death.

Let thy bowels also be full of charity towards all
men, and to the household of faith, and let virtue garnish thy thoughts unceasingly.[646]

The inverse of living these principles is living according to mores that retard or negate
priesthood power: love of money, power, and popularity (attention, recognition, and
influence). These things are highly destructive. Their common denominator is selfishness—one of Babylon's hallmark attributes. Babylon would use money, power, and
influence to compete, suppress, control, dominate, compel, gratify one's pride, and build
a personal empire on the shaky foundation of supposed security[647]—all "vain ambitions,"
according to the scripture.[648] On the other hand, Zion would use money, power, and
influence for building the kingdom of God; for shoring up the poor, thus providing equal
esteem to all people; for caring for one another's needs—blessing the sick, comforting the
afflicted, clothing the naked, feeding the hungry; and establishing peace.

The attitude of Babylon leads to pride, contention, hardened hearts, withdrawing
from the core principles of the Church, and promoting behavior akin to persecuting the
poor and afflicted. It is Satanic thought and action, idolatry, idleness and idle talk, envy,
strife, self-indulgence, lying, dishonesty, robbery, inappropriate sexual dalliance, murder,
and all manner of wickedness. Conversely, the attitude of Zion engenders the confidence
to be able to stand in the presence of God, priesthood power, a growing knowledge of the
doctrine of the priesthood, the constant companionship of the Holy Ghost, and becoming
unto God a king and priest who wields an unchanging scepter of righteousness and truth.
A Zion attitude leads to inheriting everlasting kingdoms, thrones, principalities, powers,
and dominions—the blessings of which will flow to a Zion person forever and ever.[649]

## Building a Sure House

In a speech entitled "Beware Lest Ye Fall," President George Q. Cannon exhorted us to
become identified with the few who are "chosen." Our effort will supersede any other
individual attainment, he promised, and the benefits of the priesthood will extend to
our children. How we fare in becoming one of the few will have a direct impact on our

646   D&C 121:41–45.
647   Alma 1:20–32.
648   D&C 121:37.
649   D&C 121:45–46.

descendants and our ability to build for them a "sure house." He said, "The Lord is weeding out His Church continually. The work of selection is going on. 'Many are called,' the Lord has said, 'but few are chosen.' The Lord is choosing the people now. The Lord is pulling up—in fact, they are pulling themselves up—the unfaithful, the transgressor. The work of cleansing the Church is going on perpetually, and it will continue until Christ comes. What an impressive lesson this ought to be to us! Do we desire to live and to be connected with the work of God? Do we desire our children to be numbered with the people of God? The great desire of some of the prophets and mighty men of old was that the Lord would build them a sure house."[650]

Clearly, how we respond to the priesthood "call" distinguishes the few from the "many." Of the latter group the Lord said, "When I called, ye did not answer."[651] Our response has everything to do with our eventually being "chosen" or elected. Joseph Smith was an example. Janne M. Sjodahl and Hyrum M. Smith wrote: "The Prophet Joseph was 'called and chosen' to give to the world the Book of Mormon and to engage in the ministry. God called him, through the Angel, and when he manifested his willingness to obey the call, he was chosen for the work." Then a significant observation, *"The call always precedes the election: 'Give diligence to make your calling and election sure' (2 Peter 1:10). He who is called, is sure of his election if he obeys the call."*[652]

## Mortal Tests That Challenge Our Calling

"We believe in being true," proclaims the thirteenth Article of Faith. To God, to family, to country, to our brethren, to our covenants, and to the cause of Zion, we believe in being true. The "true" are the few who are called *and* chosen. The "true" are contrasted from the many, they who are also called but *not* chosen because they are distracted by money, power, and popularity; the many are they who receive God's power and then misuse it by attempting to dominate and control. In the test of life, the "true" are the few who live their covenants despite all hazards; they flee Babylon, as they have been commanded, and they choose Zion over every other consideration. How we choose between Babylon and Zion is a pivotal element in the test of life; that choice separates the *true few* from the *untrue many*. In an article published in the *Improvement Era*, James G. Duffin wrote:

> God chooses his own way of testing men and preparing them for the work he designs them to do. "Many are called but few are chosen." The chosen ones are those upon whom he can rely under the most trying conditions. Tests, in themselves apparently trifling, may determine the integrity of those thought of for more important work. It is related of the Prophet Joseph that when he was making up his company to go West, to

650   Cannon, "Beware Lest Ye Fall," Feb. 16, 1896.
651   Isaiah 65:12.
652   Smith and Sjodahl, *Doctrine and Covenants Commentary,* 123; emphasis added.

find a suitable location for his suffering people, where
they could worship God without being molested by mob
violence, one day he invited a number of brethren to
take a horseback ride with him. As the prophet led his
little company along the road, he came to a large pool
of water, around the edge of which the road made a
curve. Without hesitating, the prophet plunged his horse
through the water. A number of those with him followed
without saying a word, while others followed the road
around the pool. It is related that when he made up his
company, Joseph selected every man who followed him
through the pool of water, and not one of the others was
chosen. "Blind obedience," says one. *The key is this: intel-
ligent beings moved by the same spirit act in unison.*[653]

Such is the test and condition of Zion people. Tests bring us to the crucible of choice.
The early Saints reached such a crucible when, impoverished and persecuted, they were
commanded to build the Kirtland Temple. The act was a kind one. The Lord knew
that the key to their deliverance and the redemption of Zion lay in receiving priesthood
ordinances and living the law of the celestial kingdom. The administration of these
ordinances and the celestial law could be received only in a temple. Thus, the Saints
understood from the outset that Zion must be their goal, and "Zion cannot be built up
unless it is by the principles of the law of the celestial kingdom."[654] When this revelation
(D&C 105) was received, "the Kirtland Temple was under construction. The faithful
were to receive 'their endowment from on high' in this House of the Lord, for 'the time
[had] come for a *day of choosing*' (D&C 105:12, 33, 35). Those 'chosen' for this blessing
would be those whose works had manifested their worthiness."[655] The few priesthood
holders who would be called and chosen would be those who lived the law of the celestial
kingdom and thus become Zion people.

Likewise, our day of choosing and our deliverance centers on the temple and the
criterion of worthiness to attend the temple. How we choose—and there are only two
choices—is our test: Will we or will we not choose to remain true to our covenants?
Elijah said it this way: "How long halt ye between two opinions? if the Lord be God,
follow him: but if Baal [a god of Babylon], then follow him."[656] We cannot have it both
ways; we must choose. If we choose to keep our covenants and separate ourselves from
Babylon, we are promised that we will be "endowed with power from on high,"[657] which
endowment is the power of deliverance, the power of godliness, and the power to bring
us back into the presence of God.[658] If, on the other hand, we choose to neglect or

653    Duffin, "A Character Test," *Improvement Era*, Feb. 1911; emphasis added.
654    D&C 105:5.
655    Brewster, *Doctrine and Covenants Encyclopedia*, 124.
656    1 Kings 18:21.
657    D&C 105:11.
658    D&C 84:20–21.

reject our covenants, we will receive the pronouncement: "Amen to the priesthood or authority of that man." Clearly, our day of choosing is today, and how we choose places us in the camp of the wise or the camp of the foolish, for, according to the scriptures, only the "wise virgins" will be ready when comes the day of choosing. "And until that hour there will be foolish virgins among the wise; *and at that hour cometh an entire separation of the righteous and the wicked;* and in that day will I send mine angels to pluck out the wicked and cast them into unquenchable fire."[659] Thus, "there are many called, but few are chosen."

## The Daunting Test of Riches

Jesus sounded a warning against our tendency to step into the snare of the love of money: "For what is a man profited if he shall gain the whole world and lose his own soul?"[660] Sadly, many priesthood holders are wont to rationalize their preoccupation with wealth, and thus they choose to remain in Babylon. When Joseph Smith was incarcerated in Liberty Jail, he issued an epistle warning the Saints about this snare. Parts of that epistle became sections 121 and 122 of the Doctrine and Covenants. Joseph admonished those Saints who would "aspire after their own aggrandizement and seek their own opulence while their brethren are groping in poverty." Care should be given, he wrote, that our hearts not be open to "such high mindedness." Otherwise a condition would prevail wherein "there are many called but few are chosen."[661]

As we have discussed, of the many who are called to eternal life, only a few will ultimately give diligent heed to their priesthood calling and move forward in faith toward Zion. The few will become the "chosen." Part of the price of becoming one of the "chosen" is choosing God over mammon—one of the most difficult tests of mortality.

When a wealthy young man went away sorrowing after having received the Lord's answer regarding the price for him to become perfect, Jesus turned to his disciples and said, "A rich man shall *hardly* enter into the kingdom of heaven."[662] Embedded in the Lord's explanation is an introduction to the law of consecration. This law is our safety net from the preoccupation of wealth, and it is a key to our becoming perfect. To the rich young man, the Lord said, "If thou wilt be perfect, go and sell that thou hast, and give to the poor."[663] Although the rich man was clearly a good man who had lived the commandments, he could not bring himself to accept the law of consecration, which would have covered him in safety and opened the door to perfection. Truly, it is *hard* for a rich man—or for that matter, a proud, selfish, power-hungry, recognition-seeking man—to lay aside the things of this world and still achieve heaven.

---

659    D&C 63:54; emphasis added.
660    Matthew 16:26.
661    Millet and Jackson, 1:471–72.
662    Matthew 19:23.
663    Matthew 19:21.

## Safety and Perfection in Consecration

We learn several important principles of Zion from the incident of the Savior and the rich young man:

1. Perfection hinges not on living the commandments alone but on living the law of consecration.
2. The ultimate test of discipleship is the law of consecration.
3. The law of consecration was instituted, in part, for our safety, because pursuing and hoarding wealth can result in the loss of exaltation.
4. The law of consecration is hard to live, but it is harder for a rich man.
5. Only divine intervention can save the rich—those who have too much of what they do not need or deserve, but that intervention is not necessarily guaranteed.
6. Consecrating our excess to the poor tends to stockpile treasure in heaven, where treasure is needed.
7. The law of consecration makes us safe and secure. The Lord invited the rich young man to "come and follow me," which implies true safety. If we are with the Lord, we are safe.
8. Consecrated sacrifices earn "an hundredfold" return. If that is true, the rich young man would have received an hundredfold more blessings than he sacrificed to bless the poor, and as the young man gave, the Lord would have kept him safe; he would have achieved perfection, and he would have earned eternal life.

Thus sang the Psalmist: "Blessed is he that considereth the poor: the Lord will deliver him in time of trouble. The Lord will preserve him, and keep him alive; and he shall be blessed upon the earth: and thou wilt not deliver him unto the will of his enemies. The Lord will strengthen him upon the bed of languishing: thou wilt make all his bed in his sickness."[664] Deliverance, preservation, safety, protection, strength, and health—these are the blessings of consecration. But only a few of the many who are called will actually embrace this celestial law of Zion and live within its safety.

## The Sacrifice of All Things—A "Hard Thing"

Seeking after and clinging to riches can be a difficult vice to overcome. Obtaining wealth often requires sidestepping the principles of Zion and embracing the principles of Babylon. Letting go of riches, a principle essential to becoming a Zion person, requires our rethinking a core Babylonian philosophy that brought us riches in the first place.

The Book of Mormon prophet, Jacob, stated emphatically that the only legitimate celestial purpose for seeking wealth is to obtain more resources to give away: "to clothe the naked, and to feed the hungry, and to liberate the captive, and administer relief to the sick and the afflicted." He said seeking the kingdom of God takes precedence over seeking riches—first one, then the other. We often try to invert this process. Only by fol-

---

664   Psalms 41:1–3.

lowing Jacob's prescribed sequence will we use wealth for its intended purpose, and that purpose is clearly *not* for personal empire building.

If we are to become Zion-like, we can harbor no selfish motive with our time, talents, or *anything* God has given us. Jacob said, "Think of your brethren like unto yourselves, and be familiar with all and free with your substance, that they may be rich like unto you."[665] Otherwise, he said, damning pride sets in, which condition God will not justify. Rather, pride condemns its victims with God's harsh judgment. A selfish attitude toward wealth is destructive and wholly Babylonian in nature; it is classified by Jacob as an iniquity and an abomination.[666] Essentially, he said, we are persecuting and afflicting the poor[667]; we are advancing inequality and promoting classes of people, which actions are contrary to the culture of Zion in every way. When such conditions exist, we hear the Lord's condemnation: "Amen to the priesthood or the authority of that man!"

Of course, many rich people would not want to hear this. It is a "hard thing"[668] to reject telestial philosophies that seem so alluring and make so much sense here. With little doubt, it is a hard thing to make the sacrifice of all things, which is the crowning sacrifice required for eternal life.[669] But that sacrifice becomes much more difficult for a rich person; he has much more to unload, and in the process he must also abandon his telestial attitude of wealth-building. While no prophet has condemned wealth, every prophet has condemned pursuing and hoarding it. Zion is described as a condition of unequalled abundance—there are simply no poor in Zion—but that abundance must be obtained in the right sequence and for the right reasons.

Only the law of consecration can protect us from the snare of wealth and provide us ultimate protection. This celestial law makes little sense in a telestial world, but it is in its application that Zion people realize great abundance and safety.

## Safety in the "Royal Law"

Love motivates us to consecrate. Because we love, we are willing to give ourselves and that which we have to building up God's kingdom, promoting the cause of Zion, and taking care of God's children. Consecration can be lived only by the law of love, which James called the "Royal Law": "Thou shalt love thy neighbour as thyself."[670]

President Marion G. Romney said we must do an about-face and begin to live according to the "royal law." This law is central to the law that governs the celestial kingdom.[671] Elder Romney taught that Zion people can be established on no other principle. Priesthood holders must fully and ungrudgingly yield obedience to the "royal law." The Lord has stated unequivocally that Zion people must become united according to the

---

665   Jacob 2:17–19.
666   Jacob 2:13–16.
667   Psalms 10:2; 2 Nephi 9:30; 28:13.
668   1 Nephi 3:5.
669   Smith, *Lectures on Faith*, 6:7.
670   James 2:8.
671   D&C 105:4–5.

"union required by the laws of the Celestial Kingdom," which stipulates that we must impart of our substance "as becometh saints, to the poor and afflicted."[672]

We should insert here that money is not the only item of wealth we must consecrate. For example, we might be rich in time, talent, or other resources the Lord has given us. Holding back and not consecrating *any* abundance that God has blessed us with is categorized, as we have said, as persecuting the poor.[673] Catastrophic consequences follow such self-dealing and selfish intent. Mormon identified ignoring the poor as a central reason for the pre-Christ destruction of the Nephite nation: "Now this great loss of the Nephites, and the great slaughter which was among them, would not have happened had it not been for their wickedness and their abomination which was among them; *yea, and it was among those also who professed to belong to the church of God. And it was because of the pride of their hearts, because of their exceeding riches, yea, it was because of their oppression to the poor, withholding their food from the hungry, withholding their clothing from the naked,* and smiting their humble brethren upon the cheek, making a mock of that which was sacred, denying the spirit of prophecy and of revelation, murdering, plundering, lying, stealing, committing adultery, rising up in great contentions, and deserting away."[674]

We must be so very careful. We must be ruled by the "royal law" and exhibit love that is deep enough to consecrate all that we are and have to God, his purposes, and his children. Love vitalizes the priesthood covenant as much as love infuses life into Zion people.

## The Dangers of Rationalization and Postponement

Consecration is the ultimate sacrifice, for it involves all that we are and have. That sacrifice, which Joseph Smith described as the "sacrifice of all things," is the *only* sacrifice that has "power sufficient to produce the faith necessary unto life and salvation."[675] Certainly this sacrifice is daunting, but it is equally certain that we must make it; and when we do, we will make it in a highly individualized way by consecration.

In advance of making this sacrifice, we must first give up the selfish, prideful telestial attitudes that have stood in the way of such a sacrifice. The price of eternal life is total devotion, which can be proven only by the sacrifice of all things. Upon this sacrifice hangs our inheritance in the celestial kingdom; thus it was designed to cause us to stretch.

Because this ultimate sacrifice is extremely difficult, we often shrink from making it; we rationalize in order to set it aside. Sometimes we try to assuage our conscience, as do the many who are called but not chosen, by saying that we are doing our best to live the commandments; but then we remember that the rich young man was also living the commandments but would not make the sacrifice and so fell short of eternal life. Or perhaps we postpone the sacrifice by saying that we would certainly be willing to live the law of consecration whenever the President of the Church sends down a new program. But the reality is that the law of consecration is neither a new law nor one that is waiting

672   Marion G. Romney, "The Royal Law of Love," 95, quoting D&C 105:1–6.
673   2 Nephi 9:30; 13:15; 28:13; Mosiah 4:26; Alma 5:55; Helaman 4:12; Mormon 8:37.
674   Helaman 4:11–12; emphasis added.
675   Smith, *Lectures on Faith,* 6:7.

for a program. Again, the Lord told the rich young man that today was the day of obedience and sacrifice; the one thing the young man lacked, *if he would be perfect*, was to sell all that he had and give to the poor *today*, with the immediate promise that he would have treasure in heaven.

As mentioned, the Savior's invitation to the rich young man is the same as his invitation to every man who makes the oath and covenant of the priesthood: "Come and follow me." When the young man declined the invitation, shrank from the sacrifice, and went away, the Lord noted that a rich man's effort to develop a new attitude toward riches is difficult indeed: "It is easier for a camel to go through the eye of a needle, than for a rich man to enter into the kingdom of God."[676] Of course, the disciples were as astonished by this doctrine as are we. They wondered aloud, who then could be saved? Jesus answered that such a feat requires God's intervention. But that statement should not be viewed as a comfort or a guarantee. The Joseph Smith Translation of this scripture reads: "It is *impossible* for them who trust in riches, to enter into the kingdom of God; but he who forsaketh the things which are of this world, it is possible with God, that he should enter in."[677]

Jesus' concluding warning to the disciples should be sobering to every priesthood holder: "But *many* that are first shall be last; and the last shall be first." Again, we see the word many and contemplate the implied condemnation: "*many* are called, but *few* are chosen." It is upon the law of consecration that the few distinguish themselves from the many and make sure their calling to eternal life.

## The Law of Restitution—An *Hundredfold* Reward

True safety and prosperity are found only in making the sacrifice of all things through consecration and by following Christ. The incident of the rich young man disturbed the Apostles so much that they began to search their souls. Evidently, they wondered if they had fully complied with the laws of sacrifice and consecration so that they might obtain eternal life. Jesus offered them an astonishing promise: "And every one that hath forsaken houses, or brethren, or sisters, or father, or mother, or wife, or children, or lands, for my name's sake, *shall receive an hundredfold, and shall inherit everlasting life.*"[678] Here the Lord makes two divine promises connected with consecration: (1) an hundredfold return, and (2) the promise of eternal life. The few priesthood holders who are called and chosen are blessed a hundred times over for their sacrifice, and they will inherit exaltation![679]

The hundredfold-reward principle is a manifestation of the law of restoration,[680] which flows from the laws of sacrifice and consecration—whatever we give the Lord in priesthood service and personal sacrifice is restored to us "an hundredfold." The Apostles had firsthand experience with the hundredfold principle on at least two occasions: first,

---

676    Luke 18:25.
677    JST, Luke 18:27; emphasis added.
678    Matthew 19:29; emphasis added.
679    Matthew 19:16–30.
680    Smith, *Teachings of the Prophet Joseph Smith*, 395.

when Jesus fed the five thousand and, second, when he fed the four thousand.[681] Each time, Jesus required the Apostles to bring (consecrate) *all* they could to the Lord. Jesus blessed their offering, and then the resource multiplied and fed many. Of significance, in each instance, the Apostles were instructed to gather up the remaining fragments and take note of the resulting quantity. Five loaves and two fishes had not only fed thousands until they were filled, but the fragments now filled twelve baskets in addition![682] *An hundredfold return!* Later, seven loaves and a few small fishes had not only fed thousands until they were filled, but the fragments now filled seven baskets more![683] *An hundredfold return!* These are lessons for every priesthood holder.

The law of restoration is a law of faith. When priesthood holders and their women counterparts consecrate our time, talents, and resources to build the kingdom of God, to promote the cause of Zion, and to bless the lives of others, we invoke a celestial law of abundance upon which Zion people and a Zion priesthood society are built. What the Lord said to his disciples, he repeats to us: "Freely ye have received, freely give"[684]; "Feed my lambs. . . . Feed my sheep."[685] Of the many priesthood holders who are called to eternal life, only a few will actually achieve it, and when they do it will be because they made a consecrated effort, allowing the law of restoration to engage, which triggers the powers of earth and heaven to work together to return to us an hundredfold reward and the promise of eternal life.

## Babylon among Us

As we've mentioned previously, when priesthood holders make the covenant of conse-cration and then neglect it or fall back into Babylon, they risk forfeiture of the Lord's blessings and their own salvation. The Mormon pioneers are examples. After they, the many who had been called to eternal life, had sacrificed everything to leave Babylon to establish Zion in the tops of the mountains, Brigham Young lamented that they, the many, had brought Babylon with them.

> The cry has come to [us]—"Separate yourselves from sinners and from sin." If we, as a people, had not believed this, we should not have been here this day. "Be not partakers of her sins, lest ye receive of her plagues, for her sins have reached unto heaven, and God hath remembered her iniquities." This we believe, consequently I have to say to the people, we have not come with any new doctrine; we have believed this ever since we were baptized for the remission of sins. Have

---

681   Mark 6:35–44; 8:1–9.
682   Mark 6:35–44.
683   Mark 8:1–9.
684   Matthew 10:8.
685   John 21:15–16.

the people come out from the nations? Yes. Have we
separated ourselves from the nations? Yes. And what
else have we done? Ask ourselves the question. Have
we not brought Babylon with us? Are we not promoting Babylon here in our midst? Are we not fostering the
spirit of Babylon that is now abroad on the face of the
whole earth? I ask myself this question, and I answer,
Yes, yes, to some extent, and there is not a Latter-day
Saint but what feels that we have too much of Babylon
in our midst. The spirit of Babylon is too prevalent
here. What is it? Confusion, discord, strife, animosity,
vexation, pride, arrogance, selfwill and the spirit of the
world. Are these things in the midst of those called
Latter-day Saints? Yes, and we feel this.[686]

Alma the Younger's people were no different. In the beginning, under the direction
of their prophet, Alma the Elder, they were the many who been called to eternal life.
Later, they had suffered greatly at the hands of their enemies. Then they had experienced deliverance. But safe in Zarahemla, they had abandoned Zion for the charms of
Babylon.[687] Brigham Young noted that the Latter-day Saints were following the same
pattern. He then issued a chilling prophecy. He foretold that the Saints would become
the richest people on earth, but he also forewarned that those same riches would become a terrible trial. That vision caused him to mourn that many of us, who are called
to eternal life like Alma's people, would fail the test of wealth and risk losing our exaltation. President Young said, "The worst fear that I have about this people is that they
will get rich in this country, forget God and his people, wax fat, and kick themselves
out of the Church and go to hell. This people will stand mobbing, robbing, poverty,
and all manner of persecution, and be true. But my greater fear for them is that they
cannot stand wealth; and yet they have to be tried with riches, for they will become
the richest people on this earth."[688]

Like us, Alma's people were divided into the many who were called and the few who
were chosen. The first chapter of Alma gives us some helpful descriptions.

The many who were called but not chosen exhibited the following characteristics:
- pride
- contention
- hardened hearts
- distancing or withdrawing from the Church
- persecuting the few
- sorceries
- idolatry

---

686    Young, *Journal of Discourses*, 17:38.
687    Alma 1:20–32.
688    Nibley, *Brigham Young*, 128.

- idleness
- babblings (idle talk)
- envy
- strife
- wearing costly apparel
- lying
- thieving
- robbing
- committing whoredoms (sexual sins)
- murdering
- all manner of wickedness

The few who were called and chosen exhibited the following characteristics:
- humility
- imparting the word of God, one with another, without money and without price
- remaining steadfast and immovable in keeping the commandments of God
- bearing persecution with patience
- leaving the cares of the world behind to hear the word of God
- not esteeming themselves above each other
- striving for equality
- laboring according to each person's individual strength
- imparting their substance according to each other's needs
- caring for the poor, the needy, the sick, and the afflicted
- dressing modestly and avoiding costly apparel
- being neat and comely in appearance[689]

Interestingly, the few who were chosen for eternal life enjoyed an incredible abundance of peace and wealth—even to exceed the riches of the many who had defected to Babylon. These few used their abundance to level up those around them and to bless those who were not members of the Church. And they accomplished this feat—becoming Zion people and establishing their Zion—in a matter of months![690]

> And thus they did establish the affairs of the church;
> and thus they began to have continual peace again,
> notwithstanding all their persecutions.
>        And now, because of the steadiness of the church
> they began to be exceedingly rich, having abundance of
> all things whatsoever they stood in need—an abun-
> dance of flocks and herds, and fatlings of every kind,
> and also abundance of grain, and of gold, and of silver,

---

689   Alma 1:20–32.
690   Alma 1:23.

and of precious things, and abundance of silk and fine-twined linen, and all manner of good homely cloth.

And thus, in their prosperous circumstances, they did not send away any who were naked, or that were hungry, or that were athirst, or that were sick, or that had not been nourished; and they did not set their hearts upon riches; therefore they were liberal to all, both old and young, both bond and free, both male and female, whether out of the church or in the church, having no respect to persons as to those who stood in need. And thus they did prosper and become far more wealthy than those who did not belong to their church.[691]

## Walking in Darkness at Noon-day

Regarding the many who fail to live up to their premortal and mortal callings those who are unwilling to face and overcome the obstacles that block their potential to receive the blessings of the priesthood and hinder them from becoming Zion people, President Harold B. Lee wrote,

"The Lord requireth the heart and a willing mind; and the willing and obedient shall eat the good of the land of Zion in these last days." (D&C 64:34.) I fear there are many among us who because of their faithfulness in the spirit world were "called" to do a great work here, but like reckless spendthrifts they are exercising their free agency in riotous living and are losing their birthright and the blessings that were theirs had they proved faithful to their calling. Hence as the Lord has said, "there are many called but few are chosen," and then he gives us two reasons as to why his chosen and ordained fail of their blessings: First, because their hearts are set so much upon the things of this world, and second, they aspire so much to the honors of men that they do not learn that "the powers of heaven cannot be controlled nor handled only upon the principles of righteousness." (D&C 121:34–36.) *All these have sinned "a very grievous sin, in that they are walking in darkness at noon-day."* (D&C 95:5–6.)[692]

---

691   Alma 1:28–31.
692   Lee, *Decisions for Successful Living,* 169; emphasis added.

They have not sinned ignorantly. They have taken upon them the oath and covenant of the priesthood and the covenant of consecration, and they have set them aside. "They are walking in darkness at noonday."

Quoting the scripture, "Many are called, few are chosen," President Wilford Woodruff grieved, "The Almighty has revealed in our day the reasons, but what a mighty host have wrecked their eternal hopes on those fatal reefs—love of the riches of this world, the honors and praises of men, and the exercises of unrighteous dominion."[693] The many know the law and yet they reject the law.

This is the day for choosing between Zion and Babylon. We cannot escape the fact that President Young's prophecy is true: Many priesthood holders are rich by the world's standard, and yet they, who long for and profess to be Zion people, are too much identified with Babylon. They are walking in darkness at noonday, according to President Lee, and their actions constitute a very grievous sin. They have agreed to follow the principles of obedience, sacrifice, and consecration, but they do not do so. President Woodruff warned that their behavior carries severe eternal risks. Their pursuit and love of riches, their selfish attitude regarding their time and talents, their insistence upon gratifying their pride with praise and honor, and their demeaning and unequal treatment of others will have the eventual effect of dashing their eternal hopes on fatal reefs. The priesthood cannot function under such conditions. Unless the priesthood many come to their senses and admit that all is *not* well in Zion, the devil will cheat their souls, as prophesied, and lead the them carefully down to hell [694] Then the priesthood becomes totally inoperative.

## The Test of Praise

Who does not feel a rush of exhilaration when praise and recognition are lavished upon him? But how many have become intoxicated by the opiate of praise, and then have fallen? Elder Harold B. Lee identified seeking worldly things and aspiring to the honors of men as the primary causes of failure in prominent men and their loss of the highest priesthood possibilities.[695] Jesus taught that it is impossible to simultaneously serve two masters.[696] We see evidence of the truth of this principle in the construct of our minds and hearts: We can neither think two thoughts at the same time, nor can we simultaneously set our hearts upon two things. Ultimately, we will "hate the one, and love the other." Therefore, when we are tempted to aspire to the honors of men, we are faced with making a choice between the honors of men and the honor of God. How we choose determines whether we are of Babylon or of Zion, whether we are of the many who are called and not chosen or the few who will respond to their priesthood calling and be chosen for eternal life. Let us make a distinction here that while we are encouraged to speak kind words to each other and to sincerely compliment each other in order that we might strengthen those we love and care for, the kind of praise we are talking about stems from other motives.

---

693   Clark, *Messages of the First Presidency,* 3:131.
694   2 Nephi 28:21.
695   Lee, Conference Report, Oct. 1965, 128.
696   Matthew 6:24.

Seeking acclaim, popularity, attention, and recognition is akin to praise-seeking. Any one of these leads to the same disastrous end. It has been observed that nothing good ever comes from seeking praise. Undisciplined, praise can only promote pride in the receiver. Moreover, this type of praise suggests that unequal levels of worth exist among God's children—one standing above the other, with the praised one standing on top. This attitude is not Zion-like and runs contrary to the priesthood, which stipulates that priesthood holders must strive to love God's children as themselves and be servants to all.[697]

Seeking and receiving praise sets in motion a destructive cycle that inevitably spirals out of control. Self-centeredness almost always follows; self-centeredness is fed by praise. Self-centeredness is the bedfellow of competition, which also loves praise. Winners receive the secondary prize of praise, which they often desire more than the primary prize of their competitive enterprise. Babylon glorifies winners and lavishes upon them the spoils of victory—money, power, popularity, and influence. Winners are set up as heroes; they are superhuman; they are gods. Consequently, winners receive our adoration and our praise. No wonder, then, that praise is a foundational principle of inequality.

We praise the beautiful, the rich, the smart, the talented, and the strong. The problem arises when we give them more acclaim than we give our God. We set them up as examples. We pay them tribute. We write about them, talk about them, and try to draw near to them. When we praise another so as to exalt and glorify him, and when the person being praised accepts the praise and becomes elevated in his own eyes, both the praiser and the praised have sinned. Both have joined the many who have broken the priesthood covenant and traded their priesthood calling for a fleeting prize.

Perhaps one of the reasons God gives us adversity is to shake us loose from praise and the vanity associated with it. Adversity is a great equalizer. It is at the common denominator of adversity that the proud and the humble, the rich and the poor, the powerful and the weak, the popular and the nobodies, and the praised and the praisers are equal. Perhaps it is by means of adversity that God tries to teach us the principle of equality. When the joy of achievement is measured by praise, when life is a contest in which everyone is constantly comparing himself to others, lives will be ruined and people will become miserable. Unfortunately, this is the sad state of the many, who "set their hearts upon the things of this world, and aspire to the honors of men," those who compete and "exercise unrighteous dominion," those whose actions grieve the Spirit and thus cause the heavens to withdraw with a sounding amen to their priesthood.[698]

Joseph Fielding McConkie and Robert L. Millet wrote, "Whenever men of any age value the approval of their fellows more than the approbation of their God, they forfeit the reward that might have been theirs. . . . President Joseph F. Smith warned against three great dangers, which the Saints of God must encounter: false educational ideas, sexual impurity, *and the flattery of prominent men* (see *Gospel Doctrine*, p. 313). To those who seek the applause of mortals, the words of the Master are clear and poignant: 'They have their reward' (Matthew 6:5)."[699]

---

697    Smith, *History of the Church*, 4:492.
698    D&C 121:37, 39.
699    McConkie and Millet, *Doctrinal Commentary on the Book of Mormon*, 1:90; emphasis added.

To forfeit the wealth of eternity for the transitory riches of this world, and to set aside the everlasting praise of God for the fickle honors of men is shortsighted and foolish. These insanities are nothing more than replays of Esau's selling his birthright for a mess of pottage. Do we really crave praise so much that we would choose it rather than the power and honor of God? If we were to ask parents what is the worst danger their children face, they would likely answer peer pressure. And yet many adults do not perceive that danger in their own lives. We crave praise and acceptance, and often we will do whatever it takes to get them. Has history taught us nothing? If Saul, David, and Solomon could fall by aspiring to the honors of men, could not we?

Our desire for praise encroaches on every area of our lives, even our attitude toward Church service. There is a dangerous tendency here: Occasionally, praise-seeking individuals are tempted to mold their callings in such a way that it draws attention to themselves. Idolatry results—the serving of false gods instead of serving the true God and his children. For example, a Young Women leader might be tempted to focus her effort on gaining the honor of her class, and soon her attempts to teach the gospel will take second place to her basking in her students' admiration and respect. She is doing a good work for the wrong reason; she has her reward—praise—but it is the wrong reward. Or a new elders quorum president, who is rightly held in esteem by his quorum, might feel invigorated and elevated as he notes that his brethren now cling to his every authoritative word. Then, rather than feeling humble and dependent upon God, he might feel powerful and important; worse, he might actively encourage more of these feelings by seeking more praise. Now, having lost view of his priesthood calling, he is in great danger of losing his authority altogether. He has "a form of godliness,"[700] but he denies the principles upon which the priesthood functions. He has the appearance of righteousness, but he is failing the test of praise. He has his reward—the wrong one—and he no longer has priesthood power. Elder Marlin K. Jensen put it this way:

> The temptation to seek personal recognition and reward from our service to others is ever-present. The pattern was established in the pre-earth life by Satan himself. . . .
>
> Those who seek honor and gain for themselves in doing the Lord's work are guilty of what the scriptures call priestcrafts. . . .
>
> Latter-day Saints whose eyes are single to God's glory see life from a vastly different perspective than those whose attention is directed elsewhere. Such members, for instance, care little about receiving credit or recognition for their good deeds. They are more interested in feeding the Lord's sheep than in counting them. In fact, they frequently find their greatest

---

700   2 Timothy 3:5.

happiness in serving anonymously, thereby leaving the
beneficiaries of their kindness with no one to thank or
praise except the Lord.

A Zion life cannot be established where there is unholy praise: seeking and receiving acclaim that leads to pride; giving recognition and acclaim to others so as to exalt them.

## "Rights of the Priesthood"

Everything basically comes down to a single lesson, and we must learn that lesson if we
hope that the priesthood will become a power and remain functional within us. The
lesson is "that the rights of the priesthood are inseparably connected with the powers of
heaven, and that the powers of heaven cannot be controlled nor handled only upon the
principles of righteousness."[701]
    The priesthood "rights" the Lord mentions here are not "rites," that is, those sacred
ordinances and ceremonies necessary for salvation. Rather, these "rights" are privileges
that flow from recognizing the source of priesthood power. This power can be accessed
only by obedience to the laws of heaven, where the power originates; this power comes
by magnifying our priesthood calling and by living a life distinguished by persuasion
rather than force, long-suffering rather than impatience, gentleness rather than harsh-
ness, meekness rather than pride, love unfeigned (genuine) rather than love contrived
(pretended or insincere), and kindness rather than abusiveness. Clearly, the priesthood is
a lifestyle. The scripture states that if we will assume the true lifestyle of the priesthood,
the Holy Ghost will distil upon us pure knowledge. It is pure knowledge that has the effect of aligning us, sincerely and without ulterior motives, with the character of God.
    Now we are in a position to have the right to the "rights" of the priesthood. One of
those priesthood rights is the right to occasionally correct people in our stewardships. We
exercise that priesthood right by "reproving betimes with sharpness, when moved upon
by the Holy Ghost; and then showing forth afterwards an increase of love toward him
whom thou hast reproved, lest he esteem thee to be his enemy."[702] Notice that this right
guarantees us the companionship of the Holy Ghost in our stewardships. The influence
of the Holy Ghost makes interactions with those in our stewardships experiences of love
rather than experiences of discouragement and embarrassment. By exercising this right
of the priesthood in occasional loving correction, we will help to increase faith, hope,
and repentance in the corrected person. Then our relationship with that person will be
strengthened, and we will come to be known by the hallmark priesthood characteristics
of virtue and charity.[703] So it is with all priesthood rights that have the power to establish
Zion in our lives.

---

701    D&C 121:36.
702    D&C 121:43.
703    D&C 121:41–45.

## "Inseparably Connected"—Righteousness and Priesthood Power

We need only scan the scriptures to glimpse the power of these priesthood rights. For example, one who is given these rights has the power to create and control the elements, to heal the sick, to raise the dead, to cast out evil spirits, to teach with the tongue of angels, to know the truth of all things, and to stand in the presence of God. Before we can obtain these rights, as we have mentioned, we must first align our lives with the characteristics of God and the laws of heaven by which these rights are governed. If we should step away from this pattern, we risk severing the cord that binds us to the source of priesthood power. Again, the scripture reads "that the rights of the priesthood are inseparably connected with the powers of heaven, and that the powers of heaven cannot be controlled nor handled only upon the principles of righteousness."[704]

If we are not experiencing the powers of heaven that flow from these priesthood rights, we might profit by first looking inward and realigning our lives with the Constitution of the Priesthood. Then we must repair the connection between ourselves and heaven.

It should be clear by now that priesthood *authority* and priesthood *power* are distinct terms. Priesthood authority is granted upon ordination, but priesthood power is dependent upon our righteousness.[705] There is a cause-and-effect at play. Unrighteous dominion is the ugly consequence of our undertaking to cover our sins, to gratify our pride or vain ambitions, or to exercise control or compulsion upon other people *in any degree of unrighteousness*. Even the slightest inclination toward these evils results in priesthood cessation: "Behold, the heavens withdraw themselves; the Spirit of the Lord is grieved; and when it is withdrawn, Amen to the priesthood or the authority of that man."[706] Of course, if the heavens withdraw, we can repent and the power of the priesthood will be restored.

Clearly, the priesthood is a way of life that Zion people follow. Taking upon us the oath and covenant of the priesthood demands that we separate ourselves from the philosophies of Babylon and exercise strict obedience to the laws that govern God's power. Thus, to the degree that we exhibit righteousness, we place ourselves in a position to have access to the "rights of the priesthood."

## Connecting to the True Vine

In book 2, we talked about how being attached to the True Vine relates to our abiding in the Covenant. Now we see that in order to access priesthood power through the rights of the priesthood we must be attached to the True Vine. Before his crucifixion, Jesus taught his Apostles concerning their priesthood calling, which, he said, they could not magnify without remaining connected to him. He called himself the True Vine, and he delineated them as the branches. We must never lose sight of the fact that these men were priesthood holders, and that they were receiving a significant priesthood lesson from the Master about the rights of the priesthood. Jesus taught:

---

704   D&C 121:36.
705   Nelson, "Personal Priesthood Responsibility," 44.
706   D&C 121:37; emphasis added.

> I am the true vine, and my Father is the husbandman.
> Every branch in me that beareth not fruit he taketh
> away: and every [branch] that beareth fruit, he pur-
> geth it, that it may bring forth more fruit. Now ye are
> clean through the word which I have spoken unto you.
> Abide in me, and I in you. As the branch cannot bear
> fruit of itself, except it abide in the vine; no more can
> ye, except ye abide in me. I am the vine, ye [are] the
> branches: He that abideth in me, and I in him, the
> same bringeth forth much fruit: for without me ye can
> do nothing. If a man abide not in me, he is cast forth
> as a branch, and is withered; and men gather them,
> and cast [them] into the fire, and they are burned. If
> ye abide in me, and my words abide in you, ye shall ask
> what ye will, and it shall be done unto you. Herein is
> my Father glorified, that ye bear much fruit; so shall ye
> be my disciples.[707]

This metaphor has a variety of applications. For instance, a man who sanctifies himself has greater power in the priesthood than a man who does not; a man or woman who sanctifies himself or herself by honoring his or her temple covenants has greater power to ask for and receive blessings than a man or woman who does not; a husband and wife who sanctify themselves in the patriarchal order of the priesthood have greater power to bless their family than a couple who does not.

We, the branches, grow from the True Vine and draw our nourishment from it. We note with interest that in Jesus' metaphor the branches are already producing, but the husbandman (the Father) wants them to produce more. Personalizing this, we might say that through ordination we received priesthood authority and are "producing" to a degree, but the Father wants us to seek priesthood power through righteousness so that we can produce more. To that end, God begins to prune—to "purge and purify"—us. We, the branches, must endure this purging and purifying process if we hope to gain greater strength in the priesthood and produce more fruit. To that end, the Husbandman cuts from us anything that depletes our strength, and he carefully directs the process of growth so that we, the branches, can perform optimally. For a while we might look (and probably feel) pitiful and barren. We might not produce much fruit for a season. But the Husbandman knows that in time the purging and purifying procedure will cause us to bring forth more than we have or ever could. Therefore, enduring the Husbandman's purging process and remaining attached to Christ, the True Vine, are key elements in obtaining the rights and power of the priesthood.

Christ's promise is this: As long as we, the branches, remain in him and he in us, our nourishment and strength will never fail. "Ye shall ask what ye will, and it shall

---

707    John 15:1–8.

be done unto you."[708] Think of the implications! To the degree that we are *in* him and he is *in* us, and to the degree that we submit to the Father's process of purification and sanctification, the Lord promises us that we may draw strength from the True Vine, ask for priesthood power, and receive the blessings associated with the priesthood rights.

## Amen to the Priesthood

Jesus said, "Not every one that saith unto me, Lord, Lord, shall enter into the kingdom of heaven; but he that doeth the will of my Father who is in heaven."[709] We should note here that no one can authoritatively utter the name of the Lord except those upon whom the Lord has placed his name[710]—Melchizedek Priesthood holders. It should go without saying, however, that just because we have been ordained to the priesthood and are going through the motions, it does not necessarily mean that we have or are doing so with power. As we have learned, by our actions we can sever us from priesthood rights and power in the same way we can sever ourselves from the True Vine. Then priesthood power comes to an abrupt amen.

Hugh Nibley wrote, "Men can confer the powers of the priesthood upon others, it is true (D&C 121:37), but only God can validate that ordination, *which in most cases he does not recognize:* 'Hence many are called, but few are chosen' (D&C 121:40). . . . The exercise of the powers of heaven 'in any degree of unrighteousness' invalidates the priesthood—'Amen to the priesthood or the authority of that man' (D&C 121:37). . . . The moment I even think of my priesthood as a status symbol or a mark of superiority, it becomes a mere hollow pretense. At the slightest hint of gloating or self-congratulation, the priesthood holder is instantly and automatically unfrocked."[711]

President John Taylor taught, "Do you think that God will give power to any man only to carry out his own contracted or selfish purposes? I tell you he never will, never, no never. . . . There is no priesthood of the Son of God that authorizes one man to oppress another or to intrude upon his rights in any way. There is no such thing in the category; it does not exist."[712]

The consequences for the poor conduct mentioned in the Constitution of the Priesthood are dire: "behold, the heavens withdraw themselves; the Spirit of the Lord is grieved; and when it is withdrawn, Amen to the priesthood or the authority of that man."[713] And it gets worse! When the Spirit of the Lord withdraws from a man, "ere he is aware," that is, before he even notices, he will be "left unto himself, to kick against the pricks, to persecute the saints, and to fight against God."[714] Thus, as if in a spiraling downward circle, that unrepentant man will become increasingly irritated with

708   John 15:8.
709   3 Nephi 14:21; Matthew 7:21.
710   Abraham 1:18.
711   Nibley, *Temple and Cosmos,* 535–36.
712   Taylor, *Journal of Discourses,* 20:262–63.
713   D&C 121:37.
714   D&C 121:38.

pure doctrine, he will find fault with those who remain true, and soon he will find himself powerless and on the outside, fighting against the God whom he had once purported to love and serve. It is a sad circumstance, the scripture says, but it is nevertheless "the nature and disposition of almost all men"—the many who are called— "as soon as they get a little authority, as they suppose, they will immediately begin to exercise unrighteous dominion."[715]

This official statement from the First Presidency appeared in 1961: "It is the doctrine that those who hold this power and authority will be chosen for an inheritance of eternal life if they exercise their priesthood upon principles of righteousness; if they walk in the light; if they keep the commandments; if they put first in their lives the things of God's kingdom and let temporal concerns take a secondary place; if they serve in the kingdom with an eye single to the glory of God. It is the doctrine that even though men have the rights of the priesthood conferred upon them, they shall not reap its eternal blessings if they use it for unrighteous purposes; if they commit sin; if the things of this world take preeminence in their lives over the things of the Spirit. It is a fearful thing to contemplate this priesthood truth: Behold, many are called to the priesthood, and few are chosen for eternal life."[716]

In an effort to call us away from danger and to help us lift our sights to the glorious "rights of the priesthood," Elder Charles W. Penrose admonished,

> If we would only live up to the things that He has revealed to us; if we would be as pure and virtuous, and honest and upright, and conscientious and patient, and long-suffering and charitable as we are commanded to be in the revelations the Lord has given unto us in these latter times, we would be better prepared for the great things yet to be unfolded. . . . For we are called with a holy calling, and if we do not live up to our professions, it were better we had never made them. *Let us return to the Lord, and the Lord will return to us; his Spirit will be manifested in our midst to a still greater degree, and His gifts and blessings will abound. Our sick will be healed as in times past. We have seen the sick healed instantaneously. The lame have been made to walk, the dumb to speak, the blind to see and the deaf to hear, by the power of God through the administrations of the servants of God. The gifts of tongues, prophecy, dreams, faith, discernment, and every gift and blessing spoken of in the Bible.*[717]

---

715    D&C 121:34–40.
716    First Presidency Message, *Improvement Era*, Feb. 1961, 115.
717    Penrose, *Journal of Discourses*, 20:297–98; emphasis added.

## Summary and Conclusion

President Stephen L Richards called Doctrine and Covenants 121:34–46 "The Constitution of the Priesthood."[718] In that significant document, the Lord restores a phrase that he originally gave to his Apostles in the parable that is often called the parable of the royal feast. That phrase is "many are called but few are chosen." As this phrase applies to the Constitution of the Priesthood, the Lord divides the totality of priesthood holders into two groups: (1) those who respond to the call to eternal life[719]: magnify their calling to eternal life, and thereafter obtain the promise of exaltation: and (2) those who neglect or reject the call to eternal life, take casually or ignore that calling, and forfeit exaltation. The Lord gives the reason for the many being placed in the second group: "Because their hearts are set so much upon the things of this world, and [they] aspire to the honors of men."[720]

In that denouncing statement, the Lord reveals Satan's latter-day strategy to convince many who have been called to eternal life to sell their blessings, as did Esau, for a mess of pottage—Love of money! Love of power! Love of popularity! Satan knows it is impossible for us to simultaneously serve both God and mammon, but he tries to convince us otherwise. When we make the attempt, we automatically step into his snare, which has the purpose of causing us to abandon our priesthood covenant and making us lose control in a downward spiral toward temporal and spiritual destruction.

At the heart of the issue of being called and chosen is the test of loyalties. Other loves, such as money, power, and popularity, are the equivalents of idolatry—gods we worship instead of the true God. The Lord has declared that we will not be held guiltless for shifting our affections. The priesthood covenant demands complete allegiance to God.

In the parable of the royal feast, the king called many of his friends and family to the marriage of his son, but few of those who should have been loyal responded to the call. We see in this division Babylon's captivating the children of Zion and convincing them to love mammon over God. How we choose to respond to the King's call determines our loyalties and identifies the group to which we belong. Everyone who has entered into the new and everlasting covenant has received the King's call; each person who has received the oath and covenant of the priesthood has received that call again. All are invited to become Zion people and to gain an inheritance in Zion. But only they who keep these covenants have actual claim to the blessings of Zion. No one can enter illegitimately.

The many who are called to eternal life and yet are not chosen include those who are going through the motions of Church activity but who have not yet made the choice between God and mammon. Of this group, the Lord says that they have spent their days working iniquity or that "grievous sin." That sin, as we have discussed, lies at the foundation of Babylon—the love of money, power, and popularity. These "loves" have always resulted in oppressive class distinction and inequality, strife, and persecu-

---

718    Richards, Conference Report, Apr. 1955, 12.
719    McConkie, *Mormon Doctrine,* 482.
720    D&C 121:35.

tion; they stand in stark contrast to the unity, equality, peace, and charity required by the celestial law of Zion.[721] The many who seek for these things will be excluded from the wedding feast.

Zion people are the few who are both called *and* chosen for eternal life. They live the celestial laws in a telestial environment. They are the elect who are invited to the marriage of the Lamb, joyfully dressed in holy garments. They embrace the oath and covenant of the priesthood, which promises them all that the Father has. To that end, they magnify their priesthood calling, which is the call to eternal life. When they have proven faithful, the announcement will come that we have been elected for exaltation.

That announcement is so central to our salvation that the head of the previous dispensation, Peter, as well as of the present one, Joseph Smith, have admonished the Saints to "give diligence to make your calling and election sure."[722]

Achieving such a lofty goal, the few must choose to abide Zion's celestial law in Babylon's telestial setting. With Zion ever on his mind, the Prophet Joseph Smith continually endeavored to establish a Zion people who could overcome Babylon and become a nation of priests and kings unto God.[723] Thus, the Prophet admonished the Saints to live up to their covenants; strive for the unity that defines Zion; become separate from Babylon; and be virtuous, holy, and thus "select," or chosen. To become the chosen few depends upon our giving "diligent heed to the words of eternal life."[724] To that end, we are commanded to magnify our singular calling. Magnification of our calling exceeds obeying the commandments, which are means and not ends to achieving the glory of Zion. President Kimball taught, "The faithful in the priesthood are those who fulfill the covenant by 'magnifying their calling' and living 'by every word that proceedeth forth from the mouth of God.'"[725] Ultimately, to magnify our priesthood calling is to one day marry in the temple and thereby enter into the order of the Gods; it is to achieve exaltation and inherit eternal lives.[726]

The Constitution of the Priesthood lists a primary distinction between those who are called and those who are chosen: the powers of heaven are accessed and controlled only upon the principles of righteousness. The inverse of these principles are those that retard or negate priesthood power: love of money, power, and popularity. When we abide the principles of righteousness and access the powers of heaven, we build a "sure house," as President George Q. Cannon taught.

To bring us to the crucible of choosing to become one of the few often requires mortal testing. These tests challenge our devotion to our covenants. If we choose to keep our covenants and separate ourselves from Babylon, we are promised that we will be "endowed with power from on high,"[727] which endowment is the power of deliverance, the

---

721    D&C 105:5.
722    2 Peter 1:10–11.
723    Exodus 19:5–6. Note: Women become priestesses and queens unto their husbands.
724    D&C 84:43.
725    Kimball, *Teachings of Spencer W. Kimball,* 496.
726    D&C 132:24.
727    D&C 105:11.

power of godliness, and the power to bring us back into the presence of God.[728] If, on the other hand, we choose to neglect or reject our covenants, we will receive the pronouncement: "Amen to the priesthood or authority of that man."

One most difficult tests of mortality is the test of wealth-seeking: Will we or will we not choose God over mammon? The Book of Mormon prophet Jacob stated that the only legitimate celestial purpose for seeking wealth is to obtain more resources to give away: "to clothe the naked, and to feed the hungry, and to liberate the captive, and administer relief to the sick and the afflicted." He taught that seeking the kingdom of God takes precedence over seeking riches—first one, and then the other. The law of consecration is our safety net from the preoccupation of wealth, and, as we learn from the Savior's encounter with the rich young man, consecration is a key to our becoming perfect. We learn several important principles of Zion from this incident:

1. Perfection hinges not on living the commandments alone but on living the law of consecration.
2. The ultimate test of discipleship is the law of consecration.
3. The law of consecration was instituted, in part, for our safety, because pursuing and hoarding wealth can result in the loss of exaltation.
4. The law of consecration is hard to live, but it is harder for a rich man.
5. Only divine intervention can save the rich— those who have too much of what they do not need or deserve, but that intervention is not necessarily guaranteed.
6. Consecrating our excess to the poor tends to stockpile treasure in heaven, where treasure is needed.
7. The law of consecration makes us safe and secure. The Lord invited the rich young man to "come and follow me," which implies true safety. If we are with the Lord, we are safe.
8. Consecrated sacrifices earn "an hundredfold" return.

The law of consecration is the vehicle for the sacrifice of all things, which Joseph Smith said was necessary to inherit eternal life. . This celestial law makes little sense in a telestial world, but it is in its application that Zion people realize great abundance and safety.

It is especially true that upon the law of consecration the few divide out from the "many." To rationalize away or postpone consecration is dangerous to our achieving eternal life. Because consecration and the sacrifice of all things are by definition the most difficult sacrifices, the many often shrink from making them; and yet, if they would summon courage and move forward in faith, the Lord would bless them according to the law of restitution with "an *hundredfold*" reward, which includes the promise of eternal life. While we are making our consecrated sacrifice, the Lord will keep us safe, however that safety might be defined.

Safety is also found in the "royal law," which is, "Thou shalt love thy neighbour as thyself."[729] Love motivates us to consecrate. Because we love, we are willing to give

---

728    D&C 84:20–21.
729    James 2:8.

ourselves and that which we have to building up God's kingdom, promoting the cause of Zion, and taking care of God's children. Consecration can be lived only by love; therefore, the principle of love is more pronounced in the few than in the many.

The choice to be one of the many or the few is ever before us. Babylon continues to be the nemesis of Zion, attempting to lure us away with enticements to money, power, and popularity. Brigham Young reminded us that his worst fear was that "we would set our hearts on riches and forget God."[730] Clearly, we have become some of the most prosperous people on earth, and therein, as President Young prophesied, is our test. The few choose to use their abundance to level up those around them, while the many exalt themselves. The many are walking in darkness at noon-day. They have agreed to be obedient, to sacrifice, and to consecrate, but they refuse. President Woodruff warned that their behavior carries severe eternal risks.

For the priesthood to become a power within us, we must remember that priesthood rights originate in heaven and can be accessed only upon our righteousness.[731] Clearly, the priesthood is a lifestyle. If we will assume the priesthood lifestyle, the Holy Ghost will distil upon us pure knowledge. These rights of the priesthood are the power to create and control the elements, to heal the sick, to raise the dead, to cast out evil spirits, to teach with the tongue of angels, to know the truth of all things, and to stand in the presence of God. Before we can obtain these rights, we must align our lives with the characteristics of God and the laws of heaven by which these rights are governed. If we are not experiencing the powers of heaven that flow from these priesthood rights, we might look inward and realign our lives with the Constitution of the Priesthood. Then we must repair the connection between ourselves and heaven. As long as we, the branches, remain in him through righteousness, our nourishment and priesthood strength will never fail. To the degree that we exhibit righteousness, we place ourselves in a position to access to the "rights of the priesthood."

The Constitution of the Priesthood lays out principles of action, inaction, and evils that divide the many who have been called to eternal life from the few who are actually chosen for eternal life. The Constitution explains the source of priesthood power and how the priesthood becomes a lifestyle for those who enter into the oath and covenant of the priesthood. That these principles apply to both men and women should be evident. Because women share in the blessings of the priesthood with their husbands, they also share in the obligations of righteous living. If worthy men and women will do so, they will not only be called to the marriage of the King's son, but they will also be among the chosen few to actually attend the wedding, clothed in beautiful wedding garments, and blessed to partake of the King's feast.

730   Nibley, *Brigham Young*, 128.
731   D&C 121:36.

# Section 5
# The Constitution of the Priesthood
## Instructing the Chosen Few

A t each milestone along the path to eternal life, both men and women receive new instructions, covenants, and ordinances that renew our initial calling and election to eternal life. For example, when we are baptized and first enter into the new and everlasting covenant, the first pillar of Zion, we receive our first "calling and election." When Sidney Gilbert received baptism and entered into the Covenant, the Lord said, 'I have heard your prayers; and you have called upon me that it should be made known unto you, of the Lord your God, *concerning your calling and election in the church,* which I, the Lord, have raised up in these last days." Then the Lord gave Brother Gilbert two charges to help him continue on the path that would lead to his calling and election being made sure. These charges are common to all of us: (1) come out of Babylon, and (2) receive the oath and covenant of the priesthood, the second pillar of Zion: "Behold, I, the Lord, who was crucified for the sins of the world, *give unto you a commandment that you shall forsake the world. Take upon you mine ordination,* even that of an elder, to preach faith and repentance and remission of sins, according to my word, and the reception of the Holy Spirit by the laying on of hands."[732] Only entering into the new and everlasting covenant, forsaking the world, receiving the oath and covenant of the priesthood (priesthood blessings for women), and bringing people to Christ can qualify us for the guarantee of eternal life.

As we have noted, the priesthood is both a way of life and the way to eternal life. The priesthood makes us "different" from the world, Elder Maxwell stated, so that we can "make a difference."[733] Sadly, many who are called to the priesthood do not bother to magnify their calling, as stipulated in the Constitution of the Priesthood,[734] and therefore they do not qualify to be "chosen" for eternal life. On the other hand, a few press forward

---

732    D&C 53:1–3; emphasis added.
733    Maxwell, *Deposition of a Disciple,* 55.
734    Richards, Conference Report, Apr. 1955, 12.

and experience the blessings of the gospel and priesthood. They will desire that everyone within their influence should escape Babylon, come to Zion, and receive these blessings. The priesthood is our power to partner with God in the work of redemption. If we honor the priesthood, we invite the Spirit, whose light *enlightens* us so that we become *lights* to point people to the *Light*[735] and show them the way out of darkness.[736] When they observe us, Elder Maxwell said, they will perceive something bright and "different." But if they detect no difference in us, they will not be drawn to the Light or feel motivated to flee the darkness.

## Stages of Progression within the Covenant

From the moment we entered into the new and everlasting covenant, we accepted a trust. At baptism, the Lord gave us his name, and we agreed to "stand as witnesses of God at all times and in all things, and in all places." [737] If we achieve eternal life, it will be because of our diligent effort in keeping this trust. At the time of our priesthood ordination, the Lord gave us his authority, and again placed upon us his name.[738] Our obligation to carry that name and become *even as he is*[739] took a substantial leap forward.

Now our call to eternal life has expanded. First we entered the new and everlasting covenant and agreed to become like the Lord; second, we received the oath and covenant of the priesthood and agreed to make God's work our work. We agreed that we would never again adopt the behavior or philosophies of Babylon. Now and forever we would be identified with Zion, and we would begin to live according to the celestial order in a telestial world.

To facilitate our ability to adopt this new way of life and to become empowered to do the works of God, the Lord revealed to us the Constitution of the Priesthood. In this document, the Lord offered a list of instructions (D&C 21:41–45) that makes the priesthood functional and sets us apart as the few who are both called and chosen. Following that list of instructions, the Lord uses the word *then* to commence the list of promises of priesthood power and exaltation: "*Then* shall thy confidence wax strong in the presence of God; and the doctrine of the priesthood shall distil upon thy soul as the dews from heaven. The Holy Ghost shall be thy constant companion, and thy scepter an unchanging scepter of righteousness and truth; and thy dominion shall be an everlasting dominion, and without compulsory means it shall flow unto thee forever and ever."[740]

Contrasting Babylon with Zion, let us examine these instructions as they apply to our representing Christ and as they summon power in the priesthood.

---

735   3 Nephi 9:18; John 8:12.
736   Matthew 5:14.
737   Mosiah 18:9.
738   Abraham 1:18.
739   3 Nephi 27:27.
740   D&C 121:45–46; emphasis added.

## No Power or Influence Can or Ought to Be Maintained by Virtue of the Priesthood

At the great council in heaven, Satan proposed a frightening doctrine that would forever differentiate his kingdom, Babylon, from God's kingdom, Zion. That doctrine would also distinguish Satan's *priestcraft* from God's *priesthood*. This doctrine was one of control and force. To become a disciple of Satan and to gain membership in his great and abominable church[741] would require the sacrifice of personal agency. From that moment until now, control and force, which limit or nullify agency, have characterized Satan's kingdom, his doctrines, and his power, or *priestcraft*.

Any manifestation of priestcraft is dangerous. When Nehor first introduced it among the Nephites, Alma the Elder quickly moved to abolish it lest priestcraft become a cancer and consume the nation. He said, "Behold, this is the first time that priestcraft has been introduced among this people. And behold, thou art not only guilty of priestcraft, but hast endeavored to enforce it by the sword; *and were priestcraft to be enforced among this people it would prove their entire destruction.*"[742] Satan's church and kingdom, Babylon, can always be detected by its implementation of force; and the worst manifestation of force is seen when it is employed to enrich, expand the influence of, or draw attention to its perpetrator. Zion people are expressly forbidden to "exercise control or dominion or compulsion upon the souls of the children of men, in any degree of unrighteousness." When a priesthood holder steps into this territory, even in the smallest degree, he suddenly ceases to represent God. Then the heavens retreat, the Spirit is grieved and withdraws, the man is left unto himself, and finally he is the subject of the pronouncement: "Amen to the priesthood or authority of that man."[743] Unfortunately, "it is the nature and disposition of almost all men [the many], as soon as they get a little authority, as they suppose, they will immediately begin to exercise unrighteous dominion."[744]

This is priestcraft; this is Babylon—the appetite for power and influence by means of control and force.

Joseph Fielding McConkie and Robert L. Millet wrote:

> The only true antidote to priestcraft is charity (see 2 Nephi 26:30–31). It is interesting to note that the opposite of charity is priestcraft. Whereas priestcrafts oppress the laborer to increase profits (priestcraft is adhered to by their proponents as a religion— "priests" who follow this philosophy), charity elevates the poor. Priestcraft draws attention to self while charity draws attention to Christ. Priestcraft seeks to

---

741   1 Nephi 13:5–34; 14:3–17; 22:13–14; 2 Nephi 6:12; 28:18; D&C 29:21.
742   Alma 1:12; emphasis added.
743   D&C 121:37.
744   D&C 121:39.

become a light while charity points to the true light.
There is no room in priestcraft for love—only profit:
"This is a business decision." Priestcrafts taken to
extreme result in murder, thievery, dishonesty, sexual
sin, envy, malice, taking God's name in vain. The
person who practices these things shall perish, while
the laborer in Zion is commanded to avoid priestcrafts and labor for Zion and not for money [riches].
This life becomes the great experiment, for the poor
are ever with us. Where is our heart, and what are
our eternal desires?[745]

## Zion's Approach to Agency

Zion's approach to power and influence is exactly opposite that of Babylon's. Because of
our approach, we Zion people qualify as the chosen few. Power and influence naturally
flow to all Zion people, both priesthood holders and faithful women, because the Lord
makes us *lights* in a dark world, and our light draws people to *the* Light, Jesus Christ.
Whereas Babylon would use the resulting power and influence to enrich and exalt
herself, Zion adopts Ammon's philosophy of being "wise, yet harmless."[746] If the Lord
empowers us by means of the priesthood, and if he shines his light on us to garner the
attention of others, we must consecrate that power and influence back to him to further
his redemptive work. If we will do so, the Lord will increase our power and influence
among his children in proportion to our righteousness and our willingness to consecrate
ourselves and engage in his work.

Being "wise, yet harmless" speaks to honoring another person's agency. As we function within the priesthood, we offer loving instruction and persuasion without force or
coercion. We create situations and an environment of choice, giving people opportunities
to use their agency to experiment with and embrace gospel principles. When we interact
with family, friends, associates, or people within our stewardship, we will honor their
agency and stand with God as our partner, never stepping in front of him and always
acting as the Holy Ghost directs. We will take Jesus Christ as our example, as President
Hugh B. Brown explained: "The Lord himself, though all powerful, refuses to use force
to accomplish his purposes. Christ's obedience was always voluntary and love-inspired.
He has said that his work and his glory is to bring to pass the immortality and eternal life
of man, but this he will not do by force."[747]

Such a course invites the Spirit, who brings with him the power and influence of
the priesthood.

---

745   McConkie and Millet, *Doctrinal Commentary on the Book of Mormon*, 3:5.
746   Alma 18:21.
747   Brown, *Continuing the Quest*, 228–29.

## Persuasion versus Babylon's Counterparts

Babylon will make its argument at all costs. Babylon is always right; she is rigid, inflexible, and unyielding. Babylon's intention is to win; therefore, we can spot the Babylonian tactic by its competitive nature. Babylon will attempt to employ negative campaigning, intimidation, manipulation, domineering speech, bullying, and coercing to beat down and discourage another person until that person surrenders. A goal of Babylon is subjugation, and Babylon will employ her overbearing manner to browbeat until she achieves victory.

Babylon enjoys debating everything. Babylon will contend, bicker, disagree, and oppose until she prevails and succeeds in wearing down her opponent until that person surrenders. Babylon will not relent; her method is loveless, and she engenders distrust, discouragement, and broken relationships. Unfortunately, many of those who are called adopt this philosophy and thereby sacrifice both their right to the companionship of the Spirit and efficacy in the priesthood.

## Zion's Patient Persuasion

Conversely, Zion, the few who are called and chosen, will entreat another person by means of patient reasoning, gentle urging, and encouragement. Zion attempts to win someone over with love and empathy. Zion is a good listener and seeks to understand the other person's concerns and points of view. Zion seeks common ground without sacrificing her standards. Zion's conversations are safe: "wise, yet harmless." There is no threat that anything will be used against the other person.

Zion is a leader who carefully draws the other person forward, attempting to induce, convince, or influence without using force. If and when another person finally aligns himself with Zion's philosophy, it will be by choice.

Zion's goal is to strengthen relationships, despite differences. In the end, love grows, understanding increases, unity comes into view, equality becomes possible, and mutual respect is achieved. Because Zion represents Christlike attributes, the Holy Ghost finds a home in a Zion-like person, and consequently priesthood power and influence increase in that person.

## Patience and Long-suffering

Babylon thinks only of herself. Babylon is impatient and intolerant of delays or opposing opinions. Babylon becomes frustrated, put out, and restless when she feels she has been imposed upon. Babylon hates being asked to wait for, wait with, or wait upon someone. Babylon is eager to move on and pursue her own desires, and she becomes agitated or irritated when she is asked to sacrifice or change her mind. Babylon despises being bothered. Babylon's time is neither given nor shared without a profitable return: *Time is money!* is her motto. Therefore, Babylon dictates the terms and the disbursement of her time. Too many of the *many who are called and not chosen* are seduced by this doctrine! And too many thereby grieve the Spirit and lose the rights to the priesthood.

Conversely, Zion's time is consecrated for the building up of God's kingdom and the establishment of Zion. Two identifying traits of a Zion person are patience and long-suffering—the unselfish giving of consecrated time for the blessing of God's children. Only the Zion-like people, the *few who are called and chosen,* will embrace this doctrine and grow in priesthood power and influence.

Let us examine these attributes separately, beginning with patience.

## Patience

Priesthood holders are commanded to be patient and long-suffering.[748] Not only in patience will we possess our souls,[749] but we will acquire an attribute of Deity. An astute institute student wrote: "Nothing could be as frightening as an impatient God." Who could believe in a God whose patience wanes or whose love is limited? There is no place for impatience in the priesthood or in Zion.

Because Zion people represent God, they are patient. As patience applies to faith in Jesus Christ, the virtue of patience constitutes waiting and anticipating with "a perfect brightness of hope"[750] for the Lord's deliverance. Therefore, patience is not waiting with the feeling of impending doom; patience, according to Elder Neal A. Maxwell, is an active principle. It is being willing to submit to God's will and submit to what the scriptures call the "process of time."[751]

Through righteous waiting we learn Godlike patience.

> Patience is waiting *for* someone.
> Patience is waiting *with* someone.
> Patience is waiting *upon,* or serving, someone.

Patience requires faith, which is often developed by the trial of our patience. Elder Maxwell warned that our trial of patience can turn to our discouragement and turning from God. Impatience, he said, suggests that we think we know better than God knows what is best, and thereby, through our impatience, we question God's omniscience. Thus, when our patience is being tried, our faith is simultaneously being tried. Our challenge, then, is to patiently and gracefully submit to those things that the Lord "seeth fit to inflict upon [us]," as did Alma's people who submitted "cheerfully and with patience to all the will of the Lord."[752]

As patience pertains to long-suffering, Elder Maxwell said our course of life is often correct enough, but we need to persist in that course long enough for the desired result.

---

748    D&C 121:41.
749    D&C 101:38.
750    2 Nephi 31:20.
751    Maxwell, "Patience," 28; referencing Moses 7:21.
752    Maxwell, "Patience," 28; see also Mosiah 3:19; 24:15.

In any case, when we discover that our patience is being tried, we might expect that our faith will also be tried; and when we discover that our capacity for patience is increasing, we might also expect that our faith is increasing. We simply cannot become like God without having developed the ability to demonstrate infinite patience with perfect faith. Therefore, it should come as no surprise that God would provide us with multiple opportunities to develop patience and faith by having them regularly tried.[753]

The law of the harvest is a product of patience. This law and the principle of patience are inseparable. "Whatsoever ye sow, that shall ye also reap."[754] Between the sowing and the reaping are patience and long-suffering. The quality of the harvest is dependent upon our patient actions *after* we sow the seed. Elder Maxwell wrote, "Paul confirms that those who 'inherit the promises' are those who have triumphed 'through faith and patience' (Hebrews 6:12). Abraham 'obtained the promise,' but only 'after he had patiently endured' (Hebrews 6:15). Long-suffering, endurance, and patience are designed to be constant companions, as are faith, hope, and charity."[755] The few who are called and chosen, who are faith-filled, patient Zion people, cling to the Lord's promise: "Verily I say unto you my friends, fear not, let your hearts be comforted; yea, rejoice evermore, and in everything give thanks; waiting patiently on the Lord, for your prayers have entered into the ears of the Lord of Sabaoth, and are recorded with this seal and testament—the Lord hath sworn and decreed that they shall be granted. Therefore, he giveth this promise unto you, with an immutable covenant that they shall be fulfilled; and all things wherewith you have been afflicted shall work together for your good, and to my name's glory, saith the Lord."[756]

If patience and faith are companions, Elder Maxwell continued, so are patience and agency. When we lose our patience, we reveal an ugly side of us that is associated with Babylon; this side becomes irritated when it feels it is being inconvenienced. We must remember that at the first moment of agitated impatience, we cross over into Babylon. On the other hand, Zion people are submissive and forbearing; they do not try to override others or hasten an outcome that would abuse another person's agency.[757] Neither God nor a Zion person would do that. As always, when we consider these things we are struck with the fact that there are only two ways: Zion's faith and patience or Babylon's selfishness and impatience. There are no other choices, and the consequences for making that choice are exact opposites.

Patience, faith, long-suffering, and endurance are inseparably connected to God's *timing*. "It is in length of patience, and endurance, and forbearance that so much of what is good in mankind and womankind is shown."[758] The Lord's timetable is proprietary to him.[759] "My words are sure and shall not fail, but all things must come to pass in their time."[760]

---

753   Maxwell, *Lord, Increase Our Faith*, 39.
754   D&C 6:33.
755   Maxwell, *Lord, Increase Our Faith*, 39.
756   D&C 98:2.
757   Maxwell, "Patience," 28.
758   "Talks to Young Men," *Improvement Era*, Sept. 1903.
759   Dallin H. Oaks, "Timing," 11.
760   D&C 64:31–32.

The fact that patience requires faith in God and his timing brings us to the issue of trust. Do we or do we not trust God and his way of doing things? Do we trust that his timing is as perfect as he is? Or do we think that he is imperfect in this one area and ought to take counsel from us about timing? Elder Maxwell wrote: "The issue for us is trusting God enough to trust also His timing. If we can truly believe He has our welfare at heart, may we not let His plans unfold as He thinks best? The same is true with the second coming and with all those matters wherein our faith needs to include faith in the Lord's timing for us personally, not just in His overall plans and purposes."[761] Both Elder Maxwell and Elder Oaks concluded that we cannot truly exhibit faith in God without also trusting in his will and timing.[762]

Priesthood holders who are classified as the few know that time is on their side because God is on their side. God will cause that "all things [will] come to pass in their time."[763] This attitude of patient long-suffering speaks to the level of faith that all Zion people develop over years of righteous living; they know that they have never been let down by God, and they know that all good things come to pass with perfect timing. Prefacing the Constitution of the Priesthood, in Doctrine and Covenants 121, the Lord rhetorically asked , "How long can rolling waters remain impure? What power shall stay the heavens?" Then he answers with a profound promise to the patient and long-suffering: "As well might man stretch forth his puny arm to stop the Missouri river in its decreed course, or to turn it up stream, as to hinder the Almighty from pouring down knowledge from heaven upon the heads of the Latter-day Saints."[764] Clearly, our prayers have been heard, blessings are being prepared, eventually those blessings will flow, and our patience will be rewarded.

Priesthood faith, Zion faith, is this: By staying our course in patience and in faith, we facilitate, rather than frustrate, God's work. Because we have developed the ability to endure in patience, and because we are sufficiently acquainted with God to know that he will not divert from his decreed course, we know that we can persist in confidence with the belief that God has a perfect and a *perfectly-timed* plan for us; we are confident that he will enact that plan "in his own time, and in his own way, and according to his own will."[765] Neither the priesthood nor Zion can function with a belief system that is otherwise placed.

## Long-suffering

Priesthood holders cannot effectively minister among God's children unless they develop the attribute of long-suffering. To suffer long with someone is to suffer [allow] him his right to preserve and exercise his agency. Thus, long-suffering is characteristic of priesthood holders in Zion. To suffer long is to suffer with a person as we watch him suffer

---

761    Maxwell, *Even As I Am,* 93.
762    Dallin H. Oaks, "Timing," 11.
763    D&C 64:31–32.
764    D&C 121:33.
765    D&C 88:68.

the consequences of his actions, even when those consequences do not motivate him to change. To suffer long is to suffer in urgent prayer that perhaps a change of heart might occur and finally drive an errant soul to the Savior, who has suffered for him. For the few who are called and chosen, such righteous long-suffering is counted as a sacrifice, and, as we know, it is sacrifice that "brings forth the blessings of heaven."[766] When we suffer long with and for "one of the least" of God's children who might be temporarily *least* because of his poor choices, the Lord counts our long-suffering as a sacrificial service to the Savior.[767] Because the Savior can be in debt to no one, he rewards our sacrifice with an incredible return—"an hundredfold."[768] Truly, he is the most generous paymaster.

President Kimball, quoting Elder Orson F. Whitney, wrote: "No pain that we suffer, no trial that we experience is wasted. It ministers to our education, to the development of such qualities as patience, faith, fortitude and humility. All that we suffer and all that we endure, especially when we endure it patiently, builds up our characters, purifies our hearts, expands our souls, and makes us more tender and charitable, more worthy to be called the children of God . . . and it is through sorrow and suffering, toil and tribulation, that we gain the education that we come here to acquire and which will make us more like our Father and Mother in heaven." Then President Kimball concluded: "Suffering can make saints of people as they learn patience, long-suffering, and self-mastery. The sufferings of our Savior were part of his education."[769]

Zion people have suffered long in the heat of the Lord's crucible and emerged as gold. Priesthood holders in Zion exercise their authority as a power by suffering long in the pursuit of righteousness. When our ability to suffer long is tried beyond our apparent limit to endure, and when we search our souls for something more to give only to find an empty reservoir, we can take comfort in Elder Maxwell's perspective: "The dues of discipleship are high indeed, and how much we can *take* so often determines how much we can then *give!*"[770] The purpose of long-suffering is growth.

Patience and long-suffering are Christlike traits that both strengthen Zion people and identify us with that holy ideal. By developing these virtues, the purposes of the priesthood find fulfillment. We become better equipped to stand as witnesses and representatives of God at all times and in all places; we provide a sacred precinct for the Holy Ghost to dwell; and our power in the priesthood increases so that we might better do the work of God.

## Gentleness and Meekness

Babylon presents itself as intense, loud, wild, nonconforming, and untamed. In dealing with people, Babylon is heavy-handed, controlling, competitive, and unkind. All these characteristics are opposite Zion's gentility and meekness. To Babylon meek is weak; she

---

766   "Praise to the Man," *Hymns*, no. 27.
767   Matthew 25:40.
768   Matthew 19:29.
769   Kimball, *Faith Precedes the Miracle*, 98.
770   Maxwell, *Notwithstanding My Weakness*, 63.

is wont to persecute those who possess this attribute.[771] Babylon flexes her muscle; she is proud, domineering, stubborn, and obstinate; she is unregenerate (meaning unrepentant), unwilling to be spiritually reformed, and loath to be reconciled to change. In her sinful state, Babylon lacks moral restraint and indulges in sensual pleasures and vices. To the degree that a person exhibits any of these traits, he is Babylonian in nature and stands opposite God. The Spirit flees such a person, and his authority in the priesthood withers, if it does not cease altogether.

On the other hand, Zion people are gentle and meek. Interestingly, the Constitution of the Priesthood combines these attributes in a single phrase: "gentleness and meekness."[772] That these traits are inseparable cannot be denied. Jesus is our example; he is both gentle and meek.[773] We see Jesus' gentleness constantly displayed as he ministered among the people. He would gently encourage them to raise their sights. To those who were sick and afflicted, he would gently take them aside and work with them to increase their faith. He would use carefully worded conversation in an effort to establish contact with them and raise their confidence. Then he would heal them. He sought no acclaim; he desired only to give freely of what he had. Jesus was gentle and meek.

Likewise, a priesthood holder in Zion is expected to be of a considerate and kindly disposition. He is amiable and tender, not harsh or severe. Mild and soft are words that describe him. He is submissive, refined, modest, and polite. Because he holds the priesthood and has been anointed to become a king and priest unto God, a priesthood holder in Zion appears noble and courteous, as did King Benjamin, whose chivalrous and kindly acts endeared him to his people. Moreover, a priesthood holder in Zion is a peacemaker, another characteristic associated with gentleness and meekness. In dealing with people and by virtue of his ordination, he can soothe, pacify, and tame the distressed or wild heart. Such a person, as we have pointed out, is like Ammon—"wise yet harmless."[774] He employs his knowledge and power not to overwhelm, astonish, or subjugate, but to engage, reason, persuade, and testify—all of which create an environment where the Spirit of the Lord might do his work of conversion.

A priesthood holder in Zion is meek like his Master, and he, like Jesus, "shall inherit the earth."[775] Meekness is a childlike quality[776] the Savior attributes to himself[777] and therefore expects of everyone who enters into his holy order. The meek are not easily incited to anger or annoyance. They are humble, teachable, and willing to listen and learn; they seek for and act upon the whisperings of the Spirit. The meek are childlike in their submission to the Lord, and they place his wisdom above their own.[778] Clearly, the priesthood would become a power in such people.

---

771   2 Nephi 9:30; 28:13; Helaman 6:39.
772   D&C 121:41.
773   Matthew 11:29.
774   Alma 18:22.
775   3 Nephi 12:6.
776   Mosiah 3:19.
777   Matthew 11:29.
778   Hinckley, *Stand a Little Taller,* 18.

Taking the Savior as their example, the meek become lowly in heart, which means they prepare themselves "to hear the word of the Lord."[779] Such priesthood holders in Zion are filled with faith in Christ; they humble themselves, repent, enter into the new and everlasting covenant through baptism, and receive a remission of sins, which "bringeth meekness, and lowliness of heart; and because of meekness and lowliness of heart cometh the visitation of the Holy Ghost, which Comforter filleth with hope and perfect love."[780]

The few who are called and chosen for eternal life, the meek of Zion and the lowly of heart, are those who "find rest to their souls."[781] This rest is the glory of the Lord.[782] Thus, priesthood holders in Zion live so as to feel the love of God and receive divine confirmation that they are right before their Maker.[783]

Such Zion people seek to become meek and lowly of heart so that they can obtain exclusive spiritual gifts: faith, hope, and charity. Any other lifestyle is defined as "vain," the scripture says, "for none is acceptable before God, save the meek and lowly in heart."[784] Moreover, priesthood holders in Zion seek to become meek because that virtue gives them access to the Lord's grace,[785] the principle of heavenly help or strength that comes through Jesus Christ.[786] Hence, they strive to become gentle, meek, lowly of heart, "humble, patient, full of love, willing to submit to all things which the Lord seeth fit to inflict upon him, even as a child doth submit to his father."[787] The Lord's promise to such priesthood holders and the faithful women who are their counterparts is that they will gain an eternal inheritance on the earth,[788] the destiny of which is to become Zion and a celestial kingdom to those who inherit it.[789] To the few who are called and chosen, the gentle and meek people of Zion, the priesthood is a living, vibrant principle of power.

## Feigned and Unfeigned Love

Babylon has a variety of definitions of love, but all are counterfeits, none of which approach the true meaning of the word. Babylon's love is *feigned love*, meaning imagined, pretended, insincere, manipulative, or contrived love. Whereas true love equalizes and unites, false love is selfish, lustful, domineering, and divisive. Babylon's love serves self, while Zion's love serves another. Babylon's love is a foolish and often extravagant passion, a temporary juvenile attraction, or an admiration that is unreasoning and short-lived. Worse, Babylon's version of love is wholly ungrounded in any spiritual activity or standard; it has no celestial underpinnings that allow it to endure. Babylon's love might start as an infatuated dream, but it will end up as a nightmare.

---

779   Largey, *Book of Mormon Reference Companion* 524.
780   Moroni 8:26.
781   Alma 37:33–34.
782   D&C 84:24.
783   Smith, *Gospel Doctrine*, 58, 125–26.
784   Moroni 7:43–44.
785   Ether 12:26–27.
786   Bible Dictionary, "Grace," 697.
787   Mosiah 3:19.
788   3 Nephi 12:5.
789   D&C 88:17–26; 130:9.

A sad expression of Babylon's love is any form of forbidden sexual dalliance, which Nephi predicted would become epidemic in the last days. In a vision of latter-day Babylon, he may have seen rampant sexual experimentation—everything from inappropriate kissing and touching to out-of-wedlock intercourse, same-sex attraction, and other loathsome sexual perversions. He was so disgusted with the scene that he described it with a single word—*whoredoms.* Then he pronounced a certain and severe penalty on those who would participate unrepentantly in such actions: "for whoso doeth them shall perish;"[790] "wo, wo, wo be unto them, saith the Lord God Almighty, for they shall be thrust down to hell!"[791] Nephi foresaw that this sexual cancer would spread throughout the world and sicken the whole of humanity; even the "chosen few" of Zion would need to beware. While mourning, he wrote: "because of whoredoms, they have all gone astray save it be a few, who are the humble followers of Christ; nevertheless, they are led, that in many instances they do err because they are taught by the precepts of men."[792]

The "chosen few" of Zion have been amply warned to beware lest Babylon's counterfeits for love become so alluring that they ensnare the elect and drag them down to hell. Clearly, there is no future in Babylon's love. It is designed to decoy and trap its victims and lead them down to misery. Those who embrace Babylon's love—and may even feel a form of real affection for a time—discover soon enough that this love is ultimately destructive and discouraging; it leads to break-ups and disdain for one another. There is no future in it; and there is no future in the priesthood for the person who engages in such actions *in any degree.* The priesthood holder who does so ceases to represent Christ, the Spirit departs, and priesthood power becomes nonexistent.

Zion's love is called charity. It is "love unfeigned." In other words, it is sincere, genuine, true, unaffected, uncontrived love. Charity has no selfish intent. It is forever giving, patient, sacrificing, loyal, and trustworthy. Zion's love flows from heaven, down through us, to a loved one or to someone we are serving; therefore, charity is forever connected to the True Vine, who makes it an eternal principle.

Significantly, this quality of love is unattainable without receiving it as a spiritual endowment. We simply cannot come by it naturally. Charity will always be a spiritual gift delivered and enhanced by the Holy Ghost. It must be sought after as we would seek after any spiritual gift, such as the gift of healing or the gift of testimony.[793] Mormon exhorted us to "pray unto the Father with all the energy of heart, that ye may be filled with *this* love."[794] Righteous priesthood holders in Zion who possess this gift will also have priesthood power.

According to President Joseph F. Smith, "Charity . . . is the greatest principle in existence."[795] Charity is the "pure love of Christ,"[796] therefore, charity is *saving* love. The Apostle John taught that the man or woman who loves best knows God best: "Beloved,

---

790  2 Nephi 26:10, 14, 32.
791  2 Nephi 28:15.
792  2 Nephi 28:14.
793  D&C 46:10–30.
794  Moroni 7:48; emphasis added.
795  Smith, Conference Report, Apr. 1917, 4.
796  Moroni 7:47.

let us love one another: for love is of God; and every one that loveth is born of God, and knoweth God." For emphasis, John rephrased this scripture to read, "He that loveth not knoweth not God; for God is love."[797] That is, the man or woman who does not love well does not know God well. The more like God we become, the more love we have to give, and the more love we have to give, the more power we have to save others. Priesthood holders in Zion can be identified by this quality of love. Such Zion people who are united in charitable love obtain saving power that is perhaps only exceeded by the saving power of God.

## What Is "True Love"?

There is a vast difference between being *in love* and being *loving*. Babylon leans one way while Zion leans the other. True love—charity—is built on three sets of triplets. The first set is that of charity's essential qualities:
1. Complete loyalty
2. Complete sacrifice
3. Complete trust

The second set has to do with patience:
1. "I will wait *for* you"
2. "I will wait *with* you"
3. "I will wait *upon* you"; that is, "I will serve you."

The third set has to do with how love is received, expressed, and given. Referencing Elder Max Caldwell, H. Wallace Goddard observed that charity has three meanings:
1. Love *from* Christ
2. Love *for* Christ
3. Love *like* Christ

The process of loving begins when we feel Jesus reaching after us *(love from Christ)*. Goddard writes:

> Somewhere along the path the miracle of His love
> breaks down our resistance. As we begin to understand
> His goodness and redemptiveness, we are changed. We
> are filled with a profound awe and gratitude for Him.
> We experience the stirrings of hope. Without this con-
> version, we are nothing spiritually (1 Cor. 13:2; 2 Nephi
> 26:30; Moroni 7:44, 46; D&C 18:19). As the amazing
> truth of His unrelenting love pierces our hearts, we are
> led to the second kind of charity, *love for Christ.* 'We

---

797   1 John 4:7–8.

love him, because he first loved us' (1 John 1:19). . . .
As soon as we glimpse His love for us we instinctively
love Him in return. We fall at His feet and bathe them
with tears of gratitude. Why would He do all He has
done to love and rescue my flawed soul? Why??? The
answer is charity. As we feel the love from Him and for
Him, we naturally *love like Him.* We become saviors on
Mount Zion with Him. "Charity is first and foremost
the redemptive love that Jesus offers all of us. It is the
love from Christ. He is the model of charity—which
never faileth."[798]

With regard to our loving *like* Christ, our salvation depends on giving charitable service.[799]

In each of these descriptions of charity, or "love unfeigned," we observe that true
love means being *loving,* which is being charitable or "purely" loving as Christ loves.[800]
Charity, then, is more than a feeling; it is a principle of power that allows us to lift and to
save another. Therefore, this quality of love is central to our inviting the Spirit into our
lives, to becoming Zion-like, and to obtaining power in the priesthood.

## To Love First

How does love begin? By someone loving first. "Herein is love, not that we loved God,
but that he loved us. . . . We love him, because he first loved us."[801]

Love grows and endures on the principle of extending love. In that way, Zion's love
is different from Babylon's love. Zion people love first, *then* love is returned—first one,
then the other. It is an oft-repeated scriptural formula that has many applications. For
example, "Blessed are the merciful: for they shall obtain mercy."[802] Giving away what we
have results in blessings returning to us with increase.[803] Loving quickly and loving first
are key qualities of true love.

Love actively seeks love; that is, love is comfortable in the company of love. Love
cleaves unto love like light cleaves unto light.[804] Moreover, as we have noted, true love—
Zion's love—is saving love, the kind of love that the scriptures say *never faileth!*[805] This
love lifts another so that both might be exalted. John Greenleaf Whittier said: "I'll lift
you, and you lift me, and we'll both ascend together."

Of course, loving in this way is fraught with risk. Love unfeigned, which is love
freely given, might not immediately be returned. Edith Hamilton wrote: "When love

798   Goddard, *Drawing Heaven into Your Marriage,* 111.
799   Jensen, "Living after the Manner of Happiness," 56.
800   Moroni 7:47.
801   1 John 4:10, 19.
802   Matthew 5:7.
803   Packer, "The Candle of the Lord," 33.
804   D&C 88:40.
805   Moroni 7:46; emphasis added.

meets no return the result is suffering and the greater the love the greater the suffering. There can be no greater suffering than to love purely and perfectly one, who is
bent upon evil and self-destruction. That was what God endured at the hands of men."[806]
Elder Maxwell explained that the pain we feel in such moments provides us with an
appreciation for the Savior, which appreciation we might not otherwise gain.[807] Nevertheless, love we must, for only love unfeigned has the power to do the redemptive work
of the Father and the Son. If we seek to love God's children back to him, which is our
covenantal obligation, we must start by loving God better. This effort increases our
capacity to love. Then we are in a position to better love someone else.

*Loving God so that we can love better* is a key to becoming both a Zion person and
a priesthood holder who wields priesthood power. Loving God so that we can love
better requires that we love for the sake of loving and with no selfish intent; that is,
we love because we are loving beings and cannot do otherwise. Although we realize
that our loving disposition might make us vulnerable (we might extend love to someone before that person returns love to us), we nevertheless love quickly and first. The
nature of the true love within us presses us to persist in loving until love breaks down
every barrier, softens a hardened heart, embraces that person in an unbreakable bond,
and finally urges that person home. Someone has said that a person is never in more
need of understanding than when he is nonapproachable, and he is never more in need
of love than when he is unlovable.[808]

Zion people love quickly and first with the pure love of Christ. They love for
the same reasons that the Lord loves—to lift, rescue, and redeem. They keep an eye
on love's perfect conclusion: to love as God loves. The priesthood flourishes in those
who love.

## Love Perfected

Being loving to another person is not only an expansive principle but a perfecting one
that draws God near. John said, "If we love one another, God dwelleth in us, and his love
is perfected in us."[809] Additionally, by loving acts we are endowed with a greater measure
of the Holy Ghost, the "vitalizer" of priesthood power: "Hereby know we that we dwell in
him, and he in us, because he hath given us of his Spirit."[810] As we abide in the cycle of
giving, receiving, and giving love again, our love grows until it eventually becomes perfect: "God is love; and he that dwelleth in love dwelleth in God, and God in him. Herein
is our love made perfect."[811] This is the condition of Zion and an essential principle upon
which priesthood authority becomes priesthood power.

---

806   Hamilton, *Spokesman for God,* 112.
807   Maxwell, "Enduring Well," 7.
808   Skidmore, "What Part Should the Teenager Play in a Family?" *Improvement Era,* Jan. 1952.
809   1 John 4:12.
810   1 John 4:13.
811   1 John 4:16–17.

## No Fear in Love

Perhaps one of the greatest benefits of loving is ceasing to be afraid: "There is no fear in love; but perfect love casteth out fear." Here we see an unmistakable contrast in Zion's and Babylon's love. If our circumstance is causing us to fear, we might reexamine the foundation upon which our love is built, "because fear hath torment." There is no future in such supposed love: "He that feareth is not made perfect in love."[812]

So what is "perfect love"? Perfect love is God's love. When we realize how perfectly he loves us, as manifested in the Atonement of his Son—whereby we are enabled to overcome all our weaknesses, all of our sins, and the things that cause us anxiety and weigh us down—we know we are covered. And because we are covered, or protected, by this perfect love, we need never fear.  Although we cannot love perfectly, or as God loves—yet, we can and must pray for charity with all the energy of our heart. And the closer we get to loving as he loves, which we can only do through the Atonement (because only in him and through him can we be made perfect), we will be able to experience that kind of perfect love and extend that love to others.

As an example, consider the terrified child who runs to its mother for comfort. Because of her love, the mother is capable of cradling the child in her arms and speaking words of consolation and reassurance. Her love casts out of the child the torment of fear. The child feels safe and secure. Moreover, because the child knows its mother's love is constant, the child has little reason to fear. By extension, when we, motivated by love, rush to the aid of someone whose circumstances have led them to fear, we have power to calm the torment and restore calm. Additionally, because we love, those with whom we associate have no reason to fear in our presence. They know that our love for them is unconditional and constant. Hence, "there is no fear in love; but perfect love casteth out fear."

To shift from Babylon's love to Zion's love, we must regroup and become loving as Jesus is loving, and then the love we give quickly and first will return to us with increase. As love grows, we will feel fear decrease. Neither Zion nor the priesthood can flourish in fear or lack of love.

## Love—The Greatest Power

Love—true love, Zion love, perfect love—is the greatest power in the universe. For that reason it is linked inseparably with the powers of the priesthood. Love motivates God to do all that he does.[813] The greatest expression of his love is to give life and to redeem his children. Inspired by love, he invites his children to experience his quality of life, for therein is his joy made full.[814] By following his example—giving life and redeeming life—our joy is also made full.[815]

---

812   1 John 4:18.
813   Moses 1:39.
814   3 Nephi 17:20.
815   Alma 26:11, 16; 3 Nephi 27:31; 28:10.

Eternal marriage is the ultimate expression of love; eternal marriage is the end purpose of the new and everlasting covenant and the oath and covenant of the priesthood. There is no truer statement than this: "All the stars in the universe and all the seraphic hosts of heaven can be traced back to two people who fell in love, knelt at an altar, and made an eternal covenant." Marriage is the perfection and hope of our love. By love, God creates children and places them on earth, and by love unfeigned he works with them and offers them salvation and exaltation.

There can be no greater power than love. By love we exemplify God. By love we pursue his lifestyle so that we might give and redeem life. By love Zion is established. By love the priesthood becomes operative.

## Kindness

Babylon is not kind. Because Babylon is self-serving and has little regard for another's feelings, she will only pretend benevolence when she can somehow benefit. Otherwise, Babylon is loath to extend warmhearted nurturing or to act considerately. Babylon insists that her personal needs be met over every other consideration. Babylon is neither humane, sympathetic, generous, nor forgiving. Babylon is friendly only when she can profit thereby. Babylon is neither forbearing nor tolerant; rather, she is thoughtless, inconsiderate, mean, merciless, cruel, and pitiless. Whenever one or any combination of these traits is exhibited in covenant people, they immediately assume the appearance of the author of these characteristics and become Babylonian. Then the Holy Ghost departs from them, they abandon Zion, and their power in the priesthood comes to an abrupt halt.

Zion people, conversely, exemplify the Savior, who is the perfection of kindness. Because Jesus is their true friend,[816] they strive to likewise be true friends. They are kind, caring, generous, and warmhearted. When they interact with other people, they are charitable, considerate, forbearing, and tolerant. They are quick to show sympathy and understanding, and they are humane and compassionate. Zion people are solicitous; that is, they are sincerely concerned, anxious to help, and eagerly attentive. They are nurturing and empathetic, unwilling to allow hurt or permit *lack* to exist among them. When they discover poverty in any form, they attack it with mercy, tenderness, pity, and kindness. Their actions qualify them to summon priesthood power from heaven, where perfect kindness governs the authority of God.

## Pure Knowledge versus False Knowledge

"Pure knowledge," according the Constitution of the Priesthood, "shall greatly enlarge the soul without hypocrisy, and without guile."[817] This statement stands in stark contrast to the reality of much of man's knowledge. Telestial knowledge, although valuable, often poses as truth, while it blinds the mind, retards the soul, and holds its captives in igno-

---

816    D&C 104:1.
817    D&C 121:42.

rance or oppressive traditions. While man fumbles around trying to discover the truth, he would be better served if he appealed to the Source of truth and admitted that all truth has a divine origin.

A reverse reading of the above scripture reveals two devious characteristics of those who tout man's knowledge as truth: hypocrisy and guile. Hypocrisy is that action and "the practice of professing beliefs, feelings, or virtues that one does not hold or possess." Hypocrisy is "falseness."[818] That is, while knowing that the "truths" he is advancing are not completely sound, the promoter nevertheless presents them as such for sole purpose of personal gain—money, power, and popularity. Such supposed "experts" are highly rewarded by the world for their "knowledge."

The second characteristic, guile, enforces the first, hypocrisy. Guile is defined as "treacherous cunning, and skillful deceit."[819] Together, hypocrisy and guile, applied to man's knowledge are, at least, risky and often destructive, and that knowledge is frequently advanced for the gain and praise of those who forward their ideas.

In the 123rd section of the Doctrine and Covenants, Joseph Smith condemned such knowledge and the perpetrators of it, and he identified the evil source and strategy. While he was held in Liberty Jail, he penned a letter to the Saints regarding their duty to expose and counter their persecutors. Much of what he said speaks to the issue of ignorance and oppressive traditions that promote guile, hypocrisy, and false knowledge. "It is an imperative duty we owe to God, to angels, with whom we shall be brought to stand, and also to ourselves, and to our wives and children, who have been made to bow down with grief, sorrow, and care, under the most damning hand of murder, tyranny, and oppression, supported and urged on and upheld by the influence of that spirit which hath so strongly riveted the creeds of the fathers, who have inherited lies, upon the hearts of the children, and filled the world with confusion, and has been growing stronger and stronger, and is now the very mainspring of all corruption, and the whole earth groans under the weight of its iniquity."

Satan is that oppressive spirit who has riveted creeds and lies upon the children of men, and the confusion he has caused is now so strong that it is the "mainspring of all corruption." The world groans under its weight. How successful has Satan been in perpetrating his lies? Apparently so successful that even he is astonished: "Which dark and blackening deeds are enough to make hell itself shudder, and to stand aghast and pale, and the hands of the very devil to tremble and palsy."

Consider the Prophet's description of this plague: "It is an iron yoke, it is a strong band; they are the very handcuffs, and chains, and shackles, and fetters of hell." As Zion people and as priesthood holders in Zion, what is our duty to dispel falsehoods and promote the truth? The Prophet gave the answer:

> Therefore it is an imperative duty that we owe, not
> only to our own wives and children, but to the widows

---

and fatherless, whose husbands and fathers have been
murdered under its iron hand. . . .

And also it is an imperative duty that we owe to
all the rising generation, *and to all the pure in heart*—

For there are many yet on the earth among all
sects, parties, and denominations, who are blinded by
the subtle craftiness of men, whereby they lie in wait to
deceive, and who are only kept from the truth because
they know not where to find it—

Therefore, that we should waste and wear out
our lives in bringing to light all the hidden things of
darkness, wherein we know them; and they are truly
manifest from heaven—

These should then be attended to with great ear-
nestness.

Our children and grandchildren, our fellow Saints, our brothers and sisters who have not
yet found the truth—all of these, including the "pure in heart," depend on us to defend
the truth and denounce error. Our future depends on it: "Let no man count them as
small things; for there is much which lieth in futurity, pertaining to the saints, which
depends upon these things."[820]

We must be so very careful in weighing man's knowledge against God's. In the last
days, many who are called to eternal life will become "foolish virgins"[821] and therefore
find themselves excluded from the marriage of the King's son. Beyond their indifferent
attitude toward preparing for the Bridegroom, these "virgins" are also foolish because
they have listened to the wrong voices. Jacob warned against such practices: "The wisdom of the learned is foolishness," he taught; "When men are learned they think they
are wise."[822]

Babylon thinks she is very wise. She examines the creations and workings of God
and attempts to explain them without adding God into the equation. Consequently,
godless teachings and theories abound. They come and go and are embraced as truth for
awhile, until finally truth rips through their fabric and they are exposed for what they
are—empty theories and falsehoods. But even when that happens, men do not repent;
they simply replace the old, godless teaching with another newer, wiser, godless teaching.

An example is the present theory of evolution. In a question-and-answer forum, gospel writer and scientist H. Clay Gorton answered the question of a young geology student
in South Africa. He wrote to the youth:

You state that the theory of evolution is demonstrable
and provable. That may be true only if you accept the *a*

---

820   D&C 123:7–15; emphasis added.
821   D&C 63:54.
822   2 Nephi 9:28.

*priori* premises on which it is based, and the methodology and accuracy of the experimental data.

The theory of evolution is based on and is a part of the more general theory of uniformitarianism, which states that changes in the earth's topology have occurred exclusively as the imperceptively slow erosion processes of rain, wind, freezing and thawing, and the counter imperceptively slow mountain uplift from tectonic plate motion. Catastrophism, the counter theory to uniformitarianism, which includes catastrophic flooding, volcanic action, earthquakes, meteoric impact and near misses by planetoids, has much more to commend it than does uniformitarianism. . . . Let me give you an example—

There is one and only one way of dating any geological, anthropological or paleontological event, and that is by the potassium-argon decay rate. Potassium, the most prevalent element in the earth's crust, has a radioisotope, K40, found in a concentration of the order of .01%. The half life of K40 is 1.8 times 10 to the 9th years, and it decays to the stable A40, which is a gas. While any rock is molten, any argon produced from K40 escapes, but if the rock is solid the argon is captured. The only dating process ever used to place a time line on any geological, anthropological or paleontological event is to measure the K40/A40 ratio in a sample of rock taken from the site. In the first place the date thus established does NOT measure the age of the site. It measures the age of the rock found at the site! Secondly, this measurement technique is highly unreliable, but its unreliability is never taken into account since it is the only possible way of dating into the distant past. So the method is accepted without question, as shown by the following experiment—

Two samples of volcanic rock were submitted for dating by the K/A decay method. One sample measured to be 65 million years old and the other, 2.5 billion years old. These two samples were taken from the lava flows from two volcanoes in Hawaii. The eruption from which the first sample was taken occurred in 1800 a.d., and the eruption from which the second sample was taken occurred in 1802 a.d.! When confronted with this data the researchers concluded that the two rocks could not have been part of the lava flow, but were picked up as debris while the flow was yet molten.

This demonstrates the tenacity with which any currently held scientific theory or method is held. Data that are contrary to the currently held theory are merely discarded. In truth, it takes a veritable scientific revolution to change the currently held theories of science. Each of the proponents of the theories of past ages, beginning with the Greeks, knew that they had the ultimate truth. But each was finally proven to be completely wrong and was replaced by the succeeding theory, in the same manner that the theories currently held to be true will also find their way into the dustbins of history.[823]

"O the foolishness of men!"[824] our Book of Mormon prophets lament, "for the reward of their pride and their foolishness they shall reap destruction; for because they yield unto the devil and choose works of darkness rather than light, therefore they must go down to hell."[825]

Babylon is the custodian and promoter of the false, transitory, foolish knowledge the world accepts as truth and wisdom. The Apostle Paul foresaw that the people in the last days would be "ever learning, and never able to come to the knowledge of the truth."[826] Nephi added, "There shall be many which shall teach after this manner, false and vain and foolish doctrines." He gives the reason: pride. People in the latter days, he said, "shall be puffed up in their hearts, and shall seek deep to hide their counsels from the Lord; and their works shall be in the dark." These false teachings will be widely accepted: "Yea, they have all gone out of the way; they have become corrupted." Why? "Because of pride, and because of false teachers, and false doctrine." Frighteningly, the children of Zion would not be exempt from buying into this counterfeit wisdom: "They have all gone astray save it be a few, who are the humble followers of Christ; nevertheless, they are led, that in many instances they do err because they are taught by the precepts of men." Nephi pronounces the Lord's curse on the wise and learned of Babylon: "O the wise, and the learned, and the rich, that are puffed up in the pride of their hearts, and all those who preach false doctrines, and all those who commit whoredoms, and pervert the right way of the Lord, wo, wo, wo be unto them, saith the Lord God Almighty, for they shall be thrust down to hell!" He pronounces a curse upon those who reject the knowledge of God and embrace the knowledge of man: "Wo unto them that turn aside the just for a thing of naught and revile against

---

823    Gorton, "My concern is that creation seems to contradict the provable and demonstrable theory of evolution of species," www.AskGramps.org
824    2 Nephi 9:28.
825    2 Nephi 26:10.
826    2 Timothy 3:7.

that which is good, and say that it is of no worth! For the day shall come that the Lord God will speedily visit the inhabitants of the earth; and in that day that they are fully ripe in iniquity they shall perish."[827]

Are we really so anxious to accept the wisdom of man when it clearly does not square with the revealed word of God? Can we become Zion people under such delusions? Can there be power in the priesthood when a man professes to embrace the truth on one hand and believe or promote falsehoods on the other?

Reviewing the near destruction of the Nephite nation prior to the birth of Christ, Mormon described the character of those who embrace Babylon and accept its teachings as truth: "O how foolish, and how vain, and how evil, and devilish, and how quick to do iniquity, and how slow to do good, are the children of men; yea, how quick to hearken unto the words of the evil one, and to set their hearts upon the vain things of the world!"[828] Gratefully, Babylon will not forever succeed in propagating its falsehoods. The Lord has stated emphatically, "The wisdom of the wise shall perish."[829]

The message should be clear: to the extent that we believe and promote the wisdom of Babylon, we shut out the Holy Ghost, who is the disseminator of all truth,[830] and thus we limit our power in the priesthood.

## Zion's Approach to "Pure Knowledge"

Zion approaches knowledge in a manner that is opposite Babylon's approach. A Zion people are taught that there is a *key* to receiving "pure knowledge." This key consists of three elements: (1) priesthood authority, (2) priesthood ordinances, and (3) the power of the Holy Ghost.[831] When these elements are in place, this key becomes functional and can be used to discover the truth in the recesses of telestial knowledge and to unlock the library of heaven. Or, as Brigham Young said, "to enable us to discern between truth and error, light and darkness, him who is of God, and him who is not of God, and to know how to place everything where it belongs. That is the only way to be a scientific Christian; there is no other method or process which will actually school a person so that he can become a Saint of God, and prepare him for a celestial glory; he must have within him the testimony of the spirit of the Gospel."[832]

According to Elder Alvin R. Dyer, "pure knowledge" is disseminated in no other way.[833] By this key—priesthood authority, priesthood ordinances, and the power of the Holy Ghost—we are promised that we might "know the truth of all things."[834]

Priesthood holders in Zion are the few who are instructed in the acquisition of "pure knowledge." They are taught that this knowledge comes only through the Spirit. They

---

827    2 Nephi 28:9, 11–12, 14–16.
828    Helaman 12:4.
829    D&C 76:9.
830    Moroni 10:5.
831    D&C 84:19–21; Moroni 10:5.
832    Young, *Discourses of Brigham Young,* 429.
833    Dyer, Conference Report, Oct. 1964, 133–34.
834    Moroni 10:5; D&C 124:97; Moses 6:61.

know that they must receive and retain the gift of the Holy Ghost or forever remain at the mercy of man's knowledge. Because the Holy Ghost is both the agent of pure knowledge and priesthood power, the sacrament covenant becomes vitally important to us. The sacrament promises the Spirit's continued companionship on the condition of worthiness. The companionship of the Holy Ghost provides us with spiritual gifts, including the gift of "pure knowledge."[835] These spiritual gifts include gifts related to priesthood rights and powers, for example, the gift of administration; understanding the operations of spirits; wisdom; faith to heal and be healed; the working of miracles; and the ability to prophesy, discern spirits, and speak with tongues and interpret tongues.[836]

Significantly, the Holy Ghost disseminates pure knowledge to our minds while priesthood ordinances unlock the door to the celestial library of knowledge. As we have demonstrated, there is an inseparable connection between priesthood power and the Holy Ghost. Any action on our part to cause the Spirit to withdraw also causes priesthood power to cease. Hence, we cannot expect to receive pure knowledge from the Holy Ghost by means of the priesthood ordinances if we are sinful or unrepentant, or if we are engaging in any of the activities that are prohibited by the Constitution of the Priesthood.

On the other hand, if we are doing all we can to abide in our covenants, honor God's laws, obey his commandments, live by every word that proceeds forth from the mouth of God, and develop the virtues listed in the Constitution of the Priesthood, we may ask for and receive "pure knowledge, which shall greatly enlarge the soul without hypocrisy or guile." This knowledge exalts man, taught Elder Alvin R. Dyer.[837] This knowledge begins as a seed, according to Alma, and must pass four tests to qualify as truth:

1.  When the seed of truth is planted in our souls, we feel something positive stirring within us.
2.  We feel invigorated, and we are motivated to become a better person.
3.  The seed of truth corresponds with, builds upon, and clarifies other ideas we have had, and it sparks new ideas.
4.  The seed of truth feels so good that we want to keep seeking after it and see it through to its perfect conclusion.

Pure knowledge is expansive, enlightening, and delicious. It increases faith; it is discernable; it is, clearly, good. If we do not neglect or reject it, this knowledge will grow into a tree that bears beautiful, delicious fruit, "which is most precious, which is sweet above all that is sweet, and which is white, yea, and pure above all that is pure."[838]

Pure knowledge is manifested to both the mind and the heart; that is, to our intellect and to our emotional center.[839] Two witnesses! Pure knowledge might be presented to us as a new idea, but it will seem reasonable (witness to the mind), and it will evoke a

835   D&C 46:18.
836   D&C 46:15–17, 19–25.
837   Dyer, Conference Report, Oct. 1964, 133–34.
838   Alma 32:26–43.
839   D&C 8:2.

positive emotion (witness to the heart). The witness to the mind and the heart may vary in sequence. The second witness may come in conjunction with the first witness or after much study, fasting, and prayer—but it will come. Otherwise, without these two witnesses, we would suspect that the idea is not grounded in truth.

The emotional witness might take any number of forms. For example, the Prophet Joseph Smith once described the manner in which such direct inspiration comes: "Yea, thus saith the still small voice, which whispereth through and pierceth all things, and oftentimes it maketh my bones to quake while it maketh manifest."[840] The quaking of the body, a burning in the bosom, or any other number of physical reactions are indications that pure knowledge is being introduced to the soul.

Likewise, the intellect might be acted upon and react in multiple ways when it is being presented with truth. Again, the Prophet taught, "A person may profit by noticing the first intimation of the spirit of revelation; for instance, when you feel pure intelligence flowing into you, it may give you sudden strokes of ideas, so that by noticing it, you may find it fulfilled the same day or soon; (i.e.) those things that were presented unto your minds by the Spirit of God, will come to pass; and thus by learning the Spirit of God and understanding it, you may grow unto the principle of revelation, until you become perfect in Christ Jesus."[841]

Those who would deny such revelations of God are of Babylon. Moroni wrote: "And again I speak unto you who deny the revelations of God, and say that they are done away, that there are no revelations, nor prophecies, nor gifts, nor healing, nor speaking with tongues, and the interpretation of tongues; Behold I say unto you, he that denieth these things knoweth not the gospel of Christ; yea, he has not read the scriptures; if so, he does not understand them. For do we not read that God is the same yesterday, today, and forever, and in him there is no variableness neither shadow of changing?"[842]

Because priesthood holders agree to "live by every word that proceedeth forth from the mouth of God"[843] by covenant, we must understand the process and obligation of obtaining "pure knowledge." Of course, one of the ultimate communications of pure knowledge is to receive the divine announcement that our calling and election has been made sure. It is imperative that we strive with all our might to magnify our calling, give diligent heed to the words of the eternal life, and live by every word that proceedeth forth from the mouth of God[844] so that we might obtain this communication of "pure knowledge." The Lord said, "It is impossible for a man to be saved in ignorance;"[845] that is, ignorant of our future with God.

Wisdom carries us to this knowledge. Wisdom begins by humbly seeking the Lord: "Let him that is ignorant learn wisdom by humbling himself and calling upon the Lord his God, that his eyes may be opened that he may see, and his ears opened that he may

---

840    D&C 85:6.
841    Smith, *Teachings of the Prophet Joseph Smith*, 151.
842    Mormon 9:7–9.
843    D&C 84:44.
844    D&C 84:33, 43–44.
845    D&C 131:6.

hear."[846] Gaining pure knowledge and wisdom becomes our challenge, said Elder Alvin R. Dyer; we are to abide faithfully in our covenants and gain wisdom upon wisdom, until we receive pure knowledge from the mouth of God and thus make our calling and election sure.[847]

## Wisdom and Pure Knowledge

Pure knowledge becomes trivia unless it is acted upon. The combination of knowledge (or belief) and action is the definition of faith; this combination produces wisdom. Wisdom is an understanding of what is true, right, or lasting. Wisdom is insight that leads to common sense and good judgment. Wisdom is selecting truth from the sum of scholarly learning, sages, and prophets, and formulating those truths into a sound outlook on life and a well-reasoned plan or course of action.[848] Priesthood holders in Zion are expected to be wise.

James, the Lord's brother, explained how we might differentiate between a wise and an unwise priesthood holder: "Who is a wise man and endued [endowed] with knowledge among you? Let him shew out of a good conversation his works with meekness of wisdom. But if ye have bitter envying and strife in your hearts, glory not, and lie not against the truth. This wisdom descendeth not from above, but is earthly, sensual, devilish. For where envying and strife is, there is confusion and every evil work. But the wisdom that is from above is first pure, then peaceable, gentle, and easy to be entreated, full of mercy and good fruits, without partiality, and without hypocrisy. And the fruit of righteousness is sown in peace of them that make peace."[849]

The scriptures paint a portrait of a wise man:
- A wise man need not be compelled to do that which is right.[850]
- A wise man is a humble man who seeks sound instruction[851] and hearkens to the wisdom that is imparted.[852]
- A wise man will pursue wisdom over riches,[853] and he will treasure up pure knowledge in his bosom.[854]
- Because the word of wisdom and the word of knowledge are spiritual gifts, which are bestowed only by the Holy Ghost, a wise man will live his life so that he can ask for and receive these gifts.[855]
- A wise man will judiciously disperse his wisdom to others so that they too might praise the Lord.[856]

846   D&C 136:32.
847   Dyer, Conference Report, Oct. 1964, 133–34.
848   *American Heritage Dictionary,* s.v. "wisdom."
849   James 3:13–18.
850   D&C 58:26.
851   D&C 1:26.
852   D&C 50:1.
853   D&C 6:7; 11:7.
854   D&C 38:30.
855   D&C 46:17–18.
856   D&C 52:17.

- A wise man's reward is much; his wisdom shall beget more wisdom,[857] and as wisdom multiplies, it shall become very great.[858]
- A wise man seeks to receive communication from God[859] so that he might enter into the joy of the Lord.[860]
- If a man is wise in mortality, he shall be counted worthy to inherit the mansions of God.[861]
- A wise man will receive the Lord's seal and blessing, guaranteeing him that in the midst of the Lord's house, he shall become a ruler in the celestial kingdom.[862]

## Reproving the Lord's Way

The Lord's call to the priesthood holders of the last days is to cry nothing but repentance to this generation.[863] We must cry repentance the Lord's way. Any person with a stewardship, whether he (or she) is a parent, a missionary, a priesthood or auxiliary leader, an instructor, or a prophet, will find himself in a situation where he must call someone to repentance. In *every* case, the directive is to seek inspiration and then speak as the Spirit gives utterance. The instruction reads: "Reproving betimes with sharpness, when moved upon by the Holy Ghost; and then showing forth afterwards an increase of love toward him whom thou hast reproved, lest he esteem thee to be his enemy. That he [the reproved person] may know that thy faithfulness is stronger than the cords of death."[864]

In such situations when reproof must be given, we teeter precariously on the edge of a precipice. If we reprove in Babylon's way—domineeringly, impatiently, angrily, harshly, proudly, insensitively, or belittlingly, without first seeking the Spirit and without regard to the person's salvation—the reproved one will become discouraged, and feel victimized and fearful. Our relationship with him will suffer—and worse, his relationship with God could suffer. Over time, he may develop a low regard for the priesthood and the gospel. If we step into that contentious arena in any degree, the Spirit leaves us and priesthood power ceases. And yet, unfortunately, this is a common occurrence among the many who are called: "We have learned by sad experience that it is the nature and disposition of almost all men, as soon as they get a little authority, as they suppose, they will immediately begin to exercise unrighteous dominion."[865]

Significantly, the directive to carefully reprove follows the directives of avoiding unrighteous dominion, exercising persuasion, being patient and long-suffering, being gentle, meek, loving, and kind, and seeking pure knowledge from the Spirit so that we do not come across as hypocritical, deceitful, or harmful. If we are such people, then we might

857   D&C 88:40.
858   D&C 76:9.
859   D&C 78:2.
860   D&C 51:19.
861   D&C 72:4.
862   D&C 101:61.
863   D&C 6:9; 11:9.
864   D&C 121:43–44.
865   D&C 121:39.

reprove as the Spirit directs, but before reproving, we might ponder this proverb: "A soft answer turneth away wrath, but grievous words stir up anger."[866]

This priesthood instruction regarding reproving and calling a person to repentance is often misunderstood. A quick review of definitions might help us comprehend the Lord's intention.

- *Reprove* means to "voice or convey disapproval of; rebuke . . . admonish. To find fault with."[867]
- *Betimes* means "In good time. early. . . . Once in a while; on occasion." Or less commonly, "Quickly; soon."[868]
- *Sharp* or *sharpness* has many definitions, but the one that seems most reasonable in this context is "Clearly and distinctly set forth."[869] (Of interest, a synonym for *sharp* is *harsh*, which is totally out of character with the priesthood.)

Therefore, we might recraft "reproving betimes with sharpness" to read: "admonishing in good time with clarity and love." Nothing about this directive gives us license to explode angrily, demean, or discourage. The entire intent of reproving by the Spirit is to point out errant behavior at the right time—early, if possible—for the purpose of correcting a person's direction and calling him back to safety. It is redemption—not discipline—that is the goal. Therefore, the correction must be delivered as the Spirit directs, but softly and accompanied by "pure testimony"[870] borne in clarity and love.

We cannot magnify the priesthood and avoid reproving. Because our calling contains the commandment to cry repentance, we are obligated to do so or forfeit our authority. To that end, the Lord explains the Zion way to reprove: "Then showing forth afterwards an increase of love toward him whom thou hast reproved, lest he esteem thee to be his enemy. That he may know that thy faithfulness is stronger than the cords of death."[871] Love must *increase*; love must become greater than it was before the reproving!

## Reproving with Love

Let us review what we have learned about love as it applies to reproof. In the first place, true love is called charity, "the pure love of Christ."[872] Therefore, the Apostle John can be confident when he says, "There is no fear in love, but perfect love casteth out fear." He goes on to say, "If we love one another, God dwelleth in us, and his love is perfected in us. Hereby know we that we dwell in him, and he in us, because he hath given us of his Spirit." That is, when it comes to loving, we must take the initiative. This pattern of loving is modeled by God toward us: "Herein is love, not that we loved God, but that

---

866    Proverbs 15:1.
867    *American Heritage Dictionary,* s.v. "reprove."
868    *American Heritage Dictionary,* s.v. "betimes."
869    *American Heritage Dictionary,* s.v. "sharp."
870    Alma 4:19.
871    D&C 121:43–44.
872    Moroni 7:47.

he loved us. . . . We love him, because he first loved us."[873] What is the result of loving Christ's way? It "never faileth!"[874]

The only proof a reproved person has that our faithfulness (our love for him and our devotion to God) is greater than the "cords of death" is our showing him "love unfeigned [unpretended]." The phrase "cords of death" evokes the image of the inevitable and unceasing draw of death as it tries to separate us. Because death signifies separation, it entails a division from our spouse, children, and friends—and from God. This division, in any of its forms, is contrary to the priesthood order of Zion, which is unity. A priesthood holder in Zion will show an increase of love after the reproof to counter the "cords of death" that might otherwise separate him from the reproved person.

## Cords of Death and Bonds of Love

Opposite death is life, the uniting of two or more things to make them one. Life is made possible only by the *At-one-ment* of Jesus Christ, which is ever pulling divided things back into their perfect, unified forms—to make them *at one*. Whereas Babylon is defined by its "cords of death," which pull us apart, Zion is defined by its "bonds of love,"[875] which pull us together. We always feel the tug of these two forces. We invoke the unifying power of the *At-one-ment* by means of love that binds, which is stronger than the cords of death. This fact is of great significance to covenant people; it should be, perhaps, of even greater significance to priesthood holders, whose responsibility it is to create an atmosphere of unity so that Zion might be established.

Elder Stephen L Richards said family ties are (or should be) the strongest bonds of love by reason of the sealing power. But next to these bonds are the bonds of the holy priesthood. By revelation, these bonds are "stronger than the cords of death," according to the Constitution of the Priesthood. Because we have made unifying covenants, the loving relationships that we form and enjoy in the Church weld us together more perfectly with each other than do any other relationships.[876] Therefore, when we serve our family or serve in the Church, especially when we are impressed by the Spirit to reprove, we must strive for the oneness characteristic of Zion. The Savior said, "Be one; and if ye are not one ye are not mine."[877] No one can be happy or effective if he is not one with his family and the Saints of God.[878]

Admittedly, the instruction to carefully reprove can be challenging for the best of us. The occasions that call for such correcting are often charged with emotion and misunderstanding. But we must remember what is at stake; if we reprove Babylon's way, we risk losing access to the Spirit and ongoing power in the priesthood. The way of Babylon, which is chosen by the many, leaves us to ourselves, defrocks us of the rights of the priesthood, destroys relationships, and binds us in the cords of death. The way of

---

873    1 John 4:10, 13, 18, 19.
874    Moroni 7:46.
875    D&C 88:133.
876    Richards, Conference Report, Oct. 1938, 114.
877    D&C 38:27.
878    Richards, Conference Report, Oct. 1938, 114.

Zion, which is chosen by the few, clothes us in the Spirit, empowers us with the rights of the priesthood, enhances relationships with added love, and wraps us in unifying bonds of charity.

## Charity toward All Men and the Household of God

The Apostle Paul foresaw that the behavior of the people of Babylon in the last days would cause "perilous" conditions to arise: "For men shall be lovers of their own selves, covetous, boasters, proud, blasphemers, disobedient to parents, unthankful, unholy, without natural affection, trucebreakers, false accusers, incontinent, fierce, despisers of those that are good, traitors, heady, highminded, lovers of pleasures more than lovers of God; having a form of godliness, but denying the power thereof: from such turn away. For of this sort are they which creep into houses, and lead captive silly women laden with sins, led away with divers lusts, ever learning, and never able to come to the knowledge of the truth."[879]

Interestingly, of all these loathsome characteristics, the first on Paul's list is "lovers of their own selves." The prophet Mormon made a similar list as he contrasted Alma's Zion people to the rest of the Nephite nation. Those who characterized Babylon were selfish, indulgent, devilish, idolatrous, immoral, jealous, and proud.[880] Again, we see self-indulgence at the top of the list.

Neither the people of Zion nor priesthood holders in Zion are selfish in any way! Zion people have consecrated all that they are and have to building up God's kingdom and establishing Zion. According to Mormon, the Zion people of the Book of Mormon were selfless, modest, and steady, and, consequently, they became rich!—"And thus, in their prosperous circumstances, they did not send away any who were naked, or that were hungry, or that were athirst, or that were sick, or that had not been nourished; and they did not set their hearts upon riches; therefore they were liberal to all, both old and young, both bond and free, both male and female, whether out of the church or in the church, having no respect to persons as to those who stood in need."[881] These people were living according to the mandate of the Constitution of the Priesthood, which states: "Let thy bowels also be full of charity towards all men, and to the household of faith."[882]

The "household of faith" constitutes the Saints of God. "All men" is everyone else. According to Alma the Elder, the charity of Zion people causes them to be "liberal to all." He said that their charity compels them to reach down to another and lift him up. Their charity will not allow them to tolerate suffering or deprivation of any kind. Wherever there is hurt, they seek to heal; wherever there is want, they apply their abundance; wherever there is need, they labor to satisfy it. They do not think of themselves; they think of others. They worship God by emulating him and caring for his children. Because they love, they are not envious; rather, they rejoice in the accomplishments and stewardships of others. By their charitable actions, they "are willing to bear one another's

---

879   2 Timothy 3:2–7.
880   Alma 1:22, 32.
881   Alma 1:30.
882   D&C 121:45.

burdens, that they may be light; yea, and are willing to mourn with those that mourn; yea, and comfort those that stand in need of comfort." Because of their charity, they qualify to be called God's people. Clothed in the mantle of charity, they humbly "stand as witnesses of God at all times and in all things, and in all places that [they] may be in, *even until death.*"[883]

To such Zion people, the power of charity enhances the power of the priesthood; charity magnifies the promises made in the oath and covenant of the priesthood, which are repeated in the Constitution of the Priesthood; and by charity, this power and these promises are made sure.

## Let Virtue Garnish Thy Thoughts Unceasingly

Babylon is characterized by immorality and amorality.

On the one hand Babylon is blatantly depraved, flaunting its wickedness and proudly waving its demonic behavior like a flag. Babylon is carnal, sensual, and devilish by design; that is, it goes out of its way to be worldly, catering to its physical and sexual appetites. It sets aside spiritual and intellectual interests, and it focuses on pampering the physical and sexual senses to provide luxuriant gratification. It is malicious, evil, mischievous, annoying, contemptible, fiendish, excessive, and extreme—in every way, Babylon is characteristic of its father, the devil, whom it worships.

On the other hand, Babylon seeks to appear moral without admitting to moral distinctions or judgments. It lacks sensibility to the traditional standard of morality; it is uncaring about right and wrong; and it is zealously tolerant of shifting values. To be immoral or amoral, to cast off discipline and entertain depraved thoughts or adopt dishonorable behavior *to any degree* results in the Holy Ghost's departure and his taking with him priesthood power.

Zion's virtue is fivefold. First, it is moral excellence, righteousness, and goodness. Second, it is chastity. Third, it is the sum of positive character attributes. Fourth, it is courage and valor. Fifth, it is power.

Moral virtue, taught Elder Gordon B. Hinckley, provides freedom from regret. Virtue is the only way to achieve peace of conscience and to lay hold on the covenantal promises of God. Jesus taught this principle in the form of a covenant: "Blessed are the pure in heart: for they shall see God."[884] As much as God has the power to fulfill that covenant, he also has the power to fulfill the covenant in the Constitution of the Priesthood: "Let virtue garnish thy thoughts unceasingly" with the promise: "Then shall thy confidence wax strong in the presence of God; and the doctrine of the priesthood shall distil upon thy soul as the dews from heaven. The Holy Ghost shall be thy constant companion, and thy scepter an unchanging scepter of righteousness and truth; and thy dominion shall be an everlasting dominion, and without compulsory means it shall flow unto thee forever and ever."[885] Elder Hinckley concluded that this promise—and

---

883   Mosiah 18:8–9; emphasis added.
884   Matthew 5:8.
885   D&C 121:45–46.

there are few promises that are greater—is extended to every virtuous man *and* woman.[886] Only to the virtuous person, he said, come the blessings of undreamed of glory, peace, love, trust, and loyalty.[887] President Heber J. Grant taught similarly that, to a great extent, the path to eternal life is maintained by those whose thoughts are garnished by virtue and whose words are gentle and pure.[888]

## Garnishing Our Thoughts with Virtue

To garnish is to embellish or adorn; it is to "enhance in appearance by adding decorative touches."[889] Virtue adds delightful color, flavor, or "trim" to our thoughts, thus inviting the Holy Ghost. The Constitution of the Priesthood instructs us to garnish our thoughts with virtue with the promise that the blessings of eternity will follow.

In Hebrew culture, a newly betrothed young man would spend the better part of a year preparing a bridal chamber for his bride. No effort was too great and no detail of craftsmanship was too insignificant; he was preparing the place he would one day bring his beloved. Therefore, with "diligent heed," he would garnish the chamber with beautiful items, sweet incense, and delicious food, so that it would be perfect for his bride.[890]

In like manner, we carefully and patiently prepare and adorn our minds with virtue so that we might invite the Holy Ghost, our beloved and constant companion, to come and reside with us. As much as the bridegroom would never offend his beloved with unholy behavior or language, and as much as he would never betray her trust, even in his thoughts, neither would we act, speak, or think anything unworthy that would dishearten our beloved Friend, whom the Savior gives to us as his precious gift. Hence, the mind that is garnished with virtue is the mind wherein the Holy Ghost is willing to comfortably and continually dwell. And where the Holy Ghost dwells, there is priesthood power.

*Then* blessings abound.

## Summary and Conclusion

The Constitution of the Priesthood begins with a sobering declaration: "Behold, there are many called, but few are chosen."[891] Unless we disbelieve the word of the Lord, we are forced to admit that many who are called to the priesthood and thus to eternal life will struggle or fail in their calling. The stated reasons for their failure are the setting of their hearts on the things of the world, aspiring to the honors of men, neglecting or rejecting the principles of righteousness, and attempting to dominate and control.

When a priesthood holder violates the oath and covenant of the priesthood "in any degree of unrighteousness, behold, the heavens withdraw themselves; the Spirit of the Lord is grieved; and when it is withdrawn, Amen to the priesthood or the authority of

---

886   Hinckley, Conference Report, Oct. 1970, 66.
887   Hinckley, Conference Report, Oct. 1970, 66.
888   Grant, Conference Report, Apr. 1937, 11–12.
889   *American Heritage Dictionary*, s.v. "garnish."
890   Nielsen, *Beloved Bridegroom*, 35–36.
891   D&C 121:34.

that man."[892] These are the beginning of his troubles. Beyond losing the Spirit and priesthood power, that man, if he remains unrepentant, will begin to spin out of control, first becoming critical of the Church and its leaders, then persecuting the Saints, and finally fighting against God.[893]

The Constitution of the Priesthood also sets forth instructions for inviting the Holy Ghost into our lives; the presence of the Holy Ghost makes the priesthood functional. A person who lives by these instructions becomes Christlike and therefore powerful in the priesthood, as was Jesus.

Avoiding the behavior of Babylon and embracing the attributes of Zion summons unimaginable rewards. That is the subject we will explore in the next and final chapter on the Constitution of the Priesthood, and the final chapter in this section of the oath and covenant of the priesthood, the second pillar of Zion.

892    D&C 121:37.
893    D&C 121:34–38.

# Section 6
# The Constitution of the Priesthood
## The Rewards for the Chosen Few

*Note: This chapter explores some of the most impressive blessings of the gospel that describe the ideal of Zion and the fulness of the priesthood. While it is true that they lie within reach of every worthy covenant person, it is also true that achieving them often requires a lifetime of effort—and that effort might extend after death up until the time of resurrection. We need only recall that both Abraham and Moses had lived to an extended age before they realized the fulness of these blessings. Therefore, this chapter is not designed to discourage, but rather to state the ideal, define terms, lift our sights, and set clear goals. We do not know the Lord's timing, but we do know that every covenant we make, including the oath and covenant of the priesthood, mandates that we persist in righteousness until we obtain these blessings. Zion people, the few who are both called and chosen, are characterized by both their pursuit and the achievement of these eternal rewards.*

*Because the quest for the highest blessings is a commandment, the Lord assumes an obligation to help us fulfill that commandment, provided we put forth the effort. Our obligation is to seek until we find. As long as we move forward on the path to eternal life, we will achieve our goal—guaranteed! We must do so. Our exaltation depends on it. What will happen along the way? Zion becomes our character, priesthood knowledge distils upon our souls, and we are filled with a greater portion of the Spirit.*

*Then come the blessings of eternity!*

*Of the many who are called to eternal life by virtue of the priesthood covenant, a few will actually heed the call of Zion, forsake Babylon and its identifying behaviors as described in the Constitution of the Priesthood, and order their lives accordingly. The blessings for doing so are the rewards listed in the oath and covenant of the priesthood: eternal life and exaltation. And lest women feel excluded, we must remember Elder McConkie's reassurance that because the promises contained in the priesthood covenant are repeated at the occasion of temple marriage, they are pertinent to both men and women.*[894]

## The Rewards

*Then* shall thy confidence wax strong in the presence of God; and the doctrine of the priesthood shall distil upon thy soul as the dews from heaven. The Holy Ghost shall be thy constant companion, and thy scepter an unchanging scepter of righteousness and truth; and thy dominion shall be an everlasting dominion, and without compulsory means it shall flow unto thee forever and ever.[895]

Notice that the word *then* prefaces the rewards. After we have qualified, *then* the blessings begin to flow:

- Our confidence grows so that we can obtain the presence of God.
- The doctrine of the priesthood distils upon our souls as the dews from heaven; that is, the Father teaches us of the priesthood covenant.[896]
- The promise of the constant companionship of the Holy Ghost is once again confirmed and renewed to us—this time, in greater measure.
- We receive a scepter of unchanging righteousness and truth, thus signifying that

---

894 McConkie, *A New Witness for the Articles of Faith*, 313.
895 D&C 121:45–46; emphasis added.
896 D&C 84:48.

we are at last true sons (or daughters) of God, kings and priests (queens and priestesses), and like him in every way.

- We receive an everlasting dominion, that is, an inheritance in the celestial world with the promise of eternal increase.
- Our kingdom will flow unto us and expand of its own accord, which is according to celestial law; that is, our *righteous* dominion grows without our compelling it and without force, or *unrighteous* dominion.

## "Then Shall Thy Confidence Wax Strong in the Presence of God"

This promise assumes that we first believe that we actually *can* stand in the presence of God—*in this life.* Such a belief might challenge our paradigm of the gospel and urge us into new territory. Before embarking on this trek, we must resist the temptation to shy away from the more impressive blessings of the gospel. It was this attitude that earned the Israelites forfeiture of Melchizedek Priesthood blessings and their opportunity to become Zion people.

We learn that Moses plainly taught . . . the children of Israel in the wilderness [that] this greater priesthood administereth the gospel and holdeth the key of the mysteries of the kingdom, *even the key of the knowledge of God.* Therefore, in the ordinances thereof, the power of godliness is manifest. And without the ordinances thereof, and the authority of the priesthood, the power of godliness is not manifest unto men in the flesh; *for without this no man can see the face of God, even the Father, and live."* Moses held this priesthood and had received its blessings; therefore, to also make his people Zion-like, Moses "sought diligently to sanctify his people that they might behold the face of God; but they hardened their hearts and could not endure his presence; therefore, the Lord in his wrath, for his anger was kindled against them, swore that they should not enter into his rest while in the wilderness, which rest is the fulness of his glory."[897]

It is hard to imagine a sadder scene. Despite their being the children of the covenant, despite their having been miraculously delivered from bondage, and despite their having been miraculously preserved by the hand of God, the Israelites desired only to live a "comfortable" gospel. They contented themselves to have their prophet see and talk with God and convey to them the Lord's communication. But when it came time for them individually to pay the price to receive the same privilege, they held back. They perceived the challenge and the invitation as being too difficult.

The Lord does not react well to our treating lightly or rejecting his invitations. Because a central purpose of the Melchizedek Priesthood is to bring people into the presence of God, the Lord had no choice except to withdraw it and leave the people with a lesser and more "comfortable" gospel law.[898] Now without the higher priesthood and its attendant covenants, laws, and ordinances, the Israelites found it impossible to become Zion people. With the lesser priesthood they could become good, but they could never become great.

---

897    D&C 84:19–24; emphasis added.
898    D&C 84:25.

In our day, the early Latter-day Saints also rejected the higher law that would have made them Zion people and eventually ushered them into the presence of God. Contrary to Moses' time, however, the Lord did not withdraw the Melchizedek Priesthood, but his wrath was, nevertheless, kindled against them. He drove the Saints into the wilderness to prepare for Zion, and we have been preparing ever since. The Lord has given us the covenants, laws, and ordinances we need to become Zion people if we will simply employ them. The call to forsake Babylon and come unto Christ—to *truly* come unto Christ—continues to be God's invitation. Will we listen this time? If we do not, we risk the Lord's wrath once again .

## Now Is the Time

In all our ponderings, duties, and devotions involving the priesthood, we must remember that regaining the presence of God is the consummate event and the pinnacle of priesthood belief. Everything about the new and everlasting covenant and the oath and covenant of the priesthood points to this singular occurrence. Our "calling" in the priesthood invites us to seek to stand in the presence of God *in this life*, and the priesthood empowers us to do so. It is not enough that our prophet stands in God's presence and receives intelligence from him; if we would avoid becoming like Moses' people, we must employ the authority, principles, and powers of the Melchizedek Priesthood to follow the path that leads to the presence of God and pursue that goal with all our heart, might, mind, and strength. We cannot become the ideal of Zion people otherwise. Elder McConkie wrote:

> We must not wrest the scriptures and suppose that the promises of seeing the Lord refer to some future day, either a Millennial or a celestial day, days in which, as we all know, the Lord will be present. *The promises apply to this mortal sphere in which we now live.* This is clearly set forth in the Vision of the Degrees of Glory. After Joseph Smith and Sidney Rigdon had seen the Father and the Son, concourses of angels, and the wonders of each kingdom of glory, and after they had written the account thereof, their continuing language says: "Great and marvelous are the works of the Lord, and the mysteries of his kingdom which he showed unto us, which surpass all understanding in glory, and in might, and in dominion; which he commanded us we should not write while we were yet in the Spirit, and are not lawful for man to utter; neither is man capable to make them known, for they are only to be seen and understood by the power of the Holy Spirit, which God bestows on

those who love him, and purify themselves before him; to whom he grants this privilege of seeing and knowing for themselves; that through the power and manifestation of the Spirit, *while in the flesh,* they may be able to bear his presence in the world of glory." (D&C 76:114–18.) While in the flesh! For those who "purify themselves before him," this is the time and the day and the hour when they have power to see their God![899]

## A Change of Paradigm

When we consider that Zion is the pure in heart,[900] and then when we consider that the pure in heart are they who see God,[901] we are suddenly faced with the uncomfortable realization that our definition of Zion might be lacking. While it is true that Zion is a land, the Church, a stake, a ward, a sealed marriage, an eternal family, and a covenant person, Zion, *the ideal,* is so much more. If we are not willing to expand the boundaries of our thinking, the most impressive blessings of Zion will remain outside of our reach.

Sometimes we imagine that the ideal of Zion is obtained by our calling and election being made sure, and therefore calling and election is the ultimate gospel experience. But it is not. Coming into the presence of God is the summit gospel peak, and the calling and election made sure is an essential step in getting there. Again, this process and ideal might require a change of thinking. Remember, Zion is the pure in heart, and the pure in heart see God. The Lord gives us instructions for rending the veil: "And again, verily I say unto you that it is your privilege, and a promise I give unto you that have been ordained unto this ministry, that inasmuch as you strip yourselves from jealousies and fears, and humble yourselves before me, for ye are not sufficiently humble, the veil shall be rent and you shall see me and know that I am—not with the carnal neither natural mind, but with the spiritual."

The inverse would also be true: jealousies, fears, arrogance, and pride will hold the veil in place. We must put off the natural man and become Saints of God, capable of being quickened by the Spirit so that we can stand in the presence of God: "For no man has seen God at any time in the flesh, except quickened by the Spirit of God. Neither can any natural man abide the presence of God, neither after the carnal mind."

The Lord is patient with us as we strive toward the goal: "Ye are not able to abide the presence of God now, neither the ministering of angels; wherefore, continue in patience until ye are perfected." But strive we must: "Let not your minds turn back; and when ye are worthy, in mine own due time, ye shall see and know. . . ."[902]

Elder McConkie listed several reasons why even the best of us shrink from the ideal of Zion: "There are, of course, those whose callings and election have been made sure

---

899    McConkie, *A New Witness for the Articles of Faith,* 495; emphasis added.
900    D&C 97:21.
901    Matthew 5:8; 3 Nephi 12:8.
902    D&C 67:10–14.

who have never exercised the faith nor exhibited the righteousness which would enable them to commune with the Lord on the promised basis. There are even those who neither believe nor know that it is possible to see the Lord in this day, and they therefore are without the personal incentive that would urge them onward in the pursuit of this consummation so devoutly desired by those with spiritual insight."[903]

Think of it this way: Having our calling and election made sure is like the final marker on the pathway that leads to a special door, or veil, that opens to the presence of the Lord. Behind that door stands the Savior, who is knocking. Listen to Jesus' words: "Behold, I stand at the door, and knock: if any man hear my voice, and open the door, I will come in to him, and will sup with him, and he with me."[904] The Lord first issued the invitation to enter when we took upon ourselves the new and everlasting covenant; he renewed the invitation when we took upon ourselves the oath and covenant of the priesthood. Will we respond to the Lord's knocking?

## Turning the *Key*

How did we arrive at this wonderful door, separated by the thickness of linen from our Lord? The answer should be obvious. We followed the Holy Ghost, who showed us the "markers" on the pathway that led to the door. These markers are priesthood markers, which consist of all the covenants and saving ordinances. These markers were laid down by Jesus Christ to guide us along the path, and they are safeguarded by the Church of Jesus Christ, the institution that is the custodian of these sacred things. Combined, these markers constitute the *key* that allows Zion people, who have received the priesthood and priesthood covenants and ordinances, to respond to the Lord's invitation and step through the door. So, again, how did we arrive at the door? By following the priesthood, which brings us to the Holy Ghost, who brings us to Christ, who brings us to the Father.

But we cannot enter the presence of God of our own accord. The law of heaven demands that, first, we must be pronounced pure, clean, true, and faithful by a righteous judge who knows us intimately; and second, that we must be escorted into the presence of the Lord by someone who knows the way. The Holy Ghost, who has always been our companion and who has guided and taught us every step of the way, is our judge, friend, and escort. Now he has brought us to the door, where he helps us respond to the Lord's invitation. He is in the unique position to recommend us to God and state our case. The Holy Ghost stands beside us, supports, prompts, and shows us how to use the key. Finally, like a father releasing his daughter into the arms of her new husband, he hands us off to the loving embrace of our Lord.

There are a number of ways to view the symbolism that represents this holy experience, but one way is to recognize all three members of the Godhead in their individual roles. At the outset of our journey to the presence of God—at baptism—each of the Godhead covenanted with us to bring us to the door and usher us into celestial glory.

---

903   McConkie, *The Promised Messiah*, 586.
904   Revelation 3:20.

As we now stand at the door, we realize that they have fulfilled their promise. There, at the threshold of eternity, as we anticipate our entrance into the Lord's presence, we look beside us and see at our side the Holy Ghost, our guide and escort; behind the door, we recognize the Father's voice, and we hear him beckoning us to him; before us is the door or veil, which we must go through to reach the Father. Paul said that Jesus Christ is the veil,[905] and we must go *through* him to reach God. To qualify to enter, we must be conversant in our covenants; they are the keys that open the door. Our faithfulness allows us to ask for a supernal gift, and when we receive it, we will finally we be invited into the embrace and fellowship of God.

## Obtaining, at Last, a Perfect Knowledge of the Savior

Coming to Jesus Christ and then to the Father *through* Jesus Christ is an experience like no other. As a reference, we have the account of Nephites, who were invited, one by one, to experience the individual nature of the Atonement firsthand.[906] Too often we wonder what part of the Atonement (if any) is uniquely for us as individuals. Such ponderings betray our ignorance of the Father and the Son's ability to indivisibly extend one hundred percent of their time and attention to *each* of us.

Allow me for a moment to form the following thoughts in first person.

What part of the Atonement is mine? *All of it!* In that tender and supernal, one-on-one experience with the Lord, when I am finally invited to touch each of the wounds in his hands, feet, and side, when I remember the great drops of blood in the Garden, the betrayal, the injustice, the mocking, the beatings, the crown of thorns, the scourging, and the Crucifixion—then I will know with a perfect knowledge that he did *all of it* for me.

This universal experience with Jesus is recorded in the Book of Mormon. Listen to the Lord's invitation, and imagine the day when he will extend it to us:

> Arise and come forth unto me, that ye may thrust
> your hands into my side, and also that ye may feel the
> prints of the nails in my hands and in my feet, that ye
> may know that I am the God of Israel, and the God
> of the whole earth, and have been slain for the sins of
> the world.
>
> And it came to pass that the multitude went forth,
> and thrust their hands into his side, and did feel the
> prints of the nails in his hands and in his feet; and
> this they did do, going forth one by one until they had
> all gone forth, and did see with their eyes and did feel
> with their hands, and did know of a surety and did bear

---

905     Hebrews 10:20.
906     3 Nephi 11:15.

> record, that it was he, of whom it was written by the
> prophets, that should come.
>
> And when they had all gone forth and had wit-
> nessed for themselves, they did cry out with one accord,
> saying:
>
> Hosanna! Blessed be the name of the Most High
> God! And they did fall down at the feet of Jesus, and
> did worship him.[907]

Again, each person who walks the path to Zion will have this experience. Therefore, each Zion person must obtain the key, and respond to the knock. To attain to this singular event may require a change of paradigm. But it is nevertheless true, and every Zion person can attest that it is true. The prophets, the scriptures, and the temple testify that the end purpose and the power of the Melchizedek Priesthood is to rend the veil and convey a man or woman into the presence of God.

Will we believe it? Will we pursue that blessing once we believe it? Will we thereby become Zion people?

The commandment is clear: "And *seek the face of the Lord always,* that in patience ye may possess your souls, and ye shall have eternal life."[908] Such is the ideal and condition of Zion people, for we read: "The Lord came and dwelt with his people, and they dwelt in righteousness."[909]

## Receiving the Greatest Comfort

Is the prize worth the price? Joseph Smith assured us that it is. If we are willing to lift our sights, believe the *entirety* of the gospel, and apply the *totality* of the priesthood, the Prophet promised that we would eventually receive the Second Comforter, even the Lord Jesus Christ. "Now what is this other Comforter? It is no more nor less than the Lord Jesus Christ Himself; and this is the sum and substance of the whole matter; that when any man obtains this last Comforter, he will have the personage of Jesus Christ to attend him, or appear unto him from time to time, and even He will manifest the Father unto him, and they will take up their abode with him, and the visions of the heavens will be opened unto him, and the Lord will teach him face to face, and he may have a perfect knowledge of the mysteries of the Kingdom of God."[910]

Elder McConkie explained that this privilege is the blessing that lies beyond the "door." It is a blessing that exceeds the blessing of having our calling and election made sure, and it is the purpose for which that assurance is given.

After the true saints receive and enjoy the gift of the Holy Ghost; after they know how to attune themselves to the voice of the Spirit; after they mature spiritually so that

---

907   3 Nephi 11:14–17.
908   D&C 101:38; emphasis added.
909   Moses 7:16.
910   Smith, *Teachings of the Prophet Joseph Smith,* 150.

they see visions, work miracles, and entertain angels; after they make their calling and election sure and prove themselves worthy of every trust—after all this and more—it becomes their right and privilege to see the Lord and commune with him face-to-face. Revelations, visions, angelic visitations, the rending of the heavens, and appearances among men of the Lord himself—all these things are for all of the faithful. They are not reserved for apostles and prophets only. God is no respecter of persons.[911]

Would not this experience—receiving the Second Comforter—give us the greatest reassurance? Should we not pursue this goal by implementing the priesthood for its ultimate intended purpose?

## Regaining the Presence of God—The End Purpose of the Priesthood

Consider the following sampling among myriad statements and promises on the subject of our regaining God's presence:

"If a man love me, he will keep my words: and my Father will love him, *and we will come unto him, and make our abode with him.*"[912]

"Sanctify yourselves that your minds become single to God, and the days will come that you will see him; *for he will unveil his face unto you,* and it shall be in his own time, and in his own way, and according to his own will."[913]

"God hath not revealed anything to Joseph [Smith], but what He will make known unto the Twelve, and even the least Saint may know all things as fast as he is able to bear them, for the day must come when no man need say to his neighbor, Know ye the Lord; for all shall know Him (who remain) from the least to the greatest."[914]

Is our faith strengthened? Will we believe it? Do we understand for what purpose we have received the priesthood and its ordinances, and will we pursue that purpose and become Zion people? Elder McConkie wrote: "All who are now striving to live the laws of Zion] to the extent of their of the ability, that is, all those who are now living the law of the celestial kingdom *are qualified to seek the face of the Lord.* The attainment of such a state of righteousness and perfection is the object and end toward which all of the Lord's people are striving. We seek to see the face of the Lord while we yet dwell in mortality, and we seek to dwell with him everlastingly in the eternal kingdoms that are prepared.[915]

## The Revealed Process for Standing in the Presence of God

What then should we do? What are the steps? The Lord gave us the simple formula: "Verily, thus saith the Lord: It shall come to pass that every soul who forsaketh his sins and cometh unto me, and calleth on my name, and obeyeth my voice, and keepeth my commandments, shall see my face and know that I am."[916]

---

911    McConkie, *The Promised Messiah,* 575; emphasis added.
912    John 14:23; emphasis added.
913    D&C 88:68; emphasis added.
914    Smith, *Teachings of the Prophet Joseph Smith,* 149.
915    McConkie, *The Promised Messiah,* 578: emphasis added.
916    D&C 93:1.

It is a covenant, or two-way promise. (1) Forsake our sins; (2) come unto Christ; (3) call on his name; (4) obey his voice; (5) keep his commandments. *Then* we shall see him. But of the many who are called only a few will follow this pattern, and therefore only a few will "receive" the Lord in this life and enter his presence. "For strait is the gate, and narrow the way that leadeth unto the exaltation and continuation of the lives, and few there be that find it, because ye receive me not in the world neither do ye know me. But if ye receive me in the world, then shall ye know me, and shall receive your exaltation; that where I am ye shall be also."[917]

We cannot fully receive Christ if we do not know him. That would be like a husband claiming to have wedded or received a wife whom he has never met. On the other hand, Zion people, the bride, know and receive the Bridegroom. They know him because he is the one who claimed them by "separating" them out from all other affections; he is the one who lovingly "received" them, his bride, unto himself.[918]

## The Priesthood Is the Power to Stand in God's Presence

Clearly, the holy priesthood is the source of confidence and the actual power to stand in the presence of God. Elder McConkie expounds:

> The priesthood is the power, authority, and means that prepares men to see their Lord; also, that in the priesthood is found everything that is needed to bring this consummation to pass. Accordingly, it is written: "The power and authority of the higher, or Melchizedek Priesthood, is to hold the keys of all the spiritual blessings of the church—To have the privilege of receiving the mysteries of the kingdom of heaven, to have the heavens opened unto them, to commune with the general assembly and church of the Firstborn, and to enjoy the communion and presence of God the Father, and Jesus the mediator of the new covenant." (D&C 107:18–19). . . . Thus, through the priesthood the door may be opened and the way provided for men [and women] to see the Father and the Son. From all of this it follows, automatically and axiomatically, that if and when the holy priesthood operates to the full in the life of any man [or woman], he will receive its great and full blessings, which are that rending of the heavens and that parting of the veil of which we now speak.[919]

917    D&C 132:22–23.
918    D&C 45:12.
919    McConkie, *The Promised Messiah,* 587–88.

Joseph Smith asked, "How do men obtain a knowledge of the glory of God, his perfections and attributes?" Then the answer: "By devoting themselves to his service, through prayer and supplication incessantly strengthening their faith in him, until, like Enoch, the brother of Jared, and Moses, they obtain a manifestation of God to themselves."[920]

Therefore, when we feel the Spirit summoning us to the temple, and when we hear the voice of God "revealing through the heavens the grand Key-words of the Priesthood,"[921] our hearts should be filled with desire and hope. We raise our eyes and cry out, "O my Father, thou that dwellest in the high and glorious place, when shall I regain thy presence and again behold thy face?"[922] Our salvation depends upon our giving diligent heed to regaining his presence and again beholding his face. Thus, we devote our lives to living and serving in such a way that we might obtain this knowledge. The Prophet Joseph Smith revealed, "It is impossible for a man to be saved in ignorance."[923] And on another occasion, "A man is saved no faster than he gets knowledge."[924] The ultimate knowledge—the knowledge of the surety of our salvation; the knowledge of our origin and destiny; the knowledge that brings us to the ideal of Zion—is the perfect knowledge of the reality of God.

## "The Doctrine of the Priesthood Shall Distil upon Thy Soul"

Joseph Smith said, "A man can do nothing for himself unless God directs him in the right way; and *the priesthood is for that purpose.*"[925]

In examining the rewards listed in the Constitution of the Priesthood, we notice that the Lord bookends the verses found in D&C 121:45–46 with promises concerning our glorious destiny. These promises are the ability to stand in the presence of God and receive our coronation. The verses sandwiched between these promises reveal the markers along the path. The first marker has to do with priesthood education: "The doctrine of the priesthood shall distil upon thy soul as the dews from heaven."[926] This statement hearkens back to the promise made in the oath and covenant of the priesthood: "And the Father teacheth [us] of the covenant which he has renewed and confirmed upon [us]."[927]

As we have discussed, the Father takes both the responsibility and the initiative to teach us concerning the priesthood covenant. By the power of the Holy Ghost, under whom angels minister, the Father will summon all the powers in heaven and earth to distil priesthood knowledge upon us as fast as we are willing to receive it. Here, then, is a key to gaining priesthood understanding and power: We are taught from on high. Elder McConkie said this doctrine is unknown in the world and not widely known in the

920    Smith, *Lectures on Faith*, 2:55.
921    Abraham, Facsimile No. 2, Explanation, Figure 7.
922    "O My Father," *Hymns*, no. 292.
923    D&C 131:6.
924    Smith, *History of the Church*, 4:588.
925    Smith, *Teachings of the Prophet Joseph Smith*, 364; emphasis added.
926    D&C 121:45.
927    D&C 84:48.

Church. The priesthood information the Father distils upon us cannot be fully learned in the scriptures or even in the teachings of the prophets, he said. God reserves the right to reveal this doctrine of the priesthood by the gift of the Holy Ghost, which will likely involve the ministering of angels.[928]

Earlier in this book, we discussed at length the doctrine of the priesthood and how the Father distils priesthood knowledge upon us. By way of review, we qualify for this personal revelation by exemplifying charity and virtue.[929] The distillation of priesthood doctrine settles upon those who love and serve God with all their "heart, might, mind, and strength,"[930] and the process occurs line upon line and precept upon precept by the power of the Holy Ghost. Soon, after having walked through the dewy grasses of priesthood doctrine, we find ourselves saturated in it.

What, then, is the doctrine of the priesthood that pivots on charity and virtue? Elder McConkie lists the following:

- The priesthood is the actual power of God, and the actual name of the power of God. It is the power by which he created and creates the heavens, and it is the power by which he governs, sustains and preserves all things. To become as he is, we must exercise his priesthood, or power, as does he.

- The priesthood is the power of faith—Faith is power and power is priesthood. Faith is a true belief or knowledge that is acted upon.[931] The priesthood is useless unless it is put into action; thus the combination of faith, truth, virtue, and priesthood results in actual power. By faith, priesthood becomes power "to put at defiance the armies of nations, to divide the earth, to break every band, to stand in the presence of God; to do all things according to his will, according to his command, subdue principalities and powers; and this by the will of the Son of God."[932] To the extent that we act with our priesthood in faith, according to charity and virtue, we become like God, who is the perfection of faith, priesthood, and power. By this means, we can lay hold on eternal life.

- The priesthood is the doctrine that "God lives and is and ever shall be. He is the Everlasting Elohim who dwells in heaven above. He is our Father, the father of our spirits; we are his children, the offspring of his begetting. He has a glorified body of flesh and bones; he lives in the family unit; and he possesses all power, all might, all dominion, and all truth. The name of the kind of life he lives is eternal life [that is, he lives in the family unit]."[933]

---

928   McConkie, "The Doctrine of the Priesthood," 32.
929   D&C 121:45.
930   D&C 98:12.
931   Alma 32:21.
932   JST, Genesis 14:31.
933   McConkie, *A New Witness for the Articles of Faith,* 704.

- The priesthood is the doctrine or lifestyle that our Heavenly Father enjoys in his exalted status—that of glory, perfection, and power, because his faith and his priesthood are perfect and infinite.

- The priesthood of God is after the order of his Son, which power, like God himself, is infinite and eternal. We who receive this endowment of power become part of that same order.

- The priesthood is a system of orders, the highest of which is named the new and everlasting covenant of marriage,[934] or the patriarchal order. Only in this order can we become like God, creating for ourselves eternal family units patterned after the family of God.

- The doctrine of the priesthood is that we can progress until we obtain the priesthood's fulness, which increasingly gives us power by faith to govern and control all temporal and spiritual things, to effect miracles, to help to perfect God's children, to stand in Father's presence, and to become like him, having developed his faith, perfections, and power.

- The priesthood is the power to do all things that are expedient: move mountains, control the elements, cast away evil spirits, defeat every enemy, conquer any adversity, provide protection, cure disease, raise the dead, bind together marriages and families, and ultimately to achieve glorious immortality in the celestial kingdom of God.[935]

## The Rights and the Doctrine of the Priesthood

Having the Father as our instructor might be considered a *right* belonging to the priesthood. These rights, as we have learned, are "inseparably connected with the powers of heaven," and they are made functional upon "the principles of righteousness."[936] These rights are part of the doctrine of the priesthood that the Father distils upon our souls as the dews from heaven. The Lord describes the glorious rights and blessings he is willing to impart to us in our priesthood instruction:

> For thus saith the Lord—I, the Lord, am merciful and gracious unto those who fear me, and delight to honor those who serve me in righteousness and in truth unto the end.
> Great shall be their reward and eternal shall be their glory.

934    D&C 131:2.
935    McConkie, "The Doctrine of the Priesthood," 32.
936    D&C 121:36.

> And to them will I reveal all mysteries, yea, all the
> hidden mysteries of my kingdom from days of old, and
> for ages to come, will I make known unto them the
> good pleasure of my will concerning all things pertain-
> ing to my kingdom.
>
> Yea, even the wonders of eternity shall they know,
> and things to come will I show them, even the things of
> many generations.
>
> And their wisdom shall be great, and their under-
> standing reach to heaven; and before them the wisdom
> of the wise shall perish, and the understanding of the
> prudent shall come to naught.
>
> For by my Spirit will I enlighten them, and by my
> power will I make known unto them the secrets of my
> will—yea, even those things which eye has not seen,
> nor ear heard, nor yet entered into the heart of man.[937]

Clearly, the doctrine of the priesthood is glorious, and few blessings could be as wonderful as receiving these priesthood rights.

## The Doctrine of the Priesthood and the Law of Asking

If we desire the doctrine of the priesthood to distil upon our souls, we must take the
initiative and ask. Becoming Zion-like and obtaining priesthood understanding is an
educational process, and we must become eager students. We open the door to revelation
by asking: "If thou shalt ask, thou shalt receive revelation upon revelation, knowledge
upon knowledge, that thou mayest know the mysteries and peaceable things—that which
bringeth joy, that which bringeth life eternal."[938] We walk through the door by diligent
pursuit. "Behold, thou shalt observe all these things, and great shall be thy reward; for
unto you it is given to know the mysteries of the kingdom, but unto the world it is not
given to know them. Ye shall observe the laws which ye have received and be faithful."[939]

The principle of asking is common to receiving all gospel blessings. We wish to
receive baptism; we wish to receive the priesthood; we want to enter the temple and
receive priesthood covenants and ordinances; we wish for a temple recommend to be
sealed to our sweetheart eternally. Why, then, if we desire some of the most impressive blessings of the gospel, do we often neglect to ask? The law of asking is immutable:
"Therefore, he that lacketh wisdom, let him ask of me, and I will give him liberally and
upbraid him not."[940] If we desire to receive revelation upon revelation concerning the
doctrine of the priesthood, or to receive the ministering of angels, or have our calling

---

937   D&C 76:5–10.
938   D&C 42:61.
939   D&C 42:65–66.
940   D&C 42:67.

and election made sure, or to become part of the general assembly and Church of the Firstborn,[941] or to become Zion people, or to finally enter into the presence of God and receive the "privilege of seeing and knowing for [ourselves],"[942] we must ask. But sadly, although asking to receive is a commandment, we do not always obey: "Behold this is my will; ask and ye shall receive; but men do not always do my will."[943]

Asking to receive is an eternal law with a promise. Notice the word *shall* indicating a promised answer: "Therefore, ask, and ye *shall* receive; knock, and it *shall* be opened unto you; for he that asketh, receiveth; and unto him that knocketh, it *shall* be opened."[944]

Asking becomes effectual only after moving forward in faith, repenting, and seeking: "Behold, I say unto you, go forth as I have commanded you; repent of all your sins; ask and ye shall receive; knock and it shall be opened unto you."[945] "Draw near unto me and I will draw near unto you; seek me diligently and ye shall find me; ask, and ye shall receive; knock, and it shall be opened unto you."[946]

The law of asking opens the door to a fulness of joy, and, implied in scripture, today is the time to start: "Hitherto have ye asked nothing in my name: ask, and ye shall receive, that your joy may be full."[947]

To distinguish ourselves in the priesthood from the "many who are called" and to be identified with the "few who are chosen," to qualify to stand with the prophets, to know what they have known, to see what they have seen, and to receive the mysteries of the kingdom in absolute clarity, we must actively and deliberately seek and ask: "Unto you it is given to know the mysteries of the kingdom of God: but to others in parables; that seeing they might not see, and hearing they might not understand."[948]

The forfeited blessings for our not bothering to ask are great. Although we might be good people, if we do not seek and ask, we might never qualify to receive more than the "lesser portion of the word." Alma taught that we must be constantly reaching heavenward for information and instruction; our complacency is at least, dangerous and, at worst, damning: "And therefore, he that will harden his heart, the same receiveth the lesser portion of the word; and he that will not harden his heart, to him is given the greater portion of the word, until it is given unto him to know the mysteries of God until he know them in full. And they that will harden their hearts, to them is given the lesser portion of the word until they know nothing concerning his mysteries; and then they are taken captive by the devil, and led by his will down to destruction. Now this is what is meant by the chains of hell."[949]

Finally, the priesthood ordinances hold the ultimate power of asking and receiving. These ordinances are sometimes called keys,[950] "by which [we] may ask and receive bless-

---

941   D&C 76:54, 94; 77:11; 78:21; 88:5; 93:22; 107:19.
942   D&C 76:117.
943   D&C 103:31.
944   3 Nephi 27:29; emphasis added; see also D&C 4:7; 66:9; 103:35.
945   D&C 49:26.
946   D&C 88:63.
947   John 16:24.
948   Luke 8:10.
949   Alma 12:9–11.
950   Smith, *History of the Church*, 4:608; 5:1–2; Smith, *Teachings of the Prophet Joseph Smith*, 226; Smith, *Juvenile Instructor*, June 1, 1892, 345; Smith, *The Words of Joseph Smith*, 54, footnote 19.

ings." We qualify to use these keys to ask and receive by being humble and without guile. Then we "shall receive of [the Lord's] Spirit, even the Comforter, which shall manifest unto [us] the truth of all things."[951]

## Lesser and Greater Portions of the Doctrine of the Priesthood

According to Alma, hardheartedness is the characteristic that results in our receiving the "lesser portion of the word." To harden one's heart is to close it off to receiving what God would give for the asking. Such people are left with the "lesser portion of the word," which consists of the gospel basics, concepts, and principles that are generally known. Of course, we all must understand the lesser portion of the word, but after we have received it, we must immediately begin to reach higher. To remain contented with the lesser portion, Alma taught, puts us at risk of being "taken captive by the devil, and led by his will down to destruction."[952] The many who are called but not chosen make up this group; they do not seek the "greater portion of the word."

Conversely, the few who are called and chosen do not harden their hearts, and they actively seek the greater portion of the word. The Lord will answer their request and give them "the greater portion of the word, until it is given unto [them] to know the mysteries of God until he know them in full." As we have noted, these mysteries are not "secrets,"[953] as Satan reveals; mysteries consist of intelligence that can be learned only by revelation from God. Mysteries distil upon our souls "revelation upon revelation" and include the rights of the priesthood, spiritual gifts, and "peaceable things—that which bringeth joy, that which bringeth life eternal."[954]

Ultimately, these few who receive the greater portion will see heaven! Surely, these mysteries can be known in no other way than by seeking and asking for them by means of the rights, or keys, of the priesthood. This privilege caused Paul to exult, "Eye hath not seen, nor ear heard, neither have entered into the heart of man, the things which God hath prepared for them that love him."[955]

## The Necessity and Power of Priesthood Ordinances

A significant right belonging to the priesthood is the Father's taking charge of our priesthood education. The oath and covenant of the priesthood states: "And the Father teacheth him of the covenant."[956] Knowing who our teacher is also identifies who distils "the doctrine of the priesthood . . . upon [our] soul[s] as the dews from heaven."[957] That is not to say that Jesus Christ and the Holy Ghost are not involved; but it does seem to indicate that the Father wants to assure us of the origin of priesthood instruction. There-

---

951    D&C 124:97.
952    Alma 12:11.
953    Moses 5:31, 49.
954    D&C 42:61.
955    1 Corinthians 2:9.
956    D&C 84:48.
957    D&C 121:45.

fore, when we worthily invoke the law of asking in faith and subsequently experience the distillation of priesthood doctrine upon our souls, we can rest assured that the Father is the source of that revelation.

Distillation of priesthood doctrine must be done in an ordered way,[958] and that ordered way is by means of *ordinances,* which are another "right" of the priesthood. Elder Dennis Neuenschwander said ordinances mark the progressive order of the kingdom of God, and as we apply the ordinances in our lives, we gain a revelation of the character of God that otherwise would be impossible.[959] Zion people receive the priesthood temple ordinances, and under the Father's tutelage they learn to use them. One of the most definitive statements in scripture on this subject is found in Doctrine and Covenants 84:19, which precedes the oath and covenant of the priesthood: "And this greater priesthood administereth the gospel and holdeth the key of the mysteries of the kingdom, even the key of the knowledge of God. Therefore, in the ordinances thereof, the power of godliness is manifest. And without the ordinances thereof, and the authority of the priesthood, the power of godliness is not manifest unto men in the flesh; for without this no man can see the face of God, even the Father, and live."[960]

The powers resident in these temple priesthood ordinances are without peer. Elder A. Theodore Tuttle taught parents that they must teach their children that becoming like God and achieving exaltation are possible only if they receive these ordinances and their attendant covenants.[961] Elder Joseph Fielding Smith likewise taught that we cannot become Zion people without the temple priesthood ordinances; neither can we achieve exaltation nor obtain "the fullness of the glory of God."[962]

Joseph Smith said, "The question is frequently asked, 'Can we not be saved without going through with all those ordinances?' I would answer, No, not the fulness of salvation . . . any person who is exalted to the highest mansion has to abide a celestial law, and the whole law too."[963] And on another occasion, "All men [and women] who become heirs of God and joint heirs with Jesus Christ will have to receive the fulness of the ordinances of his kingdom; and those who will not receive all the ordinances will come short of the fullness of that glory, if they do not lose the whole."[964]

President Kimball wrote about the necessity of ordinances and their connection to the priesthood: "Men require priesthood for exaltation. No man will ever reach godhood who does not hold the priesthood. You have to be a member of the higher priesthood—an elder, seventy, or high priest—and today is the day to get it and magnify it. Righteousness and ordinances are required. Can we conceive of the vastness of the program? Can we even begin to understand it? Remember this: Exaltation is available only to righteous members of the Church of Jesus Christ; only to those who accept the gospel; only to those who have their endowments; only to those who have been through the holy temple

958   D&C 132:8, 18.
959   Neuenschwander, "Ordinances and Covenants," 20.
960   D&C 84:19–22.
961   Tuttle, Conference Report, Apr. 1984, 33.
962   Smith, "The Duties of the Priesthood in Temple Work," 4.
963   Smith, *Teachings of the Prophet Joseph Smith,* 331.
964   Smith, *Teachings of the Prophet Joseph Smith,* 309.

of God and have been sealed for eternity and who then continue to live righteously throughout their lives."[965]

The verses (D&C 84:19–22) we have discussed clearly indicate that "the power of godliness" is manifested "unto men in the flesh" by means of the ordinances of the priesthood. The very experience we are seeking—to "see the face of God, even the Father, and live"—simply cannot happen without these priesthood ordinances. The temple endowment shows us the pattern of how this must be done—the *ordered* way by means of *ordinances*. The ordinances are "the key of the mysteries of the kingdom, even the key of the knowledge of God." Without this key, or ordinances, "the power of godliness is not manifest, and no man can see God."

## The Doctrine of the Priesthood and Revelatory "Keys"

This right of the priesthood—*ordinances*—is too sacred to discuss outside the temple except in general terms. By covenant, we guard and protect these things. When we receive information about these ordinances, it is under the direction of the Father, for he is our teacher who distils the doctrine of the priesthood upon our souls and guides our education. Under his supervision, we are informed that utilizing the ordinances appropriately opens the revelatory channel between him and us; therefore, we are given both instruction and power whereby we might ask for and receive further light and knowledge. Andrew Ehat and Lyndon Cook write:

> Joseph Smith received a revelation specifically requiring that he teach Hyrum Smith and William Law certain "keys by which they could ask and receive" (D&C 124:95, 97). In the 1879 edition of the Doctrine and Covenants, Orson Pratt indicated that these keys were "the order of God for receiving revelations"—the keys to the oracles of God. . . . Elder Charles C. Rich, a member of the Council of the Twelve, was [a] preserver of Joseph's revelations on the temple ordinances and who obviously was sensitive to the propriety of discussing endowment ordinances. Nevertheless, he publicly gave this very important account of the revelation of these keys of the priesthood, during a stake conference meeting in Idaho in 1878. "It was a long time after the Prophet Joseph Smith had received the keys of the Kingdom of God, and after Hyrum and others had received many blessings, that the Lord gave Joseph a revelation, to show him and others how they could ask for and receive certain blessings. We read in the revelations of

---

965   Kimball, *Teachings of Spencer W. Kimball*, 51.

St. John, that [of] the white stone [as follows:] 'and in the stone a new name, which no man knoweth save him that receiveth it.' Joseph tells us [in D&C 130:10–11] that this new name is a key-word, which can only be obtained through the endowments. This is one of the keys and blessings that will be bestowed upon the Saints in these last days, for which we should be very thankful" (*Journal of Discourses,* 19:250).[966]

As we can see, besides being a priesthood right, these ordinances are often referred to as "keys." (Recall, however, that this is a different use of the word *keys* than that which is typical in today's Church.) Their purpose is highly significant to people who would become Zion-like. These keys are the divinely prescribed and ordered manner by which "the power of godliness is manifest," and therefore they open the door to the presence of God: "And without the ordinances thereof [the Melchizedek Priesthood], and the authority of the priesthood, the power of godliness is not manifest unto men in the flesh; for without this no man can see the face of God, even the Father, and live."[967] In another place, the scriptures say it this way: "[These are] the keys whereby [we] may ask and receive, and be crowned with the same blessing, and glory, and honor, and priesthood, and gifts of the priesthood."[968]

These ordinances, or keys, are the only legitimate way to see God, return to his presence, and "enter into his rest, which rest is the fulness of his glory"[969]—eternal life. Therefore, it behooves a Zion person to diligently apply to temple worship and pray earnestly for light and knowledge from God concerning this essential right belonging to the priesthood.

All of the scriptures mentioned herein link our education in priesthood doctrine to the temple. By now, it should be clear that we will not, and should not, learn this doctrine in a Sunday School class or in quorum or Relief Society meetings; furthermore, we will not, and should not, hear the specifics of this doctrine preached from the pulpit. The doctrine of the priesthood is a sacred one-on-one course taught by the Father primarily in the precincts of his holy house, the temple. He expects us to prepare to enter, seek, ask, and use the keys that he has given us to open the door to the "mysteries of the kingdom," "the power of godliness," and "the knowledge of God." Therefore, Zion people are instructed to attend the temple often. There they offer proxy sacrifice and service for deceased persons who cannot receive the covenants and ordinances for themselves; and there they spend time with God as he carefully and constantly distils upon their souls the precious doctrines of the priesthood. Brigham Young said: "If the Latter-day Saints will walk up to their privileges and exercise faith in the name of Jesus Christ and live in the enjoyment of the fulness of the Holy Ghost constantly day by day, there is nothing on the face of the earth that

---

966    Smith, *The Words of Joseph Smith,* 53.
967    D&C 84:19–22.
968    D&C 124:95.
969    D&C 84:22–24.

they could ask for that would not be given to them. The Lord is waiting to be very gracious unto this people and to pour out upon them riches, honor, glory, and power, even that they may possess all things according to the promises He has made through His apostles and prophets."[970]

## "The Holy Ghost Shall Be Thy Constant Companion"

As we have discussed, the new and everlasting covenant adds layer upon layer until gospel principles are enhanced, then perfected. One of these principles is the gift of the Holy Ghost.

Upon receiving baptism, we are confirmed members of the Church, and then we receive the gift of the Holy Ghost, which includes the ministering of angels.[971] Thereafter, to retain this gift, we make the covenant of the sacrament, which ensures us that, through our faithfulness to the sacramental covenant, we will "always have his Spirit to be with [us]."[972] Then when a man receives the oath and covenant of the priesthood, he receives an added portion of the Spirit "unto the renewing of his body," and furthermore, he receives the renewed and enhanced promise of the ministering of angels.[973] The Constitution of the Priesthood (D&C 121:34–46) renews the promise of the gift of the Holy Ghost: "The Holy Ghost shall be thy constant companion."[974] That promise is perfected when we live up to the Constitution's terms of righteousness; at that point, we receive the gift of the Holy Ghost in its fulness. President John Taylor said, "Then shall you feel the power of the Holy Ghost resting upon you and its influence penetrating your soul, and then it will grow and spread until its influence extends everywhere; and then will men respect, esteem, and venerate you for your fidelity and for your adherence to the truth."[975]

In the dedicatory prayer of the Kirtland Temple, Joseph Smith connected the "fulness of the Holy Ghost" to the temple: "And do thou grant, Holy Father, that all those who shall worship in this house . . . may grow up in thee, and receive a fulness of the Holy Ghost."[976] Then supernal blessings follow. Elder Carlos E. Asay wrote: "We are told that we can speak with the tongue of angels when under the influence of the Holy Ghost (see 2 Nephi 31:13). We read that people are sealed with the Holy Ghost or the Holy Spirit of Promise (see Ephesians 1:13). We know that those who are wise receive the truth and take the Holy Spirit for their guide (see D&C 45:57). Hence, those who go to the temple and partake of its saving ordinances are endowed with power from on high, even the fullness of the Holy Ghost."[977] Such are the blessings given to priesthood holders and their female counterparts in Zion.

---

970   Young, *Discourses of Brigham Young*, 156 11, p.115.
971   D&C 84:26; 107:20.
972   D&C 20:77.
973   D&C 84:33, 42.
974   D&C 121:46.
975   Taylor, *Journal of Discourses*, 20:262–63.
976   D&C 109:14–15.
977   Asay, *Family Pecan Trees*, 220.

## The Holy Spirit of Promise

The Holy Ghost has a distinctive title that is most valuable to Zion people: The Holy Spirit of Promise. The "promise" is that of exaltation and eternal life. It is the Holy Ghost's office, explains gospel scholar Matthew B. Brown, to "bind certain acts that are performed on earth so that they will be bound in heaven. This seal validates or ratifies all earthly 'covenants, contracts, bonds, obligations, oaths, vows, performances, connections, associations, or expectations' so that they will have 'efficacy, virtue, or force in and after the resurrection from the dead' (D&C 132:7, 18–19, 26). Thus, to have an earthly act sealed by the Holy Spirit of Promise is to receive a promise or assurance that the act so sealed will be valid for eternity."[978] President Joseph Fielding Smith gave this succinct definition: "The Holy Spirit of Promise is the Holy Ghost who places the stamp of approval upon every ordinance that is done righteously; and when covenants are broken he removes the seal."[979] His final words echo the Constitution of the Priesthood's ominous indictment: "Amen to the priesthood or authority of that man."[980]

Zion people seek for the gift of the Holy Ghost and the ultimate expression of that gift—the sealing of the Holy Spirit of Promise. Elder McConkie wrote the following regarding the Holy Ghost: "He is the Comforter, Testator, Revelator, Sanctifier, Holy Spirit, Holy Spirit of Promise, Spirit of Truth, Spirit of the Lord, and Messenger of the Father and the Son, and his companionship is the greatest gift that mortal man can enjoy."[981] When we consider that the Holy Ghost is the agent the Father uses to teach us the truth of all things,[982] including the doctrine of the priesthood, and when we consider that it is the Holy Ghost that seals or makes our covenants more sure, then we should also realize that we must seek this gift at every covenant opportunity and thereafter cling to that gift with all our might until we receive its fulness. The Holy Ghost will make priesthood a power; he will purify and sanctify and make us Zion people.

## Scepters and Dominions—The Holy Interview

This section of priesthood rewards (D&C 121:45–46) ends as it began: in the presence of God, where we now receive the future promise of coronation in God's eternal kingdom: "And thy scepter an unchanging scepter of righteousness and truth; and thy dominion shall be an everlasting dominion, and without compulsory means it shall flow unto thee forever and ever."[983] According to Elder Orson Pratt, when we are standing at last in the presence of God, we will not necessarily receive our "crowns of glory" at that time. Coronation does not happen "until after the resurrection."[984] But we will receive the assurance of that coronation and a view of our eventual scepter and dominion.

---

978    Brown, *The Gate of Heaven*, 253.
979    Smith, *Doctrines of Salvation*, 1:55.
980    D&C 121:37.
981    McConkie, *Mormon Doctrine*, 359.
982    Moroni 10:5; D&C 124:97; Moses 6:61.
983    D&C 121:46; emphasis added.
984    Pratt, *Times and Seasons*, June 1, 1845.

Let us review. A central purpose of the priesthood and its ordinances is to prepare, empower, and lead Zion-like men and women into God's presence. Those who see God are the pure in heart,[985] and the pure in heart are Zion people.[986] Therefore, our abilities to see God and become the ideal of Zion people are inseparably linked with the priesthood. Unless we change our paradigm regarding the purpose of the priesthood, raise our sights, and follow the road of the priesthood to its intended destination, we will continue to languish in Babylon and remain subject to the laws and conditions of this benighted kingdom. But if we will look up and harness the power of the covenants and ordinances of the priesthood, the glorious promises of Zion will burst upon us, and we will achieve coronation, scepters, and dominions at our journey's end.

What should we expect when we at last are standing in the presence of God? A thoughtful review of scripture and the writings of righteous and qualified individuals provides examples and explanations. We must remember that God's dealings with his children are highly individualized. What might occur quickly for one person may stretch into years or even extend into the next life for another person.

One of the blessings we might expect to receive is a vision of God's creations. For example, Abraham stood in the presence of God and said, "And I saw the stars, that they were very great, and that one of them was nearest unto the throne of God; and there were many great ones which were near unto it."[987] In addition to the stars, he saw all "the intelligences that were organized before the world was," and he saw the creation of the world and of man.[988] Similarly, Moses saw the creation of the world "and the ends thereof," "the inhabitants thereof," and "many lands," even "worlds without number."[989] Lehi, Nephi, John the Beloved, Mormon, Moroni, and Joseph Smith recorded similar visions in their interviews with the Lord. Our temple experience foreshadows this future vision.[990] Therefore, it stands to reason that God would allow us to survey the kingdom we are about to inherit[991] and to gain a view of our infinite possibilities as an heir to that kingdom.

Another blessing is to be endowed with the keys to God's knowledge and power, which can be learned only by revelation. The idea of being endowed leads us back to our temple experience. *The Encyclopedia of Mormonism* states:

> As he introduced temple ordinances in 1842 at Nauvoo, the Prophet Joseph Smith taught that these were 'of things spiritual, and to be received only by the spiritual minded' (TPJS, p. 237). The Endowment was necessary, he said, to organize the Church fully, that the Saints might be organized according to the laws of God, and,

---

985   Matthew 5:8; 3 Nephi 12:8.
986   D&C 97:21.
987   Abraham 3:2.
988   Abraham 3:22; 4–5.
989   Moses 1:8, 27–29, 33–38; 2–3.
990   *Encyclopedia of Mormonism*, 455.
991   D&C 84:38.

as the dedicatory prayer of the Kirtland Temple peti-
tioned, that they would 'be prepared to obtain every
needful thing' (D&C 109:15). The Endowment was
designed to give 'a comprehensive view of our condition
and true relation to God' (TPJS, p. 324), 'to prepare the
disciples for their missions in the world' (p. 274), to prevent being 'overcome by evils' (p. 259), to enable them
to 'secure the fulness of those blessings which have
been prepared for the Church of the Firstborn' (p. 237).[992]

One of the most detailed accounts of the endowment of knowledge is that of the brother
of Jared: "And [the Lord] ministered unto him even as he ministered unto the Nephites;
and all this, that this man might know that he was God, because of the many great
works which the Lord had showed unto him. And because of the knowledge of this man
he could not be kept from beholding within the veil; and he saw the finger of Jesus,
which, when he saw, he fell with fear; for he knew that it was the finger of the Lord; and
he had faith no longer, for he knew, nothing doubting. Wherefore, having this perfect
knowledge of God, he could not be kept from within the veil; therefore he saw Jesus; and
he did minister unto him."[993]

Another blessing we might expect in our interview with the Lord is our receiving
an invitation to ask him for a special gift. For example, the brother of Jared asked, "Lord,
show thyself unto me."[994] Nephi had a similar experience: "And the Spirit said unto me:
Behold, what desirest thou? And I said: I desire to behold the things which my father
saw."[995] Nephi's vision was expanded to view of the birth of the Savior, his ministry, his
Atonement, a detailed vision of the land of promise, the rise and fall of Babylon, the
restoration of the Church of Jesus Christ, the gathering of Israel, and the establishment
of latter-day Zion.[996] Joseph Smith and Sidney Rigdon stood in the presence of God and
received a vision of the resurrections and the various kingdoms of glory.[997]

Of course, our entire gospel experience is to lead us to the blessings of Abraham.
When our great progenitor had his interview with the Lord and received the desire of his
heart, the Lord promised him blessings that we all might expect to receive: a promised
land (celestial inheritance), the promise of eternal gospel blessings and priesthood power
for us and our children, and the promise of eternal increase. The parting statement of
the interview is as follows: "Now, after the Lord had withdrawn from speaking to me,
and withdrawn his face from me, I said in my heart: Thy servant has sought thee earnestly; now I have found thee."[998] When these blessings are given to us in our interview,
we might utter the same psalm of praise.

---

992    *Encyclopedia of Mormonism*, 455.
993    Ether 3:18–20.
994    Ether 3:10.
995    1 Nephi 11:2–3.
996    1 Nephi 11–15.
997    D&C 76.
998    Abraham 2:6–12.

Another interesting blessing we might expect is being "ordained of God and sent forth,"[999] meaning, we would be instructed and sent back into the world with individualized missions to draw other people out. For example, in his intercessory prayer, Jesus stated that the Apostles were no longer part of the world, although they continued to live in the world. Then he said, "I pray not that thou shouldest take them out of the world, but that thou shouldest keep them from the evil. They are not of the world, even as I am not of the world." And then he sent them back into the world with divine commissions: "As thou hast sent me into the world, even so have I also sent them into the world."[1000] Similarly, in our interview with the Lord, we will be termed "not of the world," but we will nevertheless be "ordained of God and sent forth," back into the world with a unique mission to draw out of the world the children of God and deliver them to Christ.

## Priests and Kings, Priestesses and Queens

After we have been purified and sanctified by the Holy Ghost to the extent that our calling and election has been made sure, and after we have diligently sought the face of the Lord until we finally stand in his presence, we will receive the Lord's sure promise that in the Resurrection we will be anointed priests and kings, priestesses and queens.[1001] For Zion people, this priesthood experience is singular. What was once provisional is now made sure by divine proclamation.

"What is it to be kings and priests?" asked Elder Orson Pratt. "It is to have honour, authority, and dominion, having kingdoms to preside over, and subjects to govern, and possessing the ability ever to increase their authority and glory, and extend their dominion."[1002] Elder McConkie wrote: "Those who gain exaltation are ordained kings and queens, priests and priestesses, in which positions they shall exercise power and authority in the Lord's eternal kingdoms forever."[1003] Regarding righteous women as priestesses, he added,

> Women who go on to their exaltation, ruling and reigning with husbands who are kings and priests, will themselves be queens and priestesses. They will hold positions of power, authority, and preferment in eternity."[1004] And as queens, he said, "If righteous men have power through the gospel and its crowning ordinance of celestial marriage to become kings and priests to rule in exaltation forever, it follows that the women by their side (without whom they cannot attain exaltation) will be queens and priestesses. (Rev. 1:6; 5:10.) Exaltation

---

999   D&C 50:26.
1000   John 17:11, 15–16, 18.
1001   McConkie, *Mormon Doctrine*, 425, 613.
1002   Pratt, *Times and Seasons*, June 1, 1845.
1003   McConkie, *Mormon Doctrine*, 424; see also Revelation 1:6; 5:10.
1004   McConkie, *Mormon Doctrine*, 594.

grows out of the eternal union of a man and his wife.
Of those whose marriage endures in eternity, the Lord
says, 'Then shall they be gods' (D. & C. 132:20); that is,
each of them, the man and the woman, will be a god.
As such they will rule over their dominions forever.[1005]

Throughout his ministry, Joseph Smith sought to make his people Zion-like, that is,
a kingdom of priests through the full ordinances of the temple "as in Paul's day, as
in Enoch's day."[1006] The Prophet said, "Those holding the fulness of the Melchizedek
Priesthood are kings and priests of the Most High God, holding the keys of power and
blessings."[1007] Elder McConkie explained: "Holders of the Melchizedek Priesthood have
power to press forward in righteousness, living by every word that proceedeth forth from
the mouth of God, magnifying their callings, going from grace to grace, until through
the fulness of the ordinances of the temple they receive the fulness of the priesthood and
are ordained kings and priests. Those so attaining shall have exaltation and be kings,
priests, rulers, and lords in their respective spheres in the eternal kingdoms of the great
King who is God our Father (Rev. 1:6; 5:10)."[1008]

We are anointed to become kings, queens, priests, and priestesses now, with the
futuristic hope of the surety of that blessing. Blaine Yorgason wrote, "It was ever Joseph's
intention that these priests and kings act in their office in communing with God. Speaking to the Twelve on February 23, 1844, Joseph Smith said: 'I want every man that goes
[west to explore for a new home for the Saints] to be a king and a priest. When he gets
on the mountains [the Lord's temple] he may want to talk with his God' (*History of the
Church*, 6:224)."[1009]

Of course, in talking with our God, we would want to be as near to his presence as
possible. The priesthood ordinances are the only way to approach him and the key to doing so. These blessings are no less impressive for women. Elder James E. Talmage wrote:

> In the restored Church of Jesus Christ, . . . in accor-
> dance with Divine requirement . . . it is not given to
> woman to exercise the authority of the Priesthood
> independently; nevertheless, in the sacred endowments
> associated with the ordinances pertaining to the House
> of the Lord, woman shares with man the blessings of
> the Priesthood. When the frailties and imperfections
> of mortality are left behind, in the glorified state of the
> blessed hereafter, husband and wife will administer
> in their respective stations, seeing and understanding

1005  McConkie, *Mormon Doctrine*, 613.
1006  Smith, *The Words of Joseph Smith*, 54–55.
1007  Smith, *Teachings of the Prophet Joseph Smith*, 322.
1008  McConkie, *Mormon Doctrine*, 425.
1009  Yorgason, *I Need Thee Every Hour*, 402–3.

> alike, and co-operating to the full in the government
> of their family kingdom. Then shall woman be recom-
> pensed in rich measure for all the injustice that wom-
> anhood has endured in mortality. Then shall woman
> reign by Divine right, a queen [and priestess] in the
> resplendent realm of her glorified state, even as exalted
> man shall stand, priest and king unto the Most High
> God. Mortal eye cannot see nor mind comprehend the
> beauty, glory, and majesty of a righteous woman made
> perfect in the celestial kingdom of God.[1010]

The two callings—priest (priestess) and king (queen)—suggest the two primary functions of the priesthood: to administer the ordinances of salvation to others and to preside
as a prince (princess) of peace.[1011] The titles "king" and "queen" also suggest kingdoms
and thrones. In the Constitution of the Priesthood (D&C 121:34–46), we who become
priests and kings, with our female counterparts, receive God's renewed pronouncement
of an inheritance in his kingdom ("everlasting dominion[s]") with the authority to rule
and reign forever ("an unchanging scepter of righteousness and truth").[1012] Does not this
description suggest the ideal of Zion?

To righteous couples who are sealed by God's authority and who thereafter have
that seal confirmed by the Holy Spirit of Promise, the Lord promises "everlasting dominions" and "unchanging scepters of righteousness and truth":

> And again, verily I say unto you, if a man marry a
> wife by my word, which is my law, and by the new and
> everlasting covenant, and it is sealed unto them by the
> Holy Spirit of promise, by him who is anointed, unto
> whom I have appointed this power and the keys of this
> priesthood; and it shall be said unto them—Ye shall
> come forth in the first resurrection; and if it be after
> the first resurrection, in the next resurrection; *and*
> *shall inherit thrones, kingdoms, principalities, and powers,*
> *dominions, all heights and depths,* . . . and they shall pass
> by the angels, and the gods, which are set there, to their
> exaltation and glory in all things, as hath been sealed
> upon their heads, which glory shall be a fulness and a
> continuation of the seeds forever and ever.
>
> Then shall they be gods, because they have no
> end; therefore shall they be from everlasting to everlast-
> ing, because they continue; then shall they be above

---

1010   Talmage, "The Eternity of Sex," 602–3.
1011   Abraham 1:2; D&C 84:19.
1012   D&C 121:46.

all, because all things are subject unto them. Then
shall they be gods, because they have all power, and the
angels are subject unto them.[1013]

## Becoming Members of the Church of the Firstborn

In a remarkable vision of the kingdoms, Joseph Smith recorded the following description of those who receive all of the priesthood ordinances and thereafter strive to live the celestial law of Zion: "And thus we saw the glory of the celestial, which excels in all things—where God, even the Father, reigns upon his throne forever and ever; before whose throne all things bow in humble reverence, and give him glory forever and ever. They who dwell in his presence are the church of the Firstborn; and they see as they are seen, and know as they are known, having received of his fulness and of his grace; and he makes them equal in power, and in might, and in dominion."[1014]

Whereas The Church of Jesus Christ of Latter-day Saints is Christ's church on the earth, the Church of the Firstborn is Christ's church in heaven, "and its members are exalted beings who gain an inheritance in the highest heaven of the celestial world and for whom the family continues in eternity." We enter into the Church of Jesus Christ through the gate defined as baptism and by receiving the Holy Ghost, and we enter into the Church of the Firstborn through the higher ordinances of the priesthood. "To secure the blessings that pertain to the Church of the Firstborn, one must obey the gospel from the heart, receive all of the ordinances that pertain to the house of the Lord, and be sealed by the Holy Spirit of promise in the Celestial Kingdom of God."[1015]

Are Zion people simultaneously members of that heavenly church? Yes. If we have received the ordinances of the temple, including temple marriage, we have entered the gate of the Church of the Firstborn. Elder McConkie said, "Celestial marriage is the gate to membership in the Church of the Firstborn."[1016] Of the organization of that Church, the *Encyclopedia of Mormonism* states: "The Church of the Firstborn is the divine patriarchal order in its eternal form. Building the priesthood family order on this earth by receiving sealings in the temple is a preparation and foundation for this blessing in eternity."[1017]

We note here that while temple ordinances and sealings allow us to enter the gate of membership in the Church of the Firstborn, they do not guarantee that we will receive all of the blessings of that Church. Only faithfulness can do that. "When persons have proved themselves faithful in all things required by the Lord, it is their privilege to receive covenants and obligations that will enable them to be heirs of God as members of the Church of the Firstborn. They are 'sealed by the Holy Spirit of promise' and are those 'into whose hands the Father has given all things' (D&C 76:51–55). They will be

---

1013  D&C 132:19–20.
1014  D&C 76:92–95.
1015  *Encyclopedia of Mormonism*, 1:276; see also D&C 76:67, 71, 94; 77:11; 78:21; 88:1–5.
1016  McConkie, *Doctrinal New Testament Commentary*, 3:230.
1017  *Encyclopedia of Mormonism*, 1:276.

priests and priestesses, kings and queens, receiving the Father's glory, having the fulness of knowledge, wisdom, power, and dominion (D&C 76:56–62; cf. 107:19). At the second coming of Jesus Christ, the 'general assembly of the Church of the Firstborn' will descend with him (Heb. 12:22–23; JST, Gen. 9:23; D&C 76:54, 63)."[1018]

All of this has to do with the priesthood—patriarchal priesthood. Zion people first become members of Christ's earthly Church by priesthood covenants and ordinances; then, as they progress in the gospel and receive the fulness of priesthood covenants and ordinances, culminating with temple marriage, they achieve membership in Christ's heavenly Church.[1019] There, in the Church of the Firstborn, Zion and its people exist forever. The heavenly Church, which consists of exalted beings in the family unit, continues to function under the administrative keys of the priesthood. Elder McConkie explained:

> Members of The Church of Jesus Christ of Latter-day Saints who so devote themselves to righteousness that they receive the higher ordinances of exaltation become members of the Church of the Firstborn . . . [which consists of] the inner circle of faithful saints who are heirs of exaltation and the fulness of the Father's kingdom. (D. & C. 76:54, 67, 71, 94, 102; 77:11; 78:21; 88:1–5; Heb. 12:23.)
>
> The Church of the Firstborn is made up of the sons of God, those who have been adopted into the family of the Lord, those who are destined to be joint-heirs with Christ in receiving all that the Father hath. "If you keep my commandments you shall receive of his fulness, and be glorified in me as I am in the Father; . . . And all those who are begotten through me are partakers of the glory of the same, and are the church of the Firstborn." (D&C 93:20–22; *Doctrines of Salvation*, vol. 2, p. 9, 41–43.)[1020]

Those Zion people who travel the road leading to the Church of the Firstborn must face and survive *ordained* ordeals while remaining faithful. That road is marked by priesthood covenants and ordinances. Brigham Young said, "[No one can] dwell with the Father and the Son, unless they go through those ordeals that are ordained for the Church of the Firstborn. The ordinances of the House of God are expressly for the Church of the Firstborn."[1021]

Because Zion people are members of the Church of the Firstborn, they receive the "inheritance of the Firstborn and become joint-heirs with Christ in receiving all that the

---

1018   *Encyclopedia of Mormonism*, 1:276.
1019   McConkie, *Doctrinal New Testament Commentary*, 3:230.
1020   McConkie, *Mormon Doctrine*, 139.
1021   Young, *Journal of Discourses*, 8:54.

Father has. . . . The Lord said, 'If you keep my commandments you shall receive of his fulness, and be glorified in me as I am in the Father; . . . I . . . am the Firstborn; . . . And all those who are begotten through me are partakers of the glory of the same, and are the Church of the Firstborn.'"[1022]

## Angelic Ministers from the Church of the Firstborn

As we have discussed, the Aaronic Priesthood holds the keys of the ministration of angels,[1023] who, we would venture, are presided over by the Holy Ghost.[1024] When we are baptized and receive the gift of the Holy Ghost, we automatically receive the gift of the ministering of angels. These two gifts are renewed and enhanced in the oath and covenant of the priesthood[1025] and in the Constitution of the Priesthood.[1026]

The author of the book of Hebrews wrote to a group of Saints who were living a Zion-like life. These Saints had achieved membership in the Church of the Firstborn and thus were enjoying the ministering of angels. Consider the blessings of these Zion people: "But ye are come unto mount Sion, and unto the city of the living God, the heavenly Jerusalem, and to an innumerable company of angels, to the general assembly and church of the firstborn, which are written in heaven, and to God the Judge of all, and to the spirits of just men made perfect, and to Jesus the mediator of the new covenant."[1027] Blaine Yorgason explained, "In other words, the righteous Hebrew Saints had attained the right to the ministry and association of angelic members of Christ's heavenly Church—the general assembly and Church of the Firstborn."[1028]

The angels who minister to us from the heavenly realms are members of the Church of the Firstborn. They exist in "grades" or levels, according to President John Taylor;[1029] that is, they are variously resurrected beings,[1030] spirits of individuals made perfect,[1031] and translated beings.[1032] A fourth class, suggests Yorgason, "might be departed members of the Church [of Jesus Christ] who are still 'coming unto Christ' and yet are called, from time to time, to minister to their mortal loved ones."[1033]

Expounding on the situation of the Hebrew Saints, the Prophet Joseph Smith described the organization of angels in the Church of the Firstborn and their ministry to us: "The organization of the spiritual and heavenly worlds, and of spiritual and heavenly beings, was agreeable to the most perfect order and harmony: their limits and bounds were fixed irrevocably." Continuing, the Prophet said that the privilege of angelic ministration is a power connected with the ordinances of the priesthood: "I assure the Saints

1022  *Encyclopedia of Mormonism,* 1:276; quoting Romans 8:14–17; D&C 84:33–38; 93:20–22.
1023  D&C 13:1.
1024  2 Nephi 32:2–3; Moses 5:58; Moroni 7:36.
1025  D&C 84:42.
1026  D&C 121:46.
1027  Hebrews 12:22–24.
1028  Yorgason, *I Need Thee Every Hour,* 286.
1029  Taylor, *The Gospel Kingdom,* 31.
1030  D&C 129:1.
1031  D&C 129:3.
1032  D&C 7:6.
1033  Yorgason, *I Need Thee Every Hour,* 288.

that truth, in reference to these matters, can and may be known through the revelations of God in the way of His ordinances, and in answer to prayer."

What intelligence might we expect to receive from angels? Joseph Smith explained that if we pursue the course of the Hebrew Saints and strive to become Zion-like, as they did, our privileges will be identical: "What did they learn by coming to the spirits of just men made perfect? Is it written? No. What they learned has not been and could not have been written. What object was gained by this communication with the spirits of the just? It was the established order of the Kingdom of God: The keys of power and knowledge were with them to communicate to the Saints."[1034]

President John Taylor taught that the various types of angels sent to us from the Church of the Firstborn are our watchmen and the "police of heaven." Moreover, they gather, teach, report, and help us with our prayers: "But, without going into a particular detail of the offices and duties of the different grades of angels, let us close by saying that the angels gather the elect, and pluck out all that offends. They are the police of heaven and report whatever transpires on earth, and carry the petitions and supplications of men, women, and children to the mansions of remembrance, where they are kept as tokens of obedience by the sanctified, in 'golden vials' labeled 'the prayers of the saints.'"

He continued by stating that their influence upon us often goes unnoticed and, unfortunately, is widely disbelieved, but their influence is, nevertheless, among the greatest realities in our lives: "The action of the angels, or messengers of God, upon our minds, so that the heart can conceive things past, present, and to come, and revelations from the eternal world, is, among a majority of mankind, a greater mystery than all the secrets of philosophy, literature, superstition, and bigotry, put together. Though some men try to deny it, and some try to explain away the meaning, still there is so much testimony in the Bible, and among a respectable portion of the world, that one might as well undertake to throw the water out of this world into the moon with a teaspoon, as to do away with the supervision of angels upon the human mind."[1035]

We who have entered the gate of the Church of the Firstborn, which is the entrance to heavenly Zion, we who have received the temple ordinances and have been sealed to our eternal companion, we who have endured in righteousness—we are members of the heavenly church and therefore are privileged to associate with and receive instruction and protection from these, our fellow servants. They may come to us in the form of spirits or translated or resurrected beings—but they come. And when they come, they bless us in ways that we often fail to recognize or appreciate. These are ministers who, under the direction of the Holy Ghost, speak the words of Christ.[1036] They "interact with mortals and . . . have communion with members of the mortal church—according to their respective stewardships . . . thereby encouraging and giving power and direction"[1037] to us, their associates and charges. Their ministration is a manifestation of the love of Jesus Christ, whose servants they are.

---

1034  Smith, *Teachings of the Prophet Joseph Smith,* 325.
1035  Taylor, *The Gospel Kingdom,* 31.
1036  Moroni 7:31; 2 Nephi 32:3.
1037  Yorgason, *I Need Thee Every Hour,* 288.

## The Order of the Son of God

According to Blaine Yorgason, something of significance occurs when our calling and election has been made sure: "We are brought into what is called the order of the Son of God."[1038] Let us first state that an order of the priesthood is a group of like individuals who are one in purpose, heart, mind, and authority. By this definition, therefore, men belonging to the Order of Aaron are Aaronic Priesthood holders, and men belonging to the order of Melchizedek are Melchizedek Priesthood holders. Other priesthood orders involve both men and women (not to suggest that women are ordained to the priesthood), for example, the order of Enoch[1039] and the patriarchal order.[1040] These two priesthood orders are not separate priesthoods or offices in the priesthood; rather, the priesthood order of Enoch is comprised of people who covenant to belong to the same order as the people of Enoch, and the patriarchal order of the priesthood is comprised of sealed husbands and wives (that is, belonging to the same order as the Gods).[1041]

Every priesthood order points us to becoming gods! Being part of the order of the Son of God, we receive "an unchanging scepter of righteousness and truth," and we receive "an everlasting dominion."[1042] Elder McConkie wrote:

> Those who receive the gospel and join The Church of Jesus Christ of Latter-day Saints have power given them to become the sons of God. (D&C 11:30; 35:2; 39:1–6; 45:8; John 1:12.) Sonship does not come from church membership alone, but admission into the Church opens the door to such high status, if it is followed by continued faith and devotion. (Rom. 8:14–18; Gal. 3:26–29; 4:1–7.) The sons of God are members of his family and, hence, are joint-heirs with Christ, inheriting with him the fulness of the Father. (D&C 93:17–23.) Before gaining entrance to that glorious household, they must receive the higher priesthood (Moses 6:67–68), magnify their callings therein (D&C 84:33–41), enter into the new and everlasting covenant of marriage (D&C 131:1–4; 132), and be obedient in all things. (*Doctrines of Salvation*, vol. 2, pp. 8–9, 37–41, 59, 64–65.) Those who become the sons of God in this life (1 John 3:1–3) are the ones who by enduring in continued righteousness will be gods in eternity. (D&C 76:58.)[1043]

1038  Yorgason, *I Need Thee Every Hour*, 403–6.
1039  D&C 76:57; McConkie, "The Doctrine of the Priesthood," 32; Harold B. Lee, Conference Report, Oct. 1953, 25.
1040  Kimball, "The Fruit of Our Welfare Services Labors," 74; McConkie, "The Ten Blessings of the Priesthood," 33.
1041  McConkie, *Mormon Doctrine*, 548.
1042  D&C 121:46.
1043  McConkie, *Mormon Doctrine*, 745.

When worthy men are ordained to the Melchizedek Priesthood, they enter into The Holy Priesthood after the Order of the Son of God.[1044] Then, as men *and* women progress in priesthood principles (temple ordinances and sealings), the order of the Son of God takes on additional significance. President Ezra Taft Benson stated that the order of the Son of God is the equivalent of the fulness of the Melchizedek Priesthood, and therefore requires that we receive *every* saving and exalting ordinance available in the temple.[1045] Thus, worthy men and women can enter into the same order as Jesus Christ.

We credit Alma with having provided us one of best descriptions of the order of the Son of God:

> Now, as I said concerning the holy order, or this high priesthood, there were many who were ordained and became high priests of God; and it was on account of their exceeding faith and repentance, and their righteousness before God, they choosing to repent and work righteousness rather than to perish;
>
> *Therefore they were called after this holy order,* and were sanctified, and their garments were washed white through the blood of the Lamb.
>
> Now they, after being sanctified by the Holy Ghost, having their garments made white, being pure and spotless before God, could not look upon sin save it were with abhorrence; and there were many, exceedingly great many, who were made pure and entered into the rest of the Lord their God.[1046]

We wish that this description applied to every man ordained to the high priesthood, but it does not. Alma's representation seems to point to a higher, holier order of the Son of God, an order within the order, an order consisting of those whose worthiness elevates them into "the rest of the Lord their God." That rest, of course, "is the fullness of his glory."[1047]

When President Benson used the term *fulness of the priesthood,* he referenced the patriarchal order of the priesthood, and faithfulness to the covenants that govern that priesthood order. It is only when men and women are sealed in eternal marriage and thus enter into the patriarchal order of the priesthood that the door to priesthood fulness can be accessed. Only then can the fulness of priesthood blessings begin to flow. This "fulness" is both a doctrine and a right of the priesthood that we learn of and obtain under the Father's tutelage; he distils information upon our souls as the dews from heaven until we are saturated in priesthood doctrine and fulness. The fulness of the priesthood is a condition that characterizes Zion people.

---

1044  D&C 107:3.
1045  Benson, "What I Hope You Will Teach Your Children about the Temple," 6–10.
1046  Alma 13:10–12; emphasis added.
1047  D&C 84:24.

## The Order of the Son of God and Marriage

Another element of the order of the Son of God is its association with the patriarchal order of the priesthood. As we have said, this order of the priesthood is relevant to both men and women, and the doctrine surrounding it provides the clearest statement on receiving our scepter and our everlasting dominion. That statement, cited earlier in the section on becoming priests and priestesses, bears repeating:

> It shall be said unto them—Ye shall come forth in the first resurrection; and if it be after the first resurrection, in the next resurrection; and shall inherit thrones, kingdoms, principalities, and powers, dominions, all heights and depths . . . ; and they shall pass by the angels, and the gods, which are set there, to their exaltation and glory in all things, as hath been sealed upon their heads, which glory shall be a fulness and a continuation of the seeds forever and ever.
>
> Then shall they be gods, because they have no end; therefore shall they be from everlasting to everlasting, because they continue; then shall they be above all, because all things are subject unto them. Then shall they be gods, because they have all power, and the angels are subject unto them. Verily, verily, I say unto you, except ye abide my law ye cannot attain to this glory.[1048]

Neither Zion individuals nor Zion marriages nor the priesthood society of Zion can be established without the patriarchal order of the priesthood that is part of the order of the Son of God. President Benson stated that Adam and Eve made temple covenants and complied with the associated ordinances; then God said to them, "Thou art after the order of him who was without beginning of days or end of years, from all eternity to all eternity."[1049]

The power of this priesthood order, according to President Benson, is sufficient to bring us into the presence of God. And Zion, we recall, is comprised of pure-hearted people who are qualified to see God. Three years before Adam died, he called his righteous direct-line descendants, along with others of his righteous posterity, into the valley of Adam-ondi-Ahman. On that occasion, Adam bestowed upon them his last blessing: "And the Lord appeared unto them, and they rose up and blessed Adam, and called him Michael, the prince, the archangel."[1050] Among all the superlative events that happened at that time, we must not overlook the fact that Adam's primary intent—and the power of his priesthood—was to bring his family into God's presence.

---

1048  D&C 132:19–21.
1049  Benson, "What I Hope You Will Teach Your Children about the Temple," 6–10, quoting Moses 6:67.
1050  D&C 107:53–54.

Of that occasion, Joseph Smith said, "Adam blessed his posterity" because "he wanted to bring them into the presence of God."[1051] Because this event will play out again in the last days at Adam-ondi-Ahman,[1052] we should pay attention to the particulars. Quoting from Doctrine and Covenants 107, President Benson explained how Adam succeeded in bringing himself and his righteous posterity into the presence of God: "The order of this priesthood was confirmed to be handed down from father to son, and rightly belongs to the literal descendants of the chosen seed, to whom the promises were made. This order was instituted in the days of Adam, and came down by lineage [in order] . . . that his posterity should be the chosen of the Lord, and that they should be preserved unto the end of the earth."[1053] That is, Adam received and complied with *all* the temple covenants and ordinances and thereby entered into the *patriarchal* order of the Son of God; then he brought his family into the presence of the Lord.

The patriarchal order of the priesthood governs eternal families. Fathers and mothers preside. If we had more of the revelation of the gathering at Adam-ondi-Ahman, we would likely see Eve playing a prominent role in the gathering and in the spiritual outpouring. Likewise, fathers and mothers in Zion might draw upon patriarchal priesthood power whereby they, like Adam and Eve, might do the work of God and seek to bring their families into God's presence. By reason of their sealing, parents possess the patriarchal power to do this work. President Benson said that Adam set the example of a righteous patriarch. He entered into the patriarchal order with Eve, his wife, persisted in righteousness until he had received all the blessings of the temple, and thereby entered into the order of the Son of God. Now Adam had power to bring his posterity into the presence of God.

Because Zion is the pure in heart, and because the pure in heart are qualified to see God, the principles of the patriarchal order of the Son of God become profoundly important. Enoch, who was present at the gathering at Adam-ondi-Ahman, followed Adam's lead to establish Zion principles in the hearts of his people, and thereby brought them into the presence of God. President Benson said that Noah and Shem also followed this pattern and brought themselves and many people into God's presence. Moses understood the pattern, having achieved the blessing in his life, and attempted to bring his people into the same holy order of the Son of God and thereafter into the presence of God. But, as we have discussed, the Israelites shunned the opportunity, and the Lord withdrew the privilege of entering into his rest, "which rest is the fulness of his glory."[1054]

On that occasion, the Lord told Moses, "I will take away the priesthood out of their midst; therefore my holy order, and the ordinances thereof *shall not go before them*; for my presence *shall not go up* in their midst."[1055] In this verse we hear echoes from the denunciation found in the Constitution of the Priesthood: "Behold, the heavens withdraw themselves; the Spirit of the Lord is grieved; and when it is withdrawn, Amen to the priesthood or the authority of that man."[1056]

---

1051   Smith, *Teachings of the Prophet Joseph Smith,* 159.
1052   D&C 116:1.
1053   Benson, "What I Hope You Will Teach Your Children about the Temple," 6–10; quoting D&C 107:40–42; emphasis added.
1054   D&C 84:23–25.
1055   JST, Exodus 34:1; emphasis mine.
1056   D&C 121:37.

By obedience to the new and everlasting covenant, and by receiving ordination in the Melchizedek Priesthood and becoming part of "The Holy Priesthood after the Order of the Son of God" through obedience to the oath and covenant of the priesthood and to the Constitution of the Priesthood, we can seek and at last stand before God. Our having received and proven faithful to all the ordinances of salvation and exaltation have qualified us to be members of the sacred priesthood order called the order of the Son of God. This order is associated with the patriarchal order of the priesthood. These orders of the priesthood, along with their attendant powers, are highly relevant to Zion people—for Zion is the pure in heart, and the pure in heart are those who qualify to see God.

## The Fulness of the Priesthood

When at last we stand in the presence of God, the grand purposes of the priesthood, as they pertain to mortality, are fulfilled. Now unequalled blessings begin to flow. As we have discussed, these blessings might include a vision of the infinite kingdom that God is about to bestow upon us, an endowment of extraordinary knowledge and power, the receipt of a significant gift that corresponds with our request, and a special ordination to be sent back into the world to accomplish a unique mission among God's children.

Perhaps with this divine interview in mind, President Joseph Fielding Smith said that when we have lived faithfully and done all that the Lord has required of us, we will be given the privilege of asking for and receiving other covenants and obligations, both of which will make of us heirs and members of the Church of the Firstborn: "They are they into whose hands the Father has given all things."[1057] Such Zion people, continued President Smith, will receive of the Father's fulness and glory. Therefore, we should expend every effort to achieve this objective; only obedience and actively seeking this goal will bring us face-to-face with God, in which setting we will receive wisdom, power, and dominion. President Smith concluded by saying that the temple is where we receive the fulness of these blessings.[1058] It is there that we are taught the exalting principles and receive the essential covenants and ordinances to lay hold on the privileges and powers of the order of the Son of God. It is there that we become Zion people.

## Power in the Priesthood

Standing in the presence of God, being endowed and commissioned to do a singular work, Zion people receive a singular ordination with attendant power. Blaine Yorgason gives examples of righteous individuals who achieved the holy order of the Son of God and were given powers commensurate with their calling from the Lord.

Enoch used this power according to the holy order of the Son of God with great effectiveness. In the writings of Moses as revealed to Joseph Smith we read: "So great was the faith of Enoch, that he led the people of God, and their enemies came to battle

---

1057   D&C 76:55.
1058   Smith, Conference Report, Apr. 1969, 123.

against them; and he spake the word of the Lord, and the earth trembled, and the mountains fled, even according to his command; and the rivers of water were turned out of their course; and the roar of the lions was heard out of the wilderness; and all nations feared greatly, so powerful was the word of Enoch, and so great was the power of the language which God had given him" (Moses 7:13).[1059]

Clearly, we might not fully appreciate the power given to Zion people!

Equating the order of the Son of God with the fulness of the patriarchal order of the priesthood, Yorgason continues,

> The scriptures contain other accounts of the remarkable powers that accompany the granting of the fulness of this patriarchal order of the priesthood. For instance, we know that the Lord said to Nephi, the son of Helaman: "Behold, thou art Nephi, and I am God. Behold, I declare it unto thee in the presence of mine angels, that ye shall have power over this people, and shall smite the earth with famine, and with pestilence, and destruction, according to the wickedness of this people. Behold, I give unto you power, that whatsoever ye shall seal on earth shall be sealed in heaven; and whatsoever ye shall loose on earth shall be loosed in heaven; and thus shall ye have power among this people. And thus, if ye shall say unto this temple it shall be rent in twain, it shall be done. And if ye shall say unto this mountain, Be thou cast down and become smooth, it shall be done. And behold, if ye shall say that God shall smite this people, it shall come to pass" (Helaman 10:6–10).
>
> Moroni points to the Brother of Jared as one who gained the presence of the Lord and received exceptional power in the priesthood, according to the order of the Son of God: "There were many whose faith was so exceedingly strong, even before Christ came, who could not be kept from within the veil, but truly saw with their eyes the things which they had beheld with an eye of faith, and they were glad. And behold, we have seen in this record that one of these was the brother of Jared; for so great was his faith in God, that when God put forth his finger he could not hide it from the sight of the brother of Jared, because of his word which he had spoken unto him, which word he had obtained by faith. And after the brother of Jared had

---

1059  Yorgason, *I Need Thee Every Hour*, 407–8.

> beheld the finger of the Lord, because of the prom-
> ise which the brother of Jared had obtained by faith,
> the Lord could not withhold anything from his sight;
> wherefore he showed him all things, for he could no
> longer be kept without the veil" (Ether 12:19–21).

Commenting, Yorgason says: "Thereafter the brother of Jared ordered the mountain Zerin to remove and it was removed (see Ether 12:30). But he was given another power that is even more remarkable and that was almost the envy of the great Moroni, who wrote in prayer: 'Behold, thou hast not made us mighty in writing like unto the brother of Jared, for thou madest him that the things which he wrote were mighty even as thou art, unto the overpowering of man to read them' (Ether 12:24)."[1060]

The commission that we received at baptism to be witnesses of God,[1061] which we renew every time we partake of the sacrament, and which we renew again when we receive the oath and covenant of the priesthood, is advanced to a degree that approaches perfection when we now stand in the presence of God. In that holy encounter, we actually see God, which greatly empowers our witness. We consecrate back to him that testimony by carefully imparting it to others for the purpose of bringing them to Christ. Similarly, we consecrate back to him the endowment of knowledge and power and the special gift he gives us. We recommit to the consecration of our lives by accepting his commission to accomplish a new and special mission in the ministry of Jesus Christ. Now, more than ever before, we have become Zion people.

## "Without Compulsory Means It Shall Flow unto Thee Forever"

The Constitution of the Priesthood lists opposites—those things that bring the priesthood to a halt, and those things that bring power and blessings. One set of opposites involves the word *dominion* as it applies to the presence and the absence of compulsion.

The many (Babylon people) who are called but not chosen would use force or compulsion in "unrighteous dominion,"[1062] that is, they would focus their influence on insisting that other people conform their lives in order to match theirs. To accomplish their objective, they would exert an effort to forcibly draw others into their circle and hold them there. Conversely, the few (Zion people) who are called and chosen, they who would focus their attention on personal sanctification so that they could better extend charitable service, will receive an "everlasting dominion" that will flow unto them with-out force—"without compulsory means."[1063]

The dominions of Zion people flow unto them naturally, without being compelled. This action is like a river seeking its origin. It is like light that naturally "cleaveth unto

---

1060   Yorgason, *I Need Thee Every Hour*, 407–9.
1061   Mosiah 18:9.
1062   D&C 121:39.
1063   D&C 121:39, 46.

light,"[1064] ultimately seeking the Source of light. A sign that we are succeeding and becoming more Zion-like is that blessings begin to flow to us of their own accord. They seek us out as if they sense a home in us. This is the condition of Zion people and a right of the priesthood: "Thy dominion shall be an everlasting dominion, and without compulsory means it shall flow unto thee forever and ever."[1065]

Because the blessings listed in the Constitution of the Priesthood are so exalted, they lie outside the realm of telestial experience, and they surpass our ability to fully envision. Nevertheless, they are an important part of the gospel and of Zion. That they should be given to us in the flesh is the Father's desire and design. Notice the language Lord deliberately uses to drive home this point: "He that is ordained of God and sent forth, the same is appointed to be the greatest, notwithstanding he is the least and the servant of all. Wherefore, he *is* possessor of all things; for all things *are* subject unto him, both in heaven and on the earth, the life and the light, the Spirit and the power, sent forth by the will of the Father through Jesus Christ, his Son."[1066]

## Summary and Conclusion

The new and everlasting covenant, the umbrella gospel covenant, is the first pillar of Zion. The oath and covenant of the priesthood is the second pillar of Zion. These essential covenants stand upon the foundation of the Atonement of Jesus Christ.

Our journey to Zion begins with a covenant—the new and everlasting covenant. As we progress in that Covenant and receive all the gospel covenants, including the priesthood and temple covenants, we are following the same ancient and eternal pattern of the creation of gods. President Wilford Woodruff taught that God the Father "had His endowments long ago; it is thousands of millions of years since He received His blessings."[1067] In a temple dedicatory prayer, President Gordon B. Hinckley confirmed that the initiatory ordinances, endowment, and sealings are eternal in nature.[1068] In the same way that the Father became God, in the same way that every god became a god, we too can become gods. Like our eternal Father and Mother, our kingdom begins at an altar in a temple, where we enter into an eternal union with our spouse and make with each other and with God the covenant of exaltation.[1069] Now a new kingdom is established. On that occasion all of the blessings of the oath and covenant of the priesthood are renewed to both the husband and wife.[1070] Now the infinite and eternal purposes of the priesthood begin to come clear and Zion becomes a reality. Former BYU professor of religion Rodney Turner wrote:

> Priesthood is the authority and power to organize, sustain,
> direct, redeem and sanctify. These operations are as valid
> in terms of the home as they are in terms of a planet or a

---

1064   D&C 88:40.
1065   D&C 121:46.
1066   D&C 50:27–26; emphasis added.
1067   Woodruff, *Journal of Discourses*, 4:192.
1068   Hinckley, *Church News*, Nov. 8, 1997, 4.
1069   Smith, *Doctrines of Salvation*, 2:58.
1070   McConkie, *A New Witness for the Articles of Faith*, 313.

galaxy. The microcosm is, ultimately, the macrocosm. This
is why those who prove faithful over a few things will be
made rulers over many things. Many are called and few are
chosen to retain the priesthood in eternity because their
hearts are set upon the things of the world rather than
upon the work and the glory of that God they purport to
represent. A true priesthood father is like no other father
on earth. His children recognize the difference between
him and other men. His priesthood is a light to his family
and, therefore, to the world. Men and women can provide all of the essential ingredients of good parenthood as
defined by social scientists without being members of the
Church. Both the gospel and the holy priesthood must
make a difference for there to be a difference![1071]

As we said, our journey to Zion begins with a covenant, which is motivated by our
realization that only Jesus "can unlock the gate of heaven and let us in."[1072] Therefore, we
seek to enter into an agreement of salvation with him. The new and everlasting covenant
is that covenant, and exaltation is its end purpose. The Covenant stipulates that we
cannot achieve exaltation unless we become like Christ and bring other people to Christ.
These two essentials are impossible without the power of Christ. Therefore, to progress
in the new and everlasting covenant we seek ordination to the priesthood whereby we
enter into the order of the Son of God. This is also done by covenant—the oath and
covenant of the priesthood, which, along with the covenant of marriage and the patriarchal order of the priesthood, are called covenants of exaltation.[1073]

As we progress in the priesthood covenant, we soon learn that its blessings apply to
both men and women. We obtain these priesthood blessings in stages: first, worthy men are
ordained; second, worthy men and women are purified and endowed in the temple; third,
worthy men and women enter into the highest order of the priesthood—the patriarchal
order—the priesthood order of temple marriage that is the second covenant called  the
covenant of exaltation, because marriage is the culminating ordinance of the priesthood.

Because the "rights of the priesthood are inseparably connected with the powers of
heaven," and because the "powers of heaven cannot be controlled nor handled only upon
the principles of righteousness," the Lord revealed to us what President Stephen L Richards
called the Constitution of the Priesthood.[1074] This Constitution (D&C 121:34–46) enumerates the principles upon which the priesthood either fails or functions, and it lists the
blessings that flow from obedience. These blessings are offered to the many who are called
to the priesthood and thus to eternal life, but sadly, these blessings are achieved only by

---

1071  Turner, *Woman and the Priesthood*, 302.
1072  "There Is a Green Hill Far Away," *Hymns*, no. 194.
1073  McConkie, *Mormon Doctrine*, 167: "Ordination to office in the Melchizedek priesthood and entering into that 'order of the
       priesthood' named 'the new and everlasting covenant of marriage' are both occasions when men make the covenant of exal-
       tation, being promised through their faithfulness all that the Father hath. (D. & C. 131:1–4; 84:39–41; 132; Num. 25:13.)"
1074  Richards, Conference Report, Apr. 1955, 12.

a few who persist in priesthood principles and ultimately are chosen for eternal life. The covenantal statement of priesthood blessings is this: "Then shall thy confidence wax strong in the presence of God; and the doctrine of the priesthood shall distil upon thy soul as the dews from heaven. The Holy Ghost shall be thy constant companion, and thy scepter an unchanging scepter of righteousness and truth; and thy dominion shall be an everlasting dominion, and without compulsory means it shall flow unto thee forever and ever."[1075]

These blessings are a clear statement of the ultimate objectives of the priesthood, and the Constitution of the Priesthood is a second witness, so to speak, of the principles and blessings set forth in the oath and covenant of the priesthood. We have discussed at least eight blessings and purposes of the priesthood:

1.  To make us like Christ and his Father.
2.  To empower us to bring people to Christ.
3.  To bring us into the presence of God.
4.  To give us a view of our celestial inheritance.
5.  To endow us with the knowledge and power of God.
6.  To provide us the opportunity to ask for and receive a special gift from God.
7.  To give us a personalized commission from God to serve in the cause of Christ.
8.  To establish us in our eternal kingdoms.

Thus authorized and empowered, we receive the Lord's guarantee of eternal life and the privilege of becoming part of the order of the Son of God. The highest manifestation of that priesthood order is the patriarchal order of the priesthood, which we enter into when we are sealed to our spouse for time and eternity. Ultimately, the order of the Son of God is the power to prevail with God and at last stand in his presence. In that holy setting, we are given the promise of a scepter and a dominion; that is, we receive the promise that we will become priests and kings (priestesses and queens) with power to administer the blessings of the new and everlasting covenant to others, and we receive the promise that we will inherit dominions and rule and reign in the kingdom of God forever. We are to seek this experience while we are yet in the flesh.

The priesthood is the power to bring us to our journey's end—exaltation. The priesthood is the power to establish Zion in our lives. The priesthood opens the door to our eternal destiny.

Progression in the priesthood entails magnificent blessings. Great powers become manifest in our lives, and these powers amplify our ability to accomplish our God-given priesthood commission. One of these powers is an increase of the Spirit. The Holy Ghost enlightens us to a greater degree, and the brighter we become the more we are capable of drawing lesser lights to us. The effect of this migration of light begins to create a kingdom that flows to us forever of its own accord. Under the Father's careful supervision, the Holy Ghost distils priesthood knowledge upon our souls until that knowledge becomes perfect. It is the Holy Ghost who guides every step of our journey, and it is he who now commends and introduces us to our Heavenly Father.

---

1075  D&C 121:45–46.

Standing, finally, in the presence of God, having expended every effort to return to him, to see him, to learn from him, to be blessed by him, we proclaim, as did our father Abraham, the anthem of the priesthood: "Thy servant has sought thee earnestly; now I have found thee!"[1076] This is the consummate blessing of the few who are called to the priesthood and to eternal life and who are ultimately chosen for the most supernal blessings.

## Postlude

The second pillar of Zion is *the oath and covenant of the priesthood.* It is preceded by the new and everlasting covenant and followed by the law of consecration. According to the "Law of the Church" (D&C 42), these three covenants are sufficient to establish us as Zion people.

Now we have learned that Zion was our origin and will be our destiny. She is our ideal and the antithesis of Babylon. Moreover, Zion is the standard among celestial and celestial-seeking people.[1077] Brigham Young said, "[Zion] commences in the heart of each person."[1078] Clearly, the responsibility to become Zion people rests upon each of us, individually.

That responsibility begins with formally accepting the Atonement by receiving the new and everlasting covenant by way of baptism. The new and everlasting covenant is the "umbrella covenant," consisting of two primary covenants: (1) the covenant of baptism, and (2) the oath and covenant of the priesthood. The priesthood covenant is magnified by (1) ordination for worthy men; (2) temple covenants and ordinances for worthy men and women; and (3) the marriage sealing covenant.

The new and everlasting covenant not only provides a way to be cleansed from sin and separated from the world, it provides us a way to receive God's authority, power, and knowledge—everything we need to become like him and inherit all that he has. This is the essence of the second pillar of Zion—the oath and covenant of the priesthood.

As we have seen, this section applies to both worthy men and women. The priesthood covenant is received by men at the time of ordination, but its principles are expansive and eventually lead to the temple. There, faithful men and women are endowed with priesthood covenants and ordinances that culminate at a marriage altar. An editorial in the *Improvement Era* noted: "Now, as far as the Church of Christ is concerned, this oath and covenant is made first in baptism, when the Holy Ghost is given, and more especially when the Priesthood is conferred. It is, secondly, repeated by partaking of the Sacrament, and by entering into special covenants in holy places [the temple]."[1079] Elder Bruce R. McConkie said, "This covenant, made when the priesthood is received, is renewed when the recipient enters the order of eternal marriage."[1080] Clearly, both men and women are involved in the doctrines of the priesthood.

---

1076   Abraham 2:12.
1077   D&C 105:5.
1078   Young, *Discourses of Brigham Young,* 118.
1079   Editor's Table, *Improvement Era,* Feb. 1923.
1080   McConkie, *A New Witness for the Articles of Faith,* 313.

# Bibliography

*American Heritage Dictionary.* Boston, MA: Houghton Mifflin, 2000.

Anderson, Dawn Hall, Susette Fletcher Green, and Dlora Hall Dalton, eds. *Clothed with Charity: Talks from the 1996 Women's Conference.* Salt Lake City, UT: Deseret Book, 1997.

Asay, Carlos E. "The Oath and Covenant of the Priesthood," *Ensign,* November 1985.

—*Family Pecan Trees: Planting a Legacy of Faith at Home.* Salt Lake City, UT: Deseret Book, 1992.

—*The Seven M's of Missionary Service: Proclaiming the Gospel as a Member or Full-time Missionary.* Salt Lake City, UT: Bookcraft, 1996.

Ashton, Marvin J. "Be a Quality Person," *Ensign,* February 1993.

—"Love Takes Time," *Ensign,* November 1975.

Bednar, David A. "Pray Always," *Ensign,* November 2008.

Benson, Ezra Taft. "A Vision and a Hope for the Youth of Zion," *Devotional Speeches of the Year.* Provo, UT: Brigham Young University Press, 1978.

—*A Witness and a Warning: A Modern-Day Prophet Testifies of the Book of Mormon.* Salt Lake City, UT: Deseret Book, 1988.

—"Beware of Pride," *Ensign,* May 1989.

—*Devotional Speeches of the Year.* Provo, UT: Brigham Young University Press, 1978.

—*God, Family, Country: Our Three Great Loyalties.* Salt Lake City, UT: Deseret Book, 1975.

—"In His Steps," *Ensign,* September 1988.

—"Jesus Christ—Gifts and Expectations," *New Era,* May 1975.

—*The Teachings of Ezra Taft Benson. Salt Lake City, UT: Deseret Book, 1988.*

—"What I Hope You Will Teach Your Children about the Temple," *Ensign,* August 1985;

*Bible Dictionary.* Salt Lake City, UT: The Church of Jesus Christ of Latter-day Saints, 1989;

*Black , Susan Easton, et al. Doctrines for Exaltation: The 1989 Sperry Symposium on the Doctrine and Covenants. Salt Lake City, UT: Deseret Book, 1989.*

—*The Iowa Mormon Trail: Legacy of Faith and Courage.* Orem, UT: Helix Publishing, 1997.

Bowen, Albert E. *The Church Welfare Plan.* Salt Lake City, UT: The Church of Jesus Christ of Latter-day Saints, 1946.

Brewster, Hoyt W. Jr. *Doctrine and Covenants Encyclopedia.* Salt Lake City, UT: Bookcraft, 1988.

Brown, Hugh B. *Continuing the Quest.* Salt Lake City, UT: Bookcraft, 1961.

Brown, Matthew B. *Prophecies: The Gate of Heaven.* American Fork, UT: Covenant Communications, 1999.

—*Signs of the Times, Second Coming, Millenium.* American Fork, UT: Covenant Communications, 2006.

Budge, Ernest A. Wallis. *Coptic Martyrdoms Discourse on Abbaton. London: British Museum,* 1914.

Burton, Alma P., ed. *Discourses of the Prophet Joseph Smith. Salt Lake City, UT: Deseret Book, 1956.*

Cannon, Donald Q. *Teachings of the Latter-day Prophets.* Salt Lake City, UT: Bookcraft, 1998.

Cannon, Elaine. "Agency and Accountability." Salt Lake City, *Ensign,* November 1983.

Cannon, George Q. "Beware Lest Ye Fall." Discourse delivered at the Morgan Utah Stake Conference, Sunday, February 16, 1896.

—Gospel Truth: Discourses and Writings of President George Q. Cannon. Salt Lake City, UT: Deseret Book, 1974.

Cannon, Joseph A. "Sanctification," Mormon Times, June 12, 2008, http://www.mormontimes.com.

Clark, E. Douglas. The Blessings of Abraham—Becoming a Zion People. American Fork, UT: Covenant Communications, 2005.

Clark, J. Reuben. Church Welfare Plan: A Discussion. Salt Lake, City, UT General Church Welfare Committee, 1939.

Clark, James R., comp., Messages of the First Presidency of The Church of Jesus Christ of Latter-day Saints. Salt Lake City: Bookcraft, 1965–75.

Clarke, Adam. Clarke's Commentary on the Bible. Grand Rapids, MI: Baker Book House, 1967.

Clarke, J. Richard. "Successful Welfare Stewardship," Ensign, November 1978.

Conference Report, 1897–2009, Salt Lake City, UT: The Church of Jesus Christ of Latter-day Saints.

Cook, Gene R. "Home and Family: A Divine Eternal Pattern," Ensign, May 1984.

—"The Seat Next to You," New Era, October 1983.

Cook, Lyndon. Joseph Smith and the Law of Consecration. Provo, UT: Keepsake Books, 1991.

Cowley, Matthew. Matthew Cowley Speaks: Discourses of Elder Matthew Cowley of the Quorum of the Twelve of the Church of Jesus Christ of Latter-day Saints. Salt Lake City, UT: Deseret Book Company, 1954.

Dalrymple, G. Brent. The Age of the Earth. Stanford, CA: Stanford University Press, 1991.

Dellenbach, Robert K. "Hour of Conversion," New Era, June 2002.

DeMille, Cecil B. BYU Speeches of the Year. Provo, UT: Brigham Young University Press, May 1957.

Durham, G. Homer, ed. The Gospel Kingdom: Selections from the Writings and Discourses of John Taylor, Third President of The Church of Jesus Christ of Latter-day Saints. Salt Lake City, UT: Bookcraft, 1943.

—Gospel Ideals: Selections from the Discourses of David O. McKay. Salt Lake City, UT: Improvement Era, 1953.

Dibble, Philo. "Recollections of the Prophet Joseph Smith," Juvenile Instructor, June 1892.

Duffin, James G. "A Character Test," Improvement Era, February 1911.

Easton, M. G. Illustrated Bible Dictionary. Nashville: TN: Thomas Nelson, 1897.

"The Bondage of Sin," Improvement Era, February 1923.

Ehat, Andrew F. and Lyndon W. Cook. The Words of Joseph Smith: The Contemporary Accounts of the Nauvoo Discourses of the Prophet Joseph. Provo, UT: Religious Studies Center Brigham Young University, 1980.

Encarta World English Dictionary. New York, NY: St. Martins Press, 1999.

Eyring, Henry B. "Faith and the Oath and Covenant of the Priesthood," Ensign, May 2008.

Farley, S. Brent. "The Oath and Covenant of the Priesthood." Sperry Symposium on the Doctrine and Covenants. Salt Lake City: Desert Book, 1989.

First Presidency, "What is the Doctrine of the Priesthood?" Salt Lake City, UT:
    *Improvement Era,* February 1961.

Faust, James E. "A Royal Priesthood," *Ensign,* May 2006.

—*In the Strength of the Lord: The Life and Teachings of James E. Faust.* Salt Lake City, UT:
    Deseret Book, 1999.

—"He Healeth the Broken Heart," *Ensign* July 2005.

—"Our Search for Happiness, *Ensign,* Oct. 2000.

—"Standing in Holy Places," *Ensign,* May 2005.

—"The Devil's Throat," *Ensign,* May 2003.

—"The Gift of the Holy Ghost—A Sure Compass," *Ensign,* April 1996.

—"The Shield of Faith," *Ensign,* May 2000.

"Galaxy Map." Washington D.C.: The National Geographic Society, June 1983.

Galbraith, David B., D. Kelly Ogden, and Andrew C. Skinner. *Jerusalem—The Eternal
    City.* Salt Lake City, UT: Deseret Book, 1996.

Gardner, R. Quinn. "Becoming a Zion Society," *Ensign,* February 1979.

—"I Have a Question," *Ensign,* March 1978.

Gibbons, Ted L. *Be Not Afraid,* Springville, UT: Cedar Fort, Inc., 2009.

Goddard, Wallace H. "Blessed by Angels." *MeridianMagazine.com,* July 27, 2009.

—*Drawing Heaven into Your Marriage.* Fairfax, VA: Meridian Publishing, 2007.

Grant, Heber J. *Teachings of Presidents of the Church. Salt Lake City, UT: The Church of
    Jesus Christ of Latter-day Saints, 2002.*

Guralnik, David B., ed. *Webster's New World Dictionary, 2nd College Edition.* New York
    City, NY: The New World Publishing Company, 1970.

Hafen, Bruce C. *The Broken Heart: Applying the Atonement to Life's Experiences.* Salt
    Lake City, UT: Deseret Book, 1989.

Haight, David B. "The Sacrament and the Sacrifice," *Ensign,* November 1989.

Hamilton, Edith. *Spokesman for God. New York, NY: Norton and Company, 1977.*

Hinckley, Gordon B. "Blessed Are the Merciful," *Ensign,* May 1990.

—*Faith: The Essence of True Religion. Salt Lake City, UT: Deseret Book, 1989.*

—"Our Mission of Saving," *Ensign,* November 1991.

—"Priesthood: The Power of Godliness," *Improvement Era,* December 1970.

—*Stand a Little Taller.* Salt Lake City, UT: Eagle Gate, 2000.

—*Standing for Something.* New York, NY: Three Rivers Press, 2000.

—*Teachings of Gordon B. Hinckley.* Salt Lake City, UT: Deseret Book, 2002.

—"The Dawning of a Brighter Day," *Ensign,* May 2004.

—"The Stone Cut Out of the Mountain," *Ensign,* 2007.

—"Till We Meet Again," *Ensign,* November 2001.

—"We Thank Thee for This Sacred Structure," *Church News,* 8 November 1997.

— "Your Greatest Challenge, Mother," *Ensign,* November 2000.

Holland, Jeffrey R. "Broken Things to Mend," *Ensign,* May 2006.

—"However Long and Hard the Road," *Ensign,* September 2002.

—*On Earth As It Is in Heaven.* Salt Lake City, UT: Deseret Book, 1989.

Holzapfel, Richard Neitzel and Thomas A. Wayment, eds., *The Life and Teachings of Jesus Christ: From the Transfiguration through the Triumphant Entry.* Salt Lake City, UT: Deseret Book, 2006.

Horton, George A. "Abraham's Act of Faith Reflects 'a Soul Like Unto Our Savior,'" *LDS Church News,* April 2, 1994.

"'Hymn of the Pearl': an Ancient Counterpart To 'O My Father.'" *BYU Studies,* vol. 36, 1996–97.

*Hymns of the Church of Jesus Christ of Latter-day Saints.* Salt Lake City, UT: The Church of Jesus Christ of Latter-day Saints, 1985.

Jackson, Kent P. and Robert L. Miller. eds. *Studies in Scripture.* Salt Lake City, UT: Deseret Book 1989.

Jensen, Marlin K. "Living after the Manner of Happiness," *Ensign,* December 2002.

Jenson, Andrew, *Historical Record: A Monthly Periodical.* Salt Lake City, UT: Deseret News, 1886—1890.

Jessee, Dean. "Joseph Knight's Recollection of Early Mormon History." Provo, UT: *BYU Studies,* vol. 17, no. 1, 1976.

Johnson, Clark V. *Doctrines for Exaltation: The 1989 Sperry Symposium on the Doctrine and Covenants.* Salt Lake City, UT: Deseret Book, 1989.

Josephus. *Complete Works.* William Whiston, trans., Grand Rapids, MI: Kregal Publications, 1960.

Kimball, Spencer W. "A Gift of Gratitude," *Tambuli,* December 1977.

—"Becoming the Pure in Heart," *Ensign,* May 1978.

—*Faith Precedes the Miracle: Based on Discourses of Spencer W. Kimball.* Salt Lake City, UT: Deseret Book, 1972.

—"The Fruit of Our Welfare Services Labors," *Ensign,* November 1978.

—"The Role of Righteous Women," *Ensign,* November 1979.

—*The Teachings of Spencer W. Kimball.* Salt Lake City, UT: Bookcraft, 1982.

—"Welfare Services: The Gospel in Action," *Ensign,* November 1977.

—"Young Women Fireside 1981—In Love and Power and without Fear," *New Era,* July 1981.

Kirchhoff, Frederick. "Reconstruction of Self in Wordsworth's 'Ode on Intimations of Immortality from Recollections of Early Childhood.'" *Narcissism and the Text.* New York, NY: New York University Press, 1986.

*Kirtland Council Minute Book,* eds. Fred Collier and William S. Hartwell,  Salt Lake City, UT: Collier's Publishing, 1996.

Largey, Dennis L. *Book of Mormon Reference Companion.* Salt Lake City, UT: Deseret Book, 2003.

Larsen, Dean L. "A Royal Generation," *Ensign,* May 1983.

Larson, Stan "The King Follett Discourse: a Newly Amalgamated Text." Provo, UT: *BYU Studies,* Vol. 18, 1977–1978.

Layton, Lynne and Schapiro, Barbara A. *Narcissism and the Text: Studies in Literature and the Psychology of Self.* New York, NY: New York University Press, 1986.

Lee, Harold B. *Decisions for Successful Living.* Salt Lake City, UT: Deseret Book, 1973.

—"Stand Ye in Holy Places," *Ensign*, July 1973.

—*The Teachings of Harold B. Lee.* Salt Lake City, UT: Deseret Book, 1974.

Lightner, Mary.  Address to Brigham Young University. *BYU Archives and Manuscripts, Writings of Early Latter-day Saints,* 1905.

Ludlow, Daniel H. *A Companion to Your Study of the Book of Mormon.* Salt Lake City, UT: Deseret Book, 1976.

—*Encyclopedia of Mormonism.* New York City, NY: Macmillan Publishing, 1992.

Lund, Gerald N. *Jesus Christ, Key to the Plan of Salvation. Salt Lake City, UT: Deseret Book, 1991.*

—"Old Testament Types and Symbols," *A Witness of Jesus Christ: The 1989 Sperry Symposium on the Old Testament.* ed. Richard D. Draper, Salt Lake City, UT: Deseret Book, 1990.

Lundquist, John M. and Stephen D. Ricks, eds. *By Study and Also by Faith: Essays in Honor of Hugh W. Nibley on the Occasion of His Eightieth Birthday. Provo, UT: Maxwell Institute, 1992.*

Lundwall, N. B. *Temples of the Most High.* Salt Lake City, UT: Bookcraft, 1965.

"Map: Old Testament Stories: Part Two," *Deseret News.* Jan. 8, 1994.

Maxwell, Cory H., ed. *The Neal A. Maxwell Quote Book.* Salt Lake City, UT: Bookcraft, 1997.

Maxwell, Neal A. *A Wonderful Flood of Light.* Salt Lake City, UT: Deseret Book, 1991.

—*But for a Small Moment.* Salt Lake City, UT: Bookcraft, 1987.

—"Consecrate Thy Performance." *Ensign*, May 2002.

—*Disposition of a Disciple.* Salt Lake City, UT: Deseret Book, 1976.

—"Enduring Well," *Ensign*, April 1997.

—*Even As I Am.* Salt Lake City, UT: Deseret Book, 1991.

—*If Thou Endure It Well.* Salt Lake City, UT: Bookcraft, 2002.

—*Lord, Increase Our Faith.* Salt Lake City, UT: Bookcraft, 1994.

—*Men and Women of Christ. Salt Lake City, UT: Deseret Book, 1991.*

—*Notwithstanding My Weakness.* Salt Lake City, UT: Deseret Book, 1981.

—*One More Strain of Praise.* Salt Lake City, UT: Deseret Book, 2003.

—"Patience," *Ensign*, October 1980.

—*That Ye May Believe.* Salt Lake City, UT: Bookcraft, 1994.

—*The Promise of Discipleship.* Salt Lake City, UT: Deseret Book, 2001.

—"These Are Your Days," *New Era*, January 1985.

McConkie, Bruce R. *A New Witness for the Articles of Faith.* Salt Lake City, UT: Deseret Book, 1985.

—*Doctrinal New Testament Commentary.* Salt Lake City, UT: Deseret Book, 1972.

—*Doctrines of Salvation: Sermons and Writings of Joseph Fielding Smith,* Salt Lake City, UT: Bookcraft, 1954–1956.

—*Mormon Doctrine.* Salt Lake City, UT: Bookcraft: 1966.

—"Obedience, Consecration, and Sacrifice," *Ensign*, May 1975.

—"The Doctrine of the Priesthood," *Ensign*, May 1982.

—*The Mortal Messiah: From Bethlehem to Calvary.* Salt Lake City, UT: Deseret Book, 1981.

—"*The Probationary Test of Mortality.*" Address delivered at the University of Utah Institute, January 10, 1982.

—*The Promised Messiah: The First Coming of Christ.* Salt Lake City, UT: Deseret Book, 1981.

—"The Ten Blessings of the Priesthood," *Ensign*, November 1977.

McConkie, Joseph Fielding and Robert L. Millet. *Doctrinal Commentary on the Book of Mormon.* Salt Lake City, UT: Deseret Book, 1987–1993.

—*Joseph Smith: The Choice Seer.* Salt Lake City, UT: Bookcraft, 1996.

—*Revelations of the Restoration.* Salt Lake City, UT: Deseret Book, 2000.

McKay, David O. *Gospel Ideals: Selections from the Discourses of David O. McKay.* Salt Lake City, UT: Deseret Book, 1993.

——*Pathways to Happiness.* Salt Lake City, UT: Bookcraft, 1957.

McMullin, Keith B. "Come to Zion! Come to Zion!" Salt Lake City, UT: *Ensign*, November 2002.

*Merriam Webster's New World Dictionary, Third Edition.* New York, NY: Simon and Schuster, 1998

Middlemiss, Clare. *Man May Know for Himself: Teachings of President David O. McKay.* Salt Lake City, UT: Deseret Book, 1967.

Millet, Robert L. "Quest for the City of God: The Doctrine Of Zion In Modern Revelation," *1989 Sperry Symposium on the Doctrine and Covenants.* Salt Lake City, UT: Desert Book, 1989.

—*The Capstone of Our Religion: Insights into the Doctrine and Covenants.* Salt Lake City, UT: Deseret Book, 1989.

—*The Life Beyond.* Salt Lake City, UT: Deseret Book, 1986.

—*The Power of the Word: Saving Doctrines from the Book of Mormon.* Salt Lake City, UT: Deseret Book, 2000.

Monson, Thomas S. "In Quest of the Abundant Life." *Ensign*, March 1988.

Nelson, Russell M. "Personal Priesthood Responsibility," *Ensign*, October 2005.

—*The Power within Us. Salt Lake City, UT: Deseret Book, 1989.*

Nelson, William O. "Enoch and His Message for Latter Days," *Deseret News*, Feb. 5, 1994.

Neuenschwander, Dennis. "Ordinances and Covenants," *Ensign*, August 2001.

Nibley, Hugh. *Abraham in Egypt.* Salt Lake City, UT and Provo, UT: Deseret Book and FARMS, 2000.

—*An Approach to the Book of Mormon.* Salt Lake City, UT: Deseret Book, 1988.

—*Approaching Zion.* Salt Lake City, UT: Deseret Book, 1989.

—"Educating the Saints—A Brigham Young Mosaic." Provo, UT: *BYU Studies*, Vol. 11, Autumn 1970.

—*Nibley on the Timely and the Timeless.* Provo, UT: Religious Studies Center, Brigham Young University, 2004.

—*Teachings of the Book of Mormon.* Provo, UT: Covenant Communications, 2004.

—*Temple and Cosmos: Beyond This Ignorant Present.* Salt Lake City, UT: Deseret Book, 1992.

Nibley, Preston. *Brigham Young: The Man and His Work*, 4th ed. Salt Lake City, UT: Deseret Book, 1960.

Nielsen, Donna B. *Beloved Bridegroom*. Salt Lake City, UT: Onyx Press, 1999.

Nyman, Monte S. and Charles D. Tate, Jr., eds. *Fourth Nephi through Moroni: From Zion to Destruction*. Salt Lake City, UT: Bookcraft, 1992.

—*The Capstone of Our Religion: Insights into the Doctrine and Covenants*. Salt Lake City, UT: Bookcraft, 1989.

Oaks, Dallin H. "Good, Better, Best," *Ensign*, November 2007.

—"He Heals the Heavy Laden," *Ensign*, November 2006

—"Preparation for the Second Coming," *Ensign*, November 2004.

—"Taking Upon Us the Name of Jesus Christ," *Ensign*, May 1985.

—"The Challenge to Become," *Ensign*, November 2000.

—"Timing," *Ensign*, October 2003.

Oaks, Robert C. "The Power of Patience," *Ensign*, November 2006.

Otten, L. G. and C. M. Caldwell. *Sacred Truths of the Doctrine and Covenants*. Salt Lake City, UT: Deseret Book, 1982–1983.

Pack, Frederick J. "Was the Earth Created in Six Days of Twenty-Four Hours Each?" *Improvement Era*, October 1930.

Packer, Boyd K. "Personal Revelation: The Gift, the Test, and the Promise," *Ensign*, November 1994.

—"Restoration," *First Worldwide Leadership Training Meeting*. Salt Lake City, UT: The Church of Jesus Christ of Latter-day Saints, January 2003.

—*That All May Be Edified*. Salt Lake City, UT: Bookcraft, 1982.

—"The Candle of the Lord," *Ensign*, January 1983.

—"The One Pure Defense (An Evening with President Boyd K. Packer)," Intellectual Reserve, 2004. Address to CES Religious Educators, 6 February 2004, Salt Lake Tabernacle.

Parry, Donald W., ed. *Temples of the Ancient World: Ritual and Symbolism*. Salt Lake City, UT and Provo, UT: Deseret and FARMS, 1994.

—*Understanding the Book of Revelation*. Salt Lake City, UT: Deseret Book, 1998.

Peterson, H. Burke. "Your Special Purpose," *New Era*, October 2001.

Pratt, Orson. *Times and Seasons*, vol. 6. no. 10, 1 June 1845.

Riddle, Chauncey C. "The New and Everlasting Covenant," 1989 *Sperry Symposium on the Doctrine and Covenants*. Salt Lake City: Deseret Book, 1989.

Roberts, B.H. *Comprehensive History of the Church of Jesus Christ of Latter-day Saints*. Salt Lake City, UT: Church of Jesus Christ of Latter-day Saints, 1930.

—*Seventy's Course of Theology*. Salt Lake City, UT: Deseret Book, 1931.

Romney, Marion G. "Church Welfare Services' Basic Principles," *Ensign*, May 1976.

—"Church Welfare—Temporal Service in a Spiritual Setting," *Ensign*, May 1980

—"Priesthood," *Ensign*, May 1982.

—"'In Mine Own Way,'" *Ensign*, November 1976.

—"The Celestial Nature of Self-reliance," *Ensign*, November 1982.

—"The Oath and Covenant Which Belongeth to the Priesthood," *Ensign*, November 1980.

—"The Purpose of Church Welfare Services," *Ensign*, May 1977.

—"The Royal Law of Love," *Ensign*, May 1978.

—"Unity," *Ensign*, May 1983.

—"Welfare Services: The Savior's Program," *Ensign*, October 1980.

*Salt Lake School of the Prophets Minutes.* Salt Lake City, UT: The Church of Jesus Christ of Latter-day Saints, 1899.

"Sermon Given to Different People," *LDS Church News*, Feb. 18, 1995.

Skidmore, Rex A. "What Part Should a Teenager Play in a Family?" *Improvement Era*, 1952.

Skinner, Andrew C. *Temple Worship: 20 Truths That Will Bless Your Life.* Salt Lake City, UT: Deseret Book, 2008.

—*The Old Testament and the Latter-Day Saints.* Salt Lake City, UT: Deseret Book, 2005.

Smith, Hyrum M. and Janne M. Sjodahl. *Doctrine and Covenants Commentary.* Salt Lake City, UT: Deseret Book, 1960.

Smith, Joseph. *Evening and Morning Star*, July, 1833.

—*History of The Church of Jesus Christ of Latter-day Saints.* Salt Lake City, UT: Deseret Book, 1980.

—*Lectures on Faith.* Salt Lake City, UT: Deseret Book, 1993.

Smith, Joseph F. *Gospel Doctrine: Selections from the Sermons and Writings of Joseph F. Smith.* Deseret News Press, 1919.

—*Teachings of Presidents of the Church.* Salt Lake City, UT: The Church of Jesus Christ of Latter-day Saints, 1998.

Smith, Joseph Fielding. *Church History and Modern Revelation.* Salt Lake City, UT: The Church of Jesus Christ of Latter-day Saints, 1946.

—"Our responsibility as Priesthood Holders," *Ensign*, June 1971.

—*Teachings of the Prophet Joseph Smith.* Salt Lake City, UT: Deseret Book, 1938.

—"The Duties of the Priesthood in Temple Work," *The Utah Genealogical and Historical Magazine*, vol. 30, no. 1, January 1939.

—*The Restoration of All Things.* Salt Lake City, UT: Deseret News Press, 1945.

Snow, Lorenzo. *The Teachings of Lorenzo Snow*, Salt Lake City, UT: Bookcraft, 1984.

Sorensen, A. D. "No Respector of Persons: Equality in the Kingdom," ed. Mary E. Stoval, .*As Women of Faith: Talks Selected from the BYU Women's Conferences.* Salt Lake City, UT: Deseret Book, 1989, 55.

Stevenson, Edward. "Life and History of Elder Edward Stevenson." Provo, UT: Special Collections, Harold B. Lee Library, Brigham Young University, n.d.

Stuy, Brian H., comp., *Collected Discourses.* Burbank, CA: B.H.S. Publishing, 1988.

Summerhays, James T. "The Stripling Elect." *MeridianMagazine.com*, February 20, 2009.

Talmage, James E. *Articles of Faith.* Salt Lake City, UT: Deseret Book, 1984.

—*Jesus the Christ.* Salt Lake City: Deseret News Press, 1915.

—"The Eternity of Sex," *Young Woman's Journal*, October 1914.

—*The House of the Lord.* Salt Lake City, UT: Bookcraft, 1962.

*Tanakh: A New Translation of the Holy Scriptures According to the Traditional Hebrew Text.* Philadelphia, PA: Jewish Publication Society of America, November 1985.

Tanner, N. Eldon. "Constancy Amid Change," *Ensign*, November 1979.

Tanner, Susan W. "All Things Shall Work Together for Your Good," *Ensign*, May 2004.

—"My Soul Delighteth in the Things of the Lord," *Ensign*, 2008.

Taylor, John. *Teachings of the Latter-day Prophets*. Salt Lake City, UT: Bookcraft, 1998.

*Times and Seasons*, vol. 6. no. 10, 1 June 1845.

Thomas, M. Catherine. "Alma the Younger, Part 1," Provo, UT: Neal A. Maxwell Institute for Religious Scholarship, 1996.

—"Alma the Younger, Part 2," Provo, UT: Neal A. Maxwell Institute for Religious Scholarship, 1996.

—"Benjamin and the Mysteries of God," *King Benjamin's Speech*. Provo, UT: Foundation for Ancient Research and Mormon Studies, 1998.

Turner, Rodney. *Woman and the Priesthood*. Salt Lake City, UT: Deseret Book, 1972.

Tvedtnes, John A. *The Church of the Old Testament*. Salt Lake City, UT: Deseret Book, 1967.

—"They Have Their Reward," *MeridianMagazine.com*, February 21, 2007.

Van Orden, Bruce A. and Brent L. Top. *Doctrines of the Book of Mormon: The 1991 Sperry Symposium*, Provo, UT: Maxwell Institute, 1993.

Watt, George D., ed. *Journal of Discourses*. Liverpool, England: F.D. Richards, et al., 1854–1886.

Whitney, Newell K. in *Messenger and Advocate*, 3 September 1837.

Whitney, Orson F. *Gospel Themes*. Salt Lake City, UT: n.p., 1914.

—*Life of Heber C. Kimball*. Salt Lake City, UT: Bookcraft, 1975.

—*Saturday Night Thoughts*. Salt Lake City, UT: Deseret News, 1927.

Wickman, Lance B. "Today," *Ensign*, May 2008.

Widtsoe, John A. *An Understandable Religion*. Salt Lake City, UT: The Church of Jesus Christ of Latter-day Saints, 1944.

—*Priesthood and Church Government*. Salt Lake City, UT: Deseret Book, 1939.

—*Utah Genealogical and Historical Magazine*. Salt Lake City, UT: October 1934.

Williams, Clyde J. *The Teachings of Lorenzo Snow, Fifth President of the Church of Jesus Christ of Latter-day Saints*. Salt Lake City, UT: Bookcraft, 1984.

Wilson, Marvin. *Our Father Abraham*, Grand Rapids, MI: Eerdmans Publishing Co., 1989.

Winder, Barbara W. "Finding Joy in Life," *Ensign*, November 1987.

Wirthlin, Joseph B. "The Great Commandment," *Ensign*, November 2007.

—"The Law of the Fast," *Ensign*, May 2001.

Woodruff, Wilford. *The Discourses of Wilford Woodruff*. Salt Lake City, UT: Bookcraft, 1946.

Yarn, David H. *The Gospel: God, Man, and Truth*. Salt Lake City, UT: Deseret Book, 1965.

Yorgason, Blaine M. *I Need Thee Every Hour*. Salt Lake City, UT: Deseret Book, 2003.

—*Spiritual Progression in the Last Days*. Salt Lake City, UT: Deseret Book, 1994.

Young, Brigham in *Deseret News*, 10 October 1866.

—*Discourses of Brigham Young*. Salt Lake City, UT: Deseret Book, 1926.

—*Journal History*. 28 September 1846.

—*Millennial Star, Vol. 16*. Salt Lake City, UT: The Church of Jesus Christ of Latter-day Saints, 1840–1970.

# Index and Concordance

*This is a master index of the book series. The page number is specific to the book in which it is located. For example: 101:3 means page 101 in book 3. Marker "P" refers to Portrait of a Zion Person.*

**Aaronic Priesthood.** *See* **Oath and Covenant of the Priesthood;** *See* **Patriarchal Order of the Priesthood;** *See* **Priesthood**

>   40:2, 41:2, 12:3, 22:3, 23:3, 36:3, 39:3, 42:3, 59:3, 60:3, 76:3, 92:3, 93:3, 103:3, 104:3, 202:3, 204:3, 50:4, 131:5

**abundance**

>   5:6, 8:6, 10:6, 13:6, 17:6, 18:6, 31:6, 41:6, 44:6, 46:6, 52:6, 70:6, 82:6, 87:6, 96:6, 101:6, 103:6, 106:6, 107:6, 110:6, 111:6, 112:6, 114:6, 115:6

**Adam**

>   empowered to become a savior to his family
>   >   11:1

**adultery.** *See also* **immoral**

>   Babylon distinguished by
>   >   50:2

**adversary.** *See also* **devil;** *See also* **hell;** *See also* **Lucifer;** *See also* **Satan**

>   attacks Saints more viciously than others
>   >   44:1

**adversity.** *See also* **opposition;** *See also* **trial(s)**

>   33:2, 51:2, 54:2, 56:2, 58:2, 61:2, 34:3, 66:3, 117:3, 132:3, 186:3, 178:4, 10:5, 27:5, 30:5, 76:5, 50:6, 101:6

**affluence.** *See also* **mammon;** *See also* **riches;** *See also* **wealth**

>   85:1, 139:4, 103:5, 64:6, 71:6

**agency**

>   a discussion of
>   >   62–68:4

**Amulek**

>   52:1, 80:1, 51:2, 52:2, 55:3, 42:4, 59:4, 133:4, 180:4, 36:5, 71:5, 56:6, 104:6

**angels**

>   involved in crucible experiences
>   >   26:5

**anger.** *See also* **contention**

>   19:1, 57:1, 64:1, 75:1, 86:1, 87:1, 93:1, 96:1, 97:1, 98:1, 55:2, 23:3, 152:3, 169:3, 176:3, 5:4, 29:4, 34:4, 101:4, 111:4, 116:4, 121:4, 136:4, 165:4, 179:4, 180:4, 4:5, 15:5, 22:5, 41:5, 46:5, 79:5, 104:5, 107:5, 124:5, 17:6, 28:6, 34:6, 39:6, 60:6, 94:6, 116:6

**anti-Christ**

>   17:P, 21:1, 49:1, 50:1, 51:1, 61:1, 79:1, 84:1, 85:1, 101:1, 54:2, 67:3, 87:4, 127:4, 175:4, 176:4, 33:5, 48:5, 7:6, 47:6, 88:6

**apostasy**

>   27:1, 33:1, 34:1, 60:1, 68:1, 84:4, 108:5

**apostle**

>   59:1, 17:2

**Atonement**

6:P, 14:P, 15:P, 24:P, 42:P, 11:1, 12:1, 22:1, 23:1, 42:1, 45:1, 47:1, 66:1, 70:1, 1:2, 3:2, 6:2, 7:2, 9:2, 10:2, 16:2, 17:2, 13:2, 19:2, 20:2, 23:2, 24:2, 25:2, 26:2, 27:2, 28:2, 29:2, 30:2, 31:2, 32:2, 34:2, 35:2, 36:2, 37:2, 38:2, 39:2, 45:2, 55:2, 57:2, 66:2, 67:2, 72:2, 93:2, 98:2, 1:3, 10:3, 17:3, 20:3, 21:3, 35:3, 63:3, 70:3, 73:3, 76:3, 158:3, 180:3, 196:3, 211:3, 214:3, 1:4, 16:4, 18:4, 19:4, 20:4, 31:4, 41:4, 42:4, 56:4, 57:4, 59:4, 64:4, 99:4, 122:4, 162:4, 185:4, 1:5, 4:5, 29:5, 64:5, 84:5, 87:5, 91:5, 106:5, 107:5, 111:5, 113:5, 117:5, 129:5, 133:5, 137:5, 15:6, 42:6, 67:6, 75:6

**Babel**

a counterfeit gate of God

54:1

Nimrod established kingdom in

53:1

**Babylon.** *See also* **world**

a discussion of

49–105:1

state of mind defined by excess, self-indulgence

54:1

**baptism**

2:P, 18:P, 21:P, 25:P, 11:1, 19:1, 23:1, 9:2, 18:2, 19:2, 21:2, 28:2, 31:2, 33:2, 34:2, 35:2, 36:2, 37:2, 38:2, 40:2, 41:2, 44:2, 45:2, 49:2, 53:2, 60:2, 63:2, 64:2, 67:2, 68:2, 70:2, 73:2, 75:2, 81:2, 82:2, 91:2, 93:2, 98:2, 1:3, 2:3, 4:3, 5:3, 9:3, 10:3, 11:3, 17:3, 21:3, 23:3, 27:3, 39:3, 42:3, 66:3, 70:3, 71:3, 76:3, 80:3, 93:3, 99:3, 117:3, 143:3, 144:3, 153:3, 179:3, 187:3, 193:3, 200:3, 210:3, 214:3, 1:4, 14:4, 26:4, 39:4, 51:4, 52:4, 88:4, 142:4, 144:4, 145:4, 1:5, 17:5, 18:5, 60:5, 61:5, 62:5, 63:5, 82:5, 83:5, 106:5, 117:5, 133:5, 134:5, 135:5, 68:6, 75:6, 76:6, 106:6

**Beatitudes.** *See also* **Sermon on the Mount**

16:P, 18:P, 28:P, 28:1, 49:3, 41:5, 82:5

**believe.** *See* **faith**

in order to see

68:5

**Beloved Son.** *See also* **Christ;** *See also* **Exemplar;** *See also* **Jehovah;** *See also* **Lamb;** *See also* **Savior**

47:1, 65:3, 111:3, 55:5, 56:5, 110:5, 115:5

**Bible**

39:1, 63:1, 83:1, 54:2, 7:3, 138:3, 153:3, 203:3, 8:5

**blasphemy**

59:1, 82:3

**bloodline**

men ordained to priesthood regardless of

17:1

**Book of Mormon**

   12:P, 19:P, 21:P, 30:P, 39:P, 42:P, 1:1, 2:1, 5:1, 12:1, 17:1, 31:1, 34:1, 37:1, 61:1, 64:1, 67:1,
   70:1, 78:1, 103:1, 18:2, 51:2, 7:3, 17:3, 19:3, 45:3, 46:3, 69:3, 70:3, 92:3, 120:3, 123:3,
   132:3, 141:3, 146:3, 153:3, 163:3, 171:3, 180:3, 5:4, 26:4, 40:4, 69:4, 85:4, 97:4, 99:4, 104:4,
   108:4, 124:4, 135:4, 138:4, 139:4, 157:4, 161:4, 4:5, 8:5, 11:5, 23:5, 34:5, 59:5, 78:5, 96:5,
   103:5, 109:5, 118:5, 127:5, 129:5, 11:6, 15:6, 20:6, 25:6, 44:6, 59:6, 61:6, 63:6, 113:6

**Bridegroom.** *See also* **Christ, Jesus**

   75:1, 85:1, 58:2, 71:2, 72:2, 73:2, 74:2, 75:2, 76:2, 77:2, 78:2, 79:2, 80:2, 81:2, 82:2,
   83:2, 84:2, 85:2, 86:2, 87:2, 88:2, 89:2, 90:2, 91:2, 92:2, 93:2, 94:2, 95:2, 96:2,
   97:2, 98:2, 111:3, 161:3, 173:3, 183:3, 98:4, 11:6

**Brigham Young**

   14:P, 26:P, 39:P, 41:P, 3:1, 5:1, 6:1, 12:1, 39:1, 40:1, 44:1, 46:1, 90:1, 103:1, 1:2,
   61:2, 1:3, 3:3, 19:3, 56:3, 96:3, 101:3, 102:3, 127:3, 128:3, 142:3, 164:3, 192:3,
   193:3, 201:3, 214:3, 1:4, 10:4, 30:4, 47:4, 62:4, 75:4, 85:4, 87:4, 89:4, 97:4, 105:4,
   106:4, 109:4, 113:4, 125:4, 131:4, 132:4, 133:4, 135:4, 137:4, 140:4, 141:4, 149:4,
   150:4, 152:4, 1:5, 4:5, 11:5, 28:5, 41:5, 56:5, 73:5, 81:5, 84:5, 90:5, 91:5, 96:5, 97:5,
   99:5, 101:5, 109:5, 127:5, 134:5, 136:5, 137:5, 11:6, 20:6, 21:6, 27:6, 30:6, 31:6,
   45:6, 55:6, 56:6, 57:6, 58:6, 59:6, 61:6, 64:6, 65:6, 71:6, 105:6

**brother of Jared**

   13:1, 74:1, 58:2, 184:3, 196:3, 209:3, 210:3, 8:5, 21:5, 29:5, 32:5, 34:5, 41:5, 43:5,
   53:5, 58:5, 66:5, 68:5, 69:5, 70:5, 73:5, 86:5, 112:5, 119:5

**Bruce R. McConkie**

   34:P, 36:P, 37:P, 11:1, 45:1, 85:2, 93:2, 2:3, 9:3, 11:3, 14:3, 21:3, 25:3, 33:3, 79:3,
   214:3, 2:4, 8:4, 62:4, 68:4, 82:4, 135:4, 2:5, 7:5, 60:5, 64:5, 129:5, 58:6

**business.** *See* **mammon**

**Cain**

   13:1, 51:1, 52:1, 53:1, 54:1, 61:1, 69:1, 72:1, 74:1, 77:1, 79:1, 90:1, 101:1, 109:3, 82:4,
   127:4, 150:4, 175:4, 176:4, 47:6, 88:6

**calling and election made sure**

      chronology of

         83:3

**carnal**

   20:P, 25:P, 41:P, 19:1, 23:1, 59:1, 62:1, 70:1, 89:1, 94:1, 101:1, 102:1, 8:2, 23:2, 25:2,
   29:2, 33:2, 62:2, 23:3, 109:3, 172:3, 178:3, 64:4, 65:4, 100:4, 109:4, 149:4, 14:5,
   44:5, 67:5, 93:5, 16:6, 26:6, 76:6

**celestial kingdom**

   14:P, 16:P, 18:P, 22:P, 28:P, 34:P, 48:1, 14:2, 15:2, 16:2, 18:2, 21:2, 27:2, 37:2, 74:2,
   2:3, 22:3, 23:3, 28:3, 34:3, 69:3, 71:3, 79:3, 103:3, 115:3, 121:3, 124:3, 125:3, 153:3,
   168:3, 182:3, 186:3, 199:3, 2:4, 3:4, 4:4, 6:4, 8:4, 10:4, 15:4, 26:4, 29:4, 30:4, 38:4,
   51:4, 52:4, 54:4, 63:4, 68:4, 73:4, 77:4, 79:4, 89:4, 90:4, 91:4, 95:4, 126:4, 132:4,
   141:4, 144:4, 148:4, 150:4, 152:4, 185:4, 2:5, 11:5, 31:5, 50:5, 78:5, 120:5, 132:5, 134:5,
   135:5, 3:6, 6:6, 9:6, 13:6, 31:6, 46:6, 56:6, 66:6, 68:6, 72:6, 94:6, 105:6, 110:6

charity
>    a discussion of
>        165–184:4
>    characteristics of
>        147–173:3

chaste
>    5:2, 22:2, 66:2, 24:5, 57:5

Christ, Jesus. *See also* **Beloved Son;** *See also* **Exemplar;** *See also* **Jehovah;** *See also* **Lamb;** *See also* **Savior**
>    a discussion of
>        as Bridegroom
>            72–98:2
>        coming into his presence
>            77:2
>        taking name of, upon us
>            59:2
>    frees us from the powers of Babylon
>        26:1

city of Enoch
>    14:1, 16:1, 36:1, 5:3, 19:3, 23:5, 34:5, 72:5, 2:6

comforter. *See also* **Holy Ghost**
>    37:2, 86:2, 71:3

commerce. *See also* **mammon**
>    76:1, 79:1

compete, competition
>    79:1, 88:1, 119:3, 132:3

consecrate, consecration
>    a discussion of
>        blessings of living
>            33–50:4
>        characteristics of the law of
>            3–31:4
>        guiding principles of
>            62:4
>    living law of, brings blessings of abundance
>        18:1
>    to set apart
>        160:4

contention. *See also* **anger**
>    6:P, 12:P, 43:P, 19:1, 21:1, 24:1, 29:1, 64:1, 67:1, 79:1, 85:1, 88:1, 102:1, 8:3, 119:3, 128:3, 42:4, 48:4, 179:4, 180:4 4:5, 43:5, 102:5, 103:5, 104:5, 107:5, 108:5, 2:6, 117:6

**cooperate**
>    25:P, 6:2, 9:2, 100:5

**corn**
>    kernel of, represents potential of grace freely given
>>        55:3

**coronation**
>    1:2, 9:2, 98:2, 29:3, 30:3, 36:3, 184:3, 194:3, 195:3, 65:5, 73:5, 135:5

**counterfeit**
>    Satan always has, to God's works
>>        61:1

**covet**
>    36:P, 24:1, 70:1, 69:4, 86:4, 100:4, 102:4, 148:4, 16:6, 17:6, 18:6, 115:6

**Creator.** *See* **Christ, Jesus**

**crown.** *See* **coronation**

**crucibles**
>    angels involved in
>>        26:5
>    many, last fourteen years
>>        25:5

**deceive.** *See* **deception**

**deception**
>    victims of, will not be condemned
>>        22:1

**Deity.** *See* **God**

**deliverance**
>    20:P, 18:1, 25:1, 72:1, 8:2, 22:2, 35:2, 51:2, 52:2, 26:3, 121:3, 128:3, 140:3, 148:3, 44:4, 84:4, 125:4, 131:4, 161:4, 162:4, 163:4, 174:4, 178:4, 180:4, 185:4, 3:5, 16:5, 17:5, 19:5, 23:5, 26:5, 27:5, 29:5, 36:5, 38:5, 39:5, 40:5, 45:5, 48:5, 49:5, 50:5, 51:5, 52:5, 55:5, 57:5, 68:5, 69:5, 70:5, 71:5, 72:5, 73:5, 75:5, 76:5, 78:5, 45:6, 52:6, 101:6

**descend**
>    we must, below all things to ascend above all
>>        39:1

**devil.** *See also* **adversary;** *See also* **hell;** *See also* **Lucifer;** *See also* **Satan**
>    6:P, 35:P, 41:P, 21:1, 24:1, 44:1, 51:1, 52:1, 60:1, 61:1, 62:1, 63:1, 64:1, 68:1, 70:1, 72:1, 73:1, 84:1, 86:1, 90:1, 92:1, 100:1, 101:1, 102:1, 28:2, 32:2, 49:2, 89:2, 98:2, 97:3, 109:3, 131:3, 160:3, 163:3, 172:3, 188:3, 189:3, 19:4, 45:4, 63:4, 64:4, 65:4, 67:4, 70:4, 109:4, 113:4, 120:4, 138:4, 141:4, 149:4, 151:4, 152:4, 14:5, 18:5, 47:5, 55:5, 101:5, 104:5, 107:5, 120:5, 26:6, 27:6, 30:6, 38:6, 63:6, 65:6, 71:6, 117:6

**disputations**
>    6:P, 17:P, 26:P, 30:1, 49:1, 57:1, 19:3, 42:4, 119:4, 107:5, 108:5, 109:5, 122:5, 2:6, 37:6, 117:6

elect

> 57:1, 63:1, 85:1, 101:1, 103:1, 43:2, 48:2, 92:2, 40:3, 63:3, 79:3, 80:3, 81:3, 82:3, 84:3, 85:3, 87:3, 105:3, 114:3, 140:3, 154:3, 203:3, 73:5, 74:5, 90:5, 96:5, 7:6

Elijah

> 23:P, 35:P, 31:1, 81:2, 12:3, 13:3, 14:3, 15:3, 16:3, 17:3, 65:3, 116:3, 121:3, 66:4, 130:4, 8:5, 51:5, 70:5, 92:5, 52:6

Eliza R. Snow

> 34:1

endow, endowment

> Abraham administered, regardless of bloodline
>> 17:1

Enoch

> 3:P, 12:P, 15:P, 33:P, 37:P, 39:P, 3:1, 4:1, 6:1, 7:1, 13:1, 14:1, 15:1, 16:1, 18:1, 32:1, 33:1, 36:1, 37:1, 55:1, 58:1, 74:1, 87:1, 88:1, 103:1, 11:2, 12:2, 5:3, 7:3, 9:3, 18:3, 19:3, 20:3, 24:3, 25:3, 27:3, 30:3, 46:3, 57:3, 72:3, 73:3, 89:3, 93:3, 116:3, 184:3, 198:3, 204:3, 207:3, 208:3, 209:3, 10:4, 11:4, 82:4, 86:4, 157:4, 23:5, 34:5, 37:5, 69:5, 72:5, 86:5, 89:5, 90:5, 94:5, 96:5, 100:5, 101:5, 112:5, 124:5, 125:5, 127:5, 132:5, 1:6, 2:6

equal

> 6:P, 7:P, 12:P, 33:P, 27:1, 41:1, 57:1, 65:1, 87:1, 13:2, 64:2, 4:3, 18:3, 40:3, 41:3, 50:3, 60:3, 90:3, 105:3, 106:3, 119:3, 132:3, 200:3, 9:4, 24:4, 26:4, 27:4, 30:4, 36:4, 37:4, 38:4, 39:4, 49:4, 58:4, 59:4, 61:4, 73:4, 74:4, 77:4, 90:4, 96:4, 125:4, 156:4, 183:4, 185:4, 4:5, 122:5, 123:5, 3:6, 10:6, 45:6, 53:6, 77:6, 107:6, 116:6

exalt

> 25:P, 1:2, 9:2, 32:2, 33:2, 45:2, 54:2, 57:2, 61:2, 28:3, 59:3, 132:3, 134:3, 142:3, 146:3, 4:4, 37:4, 52:4, 56:4, 109:4, 184:4, 93:5, 26:6, 76:6, 78:6, 108:6, 116:6

Exemplar. *See also* **Christ, Jesus;** *See also* **Jehovah;** *See also* **Lamb;** *See also* **Savior**

> 39:1, 65:3

Ezra Taft Benson

> 34:P, 8:1, 24:1, 41:1, 61:1, 67:1, 26:3, 109:3, 116:3, 205:3, 6:4, 15:4, 25:4, 26:4, 27:4, 28:4, 48:4, 59:4, 1:6, 80:6, 105:6

face-to-face

> coming, with God is ultimate blessing and right of Zion people
>> 97:3

family, families

> 3:P, 4:P, 23:P, 27:P, 29:P, 31:P, 32:P, 33:P, 34:P, 36:P, 37:P, 38:P, 42:P, 43:P, 6:1, 11:1, 12:1, 13:1, 14:1, 17:1, 18:1, 24:1, 26:1, 40:1, 42:1, 43:1, 45:1, 47:1, 54:1, 89:1, 93:1, 5:2, 23:2, 29:2, 32:2, 36:2, 37:2, 41:2, 50:2, 51:2, 52:2, 53:2, 62:2, 64:2, 68:2, 80:2, 83:2, 92:2, 5:3, 8:3, 12:3, 13:3, 14:3, 15:3, 16:3, 17:3, 20:3, 25:3, 26:3, 27:3, 28:3, 31:3, 32:3, 34:3, 65:3, 69:3, 70:3, 76:3, 78:3, 92:3, 100:3, 111:3, 113:3, 120:3, 136:3, 139:3, 146:3, 170:3, 178:3, 185:3, 186:3, 199:3, 200:3, 201:3, 204:3, 206:3, 207:3, 212:3, 4:4, 6:4, 8:4, 9:4, 23:4, 26:4, 27:4, 29:4, 30:4, 39:4, 41:4, 69:4, 72:4, 73:4, 74:4, 79:4, 82:4, 84:4, 86:4,

87:4, 133:4, 134:4, 141:4, 151:4, 157:4, 170:4, 171:4, 179:4, 180:4, 4:5, 21:5, 24:5, 42:5, 50:5, 51:5, 52:5, 62:5, 66:5, 71:5, 94:5, 95:5, 104:5, 107:5, 127:5, 133:5, 134:5, 5:6, 57:6, 65:6, 78:6, 87:6, 98:6, 102:6, 103:6, 104:6, 111:6, 112:6, 113:6, 114:6, 115:6

fathers
6:P, 18:1, 28:1, 35:1, 45:1, 63:1, 81:1, 91:1, 98:1, 32:2, 75:2, 13:3, 15:3, 17:3, 23:3, 27:3, 65:3, 77:3, 91:3, 104:3, 160:3, 161:3, 207:3, 118:4, 124:4, 128:4, 137:4, 141:4, 152:4, 67:5, 109:5, 124:5, 128:5, 136:5, 4:6, 37:6, 43:6, 48:6, 60:6, 66:6

fear
11:P, 26:P, 29:P, 42:P, 43:P, 23:1, 35:1, 37:1, 40:1, 53:1, 56:1, 64:1, 84:1, 85:1, 93:1, 94:1, 97:1, 59:2, 86:2, 39:3, 128:3, 130:3, 142:3, 149:3, 158:3, 169:3, 186:3, 196:3, 4:4, 22:4, 116:4, 141:4, 171:4, 172:4, 177:4, 27:5, 37:5, 57:5, 101:5, 133:5, 1:6, 35:6, 66:6, 90:6, 97:6, 98:6, 112:6

flatter
73:1, 96:1

forgive
10:P, 39:2, 40:2, 116:4, 178:4, 183:4, 35:6, 101:6

fornication
56:1, 57:1, 58:1, 59:1, 76:1, 80:1, 93:1, 50:2, 22:5

fourteen years
many crucibles last
25:5

fruit
ripe, falls from tree of life to rot on ground
96:1

fundamentalism
definition of
83:1

Gadianton robbers. *See also* secret combinations
97:1

Garden of Eden
13:1, 77:1, 108:4, 8:5, 28:5, 36:5, 72:5, 25:6

gathering
always associated with Zion
20:1

generosity. *See* selflessness

give yourself rich. *See* abundance
8:P, 176:4, 89:6

God-like, godliness
become, by learning how to lift others
5:1

gold

28:P, 38:P, 42:P, 27:1, 50:1, 52:1, 58:1, 59:1, 62:1, 76:1, 96:1, 22:2, 80:2, 94:2, 129:3, 151:3, 9:4, 40:4, 44:4, 82:4, 101:4, 103:4, 106:4, 109:4, 116:4, 118:4, 124:4, 132:4, 139:4, 140:4, 145:4, 146:4, 3:5, 21:5, 23:5, 24:5, 25:5, 26:5, 17:6, 19:6, 22:6, 27:6, 35:6, 36:6, 44:6, 55:6, 64:6, 65:6, 68:6, 69:6, 70:6

good

definition of

9:1

goods. *See* **mammon**

**Gordon B. Hinckley**

6:P, 7:1, 28:2, 55:3, 172:3, 211:3, 37:4, 40:4, 41:4, 56:4, 59:4, 60:4, 164:4, 170:4, 87:5, 78:6, 83:6, 93:6

grace. *See also* **mercy**

15:P, 19:P, 22:P, 4:1, 6:1, 10:1, 11:1, 28:1, 42:1, 4:2, 17:2, 18:2, 19:2, 20:2, 22:2, 23:2, 26:2, 29:2, 36:2, 38:2, 43:2, 45:2, 78:2, 16:3, 21:3, 24:3, 52:3, 53:3, 54:3, 55:3, 60:3, 64:3, 86:3, 104:3, 153:3, 198:3, 200:3, 57:4, 66:4, 79:4, 89:4, 92:4, 139:4, 146:4, 174:4, 175:4, 177:4, 181:4, 184:4, 7:5, 20:5, 31:5, 32:5, 45:5, 90:5, 124:5, 64:6, 70:6, 75:6, 80:6, 81:6, 82:6, 83:6, 89:6, 90:6, 100:6, 101:6

**Harold B. Lee**

16:P, 28:P, 28:1, 82:1, 49:3, 130:3, 131:3, 204:3, 82:5, 147:5

heal

21:P, 1:1, 2:1, 46:1, 135:3, 142:3, 152:3, 165:3, 171:3, 73:4, 77:4, 142:4, 144:4, 159:4, 160:4, 161:4, 184:4, 15:5, 113:5, 68:6, 86:6

healing

we prepare for Zion by experiencing

160:4

health

23:P, 9:1, 76:1, 90:1, 100:1, 24:2, 29:2, 123:3, 18:4, 161:4, 180:4, 185:4, 15:5, 24:5, 25:5, 37:5, 57:5, 71:5, 72:5, 1:6, 86:6, 103:6, 109:6

heart

a discussion of

pure in

77–108:5

is altar of soul

49:5

must be changed to attain Zion

12:1

**Heber C. Kimball**

114:1, 83:3, 100:3, 101:3, 148:5

heir

11:1, 53:1, 101:1, 29:3, 76:3, 195:3, 45:5

**hell.** *See also* **adversary;** *See also* **devil;** *See also* **Lucifer;** *See also* **Satan**
18:P, 41:P, 47:1, 63:1, 68:1, 70:1, 72:1, 73:1, 74:1, 101:1, 102:1, 26:2, 97:3, 109:3, 128:3, 131:3, 154:3, 160:3, 163:3, 188:3, 75:4, 109:4, 112:4, 113:4, 120:4, 126:4, 141:4, 149:4, 13:5, 14:5, 47:5, 56:5, 97:5, 5:6, 26:6, 29:6, 30:6, 39:6, 46:6, 65:6

**Holy Ghost.** *See also* **comforter**
presence of, signifies we are retaining remission of sins
38:2

**homosexuality**
56:1

**Hugh Nibley**
5:P, 26:P, 33:P, 5:1, 7:1, 8:1, 33:1, 34:1, 50:1, 51:1, 56:1, 57:1, 70:1, 71:1, 75:1, 77:1, 79:1, 80:1, 89:1, 92:1, 93:1, 47:3, 109:3, 110:3, 137:3, 6:4, 7:4, 16:4, 28:4, 50:4, 56:4, 85:4, 87:4, 93:4, 94:4, 98:4, 99:4, 105:4, 108:4, 110:4, 113:4, 127:4, 132:4, 136:4, 138:4, 150:4, 21:5, 22:5, 96:5, 7:6, 8:6, 12:6, 15:6, 21:6, 25:6, 27:6, 30:6, 47:6, 56:6, 59:6, 61:6, 105:6, 116:6

**hundredfold**
8:P, 25:2, 27:2, 29:2, 123:3, 126:3, 127:3, 141:3, 151:3, 36:4, 58:4, 67:4, 92:4, 145:4, 153:4, 170:4, 177:4, 184:4, 70:5, 118:5, 3:6, 6:6, 69:6, 70:6, 72:6, 87:6, 89:6, 106:6, 107:6, 108:6, 109:6, 110:6

**husband.** *See also* **marriage**
24:2, 66:2, 75:2, 76:2, 77:2, 78:2, 79:2, 80:2, 81:2, 83:2, 84:2, 85:2, 89:2, 90:2, 94:2, 97:2, 13:3, 15:3, 17:3, 23:3, 59:3, 64:3, 85:3, 110:3, 136:3, 179:3, 183:3, 198:3, 211:3, 41:4, 43:4, 98:4, 155:4, 156:4, 157:4, 42:5, 117:5, 11:6

**hypocrisy**
80:1, 41:2, 44:3, 47:3, 108:3, 110:3, 119:3, 159:3, 160:3, 165:3, 167:3, 140:4, 64:6

**idleness**
38:P, 27:1, 56:1, 119:3, 129:3, 20:4, 39:4, 83:4, 84:4, 85:4, 86:4, 101:4, 121:4, 157:4, 18:6, 41:6, 50:6

**idolatrous**
54:1, 88:1, 54:2, 171:3, 109:4, 117:4, 27:6, 35:6

**immoral.** *See also* **adultery**
58:1, 69:1, 76:1, 87:1, 171:3, 172:3, 176:4, 88:6

**inequality**
7:P, 86:1, 114:3, 124:3, 132:3, 139:3, 19:4, 29:4, 36:4, 39:4, 73:4, 85:4, 119:4, 124:4, 125:4, 150:4, 103:5, 38:6, 44:6, 45:6, 78:6

**inherit, inheritance**
a discussion of the chosen few
63–105:3

**Israel**
26:P, 18:1, 29:1, 32:1, 36:1, 42:1, 43:1, 45:1, 46:1, 65:1, 100:1, 14:2, 72:2, 81:2, 90:2, 91:2, 94:2, 14:3, 23:3, 31:3, 70:3, 76:3, 77:3, 111:3, 176:3, 180:3, 196:3, 18:4, 73:4, 100:4, 101:4, 104:4, 106:4, 126:4, 130:4, 131:4, 135:4, 150:4, 160:4, 35:5, 36:5, 41:5, 79:5, 110:5, 111:5, 112:5, 113:5, 114:5, 132:5, 4:6, 16:6, 17:6, 20:6, 21:6, 22:6, 46:6, 52:6, 58:6

**James E. Faust**

  8:P, 83:1, 93:3, 117:3, 43:4, 156:4, 162:4, 45:5, 91:5, 142:5

**Jehovah.** *See also* **Christ, Jesus;** *See also* **Exemplar;** *See also* **Lamb;** *See also* **Savior**

  18:1, 30:3, 66:4, 98:4, 100:4, 88:5, 98:5, 12:6, 16:6

**Jerusalem.** *See also* **Salem**

  14:P, 2:1, 9:1, 15:1, 16:1, 33:1, 36:1, 37:1, 47:1, 53:1, 55:1, 61:1, 75:1, 78:1, 104:1,
  1:2, 3:2, 51:2, 97:2, 1:3, 9:3, 13:3, 49:3, 100:3, 202:3, 1:4, 41:4, 1:5, 8:5, 20:5, 23:5,
  63:5, 73:5, 87:5, 96:5, 97:5, 98:5, 113:5, 117:5, 118:5, 127:5, 128:5, 131:5, 134:5, 1:6

**John A. Widtsoe**

  8:1, 45:1, 61:1, 72:2, 164:4, 67:5, 93:6

**Joseph Fielding Smith**

  14:1, 81:1, 15:3, 21:3, 41:3, 56:3, 78:3, 102:3, 103:3, 190:3, 194:3, 208:3, 3:6

**Joseph Smith**

  4:P, 12:P, 18:P, 33:P, 39:P, 40:P, 41:P, 3:1, 5:1, 15:1, 26:1, 31:1, 32:1, 41:1, 44:1, 46:1, 48:1,
  65:1, 67:1, 72:1, 90:1, 94:1, 103:1, 1:2, 3:2, 4:2, 6:2, 10:2, 15:2, 22:2, 23:2, 25:2, 26:2,
  27:2, 28:2, 31:2, 42:2, 44:2, 45:2, 50:2, 58:2, 61:2, 62:2, 63:2, 87:2, 88:2, 90:2, 1:3, 5:3,
  6:3, 7:3, 12:3, 13:3, 14:3, 15:3, 16:3, 17:3, 18:3, 20:3, 22:3, 25:3, 30:3, 31:3, 36:3, 43:3,
  44:3, 57:3, 68:3, 69:3, 77:3, 81:3, 82:3, 83:3, 85:3, 86:3, 87:3, 88:3, 91:3, 93:3, 97:3,
  98:3, 99:3, 100:3, 101:3, 104:3, 116:3, 120:3, 122:3, 125:3, 126:3, 140:3, 141:3, 160:3,
  166:3, 177:3, 181:3, 182:3, 184:3, 188:3, 190:3, 191:3, 192:3, 193:3, 195:3, 196:3, 198:3,
  200:3, 202:3, 203:3, 207:3, 208:3, 1:4, 4:4, 7:4, 10:4, 11:4, 12:4, 13:4, 28:4, 29:4, 30:4,
  38:4, 39:4, 44:4, 45:4, 46:4, 48:4, 57:4, 61:4, 65:4, 76:4, 77:4, 78:4, 100:4, 104:4, 107:4,
  114:4, 133:4, 137:4, 142:4, 148:4, 157:4, 169:4, 171:4, 1:5, 4:5, 5:5, 8:5, 9:5, 14:5, 20:5,
  24:5, 25:5, 27:5, 30:5, 31:5, 33:5, 34:5, 42:5, 45:5, 47:5, 54:5, 55:5, 56:5, 58:5, 64:5,
  66:5, 68:5, 77:5, 81:5, 86:5, 88:5, 89:5, 93:5, 94:5, 95:5, 96:5, 97:5, 98:5, 99:5, 100:5,
  108:5, 112:5, 118:5, 119:5, 123:5, 124:5, 126:5, 127:5, 129:5, 136:5, 1:6, 3:6, 5:6, 6:6,
  16:6, 20:6, 22:6, 25:6, 31:6, 51:6, 56:6, 57:6, 60:6, 87:6, 98:6, 105:6, 106:6, 113:6, 116:6

**journey**

  a discussion of

    life's journey

      7–57:5

**J. Reuben Clark**

  44:1, 79:3, 21:4, 28:4

**justice, justification**

  discussion of

    6–17:2

  rewards those who are obedient to God's laws

    17:2

**justified.** *See* **justice, justification**

**key(s)**

  8:P, 23:P, 26:P, 2:1, 13:1, 18:1, 87:1, 101:1, 104:1, 28:2, 61:2, 22:3, 23:3, 24:3, 43:3,
  44:3, 57:3, 60:3, 76:3, 83:3, 94:3, 95:3, 97:3, 98:3, 121:3, 122:3, 136:3, 141:3, 156:3,

157:3, 164:3, 176:3, 179:3, 181:3, 184:3, 190:3, 191:3, 192:3, 198:3, 9:4, 62:4, 66:4, 89:4, 106:4, 146:4, 153:4, 159:4, 164:4, 182:4, 26:5, 46:5, 47:5, 54:5, 64:5, 66:5, 87:5, 88:5, 108:5, 134:5, 22:6, 70:6, 94:6, 106:6, 108:6

King Benjamin
20:P, 19:1, 20:1, 21:1, 22:1, 23:1, 24:1, 25:1, 26:1, 8:2, 66:2, 7:3, 8:3, 9:3, 10:3, 11:3, 20:3, 51:3, 67:3, 152:3, 9:4, 35:4, 39:4, 78:4, 120:4, 121:4, 126:4, 127:4, 170:4, 36:5, 42:5, 59:5, 62:5, 63:5, 64:5, 66:5, 106:5, 108:5, 39:6, 46:6, 48:6, 76:6, 79:6, 106:6

king(s)
15:1, 16:1, 20:1, 21:1, 23:1, 25:1, 49:1, 85:2, 90:2, 92:2, 94:2, 95:2, 5:3, 7:3, 9:3, 10:3, 11:3, 29:3, 45:3, 111:3, 112:3, 113:3, 119:3, 139:3, 152:3, 198:3, 199:3, 20:4, 39:4, 76:4, 100:4, 108:4, 134:4, 8:5, 9:5, 39:5, 51:5, 54:5, 58:5, 60:5, 62:5, 63:5, 89:5, 1:6, 2:6, 16:6, 26:6, 46:6, 58:6

Korihor
50:1, 79:1, 127:4, 175:4, 47:6, 88:6

labor. *See also* work
35:P, 37:P, 38:P, 42:P, 20:1, 24:1, 27:1, 30:1, 42:1, 84:1, 39:2, 7:3, 19:3, 55:3, 146:3, 171:3, 17:4, 19:4, 39:4, 58:4, 62:4, 70:4, 71:4, 80:4, 82:4, 83:4, 84:4, 85:4, 86:4, 87:4, 88:4, 89:4, 90:4, 91:4, 92:4, 127:4, 135:4, 136:4, 140:4, 141:4, 151:4, 152:4, 156:4, 174:4, 176:4, 183:4, 185:4, 4:5, 26:5, 32:5, 33:5, 50:5, 92:5, 93:5, 95:5, 122:5, 137:5, 48:6, 59:6, 60:6, 65:6, 66:6, 71:6, 72:6, 100:6

lack. *See* poor

Laman
101:1, 20:5, 27:5

Lamb. *See also* **Christ, Jesus;** *See also* **Exemplar;** *See also* **Jehovah;** *See also* **Savior**
18:1, 172:4, 98:6

lawyers
86:1, 90:1, 119:4, 103:5, 37:6

Lehi
17:P, 27:P, 63:1, 64:1, 74:1, 94:1, 52:2, 58:2, 78:2, 195:3, 21:4, 42:4, 59:4, 3:5, 8:5, 9:5, 10:5, 17:5, 19:5, 21:5, 23:5, 26:5, 28:5, 31:5, 34:5, 41:5, 42:5, 51:5, 52:5, 58:5, 67:5, 73:5

lies
30:P, 9:1, 18:1, 22:1, 51:1, 63:1, 72:1, 19:2, 97:2, 9:3, 55:3, 60:3, 95:3, 97:3, 117:3, 139:3, 160:3, 181:3, 13:4, 41:4, 47:4, 65:4, 74:4, 137:4, 142:4, 156:4, 166:4, 7:5, 9:5, 19:5, 26:5, 87:5, 2:6, 60:6, 67:6, 101:6, 112:6

Lorenzo Snow
78:1, 6:4, 15:4, 17:4, 31:4, 47:4, 4:5, 94:5, 95:5, 100:5, 131:5, 136:5, 148:5

love. *See also* charity; *See also* heart
2:P, 7:P, 9:P, 10:P, 11:P, 12:P, 17:P, 20:P, 21:P, 22:P, 24:P, 27:P, 28:P, 34:P, 39:P, 43:P, 19:1, 22:1, 23:1, 24:1, 26:1, 29:1, 30:1, 33:1, 34:1, 42:1, 49:1, 64:1, 65:1, 70:1, 71:1, 76:1, 77:1, 79:1, 86:1, 87:1, 89:1, 91:1, 99:1, 3:2, 4:2, 5:2, 18:2, 19:2, 27:2, 38:2, 41:2, 44:2, 50:2, 54:2, 56:2, 57:2, 60:2, 61:2, 62:2, 66:2, 67:2, 69:2, 70:2, 72:2, 73:2, 74:2, 75:2, 76:2, 77:2, 78:2, 79:2, 80:2, 81:2, 82:2, 84:2, 86:2,

93:2, 95:2, 96:2, 97:2, 98:2, 99:2, 17:3, 30:3, 33:3, 44:3, 47:3, 48:3, 49:3, 50:3, 51:3, 52:3, 56:3, 57:3, 61:3, 68:3, 74:3, 75:3, 85:3, 86:3, 87:3, 90:3, 91:3, 92:3, 93:3, 95:3, 104:3, 108:3, 109:3, 111:3, 113:3, 114:3, 117:3, 118:3, 119:3, 122:3, 124:3, 125:3, 131:3, 132:3, 134:3, 138:3, 139:3, 140:3, 141:3, 142:3, 146:3, 147:3, 148:3, 153:3, 154:3, 155:3, 156:3, 157:3, 158:3, 159:3, 168:3, 169:3, 170:3, 171:3, 173:3, 178:3, 182:3, 185:3, 189:3, 203:3, 2:4, 19:4, 21:4, 23:4, 25:4, 26:4, 27:4, 33:4, 34:4, 35:4, 37:4, 38:4, 41:4, 42:4, 47:4, 50:4, 51:4, 52:4, 54:4, 55:4, 56:4, 57:4, 58:4, 60:4, 64:4, 70:4, 72:4, 73:4, 90:4, 91:4, 93:4, 95:4, 97:4, 98:4, 99:4, 100:4, 102:4, 107:4, 114:4, 116:4, 120:4, 121:4, 123:4, 138:4, 141:4, 142:4, 143:4, 146:4, 147:4, 148:4, 149:4, 152:4, 153:4, 155:4, 156:4, 157:4, 158:4, 163:4, 164:4, 165:4, 166:4, 167:4, 168:4, 169:4, 170:4, 171:4, 172:4, 173:4, 174:4, 175:4, 178:4, 179:4, 181:4, 182:4, 183:4, 184:4, 185:4, 186:4, 2:5, 16:5, 24:5, 30:5, 33:5, 42:5, 43:5, 52:5, 64:5, 66:5, 67:5, 69:5, 70:5, 71:5, 74:5, 77:5, 78:5, 79:5, 81:5, 85:5, 89:5, 92:5, 100:5, 106:5, 107:5, 108:5, 122:5, 124:5, 127:5, 133:5, 135:5, 137:5, 2:6, 5:6, 7:6, 8:6, 9:6, 11:6, 13:6, 15:6, 16:6, 18:6, 23:6, 31:6, 35:6, 38:6, 39:6, 43:6, 61:6, 66:6, 67:6, 70:6, 78:6, 79:6, 80:6, 85:6, 86:6, 87:6, 88:6, 91:6, 93:6, 94:6, 95:6, 96:6, 97:6, 98:6, 99:6, 100:6, 101:6, 102:6, 106:6, 107:6, 108:6, 113:6, 116:6, 117:6

**low**

to make, is not demeaning
34:4

**Lucifer.** *See also* **adversary;** *See also* **devil;** *See also* **hell;** *See also* **Satan**

10:1

**lukewarm**

being, is a one-way ticket to hell
47:1

**Mahan**

51:1, 52:1, 69:1, 79:1, 127:4, 151:4, 47:6

**mammon.** *See also* **materialism;** *See also* **money;** *See also* **riches**

a discussion of
choosing, over God
99–137:4
making friends with
109:4

**mansions**

37:P, 76:1, 73:2, 82:2, 86:2, 89:2, 93:2, 168:3, 203:3, 81:4, 175:4, 50:5, 100:6

**marriage.** *See also* **new and everlasting covenant**

a discussion of
how it's likened to new and everlasting covenant
72–99:2

**martyrdom**

34:1, 58:2

**materialism.** *See also* **mammon**

25:P, 41:P, 62:1, 64:1, 68:1, 102:1, 109:4, 93:5, 26:6, 76:6

**Matthew Cowley**

3:P, 4:P, 6:1, 46:1, 105:6

**Melchizedek**

administered priesthood to Abraham/built temple in Salem

16:1

**Melchizedek Priesthood.** *See also* **Aaronic Priesthood;** *See also* **oath and covenant of the priesthood;** *See also* **patriarchal order of the priesthood;** *See also* **priesthood**

a discussion of

4–209:3

**merchandise.** *See* **mammon;** *See* **money**

**mercy.** *See also* **grace**

10:P, 17:P, 20:P, 21:P, 22:P, 23:P, 24:P, 23:1, 26:1, 30:1, 66:1, 100:1, 4:2, 6:2, 7:2, 8:2, 9:2, 10:2, 15:2, 16:2, 17:2, 18:2, 20:2, 23:2, 24:2, 26:2, 27:2, 28:2, 29:2, 30:2, 32:2, 34:2, 35:2, 36:2, 45:2, 57:2, 97:2, 54:3, 71:3, 156:3, 159:3, 165:3, 167:3, 98:4, 112:4, 122:4, 129:4, 130:4, 143:4, 148:4, 151:4, 179:4, 15:5, 16:5, 19:5, 44:5, 64:5, 77:5, 106:5, 113:5, 114:5, 124:5, 12:6, 29:6, 41:6, 49:6, 51:6, 82:6, 102:6

**miracle**

17:P, 25:1, 30:1, 66:1, 64:2, 155:3, 9:4, 36:4, 51:4, 57:4, 60:4, 67:4, 70:4, 159:4, 160:4, 162:4, 163:4, 173:4, 25:5, 32:5, 39:5, 66:5, 101:5, 109:5, 99:6

**miserable**

49:1, 50:1, 51:1, 60:1, 77:1, 78:1, 8:2, 16:2, 89:2, 132:3, 63:4, 13:5, 14:5, 16:5, 56:5, 30:6

**money.** *See also* **mammon;** *See also* **materialism;** *See also* **riches**

love of, is root of all evil

70:1

**Moroni**

1:1, 31:1, 61:1, 90:1, 91:1, 92:1, 103:1, 12:3, 65:3, 68:3, 92:3, 166:3, 195:3, 209:3, 210:3, 5:4, 6:4, 107:4, 123:4, 124:4, 149:4, 165:4, 166:4, 174:4, 175:4, 178:4, 181:4, 182:4, 183:4, 31:5, 44:5, 53:5, 55:5, 70:5, 77:5, 109:5, 112:5, 118:5, 119:5, 22:6, 23:6, 43:6, 86:6, 100:6

**mortality**

is testing ground for our genuine desires

47:1

**Moses**

4:P, 26:P, 18:1, 19:1, 28:1, 32:1, 34:1, 51:1, 74:1, 87:1, 88:1, 8:2, 22:2, 40:2, 81:2, 84:2, 14:3, 15:3, 16:3, 17:3, 18:3, 20:3, 23:3, 24:3, 40:3, 55:3, 63:3, 65:3, 66:3, 76:3, 77:3, 88:3, 89:3, 99:3, 104:3, 110:3, 175:3, 176:3, 177:3, 184:3, 195:3, 207:3, 208:3, 47:4, 50:4, 100:4, 101:4, 112:4, 118:4, 120:4, 126:4, 129:4, 151:4, 165:4, 166:4, 8:5, 9:5, 18:5, 23:5, 31:5, 32:5, 35:5, 41:5, 42:5, 54:5, 55:5, 67:5, 72:5, 74:5, 79:5, 86:5, 89:5, 112:5, 131:5, 16:6, 17:6, 29:6, 36:6, 38:6, 46:6, 49:6, 50:6, 94:6, 95:6

**mother**

46:1, 61:1, 62:1, 25:2, 51:2, 85:2, 59:3, 126:3, 158:3, 28:4, 110:4, 172:4, 21:5, 129:5, 27:6, 52:6, 98:6, 106:6, 109:6

**murder**

50:1, 53:1, 60:1, 62:1, 63:1, 69:1, 80:1, 90:1, 102:1, 96:2, 119:3, 146:3, 160:3, 53:4, 118:4, 137:4, 14:5, 108:5, 36:6, 60:6

**murmur**

22:2, 26:5

**mysteries**

26:P, 32:P, 39:P, 40:P, 18:1, 61:1, 44:2, 8:3, 10:3, 24:3, 30:3, 31:3, 43:3, 47:3, 49:3, 57:3, 72:3, 81:3, 87:3, 93:3, 95 3, 96:3, 97:3, 98:3, 176:3, 177:3, 181:3, 183:3, 187:3, 188:3, 189:3, 190:3, 191:3, 192:3, 46:4, 100:4, 108:4, 149:4, 59:5, 60:5, 66:5, 79:5, 85:5, 86:5, 87:5, 88:5, 116:5, 119:5, 16:6, 25:6, 115:6

**natural man**

25:P, 22:1, 78:1, 20:2, 21:2, 50:2, 178:3, 64:4, 95:4, 169:4, 182:4, 23:5, 25:5, 42:5, 43:5, 44:5, 45:5, 68:5, 76:5, 84:5, 91:5, 9:6, 86:6

**Neal A. Maxwell**

12:1, 40:1, 110:3, 118:3, 148:3, 15:4, 27:4, 57:4, 79:4, 148:5

**needy.** *See also* **poor**

3:1, 20:1, 24:1, 27:1, 56:1, 80:1, 91:1, 48:3, 114:3, 129:3, 7:4, 11:4, 14:4, 23:4, 24:4, 29:4, 33:4, 40:4, 54:4, 72:4, 75:4, 82:4, 90:4, 107:4, 117:4, 121:4, 122:4, 123:4, 124:4, 125:4, 126:4, 129:4, 130:4, 133:4, 139:4, 144:4, 149:4, 153:4, 158:4, 170:4, 179:4, 180:4, 71:5, 5:6, 8:6, 23:6, 36:6, 41:6, 43:6, 44:6, 45:6, 46:6, 50:6, 52:6, 56:6, 63:6, 67:6, 72:6, 76:6, 87:6, 95:6, 104:6, 105:6, 106:6, 107:6, 109:6, 113:6

**Nehor**

26:1, 84:1, 145:3

**neighbor**

7:P, 8:P, 9:P, 28:P, 30:P, 19:1, 29:1, 66:1, 18:3, 49:3, 96:3, 182:3, 21:4, 26:4, 33:4, 38:4, 56:4, 58:4, 77:4, 91:4, 100:4, 104:4, 118:4, 122:4, 158:4, 164:4, 165:4, 169:4, 184:4, 93:5, 94:5, 127:5, 16:6, 20:6, 36:6, 41:6, 77:6, 93:6, 94:6, 113:6

**new and everlasting covenant.** *See also* **marriage**

a discussion of

> how it's likened to marriage
>
> > 72–99:2

**Nimrod**

51:1, 52:1, 53:1, 54:1, 55:1, 58:1, 61:1, 101:1

**Noah**

15:P, 14:1, 15:1, 16:1, 18:1, 36:1, 53:1, 55:1, 86:1, 87:1, 101:1, 102:1, 103:1, 7:3, 27:3, 207:3, 107:4, 32:5, 88:5, 101:5, 124:5, 125:5, 127:5, 22:6

**oath and covenant of the priesthood.** *See also* **priesthood**

1:P, 6:1, 32:1, 9:2, 34:2, 36:2, 47:2, 61:2, 98:2, 1:3, 2:3, 3:3, 4:3, 6:3, 21:3, 25:3, 30:3, 33:3, 35:3, 36:3, 39:3, 40:3, 41:3, 43:3, 47:3, 49:3, 53:3, 54:3, 55:3, 58:3, 59:3,

60:3, 61:3, 63:3, 64:3, 66:3, 68:3, 71:3, 72:3, 76:3, 77:3, 78:3, 80:3, 81:3, 82:3, 85:3, 87:3, 88:3, 90:3, 93:3, 94:3, 95:3, 97:3, 98:3, 102:3, 103:3, 104:3, 105:3, 106:3, 109:3, 115:3, 117:3, 126:3, 131:3, 135:3, 139:3, 140:3, 142:3, 143:3, 144:3, 159:3, 172:3, 173:3, 174:3, 175:3, 177:3, 179:3, 184:3, 189:3, 190:3, 193:3, 202:3, 208:3, 210:3, 211:3, 212:3, 213:3, 214:3, 1:4, 2:4, 14:4, 72:4, 90:4, 129:4, 142:4, 185:4, 1:5, 2:5, 59:5, 116:5, 134:5, 135:5, 136:5, 50:6

obedience
30:P, 32:P, 41:P, 17:1, 19:1, 21:1, 48:1, 3:2, 4:2, 6:2, 7:2, 10:2, 12:2, 13:2, 15:2, 17:2, 28:2, 29:2, 33:2, 34:2, 35:2, 37:2, 38:2, 39:2, 42:2, 51:2, 61:2, 31:3, 67:3, 68:3, 71:3, 75:3, 80:3, 94:3, 118:3, 121:3, 124:3, 126:3, 131:3, 134:3, 135:3, 146:3, 203:3, 208:3, 212:3, 16:4, 18:4, 26:4, 36:4, 41:4, 45:4, 50:4, 56:4, 60:4, 65:4, 67:4, 102:4, 156:4, 180:4, 7:5, 33:5, 35:5, 36:5, 45:5, 46:5, 47:5, 81:5, 84:5, 97:5, 135:5, 18:6, 112:6, 113:6, 115:6

offence
73:1

offering. See consecration; sacrifice; See offerings

offerings
those, ordered by Satan are always rejected by God
51:1

oneness. See also unity
6:P, 18:P, 19:P, 12:1, 49:1, 92:1, 23:2, 24:2, 25:2, 27:2, 28:2, 29:2, 48:2, 71:2, 79:2, 170:3, 5:4, 18:4, 31:4, 41:4, 42:4, 43:4, 44:4, 45:4, 47:4, 59:4, 65:5, 94:5, 115:5, 123:5

opposition. See also adversity
35:P, 33:1, 36:1, 54:1, 67:1, 70:1, 19:2, 26:2, 56:2, 117:3, 45:4, 62:4, 10:5, 18:5, 49:5

ordinance
6:1, 11:1, 31:1, 51:1, 28:2, 31:2, 34:2, 36:2, 37:2, 38:2, 45:2, 53:2, 56:2, 63:2, 64:2, 67:2, 69:2, 91:2, 4:3, 6:3, 9:3, 10:3, 14:3, 16:3, 20:3, 21:3, 28:3, 29:3, 77:3, 82:3, 84:3, 87:3, 99:3, 105:3, 194:3, 197:3, 205:3, 212:3, 28:4, 43:4, 159:4, 160:4, 161:4, 162:4, 163:4, 25:5, 46:5, 60:5, 91:5, 133:5, 75:6

parent
42:1, 46:1, 168:3, 53:4, 147:4, 153:4, 16:5, 62:5, 70:6

patience
23:1, 27:1, 73:1, 22:2, 76:2, 85:2, 86:2, 29:3, 97:3, 129:3, 148:3, 149:3, 150:3, 151:3, 155:3, 178:3, 181:3, 99:4, 146:4, 155:4, 178:4, 184:4, 85:5, 15:6, 70:6, 101:6

patriarchal order of the priesthood. See also Melchizedek Priesthood; See also oath and covenant of the priesthood

Paul
27:P, 39:P, 41:1, 57:1, 59:1, 70:1, 73:1, 88:1, 89:1, 91:1, 103:1, 27:2, 63:2, 64:2, 81:2, 85:2, 31:3, 40:3, 67:3, 90:3, 100:3, 149:3, 163:3, 171:3, 180:3, 189:3, 198:3, 37:4, 99:4, 117:4, 165:4, 166:4, 184:4, 13:5, 15:5, 29:5, 89:5, 119:5, 133:5, 15:6, 35:6, 76:6, 78:6, 94:6, 95:6, 97:6, 106:6

Paymaster
8:P, 17:1, 151:3, 70:4, 71:4, 88:4, 90:4, 183:4

peace

2:P, 5:P, 8:P, 12:P, 17:P, 20:P, 26:P, 27:P, 9:1, 15:1, 16:1, 23:1, 25:1, 27:1, 30:1, 46:1, 88:1, 8:2, 24:2, 39:2, 50:2, 51:2, 61:2, 95:2, 5:3, 6:3, 7:3, 8:3, 18:3, 28:3, 29:3, 46:3, 50:3, 66:3, 70:3, 83:3, 114:3, 119:3, 129:3, 140:3, 167:3, 172:3, 173:3, 199:3, 19:4, 22:4, 40:4, 44:4, 46:4, 115:4, 118:4, 119:4, 124:4, 125:4, 137:4, 140:4, 150:4, 151:4, 152:4, 162:4, 171:4, 172:4, 178:4, 27:5, 28:5, 38:5, 44:5, 46:5, 53:5, 55:5, 81:5, 83:5, 92:5, 94:5, 103:5, 104:5, 106:5, 107:5, 122:5, 128:5, 130:5, 132:5, 133:5, 1:6, 2:6, 13:6, 34:6, 37:6, 38:6, 45:6, 60:6, 61:6, 64:6, 97:6, 98:6, 101:6

persecute

27:P, 28:P, 30:P, 61:1, 67:1, 85:1, 91:1, 137:3, 152:3, 108:4, 122:4, 123:4, 124:4, 150:4, 42:5, 26:6, 41:6, 42:6, 44:6, 77:6, 112:6, 113:6

plague

82:1, 160:3, 124:4, 38:5, 44:6

poor. *See also* **needy**

a discussion of

how we treat the,

120–137:4

popular

14:1, 66:1, 81:1, 83:1, 84:1, 87:1, 25:3, 132:3

possession. *See* **mammon**

praise. *See* **popular**

pray, prayer

80:1, 85:1, 98:1, 14:2, 20:2, 55:2, 86:2, 91:2, 92:2, 41:3, 70:3, 154:3, 158:3, 192:3, 197:3, 8:4, 9:4, 45:4, 46:4, 54:4, 60:4, 111:4, 112:4, 140:4, 162:4, 163:4, 181:4, 4:5, 19:5, 42:5, 51:5, 53:5, 67:5, 69:5, 77:5, 78:5, 87:5, 112:5, 114:5, 115:5, 116:5, 120:5, 121:5, 122:5, 123:5, 124:5, 28:6, 29:6, 64:6, 90:6, 104:6

premortal existence

mature knowledge of gospel from, planted deep in our souls

44:1

pride

neither rich nor poor exempt from

24:1

priest

17:1, 26:1, 84:1, 20:2, 41:2, 94:2, 95:2, 5:3, 6:3, 7:3, 9:3, 29:3, 42:3, 46:3, 65:3, 119:3, 152:3, 190:3, 198:3, 199:3, 88:4, 100:4, 40:5, 63:5, 89:5, 16:6

priestcraft

26:1, 51:1, 53:1, 61:1, 68:1, 84:1, 85:1, 145:3, 146:3

priesthood. *See also* **Aaronic Priesthood;** *See also* **Melchizedek Priesthood;** *See also* **oath and covenant of the priesthood;** *See also* **patriarchal order of the priesthood**

a discussion of

Melchizedek

4–11:3, 182–192:3, 204–210:3

oath and covenant of the
39–60:3
restoration of the
12–16:3,

**priesthood society**
1:P, 3:P, 4:P, 43:P, 3:1, 5:1, 6:1, 7:1, 12:1, 14:1, 46:1, 5:3, 6:3, 12:3, 21:3, 25:3, 28:3, 32:3, 35:3, 61:3, 85:3, 127:3, 206:3, 7:4, 14:4, 15:4, 22:4, 31:4, 74:4, 80:4, 90:5, 98:5, 99:5, 127:5, 87:6, 102:6, 105:6

**princess.** *See* **queen**

**prison**
88:1, 51:2, 52:2, 54:2, 88:2, 70:3, 100:3, 138:4, 139:4, 151:4, 152:4, 12:5, 29:5, 39:5, 75:5, 63:6, 116:6, 117:6

**probation.** *See* **mortality**

**progress**
perspective of our, compared to steps on an airplane
90:5

**properties.** *See* **property**

**property**
converting life into, is Satan's great secret
47:6

**prophecies**
93:1, 95:1, 97:1, 98:1, 109:3, 166:3, 4:5, 97:5, 103:5, 118:5, 119:5, 49:6

**prosper.** *See* **abundance**

**publicans**
80:1

**pure in heart.** *See also* **Zion**
2:P, 17:P, 25:P, 26:P, 38:P, 41:P, 43:P, 2:1, 3:1, 4:1, 6:1, 8:1, 12:1, 15:1, 19:1, 25:1, 33:1, 46:1, 48:1, 18:2, 47:3, 66:3, 71:3, 87:3, 161:3, 172:3, 178:3, 195:3, 207:3, 208:3, 2:4, 15:4, 16:4, 31:4, 73:4, 83:4, 95:4, 104:4, 109:4, 147:4, 1:5, 2:5, 3:5, 4:5, 18:5, 77:5, 78:5, 79:5, 80:5, 81:5, 82:5, 84:5, 87:5, 89:5, 90:5, 91:5, 93:5, 94:5, 95:5, 96:5, 101:5, 109:5, 114:5, 115:5, 116:5, 117:5, 118:5, 119:5, 120:5, 124:5, 125:5, 127:5, 130:5, 133:5, 134:5, 136:5, 9:6, 20:6, 26:6, 75:6, 76:6, 78:6, 116:6

**purification**
14:P, 18:2, 19:2, 20:2, 90:2, 91:2, 66:3, 137:3, 52:4, 162:4, 182:4, 3:5, 25:5, 26:5, 75:5, 79:5, 90:5, 115:5, 116:5, 120:5

**queen(s)**
93:1, 90:2, 93:2, 94:2, 199:3, 8:5

**rainbow**
sign of everlasting covenant
15:1

**redeem, Redeemer, redemption**
noble spirits in premortal life carried out work of
45:1

**repent**

20:P, 2:1, 10:1, 13:1, 16:1, 24:1, 70:1, 91:1, 98:1, 99:1, 5:2, 7:2, 16:2, 17:2, 19:2, 35:2, 36:2, 96:2, 5:3, 6:3, 19:3, 45:3, 46:3, 70:3, 103:3, 135:3, 153:3, 161:3, 188:3, 205:3, 37:4, 69:4, 84:4, 102:4, 111:4, 112:4, 117:4, 118:4, 121:4, 126:4, 135:4, 136:4, 148:4, 15:5, 46:5, 78:5, 82:5, 105:5, 106:5, 109:5, 2:6, 18:6, 28:6, 29:6, 35:6, 36:6, 39:6, 46:6, 47:6, 59:6, 60:6

**resurrected**

14:P, 13:1, 28:1, 64:1, 86:1, 95:1, 14:2, 26:2, 17:3, 91:3, 202:3, 203:3, 42:4, 13:5, 64:5, 105:5, 108:5, 121:5, 122:5, 132:5

**revelation**

is key to magnifying callings and to learning

95:3

**riches.** *See also* **mammon;** *See also* **materialism;** *See also* **money;** *See also* **wealth**

30:P, 32:P, 34:P, 38:P, 17:1, 27:1, 31:1, 33:1, 67:1, 71:1, 72:1, 76:1, 84:1, 86:1, 92:1, 93:1, 95:1, 96:1, 97:1, 99:1, 123:3, 125:3, 126:3, 128:3, 129:3, 130:3, 131:3, 133:3, 141:3, 142:3, 146:3, 167:3, 171:3, 193:3, 8:4, 9:4, 10:4, 26:4, 30:4, 38:4, 40:4, 69:4, 72:4, 83:4, 84:4, 85:4, 87:4, 88:4, 91:4, 93:4, 95:4, 99:4, 100:4, 101:4, 102:4, 103:4, 106:4, 108:4, 109:4, 110:4, 111:4, 113:4, 115:4, 116:4, 117:4, 118:4, 119:4, 120:4, 123:4, 124:4, 126:4, 127:4, 130:4, 132:4, 133:4, 135:4, 140:4, 142:4, 144:4, 148:4, 149:4, 150:4, 152:4, 158:4, 184:4, 44:5, 103:5, 104:5, 4:6, 7:6, 16:6, 17:6, 18:6, 19:6, 22:6, 25:6, 26:6, 28:6, 31:6, 33:6, 34:6, 36:6, 37:6, 38:6, 43:6, 44:6, 46:6, 47:6, 48:6, 51:6, 56:6, 57:6, 58:6, 65:6, 67:6, 72:6, 113:6, 114:6, 115:6

**Sabbath**

42:P, 37:1, 38:2, 39:2, 40:2, 50:2, 51:2, 72:2, 99:4, 53:5, 15:6

**sacrament**

14:P, 23:P, 29:1, 14:2, 20:2, 36:2, 38:2, 39:2, 40:2, 41:2, 60:2, 67:2, 80:2, 81:2, 82:2, 89:2, 9:3, 11:3, 39:3, 42:3, 66:3, 75:3, 93:3, 165:3, 193:3, 210:3, 46:4, 17:5, 18:5, 60:5, 61:5, 62:5, 64:5, 117:5, 121:5

**sacrifice.** *See also* **consecration;** *See also* **offering**

a discussion of

3–31:4, 33–52:4, 61–92:4

**Salem.** *See also* **Jerusalem**

3:P, 9:1, 15:1, 16:1, 5:3, 27:3, 29:3, 45:3, 1:6, 2:6

**salvation, plan of**

50:1, 54:2, 25:3, 26:3, 31:3, 36:3, 68:3, 73:3, 12:5, 126:5, 130:5

**sanctification**

14:P, 18:P, 18:2, 20:2, 21:2, 90:2, 91:2, 9:3, 56:3, 66:3, 67:3, 68:3, 69:3, 70:3, 71:3, 74:3, 75:3, 77:3, 84:3, 104:3, 137:3, 210:3, 14:4, 18:4, 21:4, 31:4, 52:4, 182:4, 3:5, 27:5, 47:5, 75:5, 79:5, 90:5, 94:5, 99:5, 115:5, 116:5

**sanctified body.** *See* **sanctification**

**sanctuaries.** *See* **mammon**

**Satan.** *See also* **adversary;** *See also* **devil;** *See also* **hell;** *See also* **Lucifer**
>     we must understand, in order to confront him
>>          55:5

**savior**
>     Adam empowered to become, to his family
>>          11:1

**Savior.** *See* **Christ, Jesus;** *See* **Exemplar;** *See* **Jehovah;** *See* **Lamb**

**saviors on Mount Zion**
>     43:1, 32:2, 40:2, 25:3, 35:3, 37:3, 43:3, 66:3, 69:3, 104:3, 156:3, 144:4, 184:4, 64:5, 116:5, 68:6

**science**
>     57:1, 81:1, 83:1, 14:2, 163:3

**seal**
>     26:1, 24:2, 76:2, 79:2, 93:2, 13:3, 16:3, 17:3, 81:3, 84:3, 99:3, 149:3, 168:3, 194:3, 199:3, 209:3, 52:4, 75:4, 108:4, 155:4, 162:4, 38:5, 58:5, 65:5, 67:5, 25:6

**secret combinations.** *See also* **Gadianton robbers**
>     49:1, 60:1, 61:1, 91:1, 97:1, 99:1, 102:5, 103:5, 108:5

**selfish**
>     9:P, 38:P, 58:1, 73:1, 89:1, 91:1, 96:1, 19:2, 32:2, 71:2, 21:3, 74:3, 88:3, 122:3, 124:3, 125:3, 131:3, 137:3, 153:3, 154:3, 157:3, 171:3, 27:4, 55:4, 82:4, 91:4, 97:4, 98:4, 112:4, 117:4, 134:4, 140:4, 141:4, 145:4, 149:4, 152:4, 156:4, 165:4, 169:4, 176:4, 94:5, 11:6, 18:6, 29:6, 30:6, 31:6, 35:6, 37:6, 45:6, 48:6, 58:6, 64:6, 65:6, 66:6, 68:6, 71:6, 72:6, 77:6, 86:6, 88:6, 94:6, 108:6, 115:6

**selfless.** *See also* **charity**
>     1:P, 8:P, 10:P, 12:P, 23:P, 25:P, 31:P, 24:1, 29:1, 5:2, 32:2, 71:2, 21:3, 51:3, 171:3, 109:4, 170:4, 93:5, 100:5, 26:6, 76:6, 87:6

**Sermon on the Mount.** *See also* **Beatitudes**
>     14:P, 16:P, 28:1, 18:2, 82:5, 118:5

**servant**
>     37:P, 16:1, 27:1, 34:2, 61:2, 62:2, 69:2, 87:2, 88:2, 91:2, 92:2, 96:2, 6:3, 30:3, 41:3, 72:3, 82:3, 100:3, 101:3, 103:3, 115:3, 196:3, 211:3, 214:3, 12:4, 49:4, 50:4, 53:4, 74:4, 75:4, 78:4, 79:4, 81:4, 89:4, 183:4, 66:5, 97:5, 110:5

**set apart.** *See* **consecration**

**sex**
>     57:1, 66:1, 76:1, 154:3, 97:4, 11:6

**single women**
>     64:3

**slippery treasures**
>     110:4, 27:6

**snare**
>     70:1, 73:1, 109:3, 122:3, 124:3, 139:3, 99:4, 103:4, 113:4, 14:5, 15:6, 19:6, 30:6, 108:6

Sodom

    1:1, 54:1, 55:1, 56:1, 57:1, 86:1, 94:1, 101:1, 102:1, 103:1, 5:4, 121:4, 23:5, 41:6

sorrow. *See also* wailing

    21:P, 34:1, 35:1, 63:1, 93:1, 102:1, 88:2, 51:3, 151:3, 160:3, 19:4, 124:4, 127:4, 136:4,
    10:5, 43:5, 44:5, 106:5, 44:6, 48:6, 59:6, 79:6

soul

    11:P, 16:P, 17:P, 23:P, 43:P, 20:1, 21:1, 22:1, 28:1, 60:1, 76:1, 8:2, 19:2, 26:2, 40:2,
    41:2, 49:2, 55:2, 59:2, 61:2, 94:2, 7:3, 19:3, 44:3, 47:3, 67:3, 69:3, 83:3, 97:3, 100:3,
    102:3, 108:3, 116:3, 119:3, 122:3, 144:3, 151:3, 156:3, 159:3, 165:3, 166:3, 172:3,
    175:3, 182:3, 184:3, 189:3, 193:3, 213:3, 2:4, 9:4, 16:4, 20:4, 50:4, 54:4, 56:4, 60:4,
    64:4, 65:4, 111:4, 114:4, 115:4, 118:4, 127:4, 140:4, 146:4, 152:4, 155:4, 160:4, 162:4,
    164:4, 166:4, 167:4, 171:4, 172:4, 174:4, 175:4, 179:4, 180:4, 182:4, 183:4, 186:4, 2:5,
    13:5, 15:5, 17:5, 44:5, 45:5, 49:5, 68:5, 71:5, 74:5, 80:5, 81:5, 84:5, 100:5, 108:5,
    122:5, 5:6, 6:6, 29:6, 30:6, 32:6, 33:6, 37:6, 48:6, 50:6, 65:6, 71:6, 85:6, 86:6, 91:6,
    95:6, 96:6, 97:6, 98:6, 100:6, 101:6, 102:6, 103:6, 108:6

Spencer W. Kimball

    8:P, 25:P, 33:P, 3:1, 7:1, 37:1, 55:1, 85:1, 21:3, 31:3, 35:3, 118:3, 140:3, 191:3, 7:4,
    9:4, 15:4, 17:4, 23:4, 30:4, 31:4, 48:4, 59:4, 83:4, 86:4, 109:4, 134:4, 172:4, 173:4,
    177:4, 37:5, 49:5, 92:5, 93:5, 98:5, 100:5, 26:6, 57:6, 76:6, 88:6, 90:6, 98:6, 99:6

stewardship(s)

    in heaven based on stewardships on earth
        50:5

storehouse

    7:P, 36:P, 17:1, 18:1, 64:2, 6:3, 38:4, 39:4, 48:4, 61:4, 71:4, 72:4, 74:4, 75:4, 77:4,
    79:4, 83:4, 88:4, 91:4, 96:4, 131:4, 10:6, 51:6, 77:6

submission

    79:1, 118:3, 152:3, 31:5

surplus

    36:P, 18:1, 48:3, 12:4, 24:4, 69:4, 74:4, 75:4, 79:4, 90:4, 91:4, 94:4, 147:4, 9:6, 114:6

telestial

    3:P, 9:P, 10:P, 12:P, 25:P, 26:P, 30:P, 31:P, 32:P, 37:P, 38:P, 3:1, 6:1, 7:1, 8:1, 10:1, 17:1,
    29:1, 39:1, 40:1, 47:1, 66:1, 80:1, 103:1, 14:2, 15:2, 23:2, 48:2, 60:2, 68:2, 69:2, 68:3,
    80:3, 89:3, 114:3, 117:3, 124:3, 125:3, 140:3, 141:3, 144:3, 164:3, 211:3, 10:4, 15:4, 18:4,
    25:4, 34:4, 35:4, 36:4, 64:4, 69:4, 73:4, 82:4, 83:4, 96:4, 101:4, 105:4, 141:4, 147:4, 148:4,
    163:4, 185:4, 11:5, 12:5, 19:5, 31:5, 36:5, 70:5, 76:5, 84:5, 85:5, 91:5, 121:5, 126:5, 10:6,
    17:6, 21:6, 66:6, 86:6, 105:6, 106:6, 107:6, 110:6, 112:6, 115:6, 116:6

temple

    covenants, necessary to establish Zion/is gathering place for Zion people
        31:1

temptation

    70:1, 133:3, 176:3, 43:4, 97:4, 99:4, 14:5, 120:5, 121:5, 11:6, 15:6

**Ten Commandments**

15:2, 100:4, 148:4, 110:5, 16:6

**ten virgins**

85:1, 103:1, 87:2, 90:2, 92:2

**terrestrial**

testimony, bearing of, purifies heart; bearing of, is an act of love

56:3

**tithes**

31:P, 34:P, 37:P, 42:P, 17:1, 37:1, 6:3, 8:4, 12:4, 13:4, 30:4, 81:4, 88:4, 89:4, 92:4, 96:4, 147:4, 118:5, 10:6, 12:6, 13:6, 51:6, 114:6, 115:6

**tradition**

98:1, 72:2, 73:2, 75:2, 84:2, 7:3, 9:3

**treasure.** *See* **mammon**

**trial(s).** *See also* **adversity;** *See also* **opposition**

29:P, 44:1, 56:2, 58:2, 83:3, 128:3, 148:3, 151:3, 124:4, 23:5, 27:5, 50:5, 58:5, 44:6, 50:6

**unite, unity.** *See also* **oneness**

4:P, 6:P, 37:P, 3:1, 9:1, 14:1, 19:1, 68:1, 77:1, 78:1, 92:1, 23:2, 24:2, 25:2, 27:2, 69:2, 93:2, 74:3, 85:3, 114:3, 116:3, 140:3, 147:3, 170:3, 2:4, 19:4, 33:4, 41:4, 42:4, 43:4, 44:4, 45:4, 46:4, 47:4, 48:4, 49:4, 50:4, 51:4, 52:4, 54:4, 55:4, 58:4, 59:4, 60:4, 62:4, 82:4, 156:4, 171:4, 183:4, 185:4, 2:5, 50:5, 73:5, 100:5, 108:5, 97:6

**universe**

composition of

89:3

**vain**

22:P, 28:P, 64:1, 66:1, 69:1, 80:1, 86:1, 97:1, 98:1, 41:2, 45:3, 47:3, 51:3, 92:3, 107:3, 110:3, 114:3, 119:3, 135:3, 146:3, 153:3, 163:3, 164:3, 99:4, 110:4, 111:4, 115:4, 117:4, 118:4, 119:4, 122:4, 124:4, 126:4, 127:4, 133:4, 149:4, 175:4, 181:4, 57:5, 71:5, 95:5, 101:5, 102:5, 104:5, 4:6, 15:6, 28:6, 33:6, 36:6, 38:6, 41:6, 42:6, 44:6, 46:6, 57:6, 79:6, 104:6

**veil**

40:1, 55:1, 80:2, 83:2, 84:2, 85:2, 95:2, 26:3, 91:3, 102:3, 178:3, 179:3, 180:3, 181:3, 183:3, 196:3, 209:3, 210:3, 54:4, 12:5, 67:5, 68:5, 79:5, 85:5, 89:5, 109:5, 131:5

**violence**

14:1, 36:1, 87:1, 93:1, 95:1, 8:3, 121:3, 108:4, 26:6

**wailing.** *See also* **sorrow**

94:1

**war**

17:P, 26:P, 42:1, 44:1, 55:1, 62:1, 69:1, 78:1, 80:1, 85:1, 91:1, 102:1, 28:2, 83:3, 108:4, 137:4, 37:5, 102:5, 103:5, 108:5, 26:6, 60:6

**warn**

95:1, 113:4, 124:4, 102:5, 103:5, 30:6, 44:6

**wealth.** *See also* **mammon;** *See also* **poor;** *See also* **riches**

    a discussion of

        proper use

            120–151:4

        seeking

            99–137:4

**weapon**

    29:P, 57:1, 71:1, 55:2, 99:4, 109:4, 132:4, 149:4, 16:6, 26:6, 56:6, 112:6

**whore.** *See* **Babylon**

**wickedness**

    today's level of, equals or exceeds times that of Noah's generation

        87:1

**widow**

    93:1, 7:4, 29:4, 104:4, 109:4, 130:4, 140:4, 146:4, 153:4, 51:5, 70:5, 20:6, 27:6, 52:6, 65:6, 70:6

**wife.** *See also* **marriage**

    45:P, 10:1, 33:1, 62:1, 24:2, 25:2, 58:2, 66:2, 74:2, 76:2, 77:2, 78:2, 79:2, 85:2, 92:2, 94:2, 95:2, 97:2, 13:3, 15:3, 17:3, 23:3, 31:3, 59:3, 82:3, 85:3, 110:3, 112:3, 126:3, 136:3, 183:3, 198:3, 199:3, 207:3, 211:3, 26:4, 41:4, 43:4, 45:4, 52:4, 98:4, 100:4, 156:4, 157:4, 10:5, 20:5, 24:5, 38:5, 42:5, 11:6, 16:6, 106:6, 109:6

**wilderness.** *See also* **Babylon**

    a discussion of

        our journey through the

            12–41:5

**Wilford Woodruff**

    40:1, 55:3, 131:3, 211:3, 148:5

**wisdom**

    21:P, 32:P, 23:1, 24:1, 26:1, 31:1, 33:1, 39:1, 59:1, 60:1, 64:1, 65:1, 78:1, 84:1, 98:1, 102:1, 45:2, 50:3, 54:3, 71:3, 93:3, 152:3, 161:3, 163:3, 164:3, 165:3, 166:3, 167:3, 168:3, 187:3, 201:3, 208:3, 6:4, 26:4, 27:4, 66:4, 77:4, 100:4, 105:4, 108:4, 109:4, 120:4, 122:4, 137:4, 141:4, 149:4, 152:4, 179:4, 65:5, 3:6, 16:6, 21:6 25:6, 27:6, 38:6, 42:6, 61:6, 66:6, 82:6, 102:6, 115:6

**work.** *See also* **labor**

    Christ's, takes priority

        30:1

**world, worldly.** *See also* **Babylon**

    in, but not of

        74:1

**yoke**

    17:P, 23:P, 28:P, 62:1, 63:1, 101:1, 92:2, 160:3, 179:4, 68:5, 69:5, 71:5, 102:6

**Zion**

    an individual with a pure heart
        12:1
    begins in each person's heart
        1:1,  12:1,  13:1
    definition of, is perfection
        12:1
    is a return to the presence of God
        47:1
    is our ideal
        6:1
    principles of
        19:1
    we are
        46:1
**Zion people**
    characteristics of
        12:1
    temple gathering place for
        14:1

# About the Author

Larry Barkdull is a longtime publisher and writer of books, music, art, and magazines. For nine years, he owned Sonos Music Resources and published the Tabernacle Choir Performance Library. He was also the owner and publisher of Keepsake Books. Over the past thirty years, he's published some six hundred products for numerous authors, composers, and artists. He's founded two nonprofit organizations: The Latter-day Foundation for the Arts, Education and Humanity (to promote LDS arts), and Gospel Ideals International (to promote the gospel of Jesus Christ on the Internet).

His books have sold in excess of 300,000 copies, and they have been translated into Japanese, Korean, Italian, and Hebrew. He is the recipient of the American Family Literary Award; the Benjamin Franklin Book Award; and *Foreword Magazine's* GOLD Book of the Year Award for best fiction. His most recent books are *Priesthood Power—Blessing the Sick and the Afflicted*; *Rescuing Wayward Children*; and *The Shepherd Song*.

He and his wife, Elizabeth, have ten children and a growing number of grandchildren. They live in Orem, Utah. Read more of his writings at Meridian Magazine.com.

www.ingramcontent.com/pod-product-compliance
Lightning Source LLC
Chambersburg PA
CBHW080552090426
42735CB00016B/3213